HOW WE LIVED

HOW

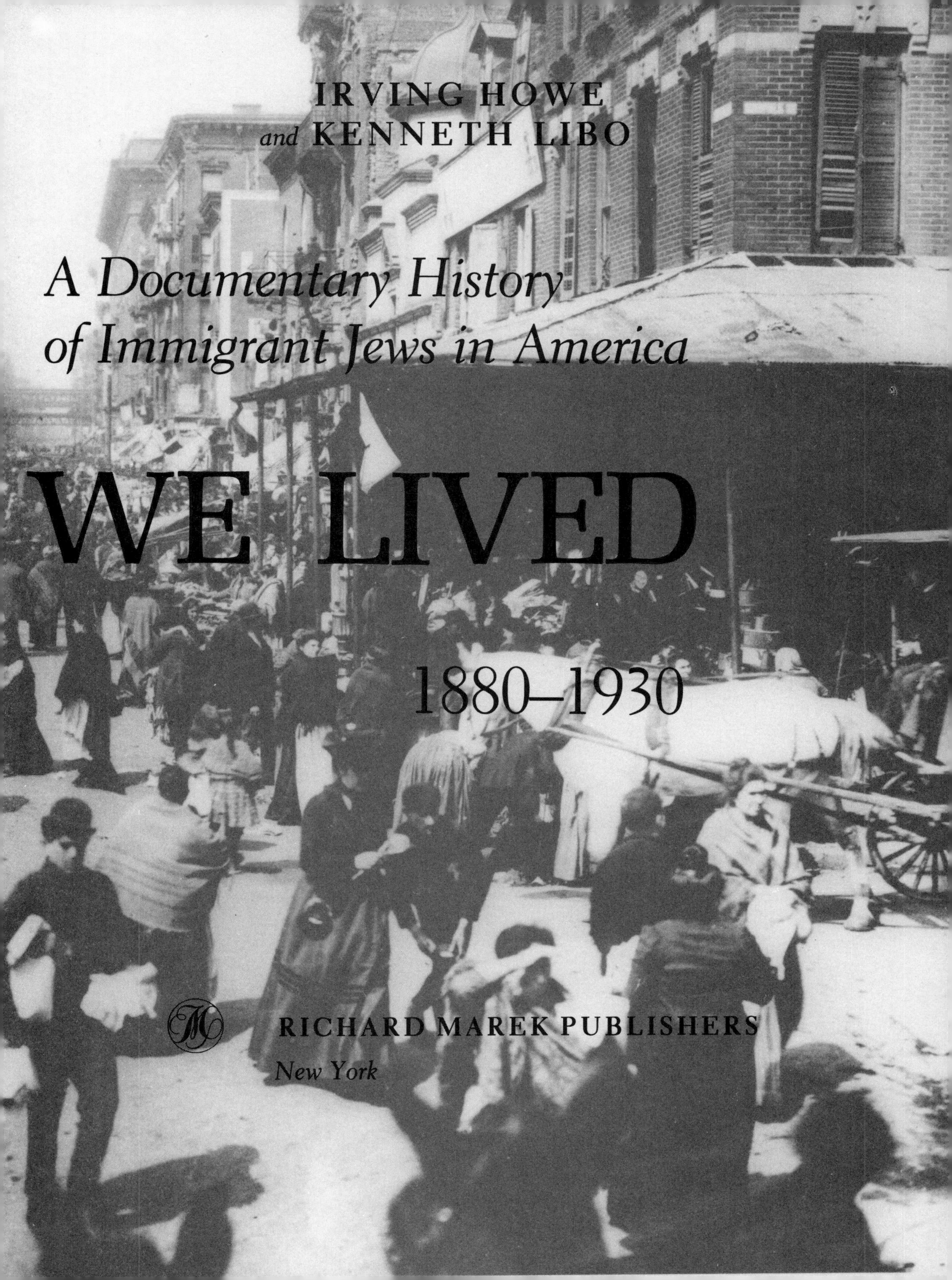

IRVING HOWE
and KENNETH LIBO

A Documentary History
of Immigrant Jews in America

WE LIVED

1880–1930

RICHARD MAREK PUBLISHERS

New York

Pages 355–360 constitute an extension of the copyright page.

Designed by Andor Braun

Typography by Fisher Composition

Library of Congress Cataloging in Publication Data

Main entry under title:

How we lived.

  Bibliography: p.
  1. Jews in New York (City)—Addresses, essays,
lectures. 2. Lower East Side, New York—Addresses,
essays, lectures. 3. United States—Emigration and
immigration—Addresses, essays, lectures.
4. New York (City)—Social conditions—Addresses,
essays, lectures. 5. New York (City)—Intellectual
life—Addresses, essays, lectures. I. Howe, Irving.
II. Libo, Kenneth.
F128.9.J5H58   974.7'1'004924   79-13391
ISBN 0-399-90051-9

Printed in the United States of America

Acknowledgments

WE WOULD LIKE TO EXPRESS our appreciation to Gershon Freidlin and Adah Fogel, dedicated Yiddishists, for translating a wealth of historical materials from newspaper and memoir accounts; to Dina Abramowicz of the YIVO Institute for Jewish Research for giving so generously of her valuable time; to Andor Braun, the designer of this book, for his sensitivity, ingenuity and artistry; to Gypsy da Silva and George Caughlan of the copyediting department for their creative concern for the pictures and expert attention to the text; to Ron Lief, production manager par excellence; and to Anne Knauerhase for her help expediting editorial preparation. Finally, special thanks to our friend and editor Joyce Engelson for her incisive recommendations and superb coordinating skills.

Contents

York/Meyer Leser: Maxwell Street/Bernard Richards: Boston/The Immigrant Jew in the United States: Philadelphia/Samuel Chotzinoff: Waterbury, Connecticut/S. N. Behrman: Worcester, Massachusetts/Irving Howe: Moving to the Suburbs

Preface

THROUGH A MATCHING of word and picture we have tried in this book to evoke an intimate yet objective sense of life in the immigrant Jewish milieu during the late years of the nineteenth century and the early years of this century. The task is more difficult than might be imagined. Not that there is any shortage of materials— on the contrary, we could easily have brought together three or four times as many documents as we have here. The problem is rather that the immigrant Jewish experience, significant as it was for the history of this country and crucial for the lives of most American Jews, is in danger of becoming a myth, often a sentimentalized myth, and thereby unavailable to serious historical understanding.

All sorts of cultural barriers and confusions of attitude stand in the way. There is first the impulse to forget, a wish to brush aside the ordeals and indignities of an earlier moment, sometimes a touch of shame at lowly origins and plebeian styles. It is an impulse as understandable as it is deplorable, and one that we ought to resist in behalf of personal—we might even say, cultural—honesty. Resist it, first of all, in ourselves, in that touch of snobbism from which few human beings are exempt. There is next, and right now more noticeable, the impulse to prettify the immigrant experience, a wish to make the past seem all quaint and "colorful," with our own little fiddlers on our own little roofs. Finally, of course, this too is a mode of forgetting and repressing.

With every ounce of our strength, we have resisted both of these impulses, and have tried instead to show the life of the immigrant Jews with its beauties and its blotches alike. We are interested here in the unvarnished truth, not in any self-serving little fables about "two cents plain." We have therefore used journalists and memoirists who see, and make others see, life as it is free of prejudice and sentimentality. And we have selected pictures that convey objective truths and human values beyond the boundaries of mere illustration. Given the scope of our subject, this book cannot be complete, but we claim that it is reasonably representative.

We have tried to portray here both the vitality and the weaknesses of the immigrant Jewish experience—the intensities of belief and aspiration toward idealistic goals, and also the high costs of suffering, frustration, and defeat. To remember the one without the other, to stress the successes without the costs, is a disloyalty to those who came before us and a disservice to those who will come after.

For reasons of dramatic concentration, we have chosen material that deals mostly with the Lower East Side of New York City—though there is one section, entitled "Beyond New York," that does offer a few glimpses of immigrant Jewish life in other places. Why did we decide to concentrate on the Lower East Side? Because this neighborhood, really an overpacked province, soon came to form the social, economic, and intellectual center of the Yiddish-speaking world in America. Here were the main writers; here, the best theaters; here, the leading intellectuals; here, the headquarters of the Jewish parties and organizations; but here, above all, during the early decades of this century, a tightly packed mass of immigrants who, in part because of their sheer density of numbers, brought to fruition the culture of Yiddish. There were, of course, other concentrations of Jewish immigrants—in Chicago, Boston, Philadelphia. No doubt each of these cosmopolitan centers had its own immigrant traits, its own idiosyncrasies of Jewish life. But we believe that, in the main, the experience of the immigrant Jews in other large cities was not very different from that on the Lower East Side. And so we have taken that to be emblematic of the others, with the admission that this surely involves simplifications. As for immigrant Jewish life in small towns, or in the South and Far West, that is another story, interesting and worth recording, but beyond our present scope.

It may interest our readers to know something about our sources. A great deal of the material in this book appears in English for the first time. We have gone through the files of the Yiddish press, especially that extraordinary paper, the Daily Forward, *which began publishing in 1897 and still appears regularly. An absolute gold mine of historical material, sociological observation, journalistic sharpness, cultural nuance—the* Forward! *It had its weaknesses, it was not so good with statistics, and it rarely satisfied latter-day notions of objectivity; but when it came to life, to vividness, to passion, there has probably never been another paper like it in America. So we took material, with occasional abridgments, from the* Forward, *material written not just with journalistic acuteness but with that larger gift that C. Wright Mills once called "the sociological imagination."*

Second only to the newspapers as a Yiddish source has been the numerous memoirs, some published in long-forgotten and inaccessible books, and others still extant in yellowing manuscript—sometimes in the invaluable archives of YIVO, that splendid center of Jewish historical material. A few of these memoirs are simplicity itself, heartfelt and honest chronicles of hope and suffering. That of David Kessler, immigrant actor and theater manager, falls into this category. Others, like that of S. Schoenfeld, Isaac Raboy, and Leon Kobrin, achieve a certain sophistication of narrative. Still others, in particular the accounts of old-time Socialists I. Benequit and Bernard Weinstein, deal intimately and intelligently with immigrant institutional life.

There are also numerous English-language sources. In the files of the Commercial Advertiser, a long-forgotten newspaper published in New York City during the peak years of Jewish immigration, and edited for a time by the journalist Lincoln Steffens, we found an embarrassment of riches—everything from articles on café intellectuals to detailed strike reports to vivid descriptions of religious holidays and celebrations. This brilliant paper, which puts to shame more recent efforts at "personal journalism," managed to be at once informal and serious, amusing and factual, lively and responsible. For a time the Yiddish editor and writer Abraham Cahan worked as a reporter for the Commercial Advertiser, and sometimes it's possible to guess which pieces about immigrant life were written by him. Also working on the Commercial Advertiser were Norman Hapgood, an accomplished drama critic who frequently reviewed Yiddish plays during the Adler-Gordin period, and his brother Hutchins, whose book The Spirit of the Ghetto (1902), a minor classic, offers the best contemporary account of the immigrant Jews by a gentile writer.

We found valuable material in the files of the settlement houses, especially the University Settlement, which issued incisive reports regularly on the customs and mores of the immigrants. Also, in the files of the Educational Alliance, that ongoing social-cultural institution of the Lower East Side, we found a number of valuable documents—see especially the amusing report about Jewish kids at camp (p. 58).

English-language memoirs and fictionalized accounts of the immigrant days are, of course, numerous, though not all of them are valuable. Here we have chosen sparingly and, we hope, with some discrimination. Some of these writers—Rose Pastor Stokes, Anzia Yezierska, Michael Gold—come to life at key points in their accounts, particularly in recollecting family tribulations, childhood adventures, and youthful expectations. Others are notable for their intellectual grasp, true witnesses to a major experience, such as the philosopher Morris Raphael Cohen and the novelist Abraham Cahan. And there are also a few about whom one can say that they are really neglected first-rate writers, such as Marcus Ravage and Samuel Chotzinoff. The case of Chotzinoff is especially interesting: He was a none-too-distinguished music critic for the New York World several decades ago who wrote, toward the end of his life, two books of recollections about his New York immigrant boyhood. The first of these, A Lost Paradise, is a masterpiece of observation, and we have drawn from it liberally.

Our book, then, lays claim to being not just a remembrance of things recently past, not just a trip to the world of our fathers and mothers; it provides historical materials previously unavailable to the English reader, or so long forgotten on dusty shelves as to have in effect been unavailable.

The story that emerges in these texts and pictures seems to us one of moral heroism. We do not use this phrase lightly or as a mere piece of self-congratulatory rhetoric. Rather, we recognize heroism in the struggle of a community torn between a commitment to preserve its own culture and a desire to plunge into the alluring possibilities of American freedom. There is, we are persuaded, genuine heroism in the conscious efforts of our fathers and mothers, our grandfathers and grandmothers, to find a way of keeping what had been brought from the old country while at the same time learning from and yielding to, criticizing and embracing the new.

Many struggled to the point of working out an accommodation of sorts with the new world, an accommodation sometimes predicated on the violation of their original ideals and aspirations. The more reflective among them came to recognize, with each measure of achievement, an equal measure of disappointment—even bitterness. For some, America came to mean a place of false hope and cruel promise. Yet the striving of these immigrants still elicits our admiration and respect—to the point of enhancing our understanding of ourselves. For how Jews lived then is very much a part of our lives today, bearing directly on our own feelings and decisions about the way we live now. This, then, is an American story, utterly part of the dominant American experience of arrival and suffering, success and self-doubt.

The Editors

ORIGINS

**EASTERN EUROPE IN THE
ERA OF THE GREAT MIGRATION**

〜〜〜〜 Boundary of the Pale of Settlement

The Old Ways

*FOR HUNDREDS OF YEARS Jews lived in eastern
Europe, subject to the tyranny of the czars, under conditions of
extreme poverty and persecution, harassed by obscurantist officials,
and helpless before the physical violence (pogroms, or
semiorganized riots) of benighted peasants. The Jews were usually
forbidden to own land—in an overwhelmingly agricultural country,
a severe economic handicap. They were forced to live within
certain prescribed areas called the Pale. There, scraping by as best
they could, they engaged in petty trading, worked at a few crafts,
and lived off their wits. (The luftmensh—the vivid Yiddish word
means someone who lives "off the air," through a deal here, a bit
of trade there, and some borrowing where possible—is a
characteristic figure of east European Jewish life.) Most of the Jews
lived in the shtetl, which was not, as sometimes supposed, a
village; it was a small town. Generations of poverty inevitably left
their mark in physical debility, social demoralization, a widespread
attitude of passivity (God would help, man could not).*

*Yet even in their impoverishment, the east European Jews
created a remarkable culture. For many centuries it was organically
religious—that is, every department of life was shaped and colored
by religious prescription and value. By the nineteenth century, it
was painfully transformed into a mixture of religious and secular,
the two linked in a tense but creative relationship. For the Jews
maintained themselves through a memory of greatness. It was not
so much the greatness of temples or ancient kings that they
remembered as it was the grandeur of their religious vision. For
them the Bible was a living reality: it was a token of promise, a
source of wisdom, a guide to conduct. As the philosopher Isaiah
Berlin has remarked, "the Jews of east Europe put all their faith in
God and concentrated all their hope either upon individual
salvation—immortality in the sight of God—or upon the coming of
the Messiah."*

*The central value of this culture, even if necessarily violated at
times in day-to-day life, was learning, a centuries-old tradition of
biblical and talmudic commentary immersed in moral judgment
and intellectual refinements. It was a tradition that sharpened wits,
even if confining them to what most present-day thinkers would
regard as too narrow, and sometimes even fanatical, an area of
inquiry. In any case, the east European Jews, even in their darkest
years, clung to intimations of renewed glory, lived by flickers of
sublimity. Their bitter life was warmed by the glow of messianic
hope. Periods of communal stagnation might set in, but they
would be followed by the return of that messianic glow, sometimes
blazing into the fires of the false messiahs of the seventeenth and
eighteenth centuries (Sabbatai Sevi, Jacob Frank) and sometimes
burning in the purer flame of Hasidic ecstasy and vision. Day by
day, amid the exhausting scramble for bread, there was spiritual
pleasure in the reenactment of ritual, the hush of ceremony, giving*

3

order to a life always threatened by external violence. Narrow, perhaps, and until the earlier decades of the nineteenth century quite cut off from the ideas and achievements of western Europe, the culture of the Jews in czarist Russia vibrated with moral and spiritual intensity.

Socially this world had not yet split into sharply defined and antagonistic classes. There were, however, fairly rigid distinctions of caste established through learning, piety, and economic position. By the middle of the nineteenth century, when Yiddish secular culture begins to appear, some east European Jews were abandoning the shtetl, *as it sank more and more deeply into destitution, and starting to move to cities like Warsaw and Lodz. A few decades later, by the 1880s, the great migration to America would begin.*

But here, meanwhile, are a few quick evocations of the world of the shtetl, *first of all, by Mendele Mokher Sforim, the pioneering Yiddish writer who in his loving satiric way lists the old-country ingredients "for enjoying prestige, for being respected and popular."*

Market day in Kazimierz, a Polish shtetl.
YIVO INSTITUTE FOR JEWISH RESEARCH

MENDELE MOKHER SFORIM

MORE THAN WEALTH was required. At one time in Lithuania—perhaps not so much today—*Torah* was held in higher esteem than money. A boor, no matter how rich, was nothing more than a boor. Never would he be voluntarily accorded a place of honor or listened to open-mouthed. Oh, no! To be worthy of that, one had to be learned, good, pious, and come of a good family. Prestige depended not on the moneybags but upon the mind and the heart.

Memories of the old country burned themselves forever into the consciousness of the immigrants, even those who felt not the slightest twinge of nostalgia. Marcus Ravage, a gifted American writer, and Morris Raphael Cohen, a distinguished philosopher and legendary teacher at the City College of New York, remembered in their later years the houses, the few pitiable luxuries, the towns of their youth.

MARCUS RAVAGE

THE HOUSES WERE LOW and made of mud, and instead of hardwood floors the ground was plastered with fresh clay—mixed with manure to give it solidity—which had to be removed every Friday. A family occupied but one room, or two at the most; but the houses were individual and sufficient, and the yard, spacious and green in summer, was filled with trees and flowers to delight the senses. . . . Homes were not furnished with parlor sets of velvet, and the womenfolks did not wear diamonds to market; but on the other hand they did not endure the insolence of [an American] installment agent, making a fearful scene whenever he failed to receive his weekly payment. No one was envious because his neighbor's wife had finer clothes and costlier jewels than his own had. The pride of a family was in its godliness and in its respected forebears. Such luxury as there was consisted in heavy copper utensils and silver candelabra, which were passed on as heirlooms from generation to generation—solid, substantial things, not the fleeting vanities of dress and upholstery

A tailor at his sewing machine, Kutno, Poland.   JEWISH DAILY FORWARD

MORRIS RAPHAEL COHEN

A VERY SERIOUS HANDICAP was the meager water supply from the few wells. There was a pond at the outskirts of the town. But as the stables of the cavalry regiment bordered on it, people did well not to drink its water, except after boiling. They supplemented the amount they bought from water-carriers by gathering in the rain in simple primitive ways. Thus, every time it rained, pots and pails were put out to catch the water that came over the massive buttresses of the military barracks.

This lack of water made people helpless against the frequent fires which in the summer would sweep away many houses—none of them insured. I remember that every time that the weekly portion of the Pentateuch began with Numbers, chapter 8, "Thou shalt kindle," we expected a fire. In one of these, the young son of a former neighbor of ours and his blind grandfather whom he was leading through a street were caught and burnt to death. When such fires broke out we used to pack up our belongings in a few bundles, carry them to a nearby field, and wait between hope and fear. One year our synagogue was burned, and later a volunteer fire company was organized. But the scant water supply limited its usefulness, and the town was almost wiped out a few years after I left. Still, even if there was no running water in any house, people never ate without previously washing their hands. There were no theaters, dance halls, or other places of public games or amusement. But there were numerous joyous occasions, besides holidays and the weekly Sabbath. There was music, and the seven days of festivities with every marriage, and every birth was likewise a joyous celebration. A rich intellectual life prevailed in the synagogues, where men would foregather in their plentiful leisure, either to study or to engage in general discussion, and where an occasional *Maggid* (lecturer on sacred themes) would hold his audience spellbound for hours with his animated discourse . . .

One of the forces that kept the Jews together under conditions of extreme adversity was their shared belief in the value—even, if you will, the sanctity—of the family. The Jewish community was not, as a rule, well organized; and what there was of communal structure was sometimes regarded as oppressive by the poorer Jews (it is bitterly satirized in the fiction of Mendele Mokher Sforim). Thus, the family became the one place of security for Jews of the shtetl. The family yielded meaning and value. It had fixed positions of status for men and women—and while today we are likely to disapprove of some of these arrangements of sexual hierarchy, they served in their time the purpose of enabling stability. Devout fathers would sometimes give themselves entirely to religious study, though it would be a sentimental exaggeration to suppose this the norm. Mothers sometimes managed little stalls in the markets or tiny shops, but their main task was to create an unbreakable circle of affection, security, ritual.

Old wooden synagogue, Radzyn, near Lublin, Poland. JEWISH DAILY FORWARD

MORRIS RAPHAEL COHEN

WITH THE AMOUNT of work that a Jewish housewife had in those days, and with the large number of children that were born, it is a wonder that any of them survived. For, in addition to the household work familiar to us, the women then had to chop wood for the oven, bake the bread, go considerable distances to draw water from some well, and carry it uphill even when the streets were covered with slippery ice. Worst of all, underwear, linen sheets, tablecloths, and the like, had to be washed in the river nearly a mile away, even in the wintry months when the washing had to be done through a hole in the ice. To press the water out of the wet things a kind of wooden hammer had to be carried, in addition to the wooden board. It was indeed a heavy load to carry home.

BERNARD HORWICH

MY MOTHER CHERISHED her husband. He came first in everything—the best food, drink, and clothes were only for him. While she ate bread and potatoes and herring, she prepared fish and meat for him. Nevertheless, she would often chide and reprimand my father for not being more aggressive—for being a *shlemiel* and letting everybody get the best of him; but then she would go off to some corner and pray to God that her husband would not think ill of her for being rude to him.

To her children, she was a loving despot. For the slightest offense she would curse, threaten, and quite often emphasize her indigna-

Jews outside Warsaw performing the rite of tashlikh. Oil painting by A. Gierymski. WARSAW NATIONAL MUSEUM

tion with slaps in the face or punches on the body, sometimes using a stick or a whip to make it more effective; but soon after she would quietly ask God to forgive her for having been so brutal to her own flesh and blood.

"Poor innocent lambs," she would whisper, "it is my fault, not theirs, that we are so poor and they do not get enough to eat, and have to wear torn shoes and clothes. Must I give vent to my troubles and bitter heart by taking it out on them?" And so it would go on.

ABRAHAM CAHAN

WE ENTER OUR HOME with a "*Gut Shabbes!*" My mother, in her spotlessly clean clothes, replies, "*Gut Shabbes!*" and glows with the Sabbath.

A holy aura surrounds the white tablecloth and the shining candlesticks with their glowing candles. My father paces back and forth across the room, excitedly singing a Sabbath song, and it is then that it seems I hear his *neshoma yeseroh* singing. I can hear it in his song. I can see it hovering over the candlesticks.

We wash our hands and take seats around the table, my father at the head, my mother on one side and I opposite her, on the sleeping bench. My father pronounces the *Kiddush* over the *challa* and cuts off a piece for me.

The *challa!* The fish! The noodles! The bit of meat and the hot tsimmes of carrots and potatoes! I liked this dessert cold, the way it would be served on the Sabbath morning. But by that time the *neshoma yeseroh* is also cold.

After the meal my father asks me to draw a straw from my mattress. He uses it as a toothpick. Then he reads the *midrash*. My mother reads her Yiddish translation of the Pentateuch. I read my *Sefer Ha-yosher* (book of morality) in Yiddish. Sometimes on these evenings my father reads aloud and makes my heart quiver.

No one who ever went to cheder *(elementary Hebrew school) in the old country was likely to forget it, both as pleasure and pain.*

MAURICE SAMUEL

... T W E N T Y O R T H I R T Y C H I L D R E N are jammed into a space of something like fifteen by fifteen feet. Except in the hot summer days, the windows are kept closed. The ceiling is low, the walls suppurate. The air in the room is indescribably foul. The youngest of the children may be four or five years old, the oldest are in their teens. From morning till night—the older ones ten or even twelve hours a day—they sit at primitive benches and they study, audibly; for audible study is meritorious, according to the sages of old, and in the *cheder* it is an accepted corollary that the greater the audibility, the higher the degree of merit. Naturally not all of them are studying the same thing. While some—the beginners—are chanting the alphabet, others are translating the week's portion of the Pentateuch into Yiddish, together with the penetrating commentaries of Rashi, perhaps the greatest of the medieval scholars; older ones—from nine up, that is—are engaged in talmudic argumentation, or conning the pages of *The Prepared Table*, a digest of the Jewish ritual code. The *rebbe* moves from group to group, chanting now with this one, now with that one. Three languages mingle in chorus: the Hebrew of the Bible and the prayers, the Aramaic of the Talmud, and the Yiddish into which both are translated.

DAVID BLAUSTEIN

... T H A T I M I G H T N O T look upon anything unclean on the way, my father wrapped me up in a *talith* and carried me in his arms to the *cheder*, which was about a mile distant from my home. I was received by the teacher, who held out to me the Hebrew alphabet on a large chart. Before starting in with the lesson I was given a taste of honey and was asked whether it was sweet, which of course I answered in the affirmative. I was then informed that I was about to enter upon the study of the Law, and that it was sweeter than honey. After that I was shown the first letter, *alef*, and was told to mark it well on my mind. I was doing that with the greatest seriousness, when suddenly a coin fell upon the alphabet. The teacher informed me that an angel had dropped it from heaven and through the ceiling, because I was a good little boy and wanted to learn.

Pesach—a time for celebrating the defeat of tyranny, the birth of a nation, spring, and renewal.

But on the heels of celebration, trepidation. No matter how secure an east European Jewish household might become in the recollection of the Exodus, never could it completely eradicate fearful thoughts of Easter violence at the hands of the Gentiles.

SHOLOM ALEICHEM

"THANK GOD there's no more *Purim*. Now we can start worrying about *Pesach*."

That's what I heard mama say as she began inspecting the four corners of the front room like a chicken about to lay an egg. While munching on my afternoon snack—a piece of bread smeared with chicken fat—I looked in.

"Aha!" mama shouted. "Standing with bread! May the devil not learn from you." As soon as mama went away, I peeked through a crack in the door. New pots! A new meat cleaver! Even a new salting board!

Pretty soon Sosil, the maid, appeared with a wet rag and a pail of whitewash. "Sosil, come here," mama ordered. Mama was dressed in white now, with even a white kerchief on her head. The two of them were as angry as could be until most of the house was whitewashed for *Pesach*.

"We'll eat *erev Pesach* in the cellar," mama told papa. Papa made faces. I couldn't understand. What was so terrible about eating next to souring pickles, fermenting cabbage, and crocks full of cheese? Who could they harm?

"While we're cleaning the cellar," mama said, "you two go up to the attic for a few hours." "Because the floors are still wet," Sosil added quickly.

From the attic window I peeked out into our own courtyard and saw all the neighbors scrubbing and washing, scraping and rubbing, making their tables and benches *kosher* for *Pesach*.

Spring was in the air; rivulets flowed down the streets. And there was Azriel, the delivery man, hauling a white horse and a load of *matzos* through the mud. We had bought ours a long time ago, in addition to eggs, a jar of *Pesach* chicken fat, two ropes of onions, and a lot of other things too. I thought of the new clothes I'd have for *Pesach* and my heart melted with joy.

ISAAC BABEL

IN A SMALL SIDE ALLEY, a peasant wearing a vest was smashing a window of a house. He was breaking the glass with a wooden mallet, swinging his whole body with it, sighing and beaming around him with the kindly smile of intoxication, sweat, and hearty vigor. The entire street was filled with the singing of cracking and splintering wood. The peasant was banging away with his mallet only because he wanted to swing, to bend, to sweat, and to shout extraordinary, outlandish words. He shouted and sang them, his blue eyes goggling, until a procession appeared in the street, coming from the town hall. Old men with dyed beards were carrying a portrait of the czar. The czar's hair was beautifully combed. Banners with pictures of sepulchered saints on them flapped over the procession. Excited old crones surged forward. The peasant in the vest caught sight of the procession, pressed his mallet to his chest, and rushed after the banners; I waited for the procession to pass, then made my way home.

"Kishinev Massacre—over 300 Killed!"—Jewish Daily Forward, *May 1, 1903. The outbreak of pogroms in 1903 throughout the Russian Pale hastened the immigration to America of hundreds of thousands of east-European Jews.*

First as a trickle, then a flood, the Western Enlightenment—ideas of secularism, science, progress, politics, history, culture—came to the east European Jews. The Enlightenment came mostly in the form of books, in Russian and German, also in Yiddish and Hebrew. Young people would turn to these books with eagerness, hungry for excluded knowledge; they often felt that the learning of the Jews had degenerated into scholasticism, mere empty formula; they wanted to know what was being thought and said in the outer world—Kant and Rousseau, Marx and Hegel, Tolstoy and Turgenev, all the thinkers, novelists and poets the religious authorities regarded as alien and threatening. As with the philosopher Morris Raphael Cohen, it wasn't only exalted reading that brought the outer world to the young Jews of the shtetl; sometimes popular romances and historical stories stirred imaginations of undiscovered worlds.

MORRIS RAPHAEL COHEN

I READ WITH ARDENT ENTHUSIASM the heroic account of Jacob Diradia, the leader of a group of Marranos who escaped from Spain and Portugal to found a Jewish community in Holland. As I recall it now, it was full of absurdly impossible exploits, such as the defeat of Spanish battleships by the refugees. But having been brought up on biblical miracles, such incidents did not seem to me unbelievable or even strange. The story that gripped me most of all was that of Bar Kochba, the leader of the final Judean revolt against Roman oppression. Reading about a handful of Jews successfully resisting the whole Roman Empire for three years fired my imagination. For some days I carried a flat piece of wood under my coat, picturing it in my mind's eye as a sword with which I, too, might someday fight the armies of my persecutors. To this day I cannot read the story of the martyrdom of Rabbi Akiba, which occurred in connection with that rebellion, without being moved to tears.

Abraham Cahan went further than Morris Raphael Cohen.
Studying a popular science text, he came to a terrifying conclusion.

ABRAHAM CAHAN

I STRUGGLED VAINLY to understand the origin of the seasons. For days I studied the text and the diagrams. The riddles plagued me even while I strolled in the streets. Then, one Saturday afternoon, everything suddenly became clear to me. There it was—day and night and winter and summer—all clear! I was ecstatic. So

Four east-European Jewish writers (left to right): Mendele Mokher Sforim (1836–1917), Sholom Aleichem (1859–1916), Mordecai Ben-Ami (1854–1932), Chaim Nachman Bialik (1873–1934).

profound and yet so simple! The excitement within me grew. My brain was in a whirl. I was overwhelmed by new questions—about God and His miracles. The answers came easily. Clearly, there were no miracles, there was no God. My first feeling was one of release. There was nothing to be afraid of. I desecrated the Sabbath, I cursed His name—aloud, without a tremor of fear, astonished at my own fearlessness. Suddenly it occurred to me that if there is no God there is no one to curse, so I stopped cursing.

I.L. Peretz is commonly regarded, together with Mendele Mokher Sforim and Sholom Aleichem, as one of the founding fathers of Yiddish literature. Living in Warsaw, immersing himself in Yiddish folk and Hasidic materials, writing his delicately ironic stories, Peretz was characteristic of those Jewish intellectuals who would live out their lives facing, so to speak, two ways: with deep affection toward the Jewish folk past, with uneasy conviction toward the growing secular culture of the Jews.

I. L. PERETZ

I FELT, THOUGH NOT CLEARLY, that I was tearing myself away from something and from somebody—from somebody I knew, from something dear to me. I didn't sleep nights, and for days on end I wandered around and beyond the highway gates. I had an inner feeling of guilt, as if I were breaking a social code. Suddenly, something in me congealed, and something within me died. I didn't believe anymore in divine metaphysics. I didn't believe anymore in heaven, nor in reward or punishment for one's acts in life. But with whom could I talk about such things? To whom could I lay bare my astounded heart? I was speechless with the people around me, for I had no words in Yiddish to express what I had read. I attempted to talk to myself, but this didn't work either.

14 *If, as a son or daughter of a* shtetl *family, you took the giant step of denying the existence of God—which also meant the most severe and lacerating wrench from parents you still loved; and if you yielded yourself as well to the new ideas of science, progress, and humanism; it was very likely that in the atmosphere of the late nineteenth and early twentieth centuries you would soon declare yourself a socialist. The socialist movement, still fresh and unsullied, was sweeping Europe, proclaiming the possibility of a better life for the oppressed and the mute. Among east European Jews, the socialist vision roused a deep response. It provided a new faith for those who had surrendered the substance of the old one but still felt a need for some terms of transcendence. The messianic hunger, so deeply ingrained in Jewish life, had a way of reappearing now in secular guise. And young Jewish intellectuals, aflame with idealism and innocence, together with many among the Jewish working class, abandoning traditional postures of passivity for the idea of assertiveness, gave themselves passionately to the socialist hope.*

ABRAHAM CAHAN

LIFE TOOK ON NEW MEANING. Our society was built on injustices that could be erased. All could be equal. All could be brothers! I divided the world into two groups: "they" and "we." I looked on "them" with pity and scorn. I thought of any friend of mine who was one of "them" as an unfortunate being. At the same time my new belief led me to speak gently even when mixing scorn with sympathy. A kind of religious ecstasy took hold of me. I did not recognize my former self. In the first weeks of my conversion, I walked in a daze as one newly in love. I even grew lighthearted about my crossed eyes. Worrying about public approval or what impression one was making on the ladies was sharply criticized. Unless it interfered with one's mission, one was expected to be contemptuous of public opinion and to maintain a serious approach to life. "Why should I be bothered by the petty fact that my eyes are not straight?" I reasoned to myself. "Who cares if my appearance is not pleasant? I am above such foolishness. There are more important things to worry about." Earlier, I had felt relief at being rid of the belief in God, hell, and punishment in the next world. Now I felt another heavy load slip off my heart.

For the Russian Jews, the outbreak of the 1905 revolution, with its apparent promise of a constitution, some democracy, and an easing of czarist anti-Semitism, brought large, perhaps excessive hopes. Most Jews sided with the forces of liberalism, on the grounds that in a free society there would be religious tolerance. Simon Dubnow, a major Jewish historian and spokesman in the east European Jewish world for the cause of Yiddish cultural autonomy, would recall in his memoirs the Jewish response to the revolution.

But there was, of course, a darker outcome. The "Black Hundreds," gangs of hoodlums surreptitiously (sometimes openly) helped by the government, began to indulge in pogroms once czarism regained the upper hand. Sholom Aleichem, the great Yiddish writer, sent a letter in November 1905 to a Yiddish newspaper in New York, vividly detailing these tragic events.

SIMON DUBNOW

... T H E   O U T B R E A K of the general strike brought about the ostensible surrender of the government on October 17. Until then, we were cut off from the world by the railroad strike—without newspapers, without correspondence, ignorant of developments elsewhere. For days there was violence and disorder. Then, abruptly, it halted. The police disappeared. The authority of the government vanished.

"Hurrah! The Revolution Grows Victorious!"—Jewish Daily Forward, December 30, 1905. A few weeks later the Forward announced to a stunned readership the collapse of the revolutionary movement throughout Russia.

Early on October 18, while in my study, I heard a ring, then voices in the vestibule. Shmarya Levin and some other people came in with the joyous announcement: "A constitution!" They brought the first news of the manifesto of October 17. The czar had granted all civic rights and a legislative Duma to be elected on the basis of universal suffrage. When I went out, it was a clear morning, not at all like autumn. Crowds had gathered on the corners and buzzed; friends greeted each other with jubilant faces and expressions. That day I wrote in my diary: "Is not this near the realization of a dream which had each day for a quarter of a century been murdered? Are we not standing at the threshold of a real constitutional order? I await with impatience news about the manifesto and newspapers."

SHOLOM ALEICHEM

TOGETHER WITH A NUMBER of families, my wife and children and I are cowering under a storm of bullets over our heads. We remain powerless, useless, paralyzed.

On the seventeenth we were "presented" with the constitution for which our brothers spilled their blood like water. On the same day a rumor was spread abroad that orders had been given to attack the Jews—and the attack began from all sides. Simultaneously, an order was issued that we should not shoot from the windows, and not throw stones. If we should do that, the soldiers would fire back and destroy our houses. Seeing soldiers on the street—and cossacks—we felt reassured; and they did help, but not us. They helped to rob, to beat, to ravish, to despoil. Before our eyes and in the eyes of the whole world, they helped to smash windows, break down doors, break locks and to put booty in their pockets. Before our eyes and in the eyes of our children, they beat Jews grievously—men, women and children—and they shouted, "Money, give us your money." Before our eyes women were hurled from windows and children thrown to the cobblestones.

The local newspapers publish only one hundredth part of the frightful details of the happenings in Kiev. Now, imagine what is happening in hundreds of Jewish towns and villages. Too dear will our freedom cost, and God only knows whether we will live to enjoy it. The tyrant will not surrender his rod, the swords are being sharpened. . . . In God's name, brethren, help. To act, to help, to resist, that we are not permitted. For the life of one drunken brute that we take when he attacks our wives and our children we pay with hundreds of innocent lives.

What shall we do? No place to hide. Gentiles will not give shelter to Jews.

Brother, do something. Publish this in English as well as in the Jewish press.

Well then, if I cannot be saved, if I must die, I am ready. Perhaps it is better that I shall fall a sacrifice with the rest. My people are being consumed. The whole of Russian Jewry is in danger.

Castle Garden, at the Battery on the southern tip of Manhattan, where immigrants were received before the opening of Ellis Island in 1892.

Off to America

Why did they come?—millions of them, Jews from Russia and Poland, Lithuania and Rumania, Hungary and Austria?

The main reason is clear: to get away. To get away from the czar and his army, which grabbed Jewish boys for incredible lengths of service (at some points for as long as twenty-five years) and sometimes subjected them to forced conversions. To get away from the stagnation, the hunger, the hopelessness. To get away from drunken policemen and brutalized peasants.

Some of us can remember the conversations of a few decades ago in immigrant homes, over glasses of tea in dimly lit kitchens, the recollections of di alte heym ("the old home") certainly not free of nostalgia and even homesickness, yet also with a shudder of horror at memories of suffering.

And then there was the lure of the new world, di goldeneh medina, ("the golden land") as the immigrants called it hopefully, though not without irony (nothing for them was without irony). Letters came back that here you could work yourself to the bone, work yourself into TB sanatoriums, but still work yourself up, in order to bring relatives over and send children to schools. The Jews who came to America were a people infatuated with ideas of the future, not so much for themselves as for their children. The future was their dream, their "fix."

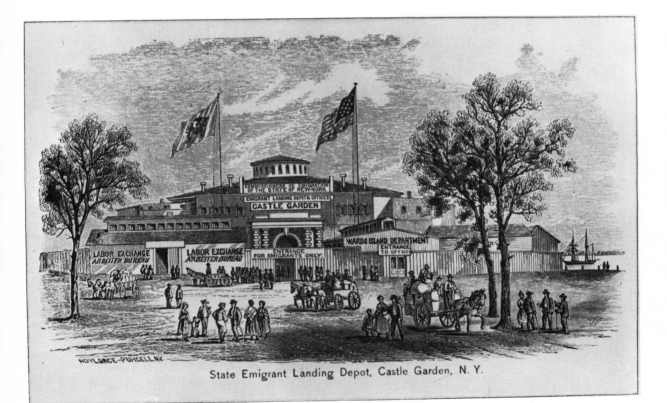

State Emigrant Landing Depot, Castle Garden, N. Y.

Here a chorus of immigrant voices, some taken from fiction, tries to explain what brought them to America—and what made them stay.

ABRAHAM CAHAN

I T   W A S   O N E of these letters from America . . . which put the notion of immigrating to the New World definitely in my mind. An illiterate woman brought it to the synagogue to have it read to her, and I happened to be the one to whom she addressed her request. The concrete details of that letter gave New York tangible form in my imagination . . . [yet,] the United States lured me not merely as a land of milk and honey, but also, perhaps chiefly, as one of mystery, of fantastic experiences, of marvelous transformations. To leave my native place and to seek my fortune in that distant weird world seemed to be just the kind of sensational adventure my heart was hankering for.

MARCUS RAVAGE

I N   T H E   Y E A R of my departure from Rumania in 1900 America had become, as it were, the fashionable place to go. Hitherto it had been but a name, and by no means a revered one. But suddenly America had flashed upon our consciousness and fanned our dormant souls to flames of consuming ambition. All my relatives and all our neighbors—in fact, everybody who was anybody—had either gone or was going to New York. Everybody who went there became a millionaire overnight, and a doctor or a teacher into the bargain. In New York, it appeared, education was to be got altogether without cost, by Jew and Gentile alike, by day or

Reading on the steerage deck of the S.S. Pennland, 1893. Photograph by Byron.
MUSEUM OF THE CITY OF NEW YORK, BYRON COLLECTION

night. The government of America not only did not exact charges for instruction; it compelled parents to send their children to school, and it begged grown-ups to come and be educated when their day's work was over. There, in America, was my future, as well as my family's. For it would take me only a few weeks to make enough money to send for them.

CHONE GOTTESFELD

WHERE DO YOU TRAVEL, and wherefore do you travel? You are heading for a corrupt and sinful land where the Sabbath is no Sabbath and the holiday no holiday. Even on the *Yom Kippur* they do not fast. And for what purpose are *you* going there? So you can eat meat every day—they say that in America people can eat meat every day. But their meat is *trayf*. No good Jew would touch such meat. I would loathe even to look at it. I would disgorge it if I accidentally ate it. Feh! Utterly disgusting.

ANZIA YEZIERSKA

...TO MY WORTHY WIFE, Masheh Mindel, and to my loving son, Susha Feifel, and to my precious darling daughter, the apple of my eye, the pride of my life, Tzipkeleh!

Long years and good luck on you! May the blessings from heaven fall over your beloved heads and save you from all harm!

First I come to tell you that I am well and in good health. May I hear the same from you.

Secondly, I am telling you that my sun is beginning to shine in America. I am becoming a person—a businessman.

I have for myself a stand in the most crowded part of America, where people are as thick as flies and every day is like market day by a fair. My business is from bananas and apples. The day begins with my pushcart full of fruit, and the day never ends before I count up at least two dollars' profit—that means four rubles. . . . I . . . Gedalyeh Mindel, four rubles a day, twenty-four rubles a week!

Thirdly, I come to tell you . . . white bread and meat I eat every day just like the millionaires.

Fourthly, I have to tell you that I am no more Gedalyeh Mindel—*Mister* Mindel they call me in America.

Fifthly, Masheh Mindel and my dear children, in America there are no mud huts where cows and chickens and people live all together. I have for myself a separate room with a closed door, and before anyone can come to me, I can give a say: "Come in," or "Stay out," like a king in a palace.

Lastly, my darling family and people of the village of Sukovoly, there is no czar in America.

CHONE GOTTESFELD

WHAT WILL PEOPLE THINK of me, I wondered, when I return from America penniless? All other men who came from America sported big diamond rings on their fingers, golden watches with heavy golden chains strung across their vests, and gold-rimmed eyeglasses on their noses, whereas I would come back just as poor as when I left—a total failure. In my hometown every American was presumed to be a wealthy person; the jewels indicated as much. And what will they say about me? Poverty is no disgrace for one who stays in town and does not venture abroad, but it is unpardonable for one who comes from the golden land.

One of the things that distinguished the Jewish migration to America, and set it apart from the journeys of other ethnic groups, is the fact that the Jews brought their intellectuals—their writers, their thinkers—with them. It isn't hard to understand why. Immigrants coming from the various European countries, especially those in the south and east of the Continent, tended to come from the poorer classes, those without jobs in the cities or land in the countryside, people who had nothing to lose. But the intellectuals, by and large, of countries like Italy and Poland stayed at home. With the Jews it was all very different. Their writers and thinkers were jammed into the constricted life of the Pale quite as the ordinary people were. There was very little place for Jewish intellectuals in the cultural life of the east European countries. Consequently, many of them came here along with the masses of ordinary Jews, thereby enriching the Yiddish culture that the immigrant would build up in America.

One of those who came, for the last few years of his life, was the great Yiddish writer—indeed, the greatest of all Yiddish writers—Sholom Aleichem. And naturally he wrote some sketches about the confusions of the journey, the bewilderment of arrival.

SHOLOM ALEICHEM

WELL, WE'RE OFF FOR AMERICA. Where it is, I don't know. I only know it's far. You have to ride and ride until you get there. And when you get there, there's a Kestel Gartel where they undress you and look you in the eyes.

"So you are going, really going to America?" says our neighbor Pesi. "May God bring you there safe and sound, and help you strike luck. With God everything is possible. Just last year our Rivele went to America with her husband, Hillel. The first few months we heard nothing from them. We thought they had fallen, God forbid, into the sea. Finally they write us, 'America is a free country where everyone is miserable making a living.' Now, I ask you, is that any way to write? Why can't they write like human beings—the what and the when and the how?" Hirsch Leib, the mechanic, says he would never think of letting *his* Pini go to America. America, he says, is *feh.*"

Now begins a new business—saying good-bye. From house to house we march, saying good-bye. We spend the whole day at our *machetunim*'s, where they give me a seat in the corner with little Alte. They call us bride and groom whenever they see us together. But they don't bother us. We sit there and talk.

"Will you write to me?" she asks.

"Why not?" I answer.

"Do you know how?"

"In America anyone can learn," I say to her, and stick my hands in my pockets. They all envy me for going to America, even Yosie, the son of Henech Vashti with the crooked eyes.

ON THE TRAIN to the border, when we hear the word *America* we rejoice.

"So you're going to New York! We're going to Philadelphia."

"What is Philadelphia?"

"A town like New York."

"Wait a minute. Philadelphia is no more like New York than Aysheshock is like Vilna or Otvozk like Warsaw."

"You seem to have been all over the world. So tell me something. What about this border? What do we do?"

"You'll do what everyone else does."

Then they huddle together and talk about stealing the border. I don't understand. What does it mean? Are we thieves? But sh! We are already there.

AT ANTWERP, waiting for the ship to take us to America, we meet Goldele, a girl with bad eyes. People tell her family to go to the doctor. So they go to the doctor. The doctor examines them and finds they are all hale and hearty and can go to America, but she, Goldele, cannot go because she has trachomas on her eyes. At first her family do not understand. Only later do they realize what it means. It means that they can all go to America but she, Goldele, will have to remain behind in Antwerp. So there begins a wailing, a weeping, a moaning. Three times her mama faints. Her papa wants to stay with her but he can't. All the ship tickets would be lost. So they have to go off to America and leave her, Goldele, here until the trachomas will go away from her eyes.

... A SUDDEN, A GREAT EXCITEMENT breaks out: passengers begin to be ordered downstairs to their little cages. They are told to go where they belong. At first politely, then

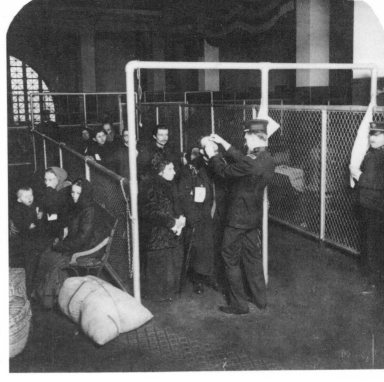

The much-feared eye examination at Ellis Island, 1907. LIBRARY OF CONGRESS

21

roughly. If you don't hurry up you get a good whack from behind. All the steerage passengers are here. It is stifling. They have locked the door and hung an iron chain across it. We have never felt so miserable as we do now. In our own eyes we look like prisoners. "For what? For when?" my chum Mendel keeps saying, while his eyes blaze and shoot fire. Come to find out, we have arrived in America.

"What will they do, pickle us?" I ask.

"No," someone answers back, "but they will take us to a certain place they call Ellis Island. There they will shut us up in a stall like calves until our friends and relatives get good and ready to take us out!" Pini almost flies out of his skin.

At Ellis Island we treat ourselves to lunch. They don't give us much, but with our hunger satisfied we begin to watch for our relatives and friends. The first one to show up is fat Pesi with her husband Moishe, the bookbinder. It costs us a quarter and we see them through the bars. Pesi's red face and fat chin are perspiring. She smiles at us from a distance. Mama nods to her and they both shed tears. From behind her broad shoulders Moishe looks out. He wears a hat now, not a cap like in the old country. We are dying to ask them a hundred questions, but cry *gevalt* you can't budge an inch.

Russian-Jewish arrival photographed at Ellis Island by Lewis Hine.
NEW YORK PUBLIC LIBRARY, LOCAL HISTORY AND
GENEALOGY DIVISION

2

THE SCENE

Relatives waiting at Battery Park for new arrivals. Photograph by Byron.

MUSEUM OF THE CITY OF NEW YORK, BYRON COLLECTION

The Shock of America

The first day in the new world, the first step upon American land, the first sight of this terrifying New York, the first emotions a compound of loneliness, bewilderment, fear and excitement—no immigrant, regardless of how dulled his memory might become through trouble or success, could ever forget that moment. Talk to one thirty, forty, even fifty years later, and he or she will always come back to that moment, with its realization that life is now forever changed, all is unfamiliar, even if in the near distance relatives are waving and Jewish officials want to help.

For who had ever seen such buildings before? Who had seen such masses of people scurrying about, their eyes fixed on some distant prospect, without apparent notice of the people near or in front of them? Noise, lights, streetcars, screaming hawkers, people shouting, "Go left, go right," children crying, yet with some undercurrent of good nature to it all?

Back home, for all its physical miseries, there had been order, sequence, assured meaning in each passage of the day. Here—what is this uncle, with his gleaming fat face, his few phrases of American speech, yelling? What does he mean by "business" and "jobs"? When do these people pray—or do they pray? How is it that a cousin, in the shtetl so mild and pious, has here gotten to be so sure of himself? And why doesn't he wear a hat?

MARCUS RAVAGE

EVERY DAY THAT PASSED I became more and more overwhelmed at the degeneration of my fellow countrymen in this new home of theirs. Even their names had become emasculated and devoid of either character or meaning. . . . It did not seem to matter at all what one had been called at home. The first step toward Americanization was to fall into one or the other of the two great tribes of Rosies and Annies.

Cut adrift suddenly from their ancient moorings, they were floundering in a sort of moral void. Good manners and good conduct, reverence and religion, had all gone by the board, and the reason was that these things were not American. . . . The ancient racial respect for elders had completely disappeared. . . . American old age had forfeited its claim to deference because it had thrown away its dignity. Tottering grandfathers had snipped off their white beards and laid aside their skullcaps and their snuffboxes and paraded around the streets of a Saturday afternoon with cigarettes in their mouths, when they should have been lamenting the loss of the Holy City in the study room adjoining the synagogue.

*It all seems to get worse, after the first two or three days of
welcome and rest. Relatives turn back to their own troubles; Jewish
agencies have ever-new flocks of immigrants to take care of; the
streets—in their winter grayness, their summer heat—seem more
alien. What have we gotten ourselves into?*

*Into the shops; into an apprenticeship often without pay, so as to
learn the rudiments of sewing and basting, cutting and pressing;
into the darkness of the tenements; into a room shared with two
other boarders; into endless hours of work. How can people labor
so long, from early in the morning till late at night? How can they
live without seeing the sun? And what is this pittance that you get
for these hours with a needle or a press iron?*

*To be an immigrant, in the first few weeks, is to know sadness,
bewilderment, loneliness . . . but not entirely. Remember what
has been left behind, the armies of the czar, the drunken police,
the peasants filled with hatred for Jews.*

*One thing is clear about the life of the Jewish immigrants. Bad
as their life might be in New York and Chicago, Boston and
Philadelphia—especially during the first waves of immigration,
from 1881 to the first two or three years of the twentieth century—
they seldom thought seriously of going back. Nostalgia,
homesickness, yes; but back to the czar, back to the shtetl, no.
They were here, for good or bad, and here they would have to
make their life.*

ISAAC RABOY

I'D NEVER HAD ICE CREAM BEFORE. It was as
new to me as America. We walked and ate. When we passed girls
my brothers wanted to give them a taste of our ice cream. The girls
refused. We reached a boulevard and stood there with other young
men who greeted my brothers.

I felt as if on coals. No word could I think of but "greenhorn."

. . . Across Delancey Street, we passed young Jewish men and
women. The girls had painted cheeks and greased netted hair with
hidden pins. As if that weren't enough, they also flashed golden
teeth. They seemed faded, withered. The males with stiff hats
tipped over their foreheads and their plastered locks, gave off an
aroma of vulgar, youthful virility. Who else was in the street?
Elderly Jews and Jewesses, their mouths filled with gold; Jews
hawking their wares from pushcarts filled with all that's exotic—I
soon decided that here Jews live in the streets.

BERNARD WEINSTEIN

THE BAD TIMES BEGAN. I took to sleeping in the streets
in express wagons. Often at night I'd feel a patrolman's club on my
feet.

Once a friend, an unemployed cigarmaker, suggested that I sleep
in the Eldridge Street police station. There they gave you a place to
sleep overnight and in the morning free breakfast, just like the
prisoners.

Rows of tenements.
CHILDREN'S AID SOCIETY OF NEW YORK

I took my friend's advice.

On a cold evening I went to the station. My heart trembled as I went to the police lieutenant and told him I'd been going around some time without work, that I had to move out of my room because I couldn't pay. I asked him to let me stay the night.

The lieutenant listened to my story, then winked to a policeman who told me to go with him. He led me into the basement, unlocked a room and let me inside. A kerosene lamp was flickering.

27

Several tramps lay on the ground. The policeman pointed to a spot on the floor, honored my back with his club, and commanded: "Lie down over there."

He left, locking the iron-grated door behind him.

I let myself down to the stone floor. I sat there a long time thinking of my life in the huge, strange city New York till sleep overcame me.

It wasn't cold there, but there was a strong odor and my neighbors snored dreadfully; yet, I slept through the night peacefully.

At dawn I heard the door being unlocked. I woke up and saw before me a policeman who was banging my feet. I rose neither dead nor alive. The room was noisy.

The policeman also tapped the others who'd been lying on the torn straw sacks, after which he had us all stand against the wall.

I considered my new companions. They were all aging tramps. I leaned over to the man nearest me and asked: "What do we do now?"

"Wait. They'll soon give us something to eat," he answered me under his breath.

It didn't take long till a second policeman entered—without a club. He carried a big rusty kettle with little tin cups. He gave each of us a cup with some murky liquid that looked like coffee. He also gave us some old rolls, and standing there, we took to our meal. When we finished breakfast the policeman opene the door and drove us into the streets.

It turned out that I would sleep again in that police station, and once I made the acquaintance of the anarchist Alexander Berkman on its stone floor.

LEON KOBRIN

SOMETIMES THERE APPEARED from a street a group of "green" Jews, straight off the ship. They cross the gutter in little bunches like new recruits. One group after another, they go, tan and weary from the sea wind and the difficult journey. They drag valises and packages and boxes and bundles and metal pots and also children on their arms, and before them goes someone from the immigrant society. . . .

The sun seems dark and worried. A weariness emanates from the Jews, from the wagons and tables and shops around which they mill, and weariness is carried from the gray walls of the tenement houses where these same Jews with their wives and children, with their . . . "boarders" and "boarderesses" choke themselves in dark rooms with no light or air . . . where bedbugs and roaches scurry around.

These Jewish streets stretch from the Bowery to the Grand Street Ferry, which ties New York to Brooklyn, and from Houston to Cherry streets.

From these streets Allen Street stands out. There, high up along the tenement houses, the "elevated" runs with a roar, the wonder of

"The First Step Toward a Maiden's Downfall"—This drawing by Samuel Zaget appeared in the early years of the century in the Yiddish newspaper **Warheit.**

TAMIMENT COLLECTION, NEW YORK UNIVERSITY

the green Jews of that time, the elevated which consisted of a few small wagons dragged by a tiny locomotive that spread around itself a thick black smoke and darkened everything and everyone around it, and there beneath the roar, an open market in human flesh is conducted.

In front of every house there stand women of every age and they call to passersby to buy their flesh.

ISAAC RABOY

AT NIGHT, when I walk in the streets of the city, all the windows are open and I can see the life inside with all its filth and sadness. Bare, scarred tables. Countless beds, with tangled sheets and blankets. The yellow gaslight, and so many, many children, and nakedness and noise . . . Life must be very bitter here, or else they wouldn't scream so loud. (When people are happy they speak quietly and calmly.) Here they yell even when they talk intimately. . . .

I sit by the open window, watching. I want to find out whether the people here really know each other, and it seems to me they don't. Very seldom, almost never, do people greet each other, or exchange a warm handclasp. . . . They're constantly rushing in all directions, as though somebody was driving them.

The days fly by so fast that often I feel as though I were leaping over a whole generation. At times I even see myself an old man, like my grandfather, but without his confidence, without his faith.

FORWARD, 6/26/'05

EVERYBODY KNOWS THE FACTS about terrible poverty in immigrant families. The following data are excerpts from the official medical report of the New York Lying-In Hospital:

Here is our doctor at the door of an apartment in 120 Delancey Street. The family arrived in America six weeks ago; the mother just gave birth to her first child. The father is an unemployed painter. The two-room apartment is occupied by the father, mother, newborn child, and eight boarders. Can you imagine the horror and debasement of giving birth in the presence of eight strangers? The mother lies on an old sofa; there are piles of dirt in all the corners. The boarders sleep on old mattresses.

68 Moore Street. This is the mother's seventh child. The family of nine lives in one room, of which the front part is the father's shoemaking "business." Here he plies his trade. The single window is also the show window. The room is indescribably filthy. The parents look to the time when the oldest boy will be twelve and go to work.

Rear view of an Allen Street tenement, and a bathtub in an airshaft between two dumbbell tenements. Designed in 1878 by James E. Ware, the dumbbell tenement earned a well-deserved reputation for providing maximum profit for the investor and maximum discomfort for the tenant. Photograph by Jacob Riis.

MUSEUM OF THE CITY OF NEW YORK, JACOB A. RIIS COLLECTION

Later generations have sometimes wondered whether the poverty of the early immigrant Jews, especially those who got here before the turn of the century, was as acute as they later remembered. We can understand the force of this question, since it's a natural temptation to exaggerate early hardships in order to make more dramatic one's escape from them. But the truth, so far as we can determine, seems to be that by and large the immigrants did not exaggerate. All the memoirs, all the contemporary accounts, all the newspaper reports, all the statistics (poor as these are for the immigrant milieu) agree. Poverty was extreme and prolonged for many of those who came from eastern Europe, and it took years before they could climb out of it.

Here are a few vignettes of these painful social conditions as they appeared in the Yiddish newspaper the Forward *a few years after the turn of the century. Being a socialist paper, and with a decided tendency toward sensationalism, the* Forward *might be suspected of overstating things. But it really wasn't . . . these are sober observations, though sometimes with somewhat lurid language. The* Forward *reflected, as no other institution in the immigrant world, the feelings and experiences of its people.*

166 Norfolk Street. The happy parents welcome their first child. They live in a furnished room, together with two other couples. There is only one bed. When the doctor asks where they sleep, they can only reply that they manage somehow. The doctor thinks they take turns, each night a different couple uses the bed. Or perhaps on an hourly schedule: One couple has the bed till midnight, then it goes to the other.

FORWARD, 2/7/'03

THE SIGNS ON THE DARK, gloomy walls of the dispensary announce that patients are received from 12:30 to 2:00 P.M. It is now after 3:00, and not a single doctor is to be seen. Nobody has the courage to ask when they will come. The employees of the free dispensary all have the same cold, contemptuous stares; every gesture shouts: "You are a charity patient, so sit and wait."

The benches are filled; men, women and children hold their numbered cards. It is a sea of troubles, pain, and tragedy. You forget your own suffering.

A forty-year-old woman sits next to me. She says her husband is the sick one, not she. He works at boys' pants, and earns about seven dollars a week. They have five children. "He started to cough, got pains in his back and chest. We don't have the fifty cents for the doctor, and we can't afford medicine. If he sits in the dispensaries, he will lose pay. So I go, while he works. I make believe I am the sick one, they give me medicine, and he takes it. He feels a little better now."

The doctors began to arrive. The woman stopped talking and gave me a farewell smile.

How immigrants in New York were forced to live— The Barracks on 98 Mott Street, built in 1884 by The Association for Improving the Condition of the Poor.
COURTESY OF COMMUNITY SERVICE SOCIETY OF NEW YORK

FORWARD, 8/1/'02

PERSONAL

My dear husband, Barney, I beg you to come home. If not, send a *get*. Your wife, Fanny. 147 Moore Street, Brooklyn.

The sister-in-law of Shlomo Cahn from Slonim is looking for him. Mathilda Cahn, 183 Osborne Street, Brownsville.

I am looking for my husband, David Silecki, the butcher from Pruzani. He is thirty-five years old, blond, of mediocre height, with a round fat face. Whoever knows about him should contact Zuckerman, 7 Orchard Street.

FORWARD, 2/8/'04

SIX IN THE MORNING. Outside of Seward Park on Division Street stands a long line of Italians with gaunt faces—several Jews among them. They've been standing since 4:00 A.M., stamp their frozen feet on the ground, and keep their icy hands on the iron fence to hold their place in line. They are waiting for a city job to sweep the snow from the streets. A short fat man arrives, selects a few, gives them tickets, appoints a foreman and sends them to another street where they will get pickaxes and shovels. The Jews know the fat Irishman doesn't like Jews; and—as the Tammany bum continues to count—he grabs a man with a long nose by the collar and wants to drag him out of line. The frightened Italian cries "Me no Jew!"—the others confirm it, and he gets a ticket. The Jews remain in line like whipped dogs.

In the life of the immigrants, space would constitute a major problem for many years. People had to crowd into tiny apartments, often sleeping three or four in a room. The shock of America meant, once you had a job, that you had no corner of your own, no bit of space in which to turn. And to help pay the rent, people had to take in boarders—there was never any shortage since young unmarried men were always coming off the ships.

    Around the boarder the immigrant world created an entire mythology of stories, jokes, songs—sometimes sad, sometimes jolly. Here the Forward, *with its lively sociological eye, offers a 1906 portrait of the boarder, his pleasures and his plight. Then comes a clever poem by A.M. Sharansky, which appeared in a 1901 issue of a Yiddish paper; it parodies Hamlet's soliloquy in bemoaning the life of the boarder.*

FORWARD, 2/12/'06

I t' s N O T G O O D to be a boarder—a fifth wheel in a strange household: with a Mrs. who measures by her stare how much soap one has used, and the spoonfuls of sugar in one's coffee; who complains that one sleeps too long or makes faces if he gets up too early. . . .

Some boarders join a family on speculation. If they like the Mrs., good; if not, they pack their laundry in their armpits, and off they go. These boarders have no easy life. They demand much more than a Mrs. is ready to offer. . . .

The boarder is an opportunist. He looks for a young widow, divorcée, grass widow or a Mrs. with a traveling husband. He tests a woman's generosity. First he sympathizes with her lot: how so gentle a lady carries coals, hovers over a hot stove. He lifts the pail of coal from her hands, grinds the coffee, pours out the soiled laundry water while she stands half naked, bare-armed over the washtub. He creates the image of the model boarder.

The Mrs. delights in his favors as when someone offers her a seat in a streetcar: the incident ends with her "Thank you."

Then he tells the Mrs., if she has a Mr., that a man should treat a woman better. If he himself had such a woman he'd carry her about on his hands and serve her nectar and ambrosia. If the woman has no husband step two is to invite her to a music hall or Yiddish theater. He urges they go out together for a good time.

The final step is suggestion—of things she's never dreamed of. At this point the good Mrs. gets angry and turns into a bad one. She contemplates her right hand: how good a fist can it form. The boarder, having failed again, packs up once more. . . .

He never really finds what he wants, although he may occasionally succeed in leading a good woman astray and destroying a peaceful family life.

Scandal is never far off where a boarder works his way in. "The Mrs. and the boarder" is an old story, yet ever played out anew.

There are also many boarders who leave their lodgings in response to a Mrs. too forward in her flirtations. Her intentions are never clear. Does she want action or just to torture? . . .

Just as there are wandering boarders there are wandering *boarderkehs* who pursue the same living patterns as the males—aging virgins who stalk male-inhabited dwellings for marriage.

Marriage between boarders rarely happens, and a Mrs. who keeps lodgers of both sexes gambles with her livelihood.

A.M. SHARANSKY

THE BOARDER'S MONOLOGUE

To move, or not to move: that is the question.
Whether 'tis better for the boarder to suffer uncomplainingly
The bittersweet words of the landlady, or courageously
To take arms against the hag. To move, to flee;
No more; and know that we escaped Gehenna and an end.
No more landlady, no more boarder; moved and done.
To move, to sleep elsewhere—perchance with board:
Ay, there is the rub; no sooner do we rid ourselves of one
And throw off the yoke of landlady
Than we get another. There is the calamity
That keeps us many years in the stuffy room.
For who would bear all the afflictions
That a wicked, garrulous woman may inflict,
Her stews and stuffed potatotes,
Her fat puddings and foul sausages,
The cousins that visit her,
The matches she proposes,
Her pretensions and her sour looks,
If we knew that there where we would move
We'll fare better than here?
But the dread of an unknown landlady
Makes cowards of us all.
Fear alone keeps us fettered fast
And the room remains rented to the last.

Problems of health and hygiene were inevitably severe in the cramped tenements of the immigrant neighborhoods. Too many people lived in too small spaces; food was poor; many people were overworked; and preventive health care was barely known. Immigrant mothers struggled heroically to care for their babies in the modern ways the Yiddish press was beginning to tell them about, but the facilities were not always available, nor the necessary cash either. One of the most moving aspects of the immigrant experience was the rise of a phalanx of pure-spirited nurses, mostly volunteers, from the Henry Street Settlement, as well as others from the board of health. A wonderful woman named Lillian Wald—nurse, protector, settlement-house leader, community spokeswoman—organized these nurses. Working tirelessly, she brought the rudiments of health care to the immigrant families.

Lillian Wald (1867–1940), nurse and founder in 1895 of the Henry Street Settlement.
LIBRARY OF CONGRESS

FORWARD, 8/16/'04

N U R S E S F I N D most problems in the back rooms of candy stores, barbershops, butcher stores, groceries, etc. The first room immediately behind the store is dark, illuminated only by gas. The next room is a little brighter, and the third can get along without gas on a sunny day. There is never any fresh air in these rooms; it is hard to imagine how people can live there, but they do. The nurse finds two babies on the bed, six-month-old twins. An eighteen-month-old baby sits on the floor chewing on paper. The nurse takes a card out of her satchel and starts to question the woman; the latter doesn't know much English, but one of the girls who had come in when the nurse arrived is ready to answer for her. The nurse asks how many windows are in the apartment, how many people live there. She writes everything on the card. Then she examines the babies. One of the twins has a banana in its mouth; the other is battling with a big pear.

"You mustn't give the babies such things," she tells the mother. When the girl interprets to the woman she gets angry: "What's her business? I'm not spending her money!"

The nurse talks directly to the mother: "Baby sick inside," pointing to her stomach. "Sick here, in the belly."

"No sick," says the mother. "Babies all right."

The nurse asks the girl to make clear to the woman that bananas will make her babies sick. The woman nods her head. Then she learns that the mother is using condensed milk, and that is no good. The mother waves her hands in despair and points to her bosom: "I ain't got none." The nurse writes down what kind of milk to buy, and where to get it. She instructs the mother to wash the babies two to three times a day in hot weather, in salt water. The mother is warned not to drink beer or tea, it makes babies sick inside. Drink milk, cocoa, or water. She should keep the babies outside. . . . In many houses the nurse's visit is a big event.

A.J. RONGY

THE PRACTICE OF MEDICINE among the immigrants was difficult. There was no family practice. It simply consisted of calls to visit the sick. It was not at all uncommon for a family to have three or four different doctors a day during a critical illness. Each doctor in turn threw away the medicine prescribed by the previous doctor, made a new diagnosis, and prescribed a "sure cure." If the patient's condition did not improve rapidly, the family became hysterical and insisted upon calling a "professor" from uptown. The East Side, therefore, became a fertile field for consultants, Jew and Gentile alike. The consultation work flourished and every budding specialist made a bid for consultations on the East Side. . . .

Backyard of the College Settlement House, circa 1900.
HARVARD UNIVERSITY, SOCIAL ETHICS COLLECTION

Some of the busy practitioners developed a fine clinical acumen and practiced medicine intelligently. There were, however, a number among them who always groped in the dark. Many interesting tales are told of how shrewdly some covered up their ignorance. A story is told of a busy practitioner who was called to see a sick child and made a diagnosis of pneumonia. Said the mother: "But, Herr Doktor, the child has no fever." The doctor quickly retorted: "Ah, my dear woman! Don't you know that there are two kinds of pneumonia, hot and cold?" Typhoid fever and malaria were popular diagnoses in those days. The physicians had to establish a definite diagnosis quickly, otherwise they were in danger of losing their patients. One of the busy practitioners on Rivington Street, who made anywhere from twenty-five to forty calls a day, when he became tired climbing stairways, stopped on the first floor, called for the patients on the floors above, asked them to describe their ailments, and rushed off, telling them that they would find their medicine in the corner drug store. Conditions like empyema, pleural effusions, appendicitis, and ectopic pregnancy were diagnoses made only by the few better-trained physicians.

Boys at the Hebrew Sheltering Guardian Society Orphanage, 1900.
MUSEUM OF THE CITY OF NEW YORK

Health exhibit sponsored in 1904 by the University Settlement, Eldridge and Rivington streets.

MOSHE NADIR

THE JEWISH DOCTOR of my insurance agency lives down the block from my house. He has just opened an office and is waiting for customers. He constantly complains that *he* is sick. When a patient drops in once in a blue moon, he takes him into the *vaytik room* (that's what Jewish patients call the waiting room) where there are numerous shelves filled with (borrowed) surgical instruments which he doesn't begin to know how to use. He lights up the electric machines with the red and green bulbs and the deafening clatter, and says, in a professorial-solemn voice: "Your stomach has to be . . . [he doesn't say what] but don't be afraid. You'll come in twice a week regularly, and we may not have to use those instruments." He points to the huge glass shelves stacked with the nickel-plated paraphernalia.

The doctor's back pockets bulge with bottles of urine, which he is constantly pulling out together with his filthy handkerchief. He is always telling my applicants that their "water" is no good.

The Yiddish writer, S. Libin, who had himself been a shop worker, wrote a series of modest little sketches about the aspirations and fears of the Jewish immigrants which appeared regularly in the Forward. *Libin had a special feeling for* dos klayne menshele *("the little man") who lived quietly, trying to keep body and soul together, making few demands upon life or the world. The tone of Libin's sketches was at once sad and ironic, not always in harmony with the rebellious voice of the* Forward. *But he was one of the authentic observers of immigrant life, as in this sketch about Sam, the capmaker, who ventures to take his family on a picnic and pays heavily for his presumptuousness—as if to say that for such people, having a good time is too much to ask.*

S. LIBIN

JUST ASK SAM, the capmaker, jokingly, whether he'd like to go for a picnic. He'll curse you as if you'd asked him to hang himself. The fact is he and his wife, Sarah, went already.

One *Shabbes* Sam came home from work and, as though alarmed at the boldness of the idea, announced, "I want to have a treat."

"What sort of a treat? A glass of water for supper?"

"Wrong."

"A pint of beer?"

"Wrong again."

"Are you going to buy more carbolic acid to drive out the bugs?"

"That's not it either."

"What do you want, the moon? Tell me once and for all and get it over with."

So Sam said, "You remember our lodge . . ."

"You don't have to remind me," interrupted Sarah. "You squandered a whole dollar there last week. What's the matter? Do you want another dollar?"

"Sarah," stammered Sam, "our lodge is sponsoring . . . I want us to go . . . on a picnic."

"A picnic!" screamed Sarah. "Why a picnic?"

"Look, Sarah. The whole year long we break our backs. It's nothing but toil and trouble. What kind of a life is that? When do we ever have a good time? We sit here day and night sweating our lives away."

"Yes, yes," sighed Sarah. So Sam spoke a little louder.

"Let's go out, Sarah. Let's enjoy ourselves together with the children. Let's have a change, even if it's only for five minutes."

"What will it cost?"

"For the children it's only thirty cents. For you and me it will be ten cents there and ten back—that makes fifty cents. I figure thirty cents for refreshments to take with us: a few bananas, a bottle of milk for the children, a few rolls—the whole thing shouldn't cost more than eighty cents at the very most."

"Eighty cents. It takes nearly a day to earn as much. For eighty cents you can buy an old icebox or a pair of trousers."

"Stop talking nonsense," Sam pleaded. "Eighty cents won't make us rich. Come on, Sarah. Let's go. It will do you good to see other people enjoying themselves. Listen, Sarah, where have you been since we came to America? Have you even seen the Brooklyn Bridge? Or Central Park?"

"You know I haven't," Sarah confessed. "I only know the way from here to Hester Street."

"America is a big place," said Sam. "But you, Sarah, know nothing at all, no more than if you had just landed. Let's go, Sarah. I'm sure you won't regret it."

"All right," said Sarah. "We'll go."

The next day, after dressing the children, Sarah took the spots out of Sam's trousers and then put on her old wedding dress. By two o'clock they were ready to go. Everything went smoothly on the streetcar until Sarah gave a start. "I don't feel so good," Sarah complained. "My head is dizzy."

"I don't feel so good either," said Sam. "Maybe it's the fresh air."

"I'm afraid for the children," said Sarah, just before they started to cry. This caused the conductor to give Sam a dirty look which frightened him so much that he dropped the handbag with the milk and bananas, ruining everything.

As soon as they got off the streetcar Sarah gave Sam a piece of her mind. "So, nothing would satisfy you but a picnic? A lot of good it will do you. You're a worker, and workers have no business going on picnics."

Sam felt his heart tighten with every word. Hush, my dears. Hush, my babies," Sam said to the children, trying to quiet them. "In just a little while mother will give you bread and sugar. Hush," he pleaded, but still the children cried.

Sam went to the refreshment stall, and asked the price of a glass of milk. "Twenty cents, mister," answered the attendant.

Sam returned to Sarah more crestfallen than ever.

"Well, *shlimazl*, where's the milk?" inquired Sarah.

"It costs twenty cents."

"Twenty cents for milk? Are you Montefiore? Maybe we should sell the bedding the next time you want to go on a picnic."

"But what are we to do?" whined Sam.

"Do?" Sarah screamed back. "Go home. This very minute!"

On the way home Sarah reminded Sam that she would settle accounts with him later. "I'll pay you back," she said, "for the bananas, for the milk, for the whole of my miserable existence."

"You're right," answered Sam. "I don't know what came over me. A picnic for a common worker like me!"

When they got home, Sarah was true to her word. There was no supper for Sam. He went to bed a hungry man, and all through the night he repeated in his sleep, "A picnic. Oy, a picnic."

S. Libin (1872–1955), *chronicler of the immigrant worker. Drawing by Bernar Gussow.*

William Dean Howells

We cannot conclude this part of the immigrant scene without including a few words from William Dean Howells, the distinguished American novelist who in 1896 paid a visit to the immigrant Jewish streets of New York's East Side and, unlike a good many of his contemporaries, responded with understanding, warmth, and kindness—a generosity of spirit that represented the best of the American tradition.

WILLIAM DEAN HOWELLS

THERE IS SOMETHING in a very little experience of such places that blunts the perception, so that they do not seem so dreadful as they are; and I should feel as if I were exaggerating if I recorded my first impression of their loathsomeness. I soon came to look upon the conditions as normal, not for me, indeed, or for the kind of people I mostly consorted with, but for the inmates of the dens and lairs about me. Perhaps this was partly their fault; they were uncomplaining, if not patient, in circumstances where I believe a single week's sojourn, with no more hope of a better lot than they could have, would make anarchists of the best people of the city.

I found them usually cheerful in the Hebrew quarter, and they had so much courage as enabled them to keep themselves noticeably clean in an environment where I am afraid their betters would scarcely have had heart to wash their faces and comb their hair. There was even a decent tidiness in their dress, which I did not find very ragged, though it often seemed unseasonable and insufficient. But here again, as in many other phases of life, I was struck by men's heroic superiority to their fate, if their fate is hard; and I felt anew that if prosperous and comfortable people were as good in proportion to their fortune as these people were they would be as the angels of light, which I am afraid they now but faintly resemble.

In the Home

Family, home, mother: These gripped the life of the immigrants and their children with iron bonds, protecting them from the chaos and brutality of the outer world, providing them an enclave of warmth and comfort, sometimes overwhelming them with heavy cares. Even for the more rebellious and "worldly" immigrants, those who thought themselves socialists and tried to keep up with the development of their movement, America still seemed strange and alien. Walk a few blocks beyond the perimeter of the Jewish neighborhood and the face of danger showed itself. A deep distrust of all Gentile institutions—understandable enough when one thinks of the history of the east European Jews—marked the life of almost all immigrants, religious and secular alike. The one certainty was the cramped little apartment, where mother and father loved and ruled, where a mishmash of values, some from the Old World and some from the new, gave one a sense of order. Testimony on this matter is all but universal, and the memoirs of Jewish sons and daughters, no matter which language they appear in, keep repeating how strong were the bonds, how painful the ruptures from immigrant parents.

In the following selections Zalmen Yoffeh, a journalist and publicist, and Sammy Aaronson, a one-time prizefighter, write about making ends meet.

ZALMEN YOFFEH

WITH . . . ONE DOLLAR A DAY [our mother] fed and clothed an ever-growing family. She took in boarders. Sometimes this helped; at other times it added to the burden of living. Boarders were often out of work and penniless; how could one turn a hungry man out? She made all our clothes. She walked blocks to reach a place where meat was a penny cheaper, where bread was a half cent less. She collected boxes and old wood to burn in the stove instead of costly coal. Her hands became hardened and the lines so begrimed that for years she never had perfectly clean hands. One by one she lost her teeth—there was no money for dentists—and her cheeks caved in. Yet we children always had clean and whole clothing. There was always bread and butter in the house, and, wonder of wonders, there was usually a penny apiece for us to buy candy with. On a dollar and a quarter we would have lived in luxury.

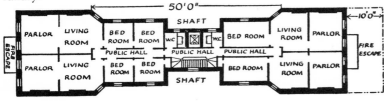

Dumbbell tenement floor plan.

SAMMY AARONSON

...EATING WAS ALWAYS A STRUGGLE. We ate when we had food in the house and our diet would give a social service worker the horrors. Meat soup was a big thing and we sometimes could have it once a week. Outside of that, the only hot food we ever had was potatoes. I never tasted anything like steak or roast beef or lamb chops until I was sixteen years old. We lived on pumpernickel, herring, bologna ends, and potatoes. The whole family could eat for fifteen or twenty cents a day, sometimes less. Mom would send me over to the delicatessen on Hester Street where we could get a pumpernickel the size of a steering wheel for a dime. We paid a penny a herring and two took care of the whole family. Another penny bought three pounds of potatoes. We always had the meat soup on Friday nights. It was made up of leftovers and ends and bones which the butcher sold for six cents a pound instead of throwing away. Three pounds was plenty for a meal for us.

MARCUS RAVAGE

CLODPATE AND INTELLIGENT dined at the same table and clashed continually—the parents enduring silent agonies over the children's disloyalty to the ancient faith, their sacrilegious mockery of the Law and its practices, their adherence to an abhorred creed, their oblivion to the ambitions that father and mother had so long entertained for them; while the youth thought of nothing but the progress of the cause and flaunted the red flag in the faces of their beloved parents in the hope of convincing them of its honesty by the simple device of getting them used to it. It needed just that element of tragedy to add to East Side radicalism the cup of martyrdom without which no religion is quite genuine.

Garter makers photographed by Lewis Hine, circa 1910.   LIBRARY OF CONGRESS

THE GROWING SENSE of superiority on the part of the
boy to the Hebraic part of his environment extends itself soon to the
home. He learns to feel that his parents, too, are "greenhorns." In
the struggle between the two sets of influences that of the home
becomes less and less effective. He runs away from the supper table
to join his gang on the Bowery, where he is quick to pick up the very
latest slang; where his talent for caricature is developed often at the
expense of his parents, his race, and all "foreigners"; for he is an
American, he is "the people," and like his glorious countrymen in
general, he is quick to ridicule the stranger. He laughs at the foreign
Jew with as much heartiness as at the "dago"; for he feels that he
himself is almost as remote from the one as from the other.

"Why don't you say your evening prayer, my son?" asks his
mother in Yiddish.

"Ah, what yer givin' us!" replies, in English, the little American-
Israelite as he makes a beeline for the street.

The boys not only talk together of picnics, of the crimes of which
they read in the English newspapers, of prizefights, of budding
business propositions, but they gradually quit going to synagogue,
give up *cheder* promptly when they are thirteen years old, avoid the
Yiddish theaters, seek the uptown places of amusement, dress in the
latest American fashion, and have a keen eye for the right thing in
neckties. They even refuse sometimes to be present at supper on
Friday evenings. Then, indeed, the sway of the old people is
broken.

"*Amerikane kinder, Amerikane kinder!*" wails the old father,
shaking his head. The trend of things is indeed too strong for the old
man of the eternal Talmud and ceremony.

HENRY ROTH

STANDING IN THE DOORWAY on the top step (two
steps led up into the front room) his mother smilingly surveyed him.
She looked tall as a tower. The old gray dress she wore rose straight
from strong bare ankle to waist, curved round the deep bosom and
over the wide shoulders, and set her full throat in a frame of frayed
lace. Her smooth, sloping face was flushed now with her work, but
faintly so, diffused, the color of a hand beneath wax. She had mild,
full lips, brown hair. A vague, fugitive darkness blurred the hollow
above her cheekbone, giving to her face and to her large brown
eyes, set in their white ovals, a reserved and almost mournful air.

"I want a drink, mama," he repeated.

"I know," she answered, coming down the stairs. "I heard you."
And casting a quick, sidelong glance at him, she went over to the
sink and turned the tap. The water spouted noisily down. She stood
there a moment, smiling obscurely, one finger parting the turbulent
jet, waiting for the water to cool. Then filling a glass, she handed it
down to him.

"When am I going to be big enough?" he asked resentfully as he took the glass in both hands.

"There will come a time," she answered, smiling. She rarely smiled broadly; instead the thin furrow along her upper lip would deepen. "Have little fear."

With eyes still fixed on his mother, he drank the water in breathless, uneven gulps, then returned the glass to her, surprised to see its contents scarcely diminished.

"Why can't I talk with my mouth in the water?"

"No one would hear you. Have you had your fill?"

He nodded, murmuring contentedly.

"And is that all?" she asked. Her voice held a faint challenge.

"Yes," he said hesitantly, meanwhile scanning her face for some clue.

"I thought so," she drew her head back in droll disappointment.

"What?"

"It is summer," she pointed to the window, "the weather grows warm. Whom will you refresh with the icy lips the water lent you?"

"Oh!" he lifted his smiling face.

"You remember nothing," she reproached him, and with a throaty chuckle, lifted him in her arms.

Sinking his fingers in her hair, David kissed her brow. The faint familiar warmth and odor of her skin and hair.

"There!" she laughed, nuzzling his cheek, "but you've waited too long; the sweet chill has dulled. Lips for me," she reminded him, "must always be cool as the water that wet them." She put him down.

IRVING HOWE

D I D S H E O V E R F E E D? Her mind was haunted by memories of a hungry childhood. Did she fuss about health? Infant mortality had been a plague in the old country and the horror of diphtheria overwhelming in this country. Did she dominate everyone within reach? A disarranged family structure endowed her with powers she had never known before, and burdens, too; it was to be expected that she should abuse the powers and find advantage in the burdens. The weight of centuries bore down. In her bones, the Jewish mother knew that she and hers, simply by being Jewish, had always to live with a sense of precariousness. When she worried about her little boy going down to play, it was not merely the dangers of Rivington or Cherry streets that she saw—though there *were* dangers on such streets; it was the streets of Kishinev and Bialystok and other towns in which the blood of Jewish children had been spilled.

The artist and his mother painted by Arshile Gorky (1904–1948). Gorky was an Armenian Jew who immigrated to America in 1920.
WHITNEY MUSEUM OF AMERICAN ART, GIFT OF JULIEN LEVY FOR MARC AND NATASHA GORKY IN MEMORY OF THEIR FATHER

*Through sheer energy and desire, the children of the immigrants
found their way. Something of their parents' ambition got
transferred to their own psyches, something of that age-old Jewish
wish to gain distinction and maybe do something useful.
Hardships, crowding, and quarrels notwithstanding, the days of
immigrant children were invigorated by a sense of possibility for
achievement—and adventure. For a child growing up in the Lower
East Side, life was endlessly absorbing. In a neighborhood bursting
with people, actually spilling out onto the streets, it was always
possible for a bright girl or boy to experience pain, sorrow, or
pleasure merely by walking around and being observant.*

SAMUEL CHOTZINOFF

IN SUMMER the fountain in Rutgers Square played all day,
and in the late afternoon and on Sundays the more adventurous
boys of the neighborhood would strip and dive into the lowest basin.
This was prohibited by law, and a warning to that effect was painted
on the basin's rim. One of us would be delegated to stand guard
over the heap of discarded pants, shirts, underwear, shoes, and

Children on Hester Street,
1898.
NEW-YORK HISTORICAL SOCIETY

48

stockings and to keep an eye open for policemen. Espying one, the lookout would let out a piercing "Cheese it—the cops!" grab a handful of garments, and make for a certain prearranged meeting place. The swimmers would scramble out of the basin and scatter in all directions. This was also prearranged to confuse our pursuer, who, not being quick enough in deciding which direction to take, would generally stand helpless for the time it took the boys to make good their escape. A few minutes later we would all have made our way, dripping but elated, to some dark tenement vestibule, or have descended to the cellar workshop and living quarters of some friendly ragpicker or shoemaker, whither our sentry had preceded us with our clothes. And sometime later we would emerge, singly, of course, to allay suspicion, and saunter nonchalantly back to the fountain, perhaps under the puzzled scrutiny of the very cop who had caused our flight. . . .

The days in summer and winter were crowded with incidents, amusing, soul-satisfying, perilous, or adventurous (at the very least, one could find satisfaction in just being an onlooker). There were gang wars to be fought, policemen to annoy and outwit, and sentimental couples to be teased and ridiculed. Standing unobserved at one's window, one could focus a burning-glass on the face of a person resting on the stone bench of the fountain and relish his annoyance and anger as he tried helplessly to locate his tormentor. From the same vantage point, one could let down a weight attached to a long string, conk the head of a passerby, and draw up the missile before the victim could look around for the offender; or, with the aid of an accomplice stationed on the curb, stretch a string head-high across the sidewalk, which, unseen by some unsuspecting pedestrian, would lift his straw hat or derby from his head and send it rolling down the street. There were the great games of leave-e-o, prisoner's base, and one-o'-cat to be played, the last limitlessly peripatetic, so that one might start to play on East Broadway and wind up, hours later, on the Bowery. There were ambulances to be run after and horsecars to hang on to—unobserved by the conductor. If one was on intimate terms with a currier in a livery stable, one could sit bareback astride a horse and ride through the streets. Something was constantly happening which one had to repair to the spot to see at firsthand. People were being knocked down by horsecars. There were altercations on every street, often ending in blows. The changing of streetcar horses at certain termini was a spectacle well worth a walk of a mile. One could run after an ambulance with a view to being in a position to give an eyewitness account of an accident to one's comrades. There were parades to be followed, also organ-grinders, bums, and itinerant sellers of cure-alls, who would assemble a crowd in a moment, deliver a stream of seemingly sensible, yet strangely incomprehensible oratory, quickly dispose

Steve Brodie's saloon on the Bowery—a glimpse of the outside world.

Playing marbles on a tenement roof.
Photograph by George Bain.

of some wares, and suddenly move on. There was Chinatown to be explored. Familiarity could not dispel the delicious fear of a walk through Mott and Pell streets or curb one's speculation on what went on behind the bamboo curtains in the dark interiors of the dimly lit shops, or, for that matter, in the inscrutable heads of the pigtailed Chinamen who shuffled along on the narrow sidewalks or sat in doorways, smoking pipes and cigarettes. . . .

In company with a playmate or two for protection in case of assault, I frequently roamed the Bowery as far north as Eighth Street and south to Chatham Square. It is true that nothing noteworthy ever happened, but the din of the elevated trains passing overhead, their engines belching smoke and sending showers of sparks and cinders down on the wagons and pedestrians below, the noise coming through the swinging doors of the many saloons, the spectacle of drunkards swaying and teetering and talking loudly to themselves, combined to give us a delicious feeling of daring and fear. Sometimes the Bowery invaded Stanton Street in the persons of derelict women we called "Mary Sugar Bums." The poor, dirty, ragged creatures would come reeling into our block, cursing and swearing, and we would run after them, calling out "Mary Sugar Bum! Mary Sugar Bum!" and they would threaten us grotesquely with their fists and lunge at us futilely when we came too close.

JACOB EPSTEIN

NEW YORK WAS AT THIS PERIOD the city of ships of which Whitman wrote. I haunted the docks and watched the ships from all over the world being loaded and unloaded. Sailors were aloft in the rigging, and along the docks horses and mules drew heavy drays; oyster boats were bringing their loads of oysters and clams, and the shrieks and yells of sirens and the loud cries of overseers made a terrific din.

At the Battery, newly arrived immigrants, their shoulders laden with packs, hurried forward, and it must have been with much misgiving that they found their first steps in the New World greeted with the hoots and jeers of hooligans. I can still see them hurrying to gain the Jewish quarter, and finding refuge amongst friends and relatives.

I often traveled the great stretch of Brooklyn Bridge, which I crossed hundreds of times on foot, and watched the wonderful bay with its steamers and ferryboats. The New York of the pre-skyscraper period was my formation ground. I knew all its streets and the waterside, I made excursions into the suburbs; Harlem, Yonkers, Long Island, and Coney Island I knew well, and Rockaway, where I bathed in the surf. I explored Staten Island, then unbuilt on, and the palisades with their wild rocks leading to the Hudson River.

In the relations between immigrant parents and American-born children—fiercely affectionate, often tense—there were also elements of comedy. Imagine the socialist Forward, *which carried on its front page a box reading "Workers of the World, Unite!," explaining to its readers that, really, it's not so terrible for the kids to play baseball—anyway, who can stop them?—and besides it's football, "the aristocratic game in colleges," that is wild and dangerous. The pressures of America and its customs were inexorable, and they made themselves felt through the pages of the* Forward, *just as much as through the pages of the other, more moderate Yiddish papers.*

FORWARD, 8/6/'03

A FATHER WROTE US that he thinks baseball is a wild and silly game. His son, who is in the upper grades, loves to play. Most of our immigrants agree with this father. But he does not make his point in an effective or interesting way:

"It makes sense to teach a child to play dominoes or chess. But what is the point of a crazy game like baseball? The children can get crippled. When I was a boy we played rabbit, chasing each other, hide-and-seek. Later we stopped. If a grown boy played rabbit in Russia they would think he had lost his mind. Here in educated America adults play baseball. They run after a leather ball like children. I want my boy to grow up to be a *mensh*, not a wild American runner. But he cries my head off."

This writer advises: Let your boys play baseball and play it well, as

Playground in a Boston tenement alley photographed by Lewis Hine, 1909. "Sometimes we played with only two forming a side, or even with three of us playing what was known as 'one o'cat' (that is, one at bat, one catching, and one pitching and fielding)."—Morris Raphael Cohen.

AMALGAMATED CLOTHING WORKERS OF AMERICA, NEW YORK

long as it does not interfere with their education or get them into bad company. Half the parents in the Jewish quarter have this problem. Chess is good, but the body needs to develop also. Jews are the most educated nation in the world; the American press writes about this all the time. The Irish boys want to be boxers and the Jews—debaters.

Baseball develops the arms, legs, and eyesight. It is played in the fresh air. The really wild game is football—the aristocratic game in the colleges. Accidents and fights occur in football, but baseball is not dangerous.

Subsisting on a scatter of pennies, the candy store came to serve as an informal social center as well as a haven of refuge from the "persecution" of the corner policeman.

UNIVERSITY SETTLEMENT SOCIETY REPORT, 1899

THE ENTIRE EAST SIDE is pretty well dotted with these stores. A careful census of the Tenth Ward alone shows the existence of fully fifty of them, nearly all of which have more or less of a clientele of these youngsters. Quite a number of these stores, some, true enough not literally candy stores (they may be cigar stores or small lunchrooms), are used as meeting places for clubs. It may be interesting to note by way of illustration that in one store alone—a cigar store—as many as eleven clubs have their meeting place. It is not at all unusual to see from twenty-five to fifty young men and boys loafing about this place in the evening.

The candy stores, however, are the true social centers. A counter along the length of the store, decked with cheap candies, and perhaps with cigars, some shelving behind filled with cigar and cigarette boxes, and invariably a soda-water fountain, make up the entire furniture of the store, if we except a few cigarette pictures on the wall. Usually the proprietor lives with his family in the rear of the store. Some stores, making a pretense to stylishness, have partitioned off a little room from the store, to which they give the elegant name of "Ice-Cream Parlor," a sign over the door to that effect apprising you of its existence. One or two bare tables and a few chairs furnish the "Ice-Cream Parlor." But this little room is very useful as a meeting place for a small club for boys, or as a general lounging room. Occasionally a dozen or more youngsters are entertained here by a team of aspiring amateur comedians of the ages of sixteen or seventeen, whose sole ambition is to shine on the stage of some Bowery variety theater. The comedian or comedians will try their new "hits" on their critical audiences (and a more critical one cannot be found).

"Soda water 5¢ a glass."

Girls had their own ways, keeping sharply apart, at least until they entered the early teens. Sometimes shyly, sometimes with astonishing force, they found their own voices and spoke of their own desires.

SOPHIE RUSKAY

CHILDREN OWNED THE STREETS in a way unthinkable to city children of today. There were a few parks, but too distant to be of any use, and so the street was the common playground. The separation of boys and girls so rigidly carried out in the public school also held on the street; *boys played with boys, girls with girls.* Occasionally we girls might stand on the sidelines and watch the boys play their games, but usually our presence was ignored. There was no doubt about it, girls were considered inferior creatures. The athletic girl, the girl who would fearlessly decide on a career or even demand the right to study a profession, was still unknown. Teaching alone was grudgingly admitted as being "respectable" for a girl. Going to college was the rare achievement for a few hardy souls, but for most, it was only a dream. We knew it to be a boy's world, but we didn't seem to mind it too much. We shared the life of the street unhampered by our parents who were too busy to try to mold us into a more respectable pattern. If we lacked the close supervision of the genteel world of maids and governesses, we gloried all the more in our freedom from restriction.

We girls played only girls' games. Tagging after us sometimes were our little brothers and sisters whom we were supposed to mind, but that was no great hardship or hindrance. We would toss them our bean bags, little cloth containers filled with cherry pits. "Now see that you play here on the stoop or you won't get any ice cream when the hokeypokey man comes along." The hope of getting that penny's worth of ice cream dished out on a bit of brown paper was sufficient to quell any incipient revolt on the part of our little charges. Thus unhampered, we could proceed to our game of potsy. Mama didn't like me to play potsy. She thought it "disgraceful" to mark up our sidewalk with chalk for our lines and boxes; besides, hopping on one foot and pushing the thick piece of tin, I managed to wear out a pair of shoes in a few weeks! I obeyed her wishes in my own way, by playing farther down the street and marking up someone else's sidewalk.

Neither my friends nor I played much with dolls. Since families generally had at least one baby on hand, we girls had plenty of opportunity to shower upon the baby brothers or sisters the tenderness and love that would otherwise have been diverted to dolls. Besides, dolls were expensive. We often stopped to look at the shop windows on Grand Street. The dolls were gorgeous: blue-eyed bits of perfection dressed in unimaginable splendor. Next to them, as if ready for a journey, were miniature trunks filled with clothes, from tiny white leather shoes to pink bonnets. What else could one do with such a doll except look at it in ecstatic wonder?

The hokeypokey man.

Necessarily thrown back on their own resources, the Jews of eastern Europe—and those in Germany and western Europe as well—had a long tradition of setting up their own institutions, ranging in purpose from education to ritual burial, from charity to labor organization. In the first several years of immigrant settlement during the 1880s, life was so hard and chaotic that most of the organizations set up by the immigrants folded. But by the 1890s the communities were at least reasonably certain of survival, and within them energetic people started creating a host of institutions.

One of the most remarkable was the Educational Alliance, on East Broadway, very near the Forward building. Originally, the alliance was started by the uptown, or German, Jews, who had gotten to America several decades before the east European Jews. Between German and east European Jews there waged a cultural war, half serious, half comic, for many decades. The Germans looked down on the east Europeans as uncouth, barbaric, ill-mannered, fanatical, while the east Europeans attacked the Germans for being wooden, materialistic, snobbish. There was a measure of truth on both sides.

Even so, some underlying bonds of solidarity held German and east European Jews together, some sense of common obligation and peril. Thus, when the east European Jews started arriving here in great numbers, the German Jews, though irritated and even alarmed, got down to the business of tsedaka, or charity, which in Yiddish points to a whole tradition of communal responsibility.

Intent upon imposing hygiene and "Americanism" on the east

Europeans, the German Jews organized the Educational Alliance. It was an astonishing institution: settlement house, educational center, night school, gymnasium, public forum, art school—truly a community home. There were lots of fights at the Alliance between those who thought it their duty to impose the values of the German Jewish donors on the east European Jewish recipients and those who thought the east European Jews should be allowed to find their own way. Still, amid all the squabbling, they worked together, bringing milk and learning, games and books, help and entertainment to the immigrants.

SAM FRANKO

AMONG THE MOST DIFFICULT and most interesting tasks that I fulfilled in the course of my years as a teacher was the training of a children's orchestra at the Educational Alliance in the Jewish quarter of New York. This class was composed of about thirty-five members, ranging from ten to fifteen years of age, and distinguished more by ambition than by talent. The parents, however, most of them immigrant Russian Jews, thought their offspring to be geniuses and were most indignant, almost insulting, when, as a result of the entrance examination, I was obliged to refuse to accept the one or the other. I have often reproached myself for the strictness and severity with which I treated these children, ill-clad and undernourished as many of them were; but they felt that it was all for their best interests and accepted my methods silently and without complaint. When the rehearsals were over, everything was forgotten; the young students never missed an opportunity of accompanying me to the station; they were not to be deterred by storm, rain, or snow. It was a sight to see so many children marching in a body through the streets of New York, each armed with a violin case! After class I often took the whole group into a restaurant and let them choose what they would from the menu, and I was often surprised by their modesty and good behavior.

MAURICE HINDUS

I DISCOVERED THE EDUCATIONAL Alliance, and I often went there to spend my leisure in the library reading room. I had never seen so many shelves of books in any one place, and I loved to take an armful of them, sit at the table and turn the pages. One evening a new librarian came to work there. She was a slender gray-haired lady with tight lips and exquisitely dressed. When she saw me bring an armful of books to the table, she came over and asked why I took so many books at once. In my imperfect English I explained that I loved to look at them, turn the pages, examine illustrations and read isolated passages. After watching me in indecision for a few minutes, she went back to her desk. I didn't like her sullen look and hoped she would never again come near

*Center of life and learning, East Broad-
way.*   JEWISH DAILY FORWARD

me. Presently she was back by my side. "Sit up straight, please," she
ordered. Startled, I looked at her with protesting eyes. I had not
been aware how I was sitting, and now that she had made me
conscious of it, I wondered what difference it made to her.
However, with no word of rejoinder I obeyed. She went away, and
while playing with the books I soon forgot myself and again leaned
my head on my elbow. In an instant she was back at my side. "I told
you to sit up straight." This time I refused to obey. I continued to
turn the pages and refrained from looking at her. Again she repeated
her order in a louder voice, and the boys and girls at my table
looked up as if expecting trouble.

"I like it better this way," I finally growled.

"You've got to sit up straight," she ordered stiffly.

Was I tearing up the books? No. Was I breaking or scratching up
the table? No. Was I calling her names? No. Why then did she
demand that I sit in a position which I disliked? Incensed with her
arbitrariness, I shoved the books off the table to the floor and dashed
out of the room. Now I knew that the things I had heard about
people uptown were true. Haughty and domineering, they didn't
like the poor people downtown, and their attendant in a library
reading room wouldn't even permit an immigrant boy to sit in
comfort. I pronounced an ugly curse on her and hoped I should
never again cross her path. To make sure of it, I never went back to
that reading room, and I decided that uptown was not real America
anyway.

EDUCATIONAL ALLIANCE REPORT, 1902

[AT THE EDUCATIONAL ALLIANCE'S Summer Camp] it is a discouraging fact, but nevertheless true, that the East Side boy despises manual labor of whatever sort. He has not learned Emerson's "nobility of labor" nor Ruskin's "duty and love for work." Apart from intellectual exertion, all labor appears menial to him. The few duties at the camp—none of them irksome or onerous—were shirked and evaded with perplexing regularity. Boys had to be literally driven to make their beds, to sweep their rooms, to act as waiters at table, to wash dishes, to clean up the camp grounds and the few other necessary things that make for the success of a camp. . . . When asked to help to remove rocks from the baseball field the reply was, "What has the camp got the farmer for?" . . . When one senior was asked about the "philosophy" of dishwashing his inquiry was, "What are the women for?" . . .

The East Side boy wants six thick slices of bread—over half a loaf to every meal. He wants chunks of meat on his plate. He wants three or four cups of coffee at a sitting. He loathes vegetables largely because he does not know them as food. Lettuce is called "grass" and not eaten; cauliflower is meant for cattle; beans are for those who are unable to get anything better. . . . Any dish not familiar to them is unfit and not edible. Fresh milk was declared to be watered, and salt butter to be rancid. Table manners and the usual conventions of decency and good breeding are woefully absent. Everybody puts his knife in his mouth and uses his personal spoon for butter, sugar, jelly, and what not else from the common plate, licking the spoon clean between self-helpings.

The greatest problems of them all are those of morality. Gambling in its various forms, from "matching pennies" and betting to playing poker for money, cropped out continually, generally under cover or in the woods some distance from the house.

Heads up—and down.
Photograph by
Jacob Riis.
MUSEUM OF THE CITY
OF NEW YORK,
JACOB A. RIIS COLLECTION

A settlement house library (unidentified) photographed by Jacob Riis.

MUSEUM OF THE CITY OF NEW YORK,
JACOB A. RIIS COLLECTION

Agricultural day.

JEWISH DAILY FORWARD

Learning to sketch at the Educational Alliance.

YIVO INSTITUTE FOR JEWISH RESEARCH

One of the most obnoxious stereotypes that has arisen about immigrant Jewish life—arisen, to be honest, among their own grandchildren—is that the immigrant streets were a vast cradle for precocious boys and girls who spent all their time studying literature, politics, and philosophy. It was not that way at all. Of course, there were many bright and scholarly kids, the intellectuals of the next generation. But there was also a healthy leavening of burly street kids, not so good at algebra but quick at making a dollar or figuring an angle. There were children of the immigrants who became prizefighters, bookies, sometimes worse. It had to be so. No culture can survive only through its minority of refinement. Every culture needs the roughness of strength, the direct physical energy, the readiness to fight for one's turf, which plebeian elements bring. And the immigrant Jews needed this more than anyone.

SAMUEL GOLDBERG

OUR HEROES WERE GREAT FIGHTERS, soldiers or strongarm hoodlums who were top gangsters. Wrongly, we tried to emulate them. Police and law-enforcement officers were our enemies. We were continually at war between ourselves or with gangs from other districts that were of different races and religions. The Irish gangs came from the East Side waterfront. They invaded our district with rocks, glass bottles, clubs, and all sorts of homemade weapons. Battles would rage in the streets, vacant lots, and even in some of the parks. Sometimes they lasted for hours or until the police would break them up. Many times I sneaked home with a bleeding head or a black eye and blamed this on a single Gentile, or *goy*, as we called them . . .

My East Side slum training stood me in good stead later in my life. The constant fighting with different gangs toughened me to withstand the blows that life would deal me. My single-handed fights with other kids, Jewish or otherwise, just for the sheer joy of supremacy, gave me knowledge of self-defense and boxing. I realized that I had more than ordinary ability and that I did excel at boxing. I won every fight I ever had, even winning with bigger and older boys.

The strong six—the Educational Alliance basketball team, 1904–1905.
YIVO INSTITUTE FOR JEWISH RESEARCH

*Benny   Leonard   (1896–1947),   world
lightweight champion, East Side hero. In
1923 Leonard successfully defended his
title in the most widely publicized and
best attended lightweight match of its
day. In later years Leonard taught scientific boxing at CCNY.*
JEWISH DAILY FORWARD

UNIVERSITY SETTLEMENT SOCIETY REPORT,

1900

A MOST IMPORTANT FACTOR in street life, and one
that easily escapes the chance observer, is the "tough" gang. These
gangs, made up of fellows from six or eight to twenty years of age,
are popularly known as "grafters," or pickpockets. . . . Their "hang-
outs" are on street corners, in alleyways, and in poolrooms
frequented only by boys and young men, where gambling at cards
goes on openly. Crowded streetcars and public parks are fruitful
fields for "grafting." . . . When a "graft" has been made the gang
adjourns to some neighboring hallway to divide the booty and then
return to renew operations. When necessary the older members of
the gang, or even some professional crook, under whom the gang
works, dispose of the plunder in a neighboring pawnshop, those less
experienced getting a small percent on the earnings of the whole.
["Fagin" schools, where boys, and sometimes girls, are trained as
pickpockets, are by no means uncommon.]

FORWARD, 4/18/'04

SHOULD BAD CHILDREN BE SENT AWAY or kept at home? Hundreds of parents are asking this question; it is not easy to drive out a child, no matter how bad, but it is being done. Hundreds of boys under twenty-one are now living away from their parents, because the situation became intolerable. Courts are filled with young criminals. The children's court in New York, which handles children under fifteen, is packed. Police courts are filled with boys over fifteen, second and third offenders who started at age thireen to fourteen.

Parents are desperate and do all in their power not to have their children sent "over the water."

The newspapers today published a story about an eighteen-year-old boy who took poison; his parents threw him out. The parents live on Second Street and the boy lived on Seventy-eighth Street. He was out of work, had no rent money, and that was probably why he killed himself. The boy had been thrown out three times. The last time was because he came home on Saturday without wages; he said he lost the money, but the parents were sure he had either spent it on a girl or gambled it away at cards. Now his parents are beside themselves with guilt. The same people who say that a bad boy should not be allowed in the house are now saying that no matter how bad a child is you should not reject him. . . .

These children must be kept at home, because if you let them out they will go to the dogs completely. They have aggressive natures; if they live elsewhere they won't pay their Mrs. rent either; if they can't get to their sister's pocketbook for a few cents, they'll try to get the money dishonestly. It is preferable that parents should suffer from their bad child.

Dopey Benny, East Side gangster.

HERBERT ASBURY

JACOB ORGEN, otherwise known as Little Augie, had been an obscure member of the Dopey Benny gang until he organized a small group which he called the Little Augies—all Jewish gunmen

The burial of Little Augie, gunman and bootlegger. UNITED PRESS INTERNATIONAL

and sluggers. Fat, flashy, and addicted to fawn-colored spats, in late 1925 Little Augie began bootlegging along Broadway, supplying liquor to speakeasies and nightclubs. Great success attended his new enterprise, and within a year he told his friends that he would soon be able to retire. But liquor peddlers whose customers he had appropriated had marked him for death, and on October 16, 1927, Little Augie was killed in front of number 103 Norfolk Street, between Delancey and Rivington, while talking to his bodyguard, Legs Diamond. Four men drove up in a black touring car, and when Little Augie turned in response to a hail, one of them shot him in the back of the head. He was buried in a massive cherry-red coffin lined with white satin, and on the lid gleamed a silver plate:

JACOB ORGEN
Age 25 years

His real age was thirty-three. But it had been eight years since he had assumed active leadership in his gang, and on that day his father had proclaimed him dead.

W. A Rogers.

Working Their Way Up

The Jewish immigrants came to America during the years of the great expansion of industrial capitalism. Years of opportunity, they were also a time of frequent depressions in which the vulnerable immigrants suffered terribly. Nevertheless, because America did offer at least some a chance to rise economically and because they were as a rule industrious, the immigrants began to better their lives. By the 1890s a tiny middle class begins to make its appearance on the East Side of New York—some even hiring newly arrived Jewish girls to work as maids. The garment industry afforded the more fortunate or ambitious the opportunity to become contractors, small middlemen who employ a few workers, and themselves work at the machines. A handful of immigrants worked their way up to become millionaires, a few in real estate. The process of class division began, and with it the steady rise of the Jews out of the working class and into the business and professional classes—a process that reached its climax after the Second World War.

Here we ought to introduce Hutchins Hapgood, who wrote the following selection on immigrant Jewish businessmen. A lively and idealistic young American, he found his way to the East Side at about the turn of the century as a reporter for the Commercial Advertiser. *The Yiddish editor Abraham Cahan became Hapgood's guide and mentor, and there followed a series of warm, brilliantly acute articles about the immigrant Jews that Hapgood brought together as* The Spirit of the Ghetto *(1902), a minor American classic.*

HUTCHINS HAPGOOD

GO TO THE GREAT pushcart markets in Hester and Ludlow streets where they join at the northwest corner of Rutgers Square . . . and study the people you see there. You will see strange types, but you will also see how strangely Americanized they are becoming, impelled by keen interest and ambition. When you notice that practically everybody is in business, you will understand why practically everybody is, to a greater or less degree, in spirit an American. . . .

The dominant effect of the life on one of these crowded downtown streets is that of business—eager, militant business, expressing itself in eternal haggling over a thousand kinds of diminutive articles. How all-absorbing this spirit of the Ghetto street is is shown by the way all the Jewish classes—no matter how unbusinesslike they naturally are—are drawn into it. In the crowds shown by our illustrations are not only the men, women and children who are exclusively merchants. A close inspection will reveal types of the scholar, the socialist, the poet, the literary man, the artist, on the one hand; and, on the other hand, the young

Carrying home pre-cut material for assembly into cheap garments, 1890. Drawing by W.A. Rogers.

Hester Street, 1898.

pickpocket of twenty, the sweat-shop girl, the agent for the "reliever" business—a business which consists in buying a poor man's new suit in exchange for a very old suit and a bit of ready cash.

The old man peddling from door to door, or tending his push-cart in the crowd, may be a poet or a scholar, with the spirit of universal brotherhood or an impassioned love of the Talmud in his soul. Some of the young women in the crowd may be fervent socialists, strike-leaders and exhorters. Complex, indeed, is this mass of human beings, representing many civilizations and many conflicting tendencies, but united—and this is the point—in one great absorbing spirit—the spirit of business; the thing that is rapidly making of them American citizens in fact as well as in name.

How persuasive is that spirit of business! If you will allow yourself to be stopped by some eager-faced Jew who wants to sell you a "reliever"—(he thinks, perhaps, that you are a young fellow who has come to the city on a spree, has spent his money and needs some ready cash to return home)—you will be (if not annoyed) charmed by his eloquence, delivered in bad English. I was once literally forced—very much against my will—to sell all my old clothes, practically for nothing, to a Jew whose appealing accents, whose serious, impassioned argument, at once poetic and logical, highly figurative and keenly unanswerable, got so firm a grip on me that he did whatever he desired. This Jew haggler seemed to me almost the youngest, most eager, and most enthusiastic thing in my experience. Certainly few of us can feel as keen a joy as falls daily to the lot of the picayune merchant of Hester Street who feels himself about to rise in the exciting world of America, and sees the old limitations of his race removed, and, behind the old barriers, a broad, fascinating field of commercial activity!

For the struggling immigrant entrepreneur, the Hebrew Free Loan Society *was an invaluable safeguard against business failure.*

STANLEY BERO

NOW THAT ITS CAPITAL has reached and overtipped the sum of $80,000, the directors of the Hebrew Free Loan Society proudly compares itself to a banking institution. But their society has this very important difference: Although it makes loans on endorsed notes, it exacts no interest, and is content with weekly part payments. The present membership is almost eighteen hundred, the majority of whom have been in this country less than twenty years.

In Russia there is not a city or village containing Jews in large numbers that has not a similar institution, and from Russia the movement has spread throughout the larger cities of the globe. Its name in Hebrew, *Gemilath Chassodim*, has unquestionably a religious influence, and this in itself assures prompter repayments than might have been the case had it been otherwise named. If figures mean anything, surely 13,143 loans and $320,740 loaned free of interest speak volumes of stories, a few of which might be well to tell in order to add life to the facts brought out in last year's balance sheet.

X had a cigar store and was compelled to buy his tobacco in small quantities and was therefore forced to pay more: with the help of

An 1898 receipt for $15 from the Hebrew Free Loan Society, located at the time on East Broadway. HEBREW FREE LOAN SOCIETY

four loans he cleared his mortgage and added considerable stock. A ladies' tailor, by making some loans, depositing them in a bank, and treating his weekly repayments thereon as part of his general expense succeeded in establishing himself on one of the city's main thoroughfares. Another man peddled, but had so little stock and so small a variety that every once in a while he would find himself having little goods and less money. A fifty-dollar loan put him on his feet.

The widespread knowledge of such incidents has gained for the society the reputation it deservedly bears.

Most of the "businessmen" in the immigrant streets were still very far from constituting a bourgeoisie; they were peddlers, petty traders, small storekeepers, hanging on for sheer life and often working at least as hard as those who went each morning to the shops. They exploited others, they exploited themselves.

"These people love fish—Shabbes fish, gefilte fish, light fish and dark fish, blue fish and white fish, fresh fish and fish not so fresh."—New York Times, 11/14/97.

SAMUEL COHEN

...AT EIGHT IN THE MORNING I put my left arm through the strap of the basket, lifting it and adjusting it on my back, the other arm through the strap of the boiler, over my neck, keeping the boiler on my chest. All you could see of me from a distance was my troublesome straw hat! My instructions were to walk up Elizabeth Street four blocks, turn east and cross the Bowery, which already had the elevated, then walk two blocks more. When I reached the blocks of private houses, I was to walk up the stoops, pull the bell, and when the door opened, to say, "Buy tinware."

At my first port of call my heart was in my mouth. I hesitated. Taking a long breath, I climbed up a stoop and yanked the bell. I was in suspense. The door opened. A redheaded young giant appeared. He looked at me and my outfit without a word. He was not a bit rough. He merely laid his hand very gently on the boiler in front of me and gave me a good shove. I descended backwards rapidly, finally landing in a sitting position in the middle of the street, my stock strewn about me in all directions. With great effort I managed to readjust my basket and wash boiler. Now what? I thought. I could not pull another bell if I tried. I turned back to Elizabeth Street. Entering a yard I saw an open door—a woman near it. I made my first sale—a cup for ten cents—the profit was not bad!

I. BENEQUIT

I WAS MAKING three dollars weekly working at shirts: making buttons and sleeves. I met a young man in a restaurant on Orchard Street who told me he peddled woven baskets near Washington Market and did very well, particularly on Saturday. I didn't feel like peddling, but I decided to try it.

I went with my *landsman* to buy the baskets, and then to

JUNE 29 1910.

Washington Market—a huge, circular, one-story building, which sold all kinds of provisions much cheaper than elsewhere. The market was near the ferry landing. The ferries brought buyers from the various towns across the Hudson. Usually the men did the buying—an old Yankee custom. Since the men felt uncomfortable carrying bundles, they eagerly bought baskets, which cost only fifteen cents. The first Saturday I earned four dollars, as did my *landsman*. During the week he only made fifty cents, so I decided to peddle only on Saturday.

Stoops and stores under the El on Division Street. *"There are fifty big dressgoods stores on the East Side. Two hundred and fifty clerks are employed in these stores. When they save a few hundred dollars, two or three get together as partners and open a store."* Jewish Daily Forward, 3/2/06.

MUSEUM OF THE CITY OF NEW YORK

ISAAC RABOY

IN THE STREET, Mannis and his grandson Isaac walked close to each other. Crowds surged up and down along the sidewalk. The stores were brightly lit. . . .

They walked along Hester Street and almost lost each other in the crush. Isaac couldn't understand why people kept grabbing him by the arm and pulling him and talking in various languages; each time Mannis had to rescue him. Mannis decided to go into a store to be safe. They went down a few steps. The store was half dark, but the moment they entered the owner lit the lights. There were many narrow lanes through which they could hardly walk. Light and dark suits hung on nails; on each suit was a card with a picture of the owner and the price. But Mannis couldn't make out what the numbers meant. The storekeeper smiled and said, "That's my secret. I have one price. First try it on, and you'll get a real bargain. So help me God."

Isaac tried on the suit, looked in the mirror, and almost burst out laughing, because he looked so comical to himself.

"A fit!" said the storekeeper.

"Like a fur coat on a *goy*," said Mannis mockingly.

"All the millionaires wear these suits. Never mind that I'm buried here on Hester Street. I should have the money you can save on Hester Street. The price is two and a half," he continued, and was immediately sorry that he had made it so cheap. Mannis complained, and the man said, "My enemies and yours should have the profit I make on it."

Mannis offered one and a half, and was sorry he had said so much. The man pleaded for another quarter, but Mannis and Isaac walked toward the door. The storekeeper ran after them: "Take it— what can I do with you? I want to earn something before I close."

As they walked along Hester Street with the package, other storekeepers shouted after Mannis:

"Mister, from him you bought a suit? It's gonna be full of holes!"

MUSEUM OF THE CITY OF NEW YORK,
PEN-AND-INK DRAWING BY MILT GROSS

BARNEY ROSS

WHENEVER A POTENTIAL CUSTOMER got close enough for me to get my hands on him, I would seize him and "pull" him inside. The approved technique was not to grab him so hard that you'd tear his clothes, but to get a good enough grip so he couldn't slip out from under . . . If he told me, "I haven't got time, I have to go," I'd tell him, "Two seconds, two seconds, it won't take more, that I swear to you on the honor of my forefathers." If he said, "I have no money, I can't buy," I'd assure him, "Forget about money, this'll cost you nothing, practically nothing." If he said, "I've got ten sweaters already," I'd tell him, "Listen, you need one real *heavy* sweater . . . it'll save you money, you won't have to buy a coat."

A small but significant number of immigrant Jewish businessmen   71
rose literally from rags to riches. In the following selection, Charles
Bernheimer describes an early phase of this development.

CHARLES BERNHEIMER

T H E   Y E A R S   (1898–1903) of unprecedented business activity
and "prosperity" for the United States caused an unusual . . .
growth of Russian Jewish fortunes in New York. Though we have
no income statistics on which to base our suppositions, there can be
not the slightest doubt that many fortunes, ranging between
$25,000 and $200,000, have been made within these years. It was
but natural that these extraordinary incomes should have been
invested in real estate, and the phenomenal growth of the so-called
ghetto, which has earned the adjective "great" (used very frequently
without the slightest suggestion of sarcasm), has had much to do
with the formation of a number of fortunes. To one who has had an
opportunity to watch the economic development of the district
south of Houston Street, the formation of a well-to-do class in the
midst of the Russian Jewish colony has been a very interesting
phenomenon. The general improvement in the character of the
stores, the sudden appearance of a dozen or more commercial
banks, the well-furnished cafés of a type utterly unknown five or six
years ago, the modern apartments "with an elevator and a 'nigger
boy' on the stoop" all tell eloquently of this growth.

*One step up—Moe Levy & Co., Fulton
Street, Brooklyn, 1907.*
MUSEUM OF THE CITY OF NEW YORK

The whole idea of community was somewhat complicated for the immigrant Jews. On the one hand, there was the enormously powerful tradition of tsedaka, *or charity in the largest sense, going back to the old country, which required Jews to look after their own—look after them in poverty and sickness, life and death. But there were also memories of a decidedly unpleasant sort regarding communal structures in the old country that had been repressive and intolerant. The Jews of the immigrant world created a vast number of institutions—synagogues, trade unions, fraternal societies, political parties, credit unions, educational societies, choral groups, and many more. Yet they were deeply, and rightly, suspicious of any effort to set up an overall communal structure that would claim to speak for all the Jews. No one could speak for all the Jews. One of the most lively and admirable features of immigrant Jewish life was precisely its pluralism of voices and opinions.*

Without putting it into so many words, either to themselves or others, immigrants wanted to keep—for a time, at least—a balance between old and new, the cultural styles they brought with them and the cultural styles they encountered in the American cities. For the Jews who came here between the early 1880s and the First World War, one of the main ways they had of keeping this precarious balance between old and new was the landsmanshaft. *This, we think, was really the most remarkable institution of the whole immigrant Jewish experience. On the one hand, it was nothing more than a society of people who had come from the same east European* shtetl *or neighborhood. They would get together, say, once a month, go through their ritual of business, play cards, reminisce about the old country, raise a few dollars for hungry relatives. On the other hand, the* landsmanshaft *became a major agency in the long, torturous process of adaptation to America. It served many of the social purposes that the welfare state would undertake on a larger scale in later decades. It was a credit union, it provided modest sick benefits, it gave some relief to destitute members, and above all, it bought land for a cemetery, so that traditional Jewish rituals for burial would be satisfied.*

At one time there were many hundreds of these landsmanshaftn. *Today a handful survive, sadly recalling the old days and having little function left but to bury a handful of survivors.*

ער זיצט מיט גוטע ברידער אין וויין־קעלער.

"He sits among his brethren in an East Side wine cellar." From The Big Stick, a Yiddish humor magazine, 9/26/13.

FORWARD, 1/17/'06

DO YOU WANT TO MEET a *landsman* from Lemberg, a freshly baked greenhorn who can give you the latest news about your city; or an Americanized *landsman* who knows how to transfer from one streetcar to the next, or whistle at the ticket chopper on the elevated? Go to the northeast corner of Clinton and Rivington streets, where you can find out about a job, family scandals, *landsleit* parties, and anything else that interests you.

I stood on that corner last week, and met an old friend. He was surprised I hadn't heard the latest. "Red—you know who I mean— has become a boss. Whenever he has to pass this corner, he stops a block before and buys a fat cigar, and watches us to make sure we see him. Once he came into our saloon and told us we should establish a society and a synagogue called Anshi Lemberg #1. The hell with him. What are we—provincials? So we got together and we're going to make a *Verein*, a union, and to spite Red we'll call it First Lemberg Ladies' and Gentlemen's Charity, Sick and Burial Society, under the patronage of the late Austrian Queen Elizabeth. A big portrait of the empress will hang over the president, and we're going to give a ball and a performance. One of our members wrote a play in seven acts, with three comedians and lots of songs, in high German. You'll see, Lemberger *landsleit* are not small-town *landsleit.*"

FORWARD, 1/17/'14

VILNA, MINSK, BERDITCHEV, HOML. Each of these cities and towns is represented by New York cafés. Odessa politics, Vilna diplomacy are reflected through representatives of these places back home who dispatch representatives to the East Side basement parliament.

Go down a few steps off the sidewalk and there's Minsk. Don't fret: A Vilner wandering into a Minsk cellar can earn a *kosher* honorary Minsk residency with a few pennies spent on a plate of cabbage with meat.

A few more blocks and we're in Vilna. The city offers cosmopolitan tolerance even though a sign reads "private restaurant." Your reporter has never seen Vilna, yet he's never been refused chopped liver or beans with potatoes. The waitress never asked for his passport but served him politely as she shouted at her thirteen-year-old boy for removing his shoes and twiddling his toes near a table. Perhaps she too was not from Vilna. . . .

. . . One feels at home in these *landsleit* cafés. The outside is shabby but inside it's clean and tidy, the floor covered by sawdust just as in Europe. White tablecloths are on the tables, and the visiting Vilner feels that his own mother is about to arrive with a Sabbath smile and the candlestickholders as she's about to bless the candles. A peaceful stillness spreads about the room. Minsk is Minsk and Vilna is Vilna. The ocean and America nothwithstanding, a familiar plate of barley soup in the basement of Vilna, Volkoviski, Shavel, or Kurenitz brings you back home. . . .

The *landsleit* in the cafés talk mainly of their societies and lodges. Each city has various benevolent societies with presidents, secretaries, and patriots. . . . Everyone defends his own society until a man with a Workmen's Circle button in his lapel gets up and says, "All your societies are small-time. I belong to the Workmen's Circle." This man is joined by the waiter who neglects the tips of

A new member bowing to his East Side lodge brethren. Drawing by L. Kidlioski.
YIVO INSTITUTE FOR JEWISH RESEARCH

the small-time benefit patriots to stand up for his own. The other patriots join forces against the Workmen's Circle but lose. The Workmen's Circle members claim to fill Chicago, St. Louis, Buffalo, and Philadelphia with strikes and lectures. The members of the smaller societies return to their coffee with lips parched by debate. . . .

On the windows of the various Russian cafés there's an added decoration: "Russian spoken here." Your reporter wanted to know if such signs indeed draw Russian clientele. Said the proprietor, "We haven't seen a real Russian yet. The writing is merely meant to attract intellectual *landsleit*. It's a treat to be given both a meal and the chance to converse in Russian."

The owner added, "If our *landsleit* in New York must eat Chicago meat at least let them chew it in with a Slutsker tongue."

S.P. SCHOENFELD

WHEN I WAS TWENTY YEARS OLD my uncle introduced me to a lodge of progressive people: The Adler's Young Men's Independent Association, Number One. I asked my uncle why such a long name. "Every word is important," he answered. First of all when a dozen young men from Kovno go to create a society the first problem is the name. There already are Kovno societies, and they'd never think to join an existing group; so the lot fell on Dr. Adler, chief rabbi in London. An impressive man—it's an honor for a society to call itself after him.

"Next, the word independent. Independent because the members did not attach themselves to an already existing body and because it was reminiscent of the Declaration of Independence."

"But why Number One, if there's no Number Two?"

"To anticipate the future when disgruntled candidates for office break off to form an organization of the same name."

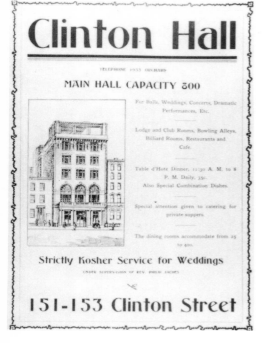

A full-page advertisement from The East Side Civic Club Journal, 1902.

AMERICAN JEWISH ARCHIVES ON THE CINCINNATI CAMPUS OF THE HEBREW UNION COLLEGE, JEWISH INSTITUTE OF RELIGION

ON SECOND STREET NEAR AVENUE A stands Mount Moriah Hospital. It deserves our attention: In a sense it's a real popular institution.

It was founded and is supported by members of the various societies affiliated with the Galicia-Bokovina League. From the pennies of its members, mostly paupers, arose the tiny, or, more nicely put, tidy and informal Mount Moriah Hospital. "It's a penny hospital," said an official who respectfully received me as a *Forward* representative. Pennies have created it.

As I go up Second Street and draw nearer to the address I see Mount Moriah, an ordinary three-story building standing much lower than the tenements that enclose it. The entranceway is simple. I felt I was entering a house and was not terrified. An employee greets me with a friendly face. How marvelous this is— I've never been met with a friendly face by a hospital official.

At first I was led to an intake room, but when they discovered my mission I was taken to the office of the superintendent. He's a middle-aged man who makes a pleasant impression, like the hospital itself. No haughtiness, just *"Sholem aleichem"*—most unsuperintendentlike.

Mt. Moriah is still an infant, having been opened this past January. The first patient arrived in February: a seventy-five-year-old man with a stomach ulcer. Since then eight hundred persons have applied for admission and four hundred accepted. Seventy-two patients now occupy beds, including ten children.

In addition to its own house physicians, patients are treated by visiting doctors from Mount Sinai Hospital as well as by prominent specialists.

The superintendent was upset that the many applicants rejected for lack of space felt insulted. Lack of room is not an excuse for a Jew. "What do you mean, 'no room,'" he retorts. "If you want to badly enough, you'll find a place. I have five children and three boarders in the same four rooms. You push the beds together and squeeze in another."

That the board of health requires a minimum fixed distance between hospital beds means nothing to the father of five and landlord of three. He waved his hand angrily and went off.

Some patients cheat the hospital. A man paid for a private room for a week, then stayed as long as he wanted without paying the rest of his bill. Since Mount Moriah serves no eviction notices the management could do no more than grumble.

I was given a tour of the various departments. Generally they are as well endowed as the richest hospitals: "all the latest improvements." Except that space is tight here. By God, it's tight. The walls need room to expand. I thought of the two adjoining tenements that squeeze the hospital building, and wished the infant Mount Moriah speedy riddance of its oppressive neighbors. More light, more air for the unfortunates whose only chance for air may be their stay in a hospital bed. . . . I wanted to shout, "Space! Space! Room! Give the sick women and children air!"

By the turn of the century, the immigrants were looking for some relief from the sweltering summers of the ghetto. All but the very poorest would manage a week or two in the Catskills, going to the kochalayns ("cook-by-yourself"), modest farmhouses turned into boardinghouses. Like certain other aspects of immigrant life, the Catskills' hotels and farmhouses later became an object of embarrassed joking to the descendants of the immigrants. But if you come to think of it, why? These people were worn out, tired, often ill-nourished; they yearned for some fresh air and grass; they found it as best they could. And what they set up in the mountains was far less vulgar than the grandiose hotels and country clubs of a later era. Milton Kutsher, now the owner of a hotel in the Catskills, spoke to us in 1978 reminiscing about the early days of his family's business.

MILTON KUTSHER

M Y F A T H E R A N D U N C L E came to the Lower East Side from Austria in 1903. My father was seventeen, my uncle twenty-seven. From working fifteen to sixteen hours a day, six days a week, my uncle's health began to deteriorate. The doctors told him it would be smart to get out of New York, so he persuaded my father to come out here and buy a farm. Everyone thought they were crazy, but they went ahead anyway and bought a farmhouse with two hundred acres of surrounding land. In order to make ends meet, they began taking in boarders in the summer, mostly people they knew from the Lower East Side.

In the early years we did practically everything ourselves, from growing sorrel (for *schav*), to cutting ice in the winter, to raising our own cows and chickens. In those days we ate chicken for dinner and farmer's cheese with sour cream for supper practically every day of

Rest day. Drawing by Abraham Walkowitz (1878–1965). As a youth growing up in the Lower East Side, Walkowitz attended art classes at the Educational Alliance. In later years, Walkowitz achieved considerable fame and remuneration for his paintings of leisure and repose. This drawing appeared in the early Twenties in Shriftn, a Yiddish journal edited by David Ignatow.

רוסטאג

א. וואלקאוויץ

Grossinger's, when it was still The Ritz.
COURTESY OF THE GROSSINGER HOTEL
AND COUNTRY CLUB

the week. In the winter months, my father peddled milk and eggs while my uncle kept busy making things with his hands. One winter it was cabinets, another winter steamer trunks. That's how we managed until we took in enough money from real estate investments to start building bungalows and tennis courts and swimming pools.

Today people expect to be entertained, but when people know entertainment isn't provided they provide it for themselves. In the old days parents played cards and sat in the sun, children fooled around in the fields, couples took walks along the country roads. On Friday night and Saturday morning my uncle conducted services; on Saturday night, in the same room, my uncle told jokes and danced the kazatska. That was the entertainment. People then didn't expect like people expect today. These were poor Jews who paid as little as five dollars a week for a bed and three meals a day. All they really wanted was the good food and the fresh air.

COMMERCIAL ADVERTISER, 9/25/'99

ONE OF THE LATEST FASHIONS among the poor people of the East Side is for the father of a family to send his wife and children to the mountains for the summer. Not that East Side prosperity has placed some of the luxuries within the reach of the poor. On the contrary, board in the Catskills has come down to a point where the "keep" of a workingman's family in a boarding-house is almost as cheap as it is at home in the city.

Competition among the boardinghouses is so rife that board is sometimes offered at less than cost price. Some of the farmers who are anxious to get started in the boarding business advertise board at four dollars. Tannersville, Pinehill, and the surrounding towns swarm with East Siders during the summer months. Many of the boardinghouses keep *kosher*, sometimes advertising that fact in Hebrew letters on the window.

An East Side physician, whose patients are almost exclusively sweatshop people, said the other day that in many instances relief is brought to otherwise hopeless cases by sending the sufferer to the mountains. "I know a man who earns fifteen dollars a week as a baster in a tailoring shop," he said. "He has a wife and two little children, one of whom was sick and needed fresh air. This did not scare him. His wife's sister and cousins and friends were going to Tannersville, he said, and if they could afford it, he could."

FORWARD, 8/9/'04

WHEN IT RAINS four or five dozen women, girls, children, and a handful of men are crowded into a small porch. If one of the girls volunteers to sing, you have to stick it out because you can't insult her by leaving; so she sings while children are crying, mothers are cursing, husbands and wives fighting, and women insulting one another. The only good thing about the Catskills is the fresh air, but instead of taking advantage of it, the women sit on the porch like a fashion show, each one showing off her clothes and jewelry. When the husband of one of these women comes for a few days, she is very proud. The other women can't stand it, so they send for their husbands who set up pinochle games and play all day, forgetting their wives.

The girls are bored and try to find boys. When a young man wanders onto a farm they do their utmost to hold him there. (There are twelve young girls to every boy in the Catskills.) If a boy doesn't come along, the girls go to look for one at a neighboring farm. Some of the hotels have dances. They are free and people come for miles around. Chinese lanterns are strung up half a mile from the hotel. The crowd in the dance hall is very happy, more than if it were a wedding. On hayrides, which are very popular, the noise becomes deafening. They sing. "Let Us All Be Happy" from Libin's *Broken Hearts* was popular this summer. . . . There are no seats on a hayride; the girls and women and few boys are all tangled up and every few minutes a girl "loses a leg."

Relaxing at Coney Island and Ulmer Park.

Manners, customs, styles of life, all underwent change, sometimes gross, sometimes subtle. In a world of tenements, hygiene was a difficulty, public baths were a necessity.

FORWARD, 1/19/'06

...S E V E R A L Y E A R S A G O the University Settlement of Eldridge Street on the corner of Rivington constructed thirty small shower rooms in its basement, charging five cents; time for undressing, bathing, and dressing was limited to twenty minutes. Several times a week these showers were made accessible to women. For the same five cents you got a towel and a piece of soap. The first year the showers were very popular; in the summer the residents of neighboring streets also used them, and the place was always packed. When it got cool, the showers were empty; obviously they were used not to wash but to cool off.

Seward Park, which was planned by reform mayor Strong and took six years to complete, offers eighty free showers—forty for men and forty for women, open every day including Sundays. These facilities are in the basement, and they are modern and beautiful, constructed of pure marble. Each bath has two small chambers: a dressing room and a shower. They are kept clean, and can be locked from the inside.

A park employee told this reporter he was surprised that the baths are not frequently used. Toward evening a few workers may come, or schoolchildren who are urged by their principals to bathe three times a week.

If workers would use these baths all year round, they would enjoy much better health.

Like all disadvantaged groups, the immigrant Jews found their way to a renewal of traditional ceremonies marking the possibilities and joys of life. How ready immigrant Jews were to spend their last dollar on a wedding—hiring a hall and a few musicians, loading down tables with shnaps and cake and sandwiches, buying a wedding dress and renting carriages.

LILLIAN WALD

W H E N W E F I R S T V I S I T E D F A M I L I E S in the tenements, we might have been misled as to the decline in the family fortunes if we judged their previous estate by the photographs hung high on the walls of the poor homes, of bride and groom, splendidly arrayed for the wedding ceremony. But we learned that the costumes had been rented and the photographs taken, partly that the couple might keep a reminder of the splendor of that brief hour, and also that relations on the other side of the water might be impressed with their prosperity.

Ladies at a Thomashefsky wedding, circa 1906. Photograph by Byron.
MUSEUM OF THE CITY OF NEW YORK, BYRON COLLECTION

Since those days the neighborhood has become more sophisticated, and brides are more likely to make their own wedding gowns, often exhibiting good taste as well as skill; though the shop windows in the foreign quarters still display waxen figures of modishly attired bride and groom, with alluring announcements of the low rates at which the garments may be hired.

NEW YORK TRIBUNE, 1/9/'98

THE CANOPY IS MADE OF VELVET and may be of any color, although it is usually purple or deep red; it is trimmed with gold lace, and has the Star of David embroidered in gold on one end. Under this canopy, which symbolizes the future home of the family, the bride is taken by her parents, and the rabbi performs the marriage ceremony. When the couple have taken wine from the same glass to show that they will be partners in joy, and the ring has been placed on the bride's finger, a glass is broken. "At no joyous occasion," explains a rabbi, "should the Jew forget that the glory of the Jewish nation is broken. The broken glass . . . also reminds the young people that sooner or later all must return to dust, and, even like the beautiful glass, be shattered and destroyed."

SAMUEL CHOTZINOFF

THE CRUNCHING NOISE set off great shouts of *"Mazel tov!"* ("Congratulations!"), the *machetunim* (in-laws) embraced, the violin, cornet, drum, and piano, which had been waiting for this very signal, broke into *"Chassen, kalleh, mazel tov!"* ("Groom, bride, congratulations!"). The married pair sailed away in a dance across the length of the room, between two long lines of guests formed to provide a narrow lane for the exhibition. These favored

Bride and groom. Drawing by Ben-Zion.
COURTESY OF BEN-ZION

guests clapped their hands in rhythm with the music, sang and laughed and called the bride and groom by their first names. Having initiated the revels, the couple retired to thronelike chairs at one end of the room to watch their guests cavort and to receive the personal felicitations of those able to make their way to them through the great press of celebrators. Strangely enough, the groom seemed to be the more popular of the pair, especially with the male guests, who flocked around him and whispered in his ear such things as made him laugh and blush. When the general exuberance had begun to subside, an impressive-looking master of ceremonies stood up on a chair, motioned the drummer to execute a roll, loud and long, and in the ensuing silence announced in a voice of thunder that supper was ready in the great room downstairs and ordered the gentlemen to escort their ladies below to the strains of a grand march that the orchestra would immediately strike up. Led by the bride and groom, with the *machetunim* following behind, a procession of couples formed and marched to the quick step of the grand march. But not for long; for some of the guests, overeager to get to the banquet hall first, broke ranks and ran ahead. In a moment the orderly march became a stampede, with the children (myself among them) snaking their way to the forefront and rushing down the wooden steps with a great clatter. Down in the dining room confusion reigned for a long time. People who had rushed to seat themselves near the bride and groom had to be forcibly dislodged by the master of ceremonies, who held a paper with the seating arrangements and could not be swerved from his determination to fill the long bridal table according to the strictest protocol.

Speak of weddings, and soon enough you speak of funerals. For an ordered community, or a community that remembered the order it had once had, this was a natural cycle, attended with outbursts of emotion unrestrained and passionate.

MICHAEL GOLD

I LIKED TO GO TO FUNERALS with the Jewish coach drivers. What glorious summer fun! Nathan was a tall Jewish ox, with a red, hard face like a chunk of rusty iron. His blustering manner had earned him many a black eye and bloody face. It was a warm bright morning. Three coaches rolled down the ramp of the livery stable on their way to a funeral. Then out bounced Nathan, cursing his horses. I begged him to let me go along. He was grouchy, but slowed down. I scrambled up beside him on the tall seat.

Three coaches and a hearse: a poor man's funeral. We rolled through the hurly-burly East Side. The sporty young drivers joked from coach to coach. The horses jerked and skipped. Nathan cursed them.

"You she-devil!" he roared in Yiddish at his white horse. "Steady down, or I'll kick in your belly!"

He tugged at the checkrein and cut the mare's mouth until it bled. But she was nervous; horses have their moods.

We came to the tenement of the corpse. Many pushcarts had to be cursed out of the way. We lined the curb. There was a crowd gathered. Weddings, sewer repairs, accidents, fires, and murders, all are food for the crowd. Even funerals.

The coffin was brought down by four pale men with black beards. Then came the wife and children in black, meekly weeping. The family was so poor that they had not the courage to weep flamboyantly.

But some of the neighbors did. It was their pleasure. They made an awful hullabaloo. It pierced one's marrow. The East Side women have a strange keening wail, almost Gaelic. They chant the virtues of the dead sweatshop slave, and the sorrow of his family.

The Old Hebrew Cemetery at Chatham Square.

They fling themselves about in an orgy of grief. It unpacks their hearts, but is hell on the bystanders.

These mourners egg on the widow; they don't want her to hide her grief; she must break down and scream and faint or the funeral is not perfect.

I sat on the high driver's seat and watched; I felt official and important somehow.

Then came the ride across the Brooklyn Bridge, with the incredible sweep of New York below us. The river was packed tight, a street with tugboat traffic. Mammoth skyscrapers cut into the sky like the teeth of a saw. The smoke of factories smeared the bright blue air. Horns boomed and wailed. Brooklyn lay low and passive in the horizon.

"A man is crazy to live in Brooklyn," said Nathan, the driver, pointing with his whip toward that side. "My God, it is as dead as a cemetery; no excitement, no nothing! Look, Mikey, down there. That's the navy yard. That's where they keep the American warships. Sailors are a lot of Irish bums. Once I had a fight with a sailor and knocked his tooth out. He called me a Jew."

"Ain't you a Jew?" I asked timidly, as my greedy eyes drank in the panorama.

"Of course I'm a Jew," said Nathan in his rough, iron voice. "I'm proud I'm a Jew, but no Irish bum can call me one."

"Why?" I asked.

I was very logical when I was seven years old.

"Why?" Nathan mimicked me with a sneer. "Why? You tell a kid something, and he asks why? Kids give me a headache!" He spat his disgust into the river. The blob fell a third of a mile.

They put the coffin in the ground. The old rabbi in a shiny high hat chanted a long sonorous poem in Hebrew, a prayer for dead Jews. A woman screamed; it was the dead man's wife. She tried to throw herself into the grave. Her weeping friends restrained her. The graveyard trees waved strangely. The graveyard sun was strange. The gravediggers shoveled earth into the grave. I felt lonesome and bewildered. I wanted to cry like the rest, but was ashamed because of Nathan.

Then it was all over. All of us went to a restaurant at the entrance to the cemetery and ate platters of sour cream, pot cheese, and black bread, the Jewish funeral food. Even the widow ate. Nathan gave me half of his portion. Then we rode home over the bridge.

I was glad to feel the East Side again engulf our coach. I lost my vague funeral loneliness in the hurly-burly of my street.

3

BINTEL BRIEF: LETTERS TO THE EDITOR

HANNE PESSL THE SECOND
drawn by Zagat

You can't say Jake Pantoffel's home life is a bed of roses.

חנה פעסיל דיא צווייטע

3. Hanne Pessl: *Golem, horse, beast! How can you start doing any cleaning without an apron? No brains at all. Look at him. Look who even got married, forgive my saying it.*

2. Hanne Pessl: *Look at him, how he sits there and reads baby stories. As if there were nothing to do. Get up, you goy. You're going to work.*

1. Jake Pantoffel: *No pal. I am not going to bum around with you. I am getting homesick. For me my home is better than Coney Island with your theaters and everything else.*

6. Hanne Pessl: *It makes you sick because I sat down for a minute to catch my breath? Nu, here is the paper! Here.*

5. Jake: *Nu, my dear little wife, I am ready, all finished. May I read the newspaper now?*

4. Hanne Pessl: *You should wash me all the dishes and wash again and put them in the closet.*

Even people who know very little about the Jewish immigrant experience have heard about the Bintel Brief ("Bundle of Letters"). Sometimes, indeed, that is the only thing they do remember. Too often this remarkable institution of Yiddish culture has been seen as mere "local color." And that's a pity, since it comes to far more than either sentiment or comedy.

In 1906 the Forward began to publish each day letters from its readers. The editor, Abraham Cahan, wanted to make his pages more vivid with the experience of the people who bought his paper; he understood that it was an experience at once significant and largely unrecorded, exciting and certain to be transient.

At first the letters were slow in coming. It wasn't an easy thing for an immigrant to take up pen and paper after a day's work and write to a newspaper: he or she felt bashful, feared the writing wouldn't be "correct," and wasn't at all sure whether to expose personal experiences to public gaze. When the letters did start coming in, the editors corrected the spelling and grammar, often cut them down (since inexperienced writers usually write too much), but tried to remain faithful to the spirit of their authors.

Were all these letters genuine? It's hard to say, but knowing the enterprise of the Forward we surmise that on "slack" days one of the reporters sat down to impersonate a reader and maybe, sometimes, did a better job of expressing what the reader felt than the reader could on his or her own.

But soon there was a flood of letters. The immigrants found an unexpected pleasure in expressing their feelings, in unpacking their hearts. To write a letter was part of the experience of freeing oneself from the constraints and repressions of the Old World—it was, in a small way, to taste freedom. It was to become persuaded that one's own life—romantic problems, loneliness, difficulties with a mother-in-law, quarrels with a business partner, ethical quandaries—also mattered. Perhaps not as much as the overall problems of the Jewish people, but at least they were now being aired.

The letters that came in were of an incredibly wide range. Topics of love naturally came first, but maybe not so naturally, for it was a relatively novel experience for east European Jews to get caught up with the entanglements of romanticism. Conflicts of opinion, difficulties of marriage, choices of career, refinements of ideology, nuances of manners, relations with Gentiles, psychological torments, generational tensions—these are only a few of the recurrent themes in the Bintel Brief.

The letters were usually answered in the early years by Cahan himself. He tried to be helpful, reasonable, calming; he tried to suggest to these often overwrought people that they should not torment themselves with excessive demands, that they should enjoy life a little bit, that they should not allow their religious or political preconceptions to stand in the way of daily need.

I'M LONELY

I FEEL THE TIME has come when I ought to get married, but when I try to talk to a lady, I do not interest her. At meetings I see young men with girls, comrades with comrades; they talk together, they laugh, they debate. And I am always alone. They never take me into their company. I do not mean to say that they are rude to me. No! They are sociable and kind, but the ladies never look at me, and when I speak, no one listens. Others say foolish things, and do not understand more than I do, and yet they make an impression. They have acquaintances and everything is rosy, and I am lonely.

I know that I am not handsome, but there are others like me, even homelier ones, and people take an interest in them, but not in me. That is why I feel very lonely, and when I go to a ball or meeting, or when there is a lecture, I do not want to remain and see how they walk out in couples and in groups. My heart yearns for love, for that natural happiness which seems to be the lot of all men except such unfortunates as myself.

SHOULD WE MARRY?

I AM A YOUNG MAN of twenty-one and would like to marry my seventeen-year-old cousin, but she's quite small and I happen to be quite tall. So when we walk down the street together, people look at us. Could this lead to an unpleasant life if we were to marry?

I AM A GIRL sixteen years old. I live together with my parents and two older sisters. Last year I met a young man. We love one another. He is a very respectable man, and makes a fine living. My sisters have no fiancés. I know that should I marry they will never talk to me. My parents are also strongly against it since I am the youngest child. I do not want to lose my parents' love, and neither do I want to lose my lover because this would break my heart. Give me some advice, dear Editor! What shall I do? Shall I leave my parents and marry my sweetheart, or shall I stay with my parents and lose the happiness of my life? Give me some advice, dear Editor!

I AM A YOUNG MAN of twenty-five, and I recently met a fine girl. She has a flaw, however—a dimple in her chin. It is said that people who have this lose their first husband or wife. I love her very much. But I'm afraid to marry her lest I die because of the dimple. *Answer:* The tragedy is not that the girl has a dimple in her chin but that some people have a screw loose in their heads.

I AM A RUSSIAN REVOLUTIONIST and a freethinker. Here in America I became acquainted with a girl who is also a freethinker. We decided to marry, but the problem is that she has Orthodox parents, and if we refuse a religious ceremony we will be cut off from them forever. I don't know what to do. Therefore, I ask you to advise me how to act. *Answer:* There are times when it is better to be kind in order not to grieve old parents.

HUSBAND AND WIFE

I HAVE BEEN HERE, in America, four years, and I earn ten dollars a week steady. But in spite of my fairly good earnings, there is really never a cent in my house. The reason is that my wife spends all the money on the peddlers and on many other unnecessary things. Originally my thought was to save a few cents and try some kind of business in order to free myself from the enslaving work. Now, however, I have had to give up the hope of establishing a business, because my words are of no avail; to take strong measures my conscience does not allow me. What then can one do?

. . . TO A MAN everything is permissible, to a woman nothing. A man is king over us and may do his will. When I argue that morality is more demanding on women, my husband gets angry and denies it with all his might. There is no such thing as a man with a bad name, but just let one spot fall upon a woman . . . Why?!

I DO NOT KNOW if all husbands are like that or if only I am punished with such a murderer of a husband. He never lets up. We are married two years, and already I am so broken and faded that I have no strength to stand on my feet. He does not care what is wrong with me: The law made him my husband, and he seeks to apply the law. He is a pious man. Yet in spite of his piety I am the victim of his animal instincts, even when the Jewish *Torah* does not permit it. I repel my husband, screaming, "*Gazlen*, murderer, with what eyes can you come to me?" He answers impudently, "You are my wife and I have the right to swallow and then spit you out whenever I want to."

I AM IN FAVOR of giving women full rights, but most of my friends are against it. They argue that the woman would then no longer be the housewife, the mother to her children, the wife to her husband—in a word, everything would be destroyed. I do not agree because a woman is a human being just like a man, and if women are recognized as human beings, they must be granted all the rights of human beings. *Answer:* Justice can reign among people only when they all have equal rights.

MY WIFE, BEFORE I MARRIED HER, knew very well that I did not believe in God and certainly not in a future world. She also expressed her opinions to me. And they agreed with mine. Soon after we married, we came to an agreement that if a boy was born to us we would not circumcise him. My wife has given birth to a son, and here began my tragedy. My wife wants a circumcision performed and nothing but, and so awful quarrels take place: I point out to her that the whole business is out of date, but she argues that the child must be circumcised. I can never allow that. If, God forbid, the baby is circumcised, I will not live through it. *Answer:* If your son ever becomes a Marx, a Lassalle, a Spinoza, or perhaps a Meyerbeer, a Halevi, a Rubenstein, it will certainly not hurt him if he is circumcised.

BREAKING DOWN

WHEN I SEE MY GIRL FRIEND, I am quite patient and calm. She is satisfied with me and I with her, but as soon as she goes away or I go away, a fire kindles within me. It happens very often that I stand whole evenings by her door; when I hear steps in the hall or on the stairs, I go away on tiptoes like a thief and the fire does not cease burning. Many times I argue with myself: What has gotten into you? How do you know? You haven't the slightest reason to think so. When I calm myself, it is really for no more than a short time. I immediately imagine crimes, embraces, passionate kisses, sweet declarations of love, and my peace is again troubled.

IS IT RIGHT?

I HAVE BEEN WORKING in a factory for over a year; I am satisfied with my job and cannot accuse the boss of any evil. On the contrary, it seems to me he is a fine man and deserves to be respected. I know only too well that he is a capitalist, but I cannot hate and curse him. Often I ask myself: Is this right?

I WAS BORN in a small town in Russia, and until I was sixteen I studied in *Talmud Torahs* and *yeshivas*, but when I came to America I developed spiritually and became a freethinker. Yet every year when the time of *Rosh Hashanah* and *Yom Kippur* approaches, I become very gloomy; my depression is so great that I cannot endure it. When I go past a synagogue during these days, my memory goes back to my childhood friends and my sweet childlike faith. So strong are my feelings that I enter the synagogue, not in order to pray to God but to heal and refresh my aching soul by sitting among *landsleit* and listening to the cantor's sweet melodies. The members of my Progressive Society don't understand. They say I am a hypocrite since I am known there as an outspoken freethinker. What is your opinion of this? *Answer:* No one can tell another what to do with himself on *Yom Kippur.*

WHY DO THE POLICE arrest workers in clothing and butcher shops on Sunday, even though they are closed on the Sabbath? Why do the police favor the clothing stores on Canal Street which remain open seven days a week? Why do the unions—which are so strong—allow people to suffer? Where else in the world do people sell their lives to make a living with no holidays and no rest? I am one of the corpses who works seven days a week in one of those electric-lit graves on Canal Street.

4

RELIGION

Disruption

If arrival in America brought shock and disruption for Jewish immigrants in general, the trauma was greater still for those who remained seriously religious. Miserable as life had been in eastern Europe, it still remained possible within the shtetl to keep intact old traditions, rituals, and modes of worship. Only with the advent of the secular enlightenment had rabbinical authority been seriously challenged—though by no means destroyed. But now, landing on strange shores, in a country where religion played no official role and the dominant faith was a Protestantism that the Jews had never directly encountered, the minority of pious Jews found itself threatened in endless ways. Observance of the Sabbath, inroads of disbelief, competition from conservative and reform congregations, the sheer difficulties of worship in busy cities and during the busy seasons of the garment industry—these were but a few of the problems. By all accounts, religious men found themselves especially threatened: they felt their authority was being undermined, they often had great difficulty in becoming breadwinners, they came to believe (not without reason) that there was hardly any place for them in di goldeneh medina ("the golden land"). Among all the memoirs written by immigrant Jews, few are more poignant than those composed by religious Jews—that of Ephraim Lisitsky, for example, a Hebrew writer who feels himself cast into an alien darkness. And even Abraham Cahan, no longer a believer though still tied emotionally to the faith he had abandoned, registers his astonishment at how different the role of the synagogue in New York is from what it was in the old country.

Still, we ought to avoid the recent sentimentalities that would make it seem that all Jews in the shtetlach and cities of east Europe were pious and that it was America that broke their faith. That simply is not true. By the late nineteenth century there was a growing secularist segment among the east European Jews, especially strong among intellectuals, the young, and the radicalized workers. The Haskalah ("Hebrew Enlightenment"), which had arisen earlier in the nineteenth century, had as its conscious intention a purification and strengthening of the faith, yet it sometimes, perhaps often, helped the trends toward disbelief. The culture of the east European Jews was no longer religiously unified—that, by the mid-nineteenth century, is the crucial fact. All the journey to America did was to hasten and make more extreme a process of inner division among the Jews that had already begun back home.

Yet, in the long run, it would be the religious Jew who held fast.

A Lower East Side church becomes a synagogue, 1898.
Drawing by W. A. Rogers for Harper's Monthly.

And the reasons seem clear. For those among whom the faith is strong, changes in external circumstances may affect minor aspects of their lives but not the core of commitment. If you hold to a belief in the Jewish God, it does not finally matter whether you live in Brownsville or Scarsdale, whether you worship in a ramshackle storefront congregation on Ludlow Street or in a synagogue designed in a suburban community by Percival Goodman: the center holds.

ABRAHAM CAHAN

WHEN IT GREW DARK and I was much in need of rest I had a street peddler direct me to a synagogue. I expected to spend the night there. What would have been more natural?

At the house of God I found a handful of men in prayer. It was a large spacious room and the smallness of their number gave it an air of desolation. I joined in the devotions with great fervor. My soul was sobbing to heaven to take care of me in a strange country.

The service over, several of the worshipers took up some Talmud folio or other holy book and proceeded to read them aloud in the familiar singsong. The strange surroundings suddenly began to look like home to me.

One of the readers, an elderly man with a pinched face and forked little beard, paused to look me over.

"A green one?" he asked genially.

He told me that the synagogue was crowded on Saturdays, while on weekdays people in America had no time to say their prayers at home, much less to visit a house of worship.

"It isn't Russia," he said with a sigh. "Judaism has not much chance here."

When he heard that I intended to stay at the synagogue overnight he smiled ruefully.

"One does not sleep in an American synagogue," he said. "It is not Russia." Then, scanning me once more, he added, with an air of compassionate perplexity: "Where will you sleep, poor child? I wish I could take you to my house, but—well, America is not Russia. There is no pity here, no hospitality. My wife would raise a rumpus if I brought you along. I should never hear the last of it."

With a deep sigh and nodding his head plaintively he returned to his book, swaying back and forth. But he was apparently more interested in the subject he had broached. "When we were at home," he resumed, "she, too, was a different woman. She did not make life a burden to me as she does here. Have you no money at all?"

I showed him the quarter I had received from the cloak contractor.

"Poor fellow! Is that all you have? There are places where you can get a night's lodging for fifteen cents, but what are you going to do afterward? I am simply ashamed of myself."

Jewish New Year Worshipers in front of a Rivington Street tenement synagogue, circa 1910. Photograph by George Bain.

"'Hospitality,'" he quoted from the Talmud, "'is one of the things which the giver enjoys in this world and the fruit of which he relishes in the world to come.' To think that I cannot offer a talmudic scholar a night's rest! Alas! America has turned me into a mound of ashes."

HIRSH MASLIANSKI

AS I LEFT BETH MEDRASH HAGODL I was shaken by what I saw. At the entrance of the *shul* half-naked Jewish boys were selling Yiddish papers. They mingled with the congregants leaving the *shul* and cried out "Two papers for a penny." Passersby and even some of the congregation bought papers as the voice of the *chazzen* could still be heard.

E. LISITSKY

I HAVE NEVER FORGOTTEN the impression of my first Saturday in Boston. I compared it to the Sabbath in Slutzk, and my heart bled. Actually there was no comparison, for Slutzk, though poverty-stricken, dressed up in glorious raiment in honor of the Sabbath. Even the horse grazing in the pasture, swishing his tail and leaping on his forelegs, bound so that he might not frisk beyond the Sabbath limits, was permitted to enjoy sabbatical rest and partake of the goodness of the luxuriant meadow. But in Boston very few Jews observed the Sabbath. In the Jewish quarter through which she had just passed they trampled with weekday shoes the train of her bridal gown. . . Leaving the synagogue after the Sabbath eve service, the observants were confronted by a tumultuous Jewish quarter: shopkeepers stood in their shop doorways; peddlers on their wagons shouted their wares. Mournfully I passed through this Jewish quarter that first Sabbath eve. As I entered our house it seemed to me that the Sabbath candles were bowed in mourning.

Everything about religious life in America seemed to be changed— and in the eyes of most pious Jews, debased. Patterns of deference and respect were broken. Traditional roles were abandoned. The sense of decorum that is so deeply a part of religious life was violated.

S. GURWITZ

ACCORDING TO AMERICAN CUSTOM, a rabbi, a *shochet* or *chazzen* is not taken on for more than a year at a time, after which they either retain him or let him go. This is not the way it was in Europe. When a rabbi, a *shochet* or *chazzen* came to town he was there for life, and even longer: if he left a son or son-in-law who could assume his place, no one else would be taken. That was his right. . . . But America doesn't care about this. If you're good, they want you; if not, they throw you out.

AARON ROTHKOFF

IN THE EARLY YEARS Old World rabbis bewailed the prevalent *cheder* system of education which produced thirteen- and fourteen-year-old youngsters who could not read the *Siddur* properly, boys who knew nothing about blessings and were ignorant of the grace before and after meals. *Kashrut* was an even more impossible situation on the immigrant scene. Unqualified immigrants became *shochetim, kosher* butchers, and supervising rabbis. This situation was further compounded by the meager regard in which true *kashrut* was held by the average housewife. Mainly interested in obtaining their meat as cheaply as possible, they were satisfied that the kosher signs in the windows of their butcher shops were a sufficient guarantee of *kashrut*. The butchers spurred the housewives on as they vied with one another in proclaiming cheaper prices without regard to their sources of supply. Sarcastically, an early religious observer cited the current adage, "*Az men ruft ihm Mendel, meg men essen fun sein fendel.*" ("As long as he's called Mendel, it's all right to eat from his pan.")

A grave difficulty on the communal scene was the lack of qualified rabbis to officiate at marriages. Numerous examples are cited of reverends permitting marriages between *kohanim* (men of Aaronic descent) and divorcées, although this was forbidden by the Torah. Men were also remarried although they had not granted *gittin* (rabbinical bills of divorcement) to their previous spouses. In cases of remarriage after the *gittin*, the reverends did not require the couple to wait the three-month period required by rabbinic decree. In one case a reverend allowed a man to marry his sister-in-law, although she already had children with his late brother. Not only was this a transgression of Torah law, but the ensuing children were also considered illegitimate by Jewish law.

Few *mohelim* or *shochetim* claimed these titles alone; their shingles usually read, "*Mohel* and Marriage Performer" or "*Shochet* and Marriage Performer." If a learned rabbi attempted to rectify these matters with dedicated sermons, the next week an anarchist paper would appear with a sarcastic rebuttal of the rabbi's sermon, and his efforts would be nullified.

"*Rabbi, is this chicken kosher?*"
DRAWING BY JACOB EPSTEIN

S.P. SCHOENFELD

ONE *SHABBES* TOWARD EVENING as the Odessa *landsleit* were sitting in *shul*, opening their hearts to one another, speaking longingly of Odessa, my father stood up for "Columbus." He pointed toward the example of the German baker from whom he got real Odessa-style baked goods very cheap.

"Do you know, Brother Shoenfeld," one of the *landsleit* called out, "why the German's stuff tastes so good? They're baked with lard."

"What?" my father shouted, grabbing his head. "I dunked them in my coffee—*fleyshiks* with *milkhiks.*"

ZALMEN YOFFEH

WE ACCEPTED UNRESERVEDLY the fact that there was a god; a Jewish god, reserved especially for us. But with us there was nothing like what I found later when I went out into the gentile world: the belief in a personal god to whom one could pray for definite, personal needs, and who would give heed to such prayers. With us prayer was an exaltation of an infinite, superior being whom one had to placate, whose laws one observed.

The observance of religious laws was, with us, such a matter of routine that we never considered their source. On Saturday morning, seated in *shul*, I muttered the prayers automatically. Never once did I think of God. It was just a matter of doing the prescribed.

One of the most interesting aspects of the immigrant Jewish experience is that it attracted the sympathetic attention of Gentile observers, some of them deeply affected, even overwhelmed, by what they saw. Two of these, Hutchins Hapgood and Ray Stannard Baker, looked closely at the practices and problems of religious life.

HUTCHINS HAPGOOD

THE PATRIARCHAL JEW devoted to the Law and prayer never does anything that is not prescribed, and worships most of the time that he is not at work. He has only one point of view, that of the Talmud; and his aesthetic as well as his religious criteria are determined by it. "This is a beautiful letter you have written," wrote an old man to his son. "It smells of Isaiah." He makes of his house a synagogue, and prays three times a day; when he prays his head is covered, he wears the black and white praying shawl, and the cubes of the phylactery are attached to his forehead and left arm. To the cubes are fastened two straps of goatskin, black and white; those on the forehead hang down, and those attached to the other cube are wound seven times about the left arm. Inside each cube is a white parchment on which is written the Hebrew word for God, which must never be spoken by a Jew. The strength of this prohibition is so great that even the Jews who have lost faith are unwilling to pronounce the word.

RAY STANNARD BAKER

...I HAVE VISITED MANY [synagogues] on Friday evenings and Saturday mornings—the two principal services of the week. Often I have found half a dozen bearded men waiting there—for what reason at first I could not understand. They would look up hopefully when I came in, and then their faces would fall when they saw that I was a Gentile and therefore would not help to make up the necessary prayer quorum of ten, without which they could not begin their services. Sometimes one of the number will go out on the street and beseech passing Jews to come in and help them with their quorum. I never shall forget one of these old Jews—his wistful eyes, his gentle, ineffectual movements—whom I saw one day stepping out like some patriarch from his fifteenth-century synagogue and seeking to stop with a call to prayer the tide of the twentieth century as it rushed through the streets.

Rabbis and Cantors

America was especially hard on the more reserved and unworldly rabbis who crossed the Atlantic. Tokens of respect, acknowledgments of authority that had simply been automatic in the old country, now had to be scrambled for. The balbatim— Yiddish for substantial congregants—played a role here they seldom could in the old country. For here money talked. And often, the more delicate among the rabbis didn't know how to talk back.

ABRAHAM CAHAN

... IN THE OLD COUNTRY, in Russia, the rabbi is a great person. He is rabbi all his life, and the only rabbi in the town, for all the Jews in every city form one congregation of which there is but one rabbi and one cantor. He is a man always full of learning and piety, and is always respected and supported comfortably by the congregation, a tax being laid upon meat, salt, and other foodstuffs for his benefit.

But in New York it is very different. Here there are hundreds of congregations, one in almost every street, for the Jews come from many different cities and towns in the old country, and the New York representatives of every little place in Russia must have their congregation here. Consequently, the congregations are for the most part small, poor, and unimportant. Few can pay the rabbi more than three or four dollars a week, and often instead of having a regular salary he is reduced to occasional fees for his services at weddings, births, and holy festivals generally. Some very poor congregations get along without a rabbi at all, hiring rabbis for special occasions, but these are congregations which are falling off somewhat from their Orthodox strictness.

The result in this state of affairs is a pretty general falling-off in the character of the rabbis. In Russia they are learned men—know the Talmud and all the commentaries upon it by heart—and have degrees from the rabbinical colleges, but here they are often without degrees, frequently know comparatively little about the Talmud, and are sometimes actuated by worldly motives. A few Jews coming to New York from some small Russian town will often select for a rabbi the man among them who knows a little more of the Talmud than the others, whether he has ever studied for the calling or not. Then again, some mere adventurers get into the position—men good for nothing, looking for a position. They clap a high hat on their heads, impose on a poor congregation with their up-to-dateness, and become rabbis without learning or piety. These "fake" rabbis—"rabbis for business only"—are often satirized in the Yiddish plays given at the Bowery theaters. On the stage they are ridiculous figures and ape American manners in bad accents.

S. GURWITZ

RABBI SLOAN TOOK CARE of his business: a whole week, slaughter; *Shabbes*, the pulpit. He never imagined the congregation would take a different *chazzen*. . . . He did not know that people thirst after a modern cantor, such as the ones on records who draw tears with their cries and tug at the heart with their wails, and penetrate the Jewish soul. Rabbi Sloan was boring people with his singing. . . . For the *bris* of his wife's brother, the Rev. D. Cantor came from Chicago. A young man, a beautiful singer . . . People heard him singing at the *bris* and held him over for *Shabbes*. He made so good an impression that they hired him as *chazzen* with a one-year contract. . . . And what about Rabbi Sloan—no longer *chazzen?* So many years he delighted people with his prayers, and now, no more. . . . When the Hebrew school was left without a teacher, congregational officials then reckoned that we must take on a young man who could function in two positions: rabbi and teacher. . . . Young applicants began to flock to us. We no longer hungered for sermons, but it took a while to find just the right man. He was Rabbi Gerstein, a young man full of personality and charm. He was intelligent with a not bad command of English. His sermons pleased because they were better than nothing. So, how do you like the exchange: two young men for one old? Greater cost, but less *Torah*.

If rabbis had trouble in adjusting to America, so too did cantors—perhaps still more so, because in the immigrant Jewish community some cantors were "stars," able to attract vast numbers of people when they sang in a congregation and commanding high salaries. Two of the greatest cantors—S. Kwartin and Yossele Rosenblatt—went through bewildering experiences, which they would later record in their memoirs. They were suddenly thrust into the status of being celebrities in the immigrant world, and the experience was deeply unsettling.

S. KWARTIN

I ASKED MY COUSIN in which *shul* I'd *daven* that *Shabbes*. I'd made clear in my letters that my first American appearance was to be in a *shul* on *Shabbes* with a real choir. . . . But my cousin answered me proudly that for my first concert they'd taken not a *shul* but the biggest hall they could find in New York, the Metropolitan Opera House where Caruso, the world's greatest singer, appears. When I heard that I felt as though someone had hit me over the head with a hammer. . . . I was terrified of the opera house: the greater the size, the greater my fear. . . . But go scream and shout.

A publicity shot of Cantor Yosele Rosenblatt for the film The Jazz Singer *(1927).*

SAMUEL ROSENBLATT

MY FATHER'S PROGRAMS in his vaudeville appearances were usually short. Two or three such favorites as "Eili, Eili," "The Last Rose of Summer," and "Duna" plus an encore was all that there was time for at a single performance. . . . The announcements on the billboards that Josef Rosenblatt would not be heard on Friday evening or Saturday matinee because he was observing his Sabbath, constituted a real *Kiddush Hashem*, a glorification of the Jewish religion. They evoked the profoundest respect and reverence in everybody. . . . However, one cannot live for months in the atmosphere of the music hall without its leaving its mark. In their eagerness to attract the public my father's managers . . . would resort to such advertisements as "The man with the $500,000 beard." In the course of time my father, too, unconsciously adopted the lingo of the stage. "One day," recorded a reporter of *Variety*, "when Bert Wheeler asked Josef Rosenblatt his routine, the tenor startled him by saying: 'I stop the show and then I sing "Eili, Eili" for an encore and pan 'em.'"

William Morris presents Sirota.

KARL SHAPIRO
THE SYNAGOGUE

The synagogue dispirits the deep street,
Shadows the face of the pedestrian,
It is the adumbration of the Wall,
The stone survival that laments itself,
Our old entelechy of stubborn God,
Our calendar that marks a separate race.

•

The altar of the Hebrews is a house,
No relic but a place, Sinai itself,
Not holy ground but factual holiness
Wherein the living god is resident.
Our scrolls are volumes of the thundered law
Sabbath by sabbath wound by hand to read.

•

Our wine is wine, our bread is harvest bread
That feeds the body and is not the body.
Our blessing is to wine but not the blood
Nor to sangreal the sacred dish. We bless
The whiteness of the dish and bless the water
And are not anthropophagous to him.

Early immigrant congregations often met in basements, tiny apartments, ramshackle stores: God, it was assumed, cared about the authenticity of worship more than the grandeur of architecture.

UNIVERSITY SETTLEMENT SOCIETY

REPORT, 1899

AN EXACT ESTIMATE of the number of congregations in the district is almost impossible. A canvass of twenty-five streets, made some time ago, at the instance of Dr. Blaustein of the Educational Alliance, showed fully one hundred organizations of sufficient size and permanence to display a sign over the door. It is safe to assert that there are at least as many more which meet in tenement houses. This estimate leaves entirely out of account the host of others which, at holiday time, spring up in lodge rooms, dance halls, and lofts, only to go out of existence when the solemn days of *Rosh Hashanah* and *Yom Kippur* are over.

The first two classes include in their membership not far from forty percent of the adult Jewish population of the district. Of this number at least one-half have no other means of social gratification than that obtained from the synagogue and the streets. Daily— morning, noon, and night—a little company of small-shop keepers, peddlers, and "out of works" gather to offer up the prayers of the day. Such rigidity of discipline is possible, however, only to the few. Most must content themselves with one or more services on *Shabbes*. As in most cases, particularly in the smaller synagogues, the members are emigrants from some town in Russia, Poland, or Roumania. These synagogue meetings then serve as a means of keeping them in touch with the old home. A new immigrant coming to the city finds himself immediately included in a little circle of people he has known on the other side. The congregation, anxious to increase the membership, is sure to seek him out, and if he is in need, to assist him with that charity which is the most generous of all, the charity of the tenement house.

ABRAHAM CAHAN

THE ORTHODOX SYNAGOGUE is not merely a house of prayer; it is an intellectual center, a mutual aid society, a fountain of self-denying altruism, and a literary club, no less than a place of worship. The study rooms of the hundreds of synagogues, where the old people of the ghetto come to read and discuss "words of law" as well as the events of the day, are crowded every evening in the week with poor street peddlers, and with those gray-haired, misunderstood sweatshop hands of whom the public hears every time a tailor strike is declared. So few are the joys which this world has to spare for those overworked, enfeebled victims of "the inferno of modern times," that their religion is to many of them the only thing which makes life worth living. In the fervor of prayer or the abandon of religious study they forget the grinding poverty of their homes. Between the walls of the synagogue, on the top floor of some ramshackle tenement house, they sing beautiful melodies, some of them composed in the caves and forests of Spain, where the wandering people worshiped the God of their fathers at the risk of their lives; and these and the sighs and sobs of the Days of Awe, the thrill that passes through the heartbroken *tallis*-covered congregation when the *shofar* blows, the mirth which fills the house of God and the tenement homes upon the Rejoicing of the Law, the tearful greetings and humbled peacemakings on Atonement Eve, the mysterious light of the *Chanukah* (a festival in memory of the restoration of the Temple in the time of the Maccabeans) candles, the gifts and charities of *Purim* (a festival commemorating the events in the time of Esther), the joys and kingly solemnities of Passover— all these pervade the atmosphere of the ghetto with a beauty and a charm without which the life of its older residents would often be one of unrelieved misery.

Everyone knows about the Forward, *the Yiddish socialist paper that played so central a role in the immigrant milieu. But there were, of course, other papers. One of the* Forward's *fiercest competitors and severest critics was the* Tageblatt, *which around the turn of the century and for some years later spoke in behalf of religious orthodoxy. It was a paper, as J. Chaiken, the historian of Yiddish journalism, has remarked, that "synthesized shtetl religiosity with American sensationalism." In this respect, the* Tageblatt *wasn't alone; its sensationalism was not very different in character, though perhaps a shade less skillful, than that of the* Forward. *To catch the eye of busy, tired, overworked immigrants, things had to be put briefly, vividly, simply.*

TAGEBLATT, 11/24/'12

IN THE SHOMRE EMUNAH SYNAGOGUE, Fifty-third Street and Fourteenth Avenue, Boro Park, the congregants will now be able to take snuff as much as they please. Rabbi Abraham Geller, who did not tolerate the beadle's distributing snuff during his sermons, is no longer there.

As has already been reported, some of the snuffers wanted to get rid of the rabbi in the easiest way. They just threw him off the pulpit. Indeed the rabbi protested the incident and a hearing has been set for Friday in the Flatbush court. However, a committee was chosen from the congregation to negotiate with the rabbi for a more peaceful solution. The rabbi agreed to give up his position for $1,300.

TAGEBLATT, 3/9/'06

...THE RADICALISM THAT IS FEARED and kept out of the Jewish pulpit is not so much of a general social and religious nature as is the radicalism that concerns the future of the Jew as a Jew, that aims at the preservation of our nationality, in a

word, the radicalism of Jewish restoration. The heart of the Jewish rabbi surely feels the throb of the great struggle for self-preservation that now animates all Jewish life; the soul of the rabbi is surely stirred by the great awakening of Jewish consciousness, but the Jewish purse, what does it say? It says nothing. It appoints a board of trustees made up of eminent Jews. And the rabbis? One wonders why they preach so persistently against Zionism, against nationalism, against Jewish restoration, against fighting for Jewish life, against distinct Jewish art, against everything that justifies the existence of the Jew. One begins to wonder why there are temples, why there are rabbis if, as the rabbis tell us, there is no Jewish people and there is no Jewish destiny.

TAGEBLATT, 3/16/'06

A RE OUR RABBIS men of independence or are they slaves? Have our rabbis the right to think and to speak and to act according to the dictates of their conscience or according to the will or the whim of the congregation, or of a board of trustees? These questions have been raised by the Rev. Dr. Stephen S. Wise.

Almost every son and daughter of immigrant Jewish parents can remember the childhood experience of going to Hebrew school, or cheder—an experience often desultory and depressing. American-born children would often feel that having to go to Hebrew school after a full session in the American public schools was an assault on their free time. The ill-paid, overworked, and often untrained teachers at these Hebrew schools resented, and suffered from, the indifference, even hostility, of their students. So the main pattern goes—though with happy exceptions, of course—both in the Orthodox schools and the secular Yiddish schools.

Yeshiva boys on Grand Street, 1910.

ALEXANDER DUSHKIN

TODAY MANY OF THE NEW YORK *chederim* are taught by men who were formerly teachers in eastern Europe. These men came to this country too late in life to make new adjustments, and they therefore continued in the only occupation which they knew in the land of their birth. The lot of these earnest, medieval men, zealously trying to impart unwished-for-knowledge to the unwilling youngsters of New York, is a sad one indeed. But there are many other *chederim* kept by those who are less worthy. These are usually ignorant men who spend their mornings in peddling wares or in plying some trade, and who utilize their afternoons and evenings for selling the little Jewish knowledge they have to American children, at so much per session (10¢ - 25¢ per week, for 10 or 15 minutes' instruction daily). The usual procedure is for a group of boys to gather in the home of the self-appointed *rebbe*, and to wait their turn, or "next." While one pupil drawls meaninglessly the Hebrew words of the prayer book, the rest play or fight, with the full vivacity of youth. The ideal of many parents contains but three elements: (1) fluency in the mechanical reading of Hebrew prayers *(ivre)*; (2) knowledge of the *Kiddush*, or Sabbath eve benediction, and the *Kaddish*, or prayer for the dead; (3) ability to read the portion of the Torah assigned at the *Bar Mitzva* initiation ceremony, and to deliver a "confirmation speech."

EVENING POST, 8/3/'01

THE *MELAMED HAS TWO TEACHING* functions not entirely separated from each other. He instructs the Hebrew children in the Hebrew tongue. He also teaches the boys the principles of their religion, drills them in the *ivre*, or prayers, and discourses to them on talmudic laws . . .

Instruction begins with the Hebrew letters and pronunciation. Then comes the *ivre*, or collection of prayers, which are all committed to memory. Next the *Chumash*, or Pentateuch, is taken up in the same way. Pupils are sometimes able to repeat almost the entire work before they have the slightest inkling of what it is all about. At last the teacher begins to translate for his pupils. Sometimes a book is used in which the Yiddish and classic Hebrew are placed side by side and in this manner the student finally gathers a more or less faint idea of the text. The *Gemara*, or commentaries and talmudic studies, follows. In this country the Talmud is usually taught superficially. The best of the *melameds* have a deep knowledge of these studies and sometimes pour out to their pupils a rich store of history and tradition.

Under the most favorable of circumstances these teachers earn but a pittance. Their prices for lessons are varied. They charge in fact whatever the parents are able or willing to pay. A dollar a month is a good average price for each pupil. It is considered the proper thing to charge more for advanced pupils than for those just beginning.

COMMERCIAL ADVERTISER, 7/23/'98

A BONNETLESS YOUNG WOMAN with a letter in her hand was gazing about her, as if in search of something, as she leisurely proceeded on her way along Ludlow Street.

"Buy fish? cucumbers? horseradish? Sabbath loaves?" several market women clambered in chorus, tugging the bashful pedestrian by the arm or skirt as she passed them.

"No," was the woman's invariable reply.

"Oh, I know what she wants!" broke in a little boy, the son of one of the fishmongers. "She wants to have a letter written; don't you, missus?"

"Sure, I do. How did you guess it?" the young housewife said gratefully. "Do you know a letter writer around here?"

"My rabbi writes letters cheap and good. He lives around the corner. Shall I show you where it is?"

Presently the boy stopped in front of a basement window with a little signboard which read: Hebrew taught. Letters written in Yiddish, English, German, Russian and Hebrew. The rabbi was found at the head of a class of dirty boys lazily singing over huge open books. "Louder or I'll break every bone in . . ." The threat was suddenly broken off by the appearance of the newcomers. The boys cast furtive glances at the strangers. "Where do you keep your eyes, Gentile boys that you are? Look at your Bible or I'll make you look the Angel of Death in the face."

The chapter finished, the rabbi reached out his hand for the woman's letter. "Have you anything particular to write, young woman?"

"Tell my sister that I am sending her ten American dollars, and that I hope to the uppermost that her husband will get well. Tell her also that mother sends her love. Tell her also that God has given me a crown for a husband and that he kisses my footprints and that he sends the money gladly, and . . . and . . . and. . . . Don't you know of anything else to write, rabbi?"

"You have got enough. You don't want me to be writing a whole year for five cents, do you?"

HENRY ROTH

THE BOY BEGAN TO READ. Though a big boy, as big as any that preceded him, he read more slowly and faltered more often than any of the others. It was evident that the rabbi was restraining his impatience, for instead of actually striking his pupil, he grimaced violently when he corrected him, groaned frequently, stamped his foot under the table and gnawed his underlip. The other students had grown quiet and were listening. From their strained silence—their faces were by now half obscured in shadow—David was sure they were expecting some catastrophe any instant. The boy fumbled on. As far as David could tell, he seemed to be making the same error over and over again, for the rabbi kept repeating the same sound. At last, the rabbi's patience gave out. He dropped the pointer; the boy ducked, but not soon enough. The speeding plane of the rabbi's palm rang against his ear like a clapper on a gong.

"You plaster dunce!" he roared, "when will you learn a *baiz* is a *baiz* and not a *vaiz*. Head of filth, where are your eyes?" He shook a menacing hand at the cringing boy and picked up the pointer.

But a few moments later, again the same error, and again the same correction.

"May a demon fly off with your father's father! Won't blows help you? A *baiz*, Esau, pig! A *baiz*! Remember, a *baiz*, even though you die of convulsions!"

The boy whimpered and went on. He had not uttered more than a few sounds, when again he paused on the awful brink, and as if out of sheer malice, again repeated his error. The last stroke of the bastinado! The effect on the rabbi was terrific. A frightful bellow clove his beard. In a moment he had fastened the pincers of his fingers on the cheeks of his howling pupil, and wrenching the boy's head from side to side roared out:

"A *baiz*! A *baiz*! A *baiz*! All buttocks have only one eye. A *baiz*! May your brains boil over! A *baiz*! Creator of earth and firmament, ten thousand *cheders* are in this land and me you single out for torment! A *baiz*! Most abject of God's fools! A *baiz*!"

While he raved and dragged the boy's head from side to side with one hand, with the other he hammered the pointer with such fury against the table that David expected at any moment to see the slender stick buried in the wood. It snapped instead!

"He busted it!" gleefully announced the boy sitting near.

"He busted it!" the suppressed giggle went round. Horrified himself by what he saw, David wondered what the rest could possibly be so amused about.

"I couldn't see," the boy at the table was blubbering. "I couldn't see! It's dark in here!"

"May your skull be dark!" the rabbi intoned in short frenzied yelps, "and your eyes be dark and your fate be of such dearth and darkness that you will call a poppyseed the sun and a carroway the moon. Get up! Away! Or I'll empty my bitter heart upon you!"

Tears streaming down his cheeks, and wailing loudly, the boy slid off the bench and slunk away.

"Stay here till I give you leave to go," the rabbi called after him. "Wipe your muddy nose. Hurry, I say! If you could read as easily as your eyes can piss, you were a fine scholar indeed!"

The boy sat down, wiped his nose and eyes with his coatsleeve and quieted to a suppressed snuffling.

> *The troubles, indeed the agonies, of trying to maintain traditional Jewish scholarship in an American setting became part of the folklore of immigrant Jewish life.*

TAGEBLATT, 1/21/'06

IN THE YESHIVA Rabbi Isaac Elchanan, 156 Henry Street, an altercation between the directors and the students resulted in a strike which has been temporarily postponed, but which is liable to be resumed next week or the week after. Strained relations between the talmudic students and what may be called the faculty are chronic in the establishment, and a sporadic flaring up of bad temper brings out every now and then hard words and bitter feeling. Indeed, there is cause for sorrow on beholding how this ultra-Orthodox rabbinical institution . . . is debasing itself, and turning itself into "copy" for the dailies and, in time, perhaps, for the comic weeklies.

One of the demands of the strikers is that students be allowed to study the English language, together with some science and literature. The *yeshiva* keeps two teachers in secular subjects, to teach the rudiments of English grammar and arithmetic, but here it puts obstacles in the path by not giving the boys enough books. The little secular instruction afforded is purely a sop. . . .

So anxious are the students for worldly knowledge that out of the three dollars a week they are given by the institution for board and lodging, they spare money for engaging private teachers and entering preparatory schools. Now comes the very worthy directorate and wants to prohibit the students from making any attempts at self-instruction. The time was when the friends of the *yeshiva* fondly hoped that it would prove to be a guiding pillar of fire for Israel. As it is, the place radiates darkness.

E. LISITSKY

BEFORE LONG I was seized with a desire to enroll in an American school. This was in conflict with my ambition for the rabbinate, which still persisted. I reconciled the conflict by pretending that a general education would advance my career as a rabbi. English was still as foreign to me as on the day I landed in America, so I set about learning the rudiments of the language. I acquired a copy of the Pentateuch with an English translation, and I began to study it every day. . . . When the public school semester approached, the *yeshiva* supervisory board issued an order that its students henceforth were to devote the entire day to their *yeshiva* studies. The students were divided in their reactions: Some submitted; others, myself included, revolted and decided to leave the *yeshiva* altogether. I had been studying at the Rabbi Isaac Elchanan Yeshiva for only half a year, and I had not developed any attachment to it. Still, it was hard for me to part from it, for it meant abandoning a lofty ideal to which I had consecrated myself as a boy.

HIRSH MASLIANSKI

A PROFESSOR AT Hebrew Union College in Cincinnati . . . visited me in my hotel and invited me in the name of Dr. Isaac M. Wise, founder of Reform Judaism in America, to speak . . . in Hebrew to professors and students.

"Who's there to understand me?"

"Ten from the faculty and some twenty of the students. We have a number of students who are emigrants from Russia—talmudists, Hebraists who studied in the *yeshivas* of Telz and Volozhin; they'll understand."

I accepted the invitation. . . .

I spoke a full hour in Hebrew to my unknown brothers, strange to me in both language and concept. I spoke calmly and slowly in order that they should understand me. More or less, they did. I told of our eight million brothers and sisters overseas living a gruesome existence in Russia. I told of the sad but wholly idealistic life of their fellows in the *yeshivas*, studying with utter devotion—studying not for careers, for the wealthy congregations that await them, but just for the sake of Torah itself. . . .

When I sensed that almost all had understood me, I shouted: "My dear young brothers, sons of Abraham, Moses and David; pupils of Isaiah, Hillel, and Rabbi Yokhanan ben Zakai, don't you feel with me the pain and shame of a Jewish speaker coming to a Jewish seminary speaking in Hebrew and a big part of the audience does not understand him? And of those who do, they still look at him with such amazement in their eyes as though he were speaking one of the archaic tongues like Latin or Greek. . . ."

Then I turned to the venerable founder of Reform, Dr. I.M. Wise, sitting near me. "And now I want to address you, most praiseworthy, sagacious teacher in Israel: Did you know that . . . one of your pupils . . . just one month ago, created such a gross scandal that terrified the hearts not only of my Orthodox brothers . . . even your real reformed were shaken. . . . He took our holy Torah scrolls out of the ark, put them in the basement and in their stead placed an English Bible."

Orthodox and Secular

What were the religious (or antireligious) convictions of the majority of the immigrant Jews? It's a question easy to ask but surprisingly difficult to answer. Some things we do know: there was a firm minority of seriously religious Jews, just as there was an equally firm minority of antireligious Jews. But beyond that?

Our impression is that the bulk of the immigrant Jews were neither entirely pious nor entirely skeptical. By the time many of them got to America, the intensity of their faith had been weakened, yet the power of memory and habit, all that had been instilled in them during their childhood, remained very strong. There were many—perhaps the majority?—of immigrants who went to shul ("synagogue") only on the high holy days and intermittently throughout the year, who continued to obey some ritual prescriptions but by no means all, and who gradually drifted into an increasingly secular mode of life. Yet, if not Orthodox, it was Orthodoxy that had shaped them. On the other hand, some of the militantly secular Jews, those who had programmatically repudiated the synagogue, still showed the marks of their upbringing—their antireligious speeches, for example, bearing religious metaphors.

Between the extremes of Orthodox and secular there was a kind of spiritual civil war in the immigrant quarters, especially during the years before the First World War. Later, this conflict grew softer, tempers cooled, fanaticism abated. For the bulk of the immigrants, what was beyond question was the experience of being a Jew, which also meant retaining one or another portion of religious observance and feeling.

Leon Kobrin, a prolific Yiddish writer of novels, plays, and stories, wrote a sketch in the early immigrant days about the doubts and guilts of radical Jewish parents who had brought up their children in a completely nonreligious, indeed, non-Jewish, way. This sketch, the first expression of nationalism presented in the American Yiddish Socialist press, drew violent protests from readers against the Abendblatt staff.

"Forward *Masquerade Ball—Shabbes, the 27th of January 1906, in Madison Square Garden*"—*an advertisement in the* Jewish Daily Forward.

LEON KOBRIN

"T R A N S I T I O N A L P E O P L E!" *Akh,* if that would be true: if, having torn ourselves away from the old, we could arrive at the new, everything would be fine. But, oh, the doubts, my questions. If I'd disclose them to my husband, that fervent cosmopolitan, he'd laugh at me. "Silly woman," he'd say, "you talk this way because in your gut there's still the taste of *tsimmes* and *kugel.* That's what you long for."

Would that be an answer to my yearnings? No, my husband knows I'm as free of religious folly as he. . . .

What does my five-year-old, Nikolai Tchernishevski, my darling boy, know of being a Jew. . . . He knows of no *Shabbes* or holiday; yet Christian children call him *sheeny,* my parents call him *goy* and in their hearts, *bastard.*

So you thought you'd get out of the darkness of the East into the light of the West. A youthful fantasy. What have you found: a night as black as the one you left, the only difference being that in that night you were warmed, and in this one you freeze.

Last Christmas our Christian neighbors put up a Christmas tree for the children. Seeing that, my Nikolai came to me with a query: "Where's my Christmas tree, mama?"

"We're not Christians," I answered.

My Nikolai was satisfied and did not question further.

Comes Passover and our Jewish neighbors dress up their children, make a real *seder.*

Nikolai runs to me again. "Mama, where are my new clothes?"

I answer: "We don't keep holidays."

Nikolai cries, twists his lips and cries.

"Why are you crying, my child?"

"Are we *sheenies,* mama?"

"What are you talking about?"

"No Christmas tree, no holiday with clothes and wine—we must be *sheenies.*"

My heartstrings tugged. What could I answer? That we're freethinkers? That we're socialists? That our holidays are in the future?

Where is the poetry in my Nikolai's childhood? . . .

All members of this transitional generation, children of the rich as well as the poor, recall with longing and trembling heart the marvelous moments of our childhood. The holy brightness of the candles that graced the *Shabbes* . . . the holiday faces of our near and dear. . . .

No more. Around us there is no life, no vitality; no life, no warmth. And from this chaos and void my child too will grow up empty and chaotic.

One of the major Yiddish intellectuals, Chaim Zhitlovsky, worked out an elaborate system of ideas: he rejected traditional religion yet saw in it a home of deep-seated Jewish experiences and feelings; he wanted Jewish life to remain coherent and rich, through developing the culture of Yiddish; he strongly opposed assimilation. History does not seem to have worked according to his prescription, but for a time his influence was considerable.

CHAIM ZHITLOVSKY

WE REJECT ALL RELIGIOUS TEACHING as a basis for our national existence and productivity, because religious teaching, if it is to be truly religious, cannot be national in character; because it fetters free thought; because it tends to sunder the bonds that tie parents to children and integrate members of a people into one folk; because it tends to isolate a nation and doom it to stagnation; because constricted religious teaching is no safeguard against language assimilation, the most dangerous foe of our normal existence and of our free development as a progressive people among modern nations. . . .

IF THE BRANCH CALLED religion should ever wither away and fall off the cultural tree of mankind—something I cannot possibly conceive—there will still be left in the possession of man the noblest heritage in the form of the finest and most exalted feelings . . . even the darkest religion has its bright side, to which should be credited the fact that it has taught the human soul to sense holiness and the infinite.

In The New Era, *a long-forgotten Jewish journal, Bernard Richards tries to reassure his readers (or himself) that the deserters from the faith will come back.*

BERNARD RICHARDS

THOSE OF OUR PEOPLE who seek spiritual consolation in worlds beyond their own ken remind me of the Jewess who, leaving the synagogue on the Day of Atonement, said: "Lord of the Universe, if Thou wilt grant me a good year, well and good; if not, I will leave this town and go to live with my sister in Wilna." The same light shines in Wilna as in Keidan and the same darkness envelops all places. Over the door of life everywhere hangs the sentence of death and the evil decree can be averted only by true words, lofty thoughts, and good deeds. And a man can live the best life, can find the most consolation, only when he is most at home.

The world is large when we stay where we belong: when we go beyond our sphere we find that there is no room for us. How many of us have wandered and wandered and wandered only to come back and learn the meaning of life from a poor, bewigged, ignorant old woman we used to be ashamed of? A tender embrace, a cry of joy, a loving word and all was clear to us.

What does Fanny say in Gordin's *Emmese Kraft?* "God or no God, but there must be something. When there is nothing it is terribly lonesome." For that "something," without which we cannot live, the wanderers, the lost sheep—at least the best of them—will come home, and they will find it in the form of either rejuvenated Judaism or a glowing nationalist ideal—at any rate in the shape of a swaying enthusiasm that will give zest to our life and fill even the reformed temples with warmth—warmth that does not come from steam heat, but from beating hearts.

When the dead, the indifferent Jews awaken they will realize that there is but one life for a Jew and that is the life of a Jew. A Jew can be a good Jew, a kind Jew, a wise Jew, a great Jew; but when he tries to be a Gentile all he can ever be is a very mediocre *goy*. Assimilation is self-assassination, and universal brotherhood is an extravagant and dangerous figure of speech. At any rate, if we are to help toward the attainment of the higher ideals of life, those who are most alike, who feel together, should unite and begin to improve the world by improving their own condition. The Jew must be himself or cease to be anything. He must help himself or anything else that he does will be in vain.

In any event most of those who have departed will come back, so do not fear or worry, my friends. "Your son will come back," says Techeref to the distracted father in Gorky's masterly *Meschanie.* "He will come back and rearrange the furniture of this house and live as you have lived."

And here are two poems by major Jewish writers, the first, Maurice Samuel, best known as the translator of Sholom Aleichem and Peretz, and the second, Itzik Manger, a gifted Yiddish poet.

MAURICE SAMUEL

AL HAREI CATSKILL

And here in Catskill what do Jews believe?
In *kosher*, certainly; in *Shabbes*, less,
(But somewhat, for they smoke in secret then.)
In *Rosh Hashanah* and in *Yom Kippur*,
In charity and in America;
But most of all in pinochle and poker,
In dancing and in jazz, in risqué stories,
And everything that's smart and up-to-date.

ITZIK MANGER

I SHALL TAKE OFF MY SHOES

My God, my Lord, my Creator,
Purify me in your light.
I lie on a cloud before you.
Rock me to sleep in the night.

And speak to me words of kindness.
"My child, my child," to me say.
And with a kiss, from my forehead
Take the signs of my sins away.

My God, my Lord, my Creator,
Purify me in your light.
I lie on a cloud before you.
Rock me to sleep in the night.

For many immigrant Jews—pious, occasionally observant, even largely secular—the religious tradition continued to provide meaning, ceremony, pleasure. For religion among Jews has never been a mere matter of belief or worship; it has been, or claimed to be, a total way of life, shaping and coloring everything from birth to death. Often, as the strictly religious component of tradition grew weaker, there occurred among the immigrants a compensating growth of attachment to ritual, celebration, and ceremony— sometimes with a tacit sense that they had to live with fragments of the past, sometimes with a thoughtless but telling attachment to the external forms of an ebbing tradition.

COMMERCIAL ADVERTISER, 3/5/'98

"WILL PURIM BE OBSERVED this year, as usual?" was asked of a representative denizen of the ghetto.

"Why not?" he answered. "Have we not our Hamans today? Is not Esterhazy [the accusor of Dreyfus] an enemy of the Jews? Doesn't he speak of exterminating our people? Yes, we are going to celebrate *Purim*, just to spite Esterhazy and his gang."

MORGAN ZHURNAL, 4/3/'50

FIFTY YEARS AGO, Jews of New York did not need a calendar to tell them when the high holidays arrived; nor an alarm clock, because they were awakened earlier than the clock. It is no exaggeration that there were two or three small synagogues and places of worship on every block; and on the first day of Elul every one of them sounded the *shofar* in the early hours of the morning, continuing throughout the month.

Every *shul* and fraternal group was busy selecting a committee to sit outside and sell tickets, and another one to audition a cantor. During the year they never needed a cantor; any member of the congregation who felt like it could go up and sing or pray. They needed a cantor for the high holidays because they wanted a special service, and because they couldn't sell tickets unless they had a world-famous singer. After all, the *shul* next door had a cantor with a choir.

Auditions were distressing for the candidates as well as for the committee, which interviewed cantors until late at night. Suddenly, hundreds of East Side Jews became experts in selecting as well as singing. An ordinary, illiterate Jew, who was a committee member, became an authority in discarding a singer. Top salary for a cantor was forty dollars, and only if he had a reputation. But the committee bargained, maintaining that this was lots of money for

Performing the rite of tashlikh *on the Brooklyn Bridge, 1910. Photograph by George Bain.*
LIBRARY OF CONGRESS, BAIN COLLECTION

doing nothing, "because a Jew has to pray anyhow." The cantor just has to sing a little louder than the rest of the congregation. He gets paid for "setting the tone," and it's really found money.

Candidates compensated for the "easy job" by running around a full month looking for work, straining their throats at auditions, and enduring insults from skeptical committee members. After several auditions in one night, most of them were hoarse and couldn't get the job.

Sidewalks were clotted with *shul* members selling their red, yellow, green, or white tickets, all promising "the famous cantor so and so," although he was unknown. Ticket sales went on until late at night. Young men who hadn't bought tickets used the first *sliches* as a testing ground to determine which cantor was best; that night they ran from *shul* to *shul* listening to the various singers. On *Rosh Hashanah* one could really see how the Jewish population had grown; all the big and little synagogues were packed. The back rooms of East Side saloons and empty stores were transformed into prayer halls—a *minyan* with a cantor. Yiddish theaters became synagogues, too.

117

COMMERCIAL ADVERTISER, 9/26/'98

T H I S I S *Yom Kippur*, the Day of Awe and Atonement. It is a terrible day in Israel, the day of days upon which depends the fate of every living creature, and with few exceptions it is observed and spent in fasting and prayer by every adult Hebrew in town. Whatever one does the whole year, however neglectful one may be of his religion on any other holiday, on this day of *Yom Kippur* one is sure to be at his synagogue and *makhzor* ("prayerbook") in hand follow the *chazzen* ("cantor") and his chorus, strike his heart while enumerating the sins he has committed and pray for mercy and an enrollment in the Book of Life.

The most important part of the service in the synagogues today is the chanting of a series of hymns. "The great trumpet is sounded," reads a passage: "a dull, murmuring noise is heard; the angels shudder; fear and trembling seize them. 'Ha!' they cry; 'it is the Day of Judgment; the heavenly choir are to be visited in judgment, for in justice even they are not found faultless before Thee. All who are about to enter into the world now pass before Thee, as a herd of sheep, as a shepherd numbereth his flock and passeth under his crook so dost Thou cause to pass, number and appoint every living soul, fixing the limitation of all creatures, prescribing their destiny. But penitence, prayer, and charity can avert the evil decree!"

This is first sung by the cantor and his choir in a melancholy tune of his own composing, but the underlying theme of the melody is borrowed from the sweet and heartrending songs composed in the "Exile of Spain" in the reign of Isabella, when the Jews had to hide in caves and forests to serve their God without incurring the risk of the auto-da-fé. The songs speak of centuries of persecution, of streams of tears and blood.

Every married man wears today the long white gown called *kittel*, the praying shawl, the skullcap of white or black satin, and stands before his Judge in his stocking feet. The women in the galleries above are arrayed in their best dresses, wigs, kerchiefs, and bonnets, but few of them have their finery on. It is no time for exhibiting one's diamond earrings or gold watch and chain. There will be plenty of time for that, for following upon *Yom Kippur* is *Succoth*, the great merry Feast of Tabernacles.

THE IMMIGRANT, 11/21/'21

T W O L A R G E R O O M S at Ellis Island were improvised for purposes of worship on *Rosh Hashanah* and *Yom Kippur*, services being conducted there for Jewish immigrants. . . . After *Yom Kippur* services, previous to a dinner of soup, fish, lamb and *pflommen* ["prunes"] furnished by HIAS, large pitchers of hot tea and cake were served, so that the fast might be immediately broken. At dinner, paper plates were used instead of the usual china to give the immigrants the assurance that everything was strictly *kosher*.

The ends sanctify the means—a movie theater becomes a synagogue for high holiday services. Photograph by George Bain.

Before leaving the dining room, each person was given an apple and an orange, the fruit for the holidays being provided by the Council of Jewish Women.

Passover is one of the happiest of Jewish holidays, uniting observance with celebration. In his brief role as reporter for the Commercial Advertiser (before he became editor of the Forward), Abraham Cahan vividly described in an 1899 issue the days before Passover on the Lower East Side. The Tageblatt offers in 1906 a more intimate look at Passover.

COMMERCIAL ADVERTISER, 3/16/'99

THE GHETTO is in a flutter. This is *Erev Pesach* ("Eve of Passover"), the busiest season in the Jewish year. The great festival, which will begin on Saturday, March 25, is to last eight days. All cooking utensils must be changed; *matzo* (unleavened bread) must take the place of the ordinary loaves; the house and every member of the family must be adorned for the celebration of Israel's Independence Day.

Not a crumb of leavened bread is to be allowed in the house, and every vessel and every bit of food that comes in contact with them are *khometz* ("proscribed"). On the eve of the first day of Passover, therefore, the head of the family, armed with a ladle, a feather brush, and a candle, inspects every crack and cranny in the house for lurking bits of leaven.

119

Distributing Passover matzos to the poor, 1908. Photograph by George Bain.
LIBRARY OF CONGRESS, BAIN COLLECTION

"Blessed art Thou, Our Lord, King of the World, Who hast sanctified us with Thy commandments and commanded us to clear the leaven!" The old man utters the benediction with special solemnity. The housewife follows him with smiling eyes, which seem to say: "Search away, Jacob! It will be a cold day in Tanus [July] when you catch a crumb after I have scrubbed and cleaned the house."

TAGEBLATT, 4/3/'06

WHAT CAN COMPARE with the joy of the Jewish housewife when she sees the ferment rising out of the hole in the *med* barrel? She knows then that her *seder* table will be real *Yiddishlach*, and that the *arba kosos* will contain the nectar of the gods. Ah, the joy of *med* brewing, rivaled only by the delights of *eingemachts preglen*.

Did you ever help to brew *med*? I remember when I was a kid how jealously I prized that privilege.

We would be routed out of bed in time for an early breakfast. Clean, new wooden pails containing honey and bags of granulated sugar greeted our sleep-laden eyes. We would eat hastily and then roll up our sleeves and proceed to work. Water was poured into the honey, just enough to liquefy the sweet mass. Then a great stirring would ensue, until the honey was softened to the right degree of smoothness . . . a sheet of cheesecloth would be fastened over the top of a near wash boiler, which we held on to for dear life. Water, pails and pails of water, would then be strained through. Finally, the bags containing the hops would be put into the wash boiler. Soon, as the concoction began to boil, the air in the house would become heavy with the pungent but not unpleasant odor of the hops. Hour upon hour the boiling continued. Toward evening a solemn air of expectancy would overtake us: The *med* was about through boiling. First one would have a taste, and then another; we would smack our lips and pass judgment.

"It ought to boil a little longer," one would say.

"Ah, what do you know about making *med?*" would come the retort.

Finally the experts would compromise. . . . When the *med* was done brewing, the wash boiler was lifted off the stove and the sweet-bitter liquid, having cooled sufficiently, carefully ladled out and poured through a funnel into the *med* barrel, which meanwhile had been brought up from the cellar bin where it had been stored away since last *Pesach.*

In a day or two a little froth would appear around the bunghole of the *med* barrel. How complacently we would look about the house then. There was the *med* frothing and fermenting merrily; the bundles of *matzos* had the place of honor on the top of the bureau; the beets were souring, and all was ready for the gladsome *Pesach.* . . . Spring has many joys, but what joys of spring can compare with those that belong to the Jewish household.

Bar Mitzva *day at the Hebrew National* **Orphan Home.**
YIVO INSTITUTE FOR JEWISH RESEARCH

Ritual persisted—as the remains of faith? as a substitute for faith? as the yearning for faith among people who did not otherwise know how to achieve it? We would not presume to say. Probably all these explanations are true, and more as well.

For the American Jewish writers who turned back to their childhood or were stirred in adulthood by experiences recalling the past, ritual became a way of structuring their fictions. Charles Angoff, a life-long chronicler of immigrant life, recalls his Bar Mitzva *in conditions of immigrant poverty.*

CHARLES ANGOFF

I WAS *BAR MITZVA* ON THURSDAY. My father woke me up at 6:30 in the morning and took me to *shul*. There were about thirty people at the service. I was called to the Torah for the first time—and that was *Bar Mitzva*. Some of the other congregants came over to me and wished me *mazel tov*. My father bashfully put his arm around me and also congratulated me. Then he and I walked a bit and he went off to work. I turned toward home feeling terribly lonely. I had become a full, mature Jew—and most of Boston was asleep, and didn't care. The few people who passed me on the street didn't care either. When I reached our house, as soon as I put my hand on the doorknob my mother opened the door and threw her arms around me and kissed me and hugged me and kissed me again. Her arm around me, she took me to the kitchen, and there on the table was the *Shabbes* tablecloth. To my mother it was *yom tov*. She had the usual *boolkes* on a platter, but there was also a platter of the kind of cinnamon cakes I liked, and a smaller platter of ginger jam, another favorite of mine. Also a cup of cocoa. "Eat, Shayel, eat," said my mother. I suggested she have some cocoa too. "No, I'm not hungry." I ate. I was conscious that she was looking at me with great appreciation of what had happened to me. Her oldest son was now a full man in Israel. I was embarrassed, but I was also delighted. I finished my cocoa, and mother said, "Have another cup." The last time she had suggested I have another cup of cocoa was when I was convalescing from a cold that had almost turned into pneumonia. I had another cup. When I was finished with my special breakfast, mother said, "Father had to go to work. He had to. You understand."

"Sure," I said.

"But we'll have a small reception on Saturday night, after *mincha*. We've invited the relatives and some friends. So we'll have a little reception."

"Oh," I said, too moved to say anything else.

She got up, came to me, patted my head and then kissed me slowly. "Maybe you're a little sleepy, Shayel. Maybe you want to sleep a little more. I'll wake you up in time for your school."

"Yes, I think I'll have a little more sleep," I said.

I didn't want any more sleep. I lay down on the bed. I was profoundly happy. Everything was good. Everything was very good.

5

WOMEN

Mothers and Daughters

Can one say anything about the situation of women in the immigrant Jewish world that will not be open to misinterpretation, or to that more subtle kind of misunderstanding that consists in seeing the past through the lenses of the present? Jewish mothers, especially, have been subjected to dripping sentimentalism and to vindictive caricature, both of them screens blocking the truth. So, in this part of the book, we have been especially concerned to present direct testimony—much of it from Jewish immigrant daughters. At the very start of this section you'll hear the voices of two such immigrant daughters: first, Rose Pastor Stokes, once a famous firebrand socialist and feminist, writing in an unpublished memoir about her mother and herself; and Rose Cohen, a less famous but equally sensitive daughter, about the way her mother gradually emerged from Old World habits. As for the mothers, they themselves wrote very rarely: they were more concerned with living. What can be said about them was said by those who were close to them, their sons and daughters especially.

Any consideration of this topic has to begin with the family: the closeness of mothers and daughters, the clashes so frequently induced by American circumstances, between mothers living by traditional values of self-sacrifice and stoicism and daughters vibrating to the idea of new kinds of personal fulfillment and assertion. The situation has its pain, shared by those of both generations, and that is why here, even more than in other sections, one wants to hear the voices of survivors themselves, nuanced, troubled, loving.

ROSE PASTOR STOKES

WE SIT ABOUT THE TABLE—four little children and I. Through the hall door comes my mother. She washes at a basin in the far corner of the room and, weary, draws a chair to the meal. Her eyelids are very red. She sits silent. . . . We eat. She is tired—too tired to talk. Only the children chatter. . . . After the long day in the stogie factory, and after supper and the chores for mother, there was my book—*Lamb's Tales*. Before the kitchen stove, when the house was asleep, I'd throw off my shoes, thaw out the icy tissues that bit all day long in my consciousness, and lose myself. I read and reread the tales with never-flagging interest. . . . On our day off much "company" came to our tenement rooms. They stayed late in the evenings, and talked of many things. My mother was the life of these gatherings. She argued, opposed, attacked, defended. When the company wearied of talking, someone would start singing—usually my mother. Her voice was clear and sweet, and every word of her song was heard. Her singing was so heartsome that soon all would be joining in, while she would serve tea in tall glasses.

Selling eggs on Hester Street, 1897. Photograph by Alice Austen.
STATEN ISLAND HISTORICAL SOCIETY

ROSE COHEN

MOTHER HAD BEEN HERE only a short time when I noticed that she looked older and more old-fashioned than father. I noticed that it was so with most of our women, especially those that wore wigs or kerchiefs on their heads. So I thought that if I could persuade her to leave off her kerchief she would look younger and more up-to-date. But remembering my own first shock, I decided to go slowly and be careful not to hurt her feelings. So, one day, when I happened to be at home and the children were playing in the yard, and we two were alone in the house, I asked her playfully to take off her kerchief and let me do her hair, just to see how it would look. She consented reluctantly. She had never before in her married life had her hair uncovered before anyone. I took off her kerchief and began to fuss with her hair. It was dark and not abundant but it was soft and had a pretty wave in it. When I parted it in front and gathered it up in a small knot in the middle of the back of her head, leaving it soft over the temples, I was surprised how different she looked. I had never before known what a fine broad forehead my mother had, nor how soft were her blue-gray eyes, set rather deep and far apart. I handed her our little mirror from Cherry Street. She glanced at herself, admitted frankly that it looked well, and began hastily to put on her kerchief as if she feared being frivolous too long. I caught hold of her hands.

"Mama," I coaxed, "please don't put the kerchief on again—ever!"

At first she would not even listen to me. But I sat down in her lap and I began to coax and beg and reason. I drew from my year of experience and observation and pointed out that wives so often looked so much older because they were more old-fashioned, that the husbands were often ashamed to go out with them. I told her that it was so with Mrs. Felesberg and Mrs. Cohen. "And this nice woman upstairs," I said, "if she would only take off her wig and—"

Mother put her finger on my lips.

"But father trims his beard," I still argued. Her face looked sad. "Is that why," she said, "I too must sin?"

But I finally succeeded.

When father came home in the evening and caught sight of her while still at the door, he stopped and looked at her with astonishment. "What!" he cried, half earnestly, half jestingly. "Already you are becoming an American lady!" Mother looked abashed for a moment; in the next, to my surprise and delight, I heard her brazen it out in her quiet way.

"As you see," she said, "I am not staying far behind."

ELIZABETH STERN

IT WAS MY FIRST SCHOOL PARTY which made me realize how different was my mother from the mothers of all the girls who were now my friends. There was no mother . . . I had ever seen . . . who could approach my mother. I was very proud of the little curls blowing about her rosy cheeks, of her trim, plump little figure in its close-fitting waist and apron. On holy days she dressed in neat sateen, or even in cashmere.

All my standards fell before the vision of the strange mother I saw at the party given by my classmate. I could not believe that the woman who opened the door to my knock was my friend's mother. A woman in *white!* Why, mothers dressed in brown and black, I always knew. And this mother sang to us. She romped through the two-steps with us, and judged the forfeits. I had always thought mothers never "enjoyed," just worked. This strange mother opened a new window to me in the possibilities of women's lives. To my eyes my mother's life appeared all at once as something to be pitied—to be questioned.

As mother helped me off with my things when I came home she asked, as was customary between us, "Did you have a good time, childie?" While I described all that happened she smiled and nodded alternately. I could not have explained why I hesitated until the very end before I told her of my friend's mother. Somehow I was afraid that mother would be hurt at the picture of that white-gowned, laughing, young mother of my classmate, and something cut into my heart at the thought of hurting her. When finally I did describe her, and her dress, and her gay romping with all the young girls and boys, mother's eyes came to mine. I dropped my own until I had finished; I could not endure to see that strange look which for the first time in my life mother turned to me. Then mother said simply, "It is very late and you must go to bed, daughter."

Daughters and Fathers

By and large, immigrant parents expected their daughters to conform to traditional values. Marie Syrkin's father, pioneer Zionist Nachman Syrkin, was extraordinary in his willingness to provide Marie with the fruits of his own learning—though even he, a committed egalitarian, could go only so far.

MARIE SYRKIN

[MY FATHER'S] ZEAL for my intellectual progress was high but unsustained. I had been a precocious child and my father was not likely to be less enthusiastic about his daughter than about other matters which engaged his emotions. But I cannot say that his instruction was methodical. Periodically he would start a reading and study project. Three books were the *bêtes noires* of my early adolescence: the Bible in Hebrew; *Das Kapital* in German; and Spinoza's *Ethics* in Latin. Every once in a while, on a Saturday or Sunday when I was not in school and he was free, he would sit me down for an hour of learning; however, the interruptions were so many, the lapses between one lesson and the next so long, that I never seemed to get beyond the first chapter of these volumes. In addition, by the age of fifteen, I had developed a passion for the English romantic poets and my father was dismayed at my frivolity in preferring Shelley to Spinoza.

In other respects, too, he found the education of a young girl trying. He had fed me the complete idealistic pabulum of his generation: the freedom of women, the equality of the sexes, the absurdity of conventions, the innate goodness of man. To the pure all things are pure and the inner light is a maiden's best guide. Very fine, but by the time his daughter was fifteen he disclosed a troublesome inconsistency. A nice young man who invited me to a concert was informed that I might go provided a chaperon accompanied us to Carnegie Hall—to the discomfort of all three in the party. Another nice young man who wanted to call had to be informed by me that my father, forgetting about the equality of sexes, had decided that distinctions existed and that he considered me too young for callers; the young man could write letters. So all that spring, the young man dwelling in Brooklyn wrote me long, formal letters to the Bronx, chiefly about Henri Bergson. Since I knew nothing about Bergson, I delighted my father temporarily by my unexpected interest in the French philosopher. After a while, however, it dawned on him that my leading questions were designed to extract replies likely to impress my Brooklyn correspondent.

Yet after behaving briefly like a Victorian ogre he capitulated completely. Our debates on his bourgeois deviations from principle, plus counsel from Mrs. Katz, the unwilling chaperon who thought

he was too strict, plus pointed reminders of what Mr. Barrett did to
Elizabeth, proved too much. As usual, there were no half
measures. Since the Strunskys, friends of his, owned the Atlantic
Hotel in Belmar, New Jersey, he decided that the seashore would be
an appropriate place for me to get fresh air and improve my mind.
Besides, the Strunskys, knowing his circumstances, were generous
enough to give him reduced rates. My independent career, as well
as my troubles with my father, had begun.

GOLDA MEIR

. . . THERE WERE CLASHES between my parents and
me. When I finished elementary school, I wanted to go to high
school. Almost from the first day I registered in primary school I
made up my mind to be a teacher. In those years there was a law in
the state of Wisconsin that a married woman could not be a teacher.
Mother was terribly worried: If I became a teacher, that meant I
would not get married. When I graduated from elementary school,
mother decided that I should not go to high school, because if I did,
there was a real danger that I might succeed in becoming a teacher
and a spinster.

Father agreed that there was no future in my becoming a teacher;
anyway, he supported mother. Then we had a really big quarrel. . . . Father was deeply hurt not only because of his love for me,
but because of my behavior: How could a girl act this way?

129

ROSE COHEN

FATHER DID NOT TAKE KINDLY to my reading.
How could he! He saw that I took less and less interest in the home,
that I was more dreamy and kept more to myself. Evidently reading
and running about and listening to "speeches," as he called it, was
not doing me any good. But what father feared most was that now I
was mingling so much with Gentiles, and reading Gentile books, I
would wander away from the Jewish faith. This fear caused great
trouble and misunderstanding between us. Of that period this is the
first outbreak I recall.

One day my brother . . . on looking through my library book,
found the word Christ. At once he took the book to father and
pointed out the offending word. Father became terribly angry. . . .
He caught up the book and flung it out of the window. When I
looked out and saw the covers torn off and the pages lying scattered
in the yard I . . . wept aloud that I had a right to know, to learn, to
understand . . . that I was horribly ignorant; that I had been put
into the world but had been denied a chance to learn. Father and
mother stood staring at me. "Wild talk," they said. . . . I myself
. . . could not have told when those thoughts first began, whom I
was blaming, who was to blame!

After this there were long periods when father and I did not talk to
each other.

ANZIA YEZIERSKA

"THEY HAVE THEIR OWN HUSBANDS to look
after. You're my only unmarried daughter. *Your first duty to God is
to serve your father.* But what's an old father to an *Amerikanerin,* a
daughter of Babylon?"

"Your daughter of Babylon brought you a hundred dollars."

"Can your money make up for your duty as a daughter? In
America, money takes the place of God."

"But I earned that money with my writing." For all his scorn of
godlessness, I thought he would take a father's pride in success.
"Ten thousand they paid me . . ."

He wouldn't let me finish. He shook a warning finger in my face.
"Can you touch pitch without being defiled? Neither can you hold
on to all that money without losing your soul."

How did it feel to be a young woman in the immigrant Jewish world—to be tied to one's family yet eager to break into the outer, beckoning world; to feel respectful toward all the old ways yet drawn irresistibly to things modern and untested? Rose Schneiderman, a pioneer union organizer, remembers her adolescence with accuracy and strong feeling.

ROSE SCHNEIDERMAN

MY ADOLESCENCE WAS A far from happy one. All the romantic novels I consumed made me a most romantic young woman, and when I looked at myself in a full-length mirror I was very unhappy. Then I would despair. I wanted to be tall, and I thought I had several other counts against me. First of all, I was a redhead with curly hair, and neither the color nor the texture was stylish at that time. Then, you were supposed to have a bosom, the larger the better, and good-sized hips. I possessed neither of these, but the hips I could do something about. I discovered that if you wore a short corset and laced it tight, your hips stuck out. The bosom was more difficult, even though I wore corset covers. I weighed only a little over ninety pounds but I was small boned and not skinny, and with my eighteen-inch waistline I would be right in style today.

From the books I read I had also developed a special taste in men. Among other traits, I wanted them well-read and cultured. I never dreamed of marrying a rich man. That was entirely out of my ken. My idea of what a man should be didn't quite match up with the boys Ann Cypress and I were meeting at the Saturday-night dances in the neighborhood. Most of them were loud and dull and suffered when compared with the heroes in my books. I didn't enjoy their company, but I did love to dance and was pretty good at it, so I put up with them.

Abraham Reisen was a Yiddish writer, living first in Russia and then in New York, who wrote delicate, endlessly compassionate sketches and poems about the experiences and feelings of his fellow Jews. Here is one of his pieces about Lena, a shopgirl who fantasizes and suffers.

ABRAHAM REISEN

AFTER THE "SEASON," Lena is left with a few ten-dollar bills to carry her through several months of "slack" time. She is careful with her savings. She budgets her expenses so she will not have to suffer, and for that reason she is able to leave a dollar in her postal savings account until the coming of the next season. Lena does not wait for the last minute, but as soon as she has reached her last ten dollars she begins to look for work. Every Sunday morning she buys a *World* for five cents.

She does not turn to the want ads immediately. First she inspects all the pictures in the magazine section before browsing through the feature stories about actresses and singers and dancers. One actress, she learns, earns two hundred thousand dollars a year just for her beautiful black eyes. Lena goes to the mirror and looks at her eyes. She is sure that they are just as nice. So why has she been overlooked for the job, especially since the other one can't even act. Lena feels insulted and hurt. Now she reads about a girl with a three million dollar inheritance who has just married a poor student. Lena figures out that for three million dollars all the girls she knows could be married. But if she had the three million she wouldn't marry, because it is simply impossible to find love with so much money.

Finally, Lena reminds herself that what she wants from the *World* is not romance but the right want ad. Tomorrow she must rise early, hurry to the waiting lines and bide her time patiently until some total stranger gives her a job. Lena looks at her eyes again. She realizes that no one will give a cent for them. All they need is her hands.

Early the next morning Lena is already at work at a small table. Next to her is a new acquaintance. She looks at the eyes of her new friend, and it seems to her that they too are just as beautiful as the eyes of that actress.

When they go out for lunch to a nearby restaurant Lena cannot contain herself: "Do you read the *World*?" she asks.

"From time to time," the other answers. "Why?"

"I read in yesterday's *World* that there's an actress who gets two hundred thousand dollars a year just for her beautiful eyes."

"I see her in the movies," her friend answers with pleasure. "I see her all the time. Her eyes are beautiful, very beautiful."

Lena looks at her friend. What a fool, she says to herself. She does not understand that *her* eyes are just as beautiful and that it is only an accident that she is working in a shop for practically nothing while the actress is making movies for two hundred thousand dollars a year. But Lena must keep her thoughts to herself. Her friend will never understand.

Glitter and finery on Division Street.

134 *Who hasn't heard about "Di Grine Kuzine" ("The Greenhorn Cousin")? She first came into existence as a song in a Yiddish theatrical production, but then quickly became a living presence, a folk legend. Here she is in Yiddish and English.*

DI GRINE KUZINE

Es iz tsu mir gekumen a kuzine
Sheyn vi gold iz zi geven, di grine
Di bekelekh vi royte pomerantsn
Fiselekh vos betn zikh tsum tantsn.

Once a cousin came to me
Pretty as gold was she, the greenhorn,
Her cheeks like red oranges,
Her tiny feet begging to dance.

Nit gegangen iz zi—nor geshprungen
Nit geredt, nor gezungen
Freylekh, lustik iz geven ir mine
Ot azay geven iz mayn kuzine.

She didn't walk, she skipped along,
She didn't talk, she sang,
Her manner was gay and cheerful,
That's how my cousin used to be.

Ikh bin arayn tsu mayn nekst-dorke
Vos zi hot a milineri-storke

A dzhab gekrogn hob ikh far mayn kuzine
Az lebn zol di goldeneh medina.

I found a place with my neighbor,
The one who has a millinery store,
I got a job for my cousin,
Blessed be the golden land.

Avek zaynen fun demolt on shoyn yorn
Fun mayn kuzine iz a tel gevorn
Peydes yorn lang hot zi geklibn

Biz fun ir aleyn iz nisht geblibn.

Since then many years have passed.
My cousin became a wreck
From many years of collecting wages
Till nothing was left of her.

Unter ire bloye sheyne oygn

Shvartse pasn hobn zikh fartsoygn
Di bekelekh, di royte pomerantsn
Hobn zikh shoyn oysgegrint in gantsn.

Underneath her pretty blue eyes
Black lines now are drawn,
Her cheeks, once like red oranges,
Have now turned entirely green.

Shopworker making artificial flowers. Photograph by Lewis Hine.
NEW YORK PUBLIC LIBRARY, LOCAL HISTORY AND
GENEALOGY DIVISION

Haynt, az ikh bagegn mayn kuzine	Today, when I meet my cousin
Un ikh freg zi: "Vos zhe makhstu, grine?"	And ask her: "How are you, greenhorn?"
Entfert zi mir mit a krumer mine	She answers with a grimace,
"Az brenen zol Kolumbuses medina!"	"To the devil with Columbus's land!"

Women at Work

For most Jewish girls there was one probable fate: to go to work in the sweatshops, huddled over sewing machines, hour after hour, to earn a few dollars that could be brought back home to help the family make ends meet. At the age when our children today are entering college or going off for trips to Europe, the daughters of the immigrants were consigned to the darkness of the shops. It was, for many of them, a trauma they would never forget. Rose Cohen, whose memoir follows, writes that "My hands trembled so that I could not hold the needle properly." For many, it was a lifelong sentence. Some resigned themselves; the more spirited among them rebelled, becoming pioneers of union organization.

Jewish girls born in America, even into immigrant families, could sometimes better their lot: They spoke without accents, they had a smattering of education, they could become librarians or office workers or teachers. But for those who came here at an early age, it was into the shops—unless and until they married.

ROSE COHEN

ABOUT THE SAME TIME that the bitter cold came father told me one night that he had found work for me in a shop where he knew the presser. I lay awake long that night. I was eager to begin life on my own responsibility but was also afraid. We rose earlier than usual that morning for father had to take me to the shop and not be over late for his own work. I wrapped my thimble and scissors, with a piece of bread for breakfast, in a bit of newspaper, carefully stuck two needles into the lapel of my coat and we started.

The shop was on Pelem Street. . . . I groped my way to the top of the stairs and, hearing a clattering noise of machines, I felt about, found a door, and pushed it open and went in. A tall beardless man stood folding coats at a table. I went over to him. "Yes," he said crossly. "What do you want?"

I said, "I am the new feller hand." He looked at me from head to foot. My face felt so burning hot that I could scarcely see.

"It is more likely," he said, "that you can pull bastings than fell sleeve lining." Then turning from me he shouted over the noise of the machine: "Presser, is this the girl?" The presser put down the iron and looked at me. "I suppose so," he said, "I only know the father."

The cross man looked at me again and said, "Let's see what you can do." He kicked a chair, from which the back had been broken off, to the finisher's table, threw a coat upon it and said, raising the corner of his mouth: "Make room for the new feller hand."

One girl tittered, two men glanced at me over their shoulders and pushed their chairs apart a little. By this time I scarcely knew what I was about. I laid my coat down somewhere and pushed my bread into the sleeve. Then I stumbled into the bit of space made for me at the table, drew in the chair and sat down. The men were so close to me at each side I felt the heat of their bodies and could not prevent myself from shrinking away. The men noticed and probably felt hurt. One made a joke, the other laughed and the girls bent their heads low over their work. All at once the thought came to me: "If I don't do this coat quickly and well he will send me away at once." I picked up the coat, threaded my needle, and began hastily, repeating the lesson father impressed upon me. "Be careful not to twist the sleeve lining, take small false stitches."

My hands trembled so that I could not hold the needle properly. It took me a long while to do the coat. But at last it was done. I took it over to the boss and stood at the table waiting while he was examining it. He took long, trying every stitch with his needle. Finally he put it down and without looking at me gave me two other coats. I felt very happy! When I sat down at the table I drew my knees close together and stitched as quickly as I could.

MARIE GANZ

WE SAT IN LONG ROWS, our bodies bent over the machines, the work we turned out fell into wooden bins attached to the part of the machine facing us. No one girl made an entire garment. As each girl completed her part the garment was passed on to the next girl by Levinson, who was always walking back and forth urging us on. Should a girl lag behind he would prod her, sometimes pulling on the garment to hurry it on to another worker.

"Hurry! Don't you see that the sleevemaker soon will have no work?" he would shout.

This sort of thing created a spirit of competition for self-preservation that ended only when the worker, too weak to compete longer with a stronger sister, broke down.

Before many days I discovered another phase of the speed-up system. At the end of each week the girl who had turned in the least work was dropped from the payroll. Knowledge of this fact had the effect of keeping the girls working like mad.

ANONYMOUS

I LIVED AT THIS TIME with a girl named Ella, who worked in the same factory and made five dollars a week. We had the room all to ourselves, paying a dollar and a half a week for it, and doing light housekeeping. It was in Allen Street, and the window looked out of the back, which was good, because there was an elevated railroad in front, and in summertime a great deal of dust and dirt came in at the front windows. We were on the fourth story and could see all that was going on in the back rooms of the houses behind us, and early in the morning the sun used to come in our window.

We did our cooking on an oil stove, and lived well, as this list of our expenses for one week will show:

Ella and Radie for Food (one week)	
Tea	$0.06
Cocoa	.10
Bread and rolls	.40
Canned vegetables	.20
Potatoes	.10
Milk	.21
Fruit	.20
Butter	.15
Meat	.60
Fish	.15
Laundry	.25
Total	$2.42
Add rent	1.50
Grand Total	$3.92

Of course, we could have lived cheaper, but we are both fond of good things and felt that we could afford them. Some people who buy at the last of the market, when the men with the carts want to go home, can get things very cheap, but they are likely to be stale, and we did not often do that. Things that kept well we did buy that way and got good bargains. Tomatoes, onions and cabbages we bought that way and did well, and we found a factory where we could buy the finest crackers for three cents a pound and another place where we got broken candy for ten cents a pound. . . . It cost me two dollars a week to live, and I had one dollar a week to spend on clothing and pleasure, and I saved the other dollar.

S.P. SCHOENFELD

MY CAPABLE FOURTEEN-YEAR-OLD SISTER had a diploma from an Odessa junior high school. I wanted her to continue her studies but my uncle was opposed. "In America," he said, "everyone has to work. Working is no shame; even a president's daughter works." He did not say whether he meant the president of a railroad or a poorhouse.

My sister went off to sew buttons in a tailor's shop for two dollars a week, but she couldn't adjust to the shop—she could not stand the vulgar comments made at her expense. Nor could she satisfy the owner: She'd not sit bent over enough while working. "Mademoiselle," he'd say sarcastically, "the way you sit you read a book, not sew buttons." At home we sympathized with her . . . and told her not to go back. She stayed home more than she went.

Always on the lookout for injustice to expose and causes to espouse, the Forward *wrote with a special keenness about the lives of the young women from the East Side—and equivalent neighborhoods throughout the country—who had to earn their own livings. It seemed made to order as a topic for socialist exhortation, but it also stirred the hearts of Yiddish writers and readers, for these were their own children.*

FORWARD, 12/24/'03

THE MORE GENTEEL the profession, the more intellect required, the less a girl gets paid. Take . . . a librarian. A girl gets three dollars a week to start, and, except in the rare circumstance of her becoming chief librarian, will go no further.

Even at prosaic store clerking, for the privilege of standing behind a counter, one girl works almost for nothing. A public school graduate can expect ten dollars a month. Meanwhile she's on her feet all day running about like crazy, from floor to floor, forbidden the use of the elevator.

Thus, as bad as shop or factory pay is, it's much better than where a girl uses her mind. The more genteel the occupation, the greater the exploitation.

FORWARD, 2/2/'06

SO MUCH IS SAID of factory servitude and the overall condition of the poor that we forget the suffering serving girls who work in comfortable homes.

If a servant girl pours out her heart to you, believe her. Likely as not, in our blessed New York, her mistress hits her. The same lady remembers how the fishmonger once smacked her across the face with a flounder. Recalling her early years, she wants to share them with her servant. God forbid the girl should appear in a nice dress or stylish brassiere, or in the company of a good-looking young man waiting for her in the kitchen. Such *chutzpa*—"a maid pretending she's somebody!"—can often cost a girl her job.

A hot bite in the cold.
NEW YORK PUBLIC LIBRARY,
LOCAL HISTORY AND
GENEALOGY DIVISION

FORWARD, 8/8/'05

M A N Y J E W I S H T Y P I S T S live in two distinct worlds. At work a girl's in a light, attractive office among well-dressed people. She shares important business secrets. She hears and speaks English only. Her betters treat her with respect and speak to her like a countess. She's called "Miss," and is asked how she feels and what she thinks. But at home, living in dirty rooms, she's plain "Beyle" or "Khontshe." Her parents speak crudely to her. They pounce upon her if she expresses an interest in a new hat. If she mentions a ball, they tell her to dance with the laundry.

Some typists face a different situation. They too live in different worlds but in a reverse fashion. A cultivated typist receives like-minded guests at home; whereas, at work the boss is a nouveau riche furrier who keeps a typist because he can barely spell. The girl begs him, "Please, Mr. Grossman, listen to me. Tell me what you want to say, and I'll word it myself."

"Hey! What do you know?" he answers. "I don't know how to prepare a business letter? If I could write, you'd all have to hide. What can I do? The thoughts are here"—he points to his head— "but I can't get them down; so, I have to depend on *nudniks* like you."

In the early struggles of Jewish unionism, women played a
remarkable role. Garment workers had been trying to form stable
unions since the 1880s, but despite repeated heroic, self-sacrificing
strikes followed by momentary victories, they had never been able
to establish stable organizations. With the famous shirtwaist makers
strike of 1909, in which thousands of young women, mostly
Jewish, won a major victory, the garment unions in America began
to dig in as solid institutions.

Often the women were the most fiery and self-sacrificing
workers, the most ready to struggle and strike. Sometimes they were
known in the Jewish quarter as the farbrente, the fiery, or fervent,
ones. Perhaps they felt freer than the men to take chances because
usually they didn't have children to feed. Perhaps they were shaken
by early visions of independence bringing together socialist and
feminist ideas. Whatever the reason, they won the admiration of
the entire Jewish quarter—and of many outside it as well.

ROSE SCHNEIDERMAN

WE HAD HAD NO IDEA that there was a union in our
industry and that women could join it. Nor did we have a full
realization of the hardships we were needlessly undergoing. There

Union leader Rose
Schneiderman (1882–1972)
at her sewing machine.
TAMIMENT COLLECTION,
NEW YORK UNIVERSITY

140

Shop organizers.

was the necessity of owning a sewing machine before you could
work. Then you had to buy your own thread. But the worst of it was
the incredibly inefficient way in which work was distributed.
Because we were all pieceworkers, any time lost during the season
was a real hardship. But because of poor management there never
seemed to be any synchronizing between our available time and the
supplying of materials we needed. . . .

Bessie Braut pointed out all these things and more, insisting that
it was possible for us to have these hardships corrected if we
complained as a group. An employer would think twice before
telling a group what he would not hesitate to tell an individual
employee: that if she didn't like it, she was welcome to take herself
and her machine and go somewhere else where things would most
likely be just as bad or perhaps worse.

. . . As her words began to sink in, we formed a committee
composed of my friend Bessie Mannis, who worked with me,
myself, and a third girl. Bravely we ventured into the office of the
United Cloth Hat and Cap Makers Union and told the man in
charge that we would like to be organized. . . .

We were told that we would have to have at least twenty-five
women from a number of factories before we could acquire a
charter. Novices that we were, we used the simplest methods. We
waited at the doors of factories and, as the girls were leaving for the
day, we would approach them and speak our piece. We had blank
pledges of membership ready in case some could be persuaded to
join us. Within days we had the necessary number, and in January
1903 we were chartered as Local 23, and I was elected secretary.

141

It was such an exciting time. A new life opened up for me. All of a sudden I was not lonely anymore. I had shop and executive board meetings to attend as well as the meetings of our unit. I was also a delegate to the Central Labor Union of New York, which was a remarkable experience for me. The central body was in many ways an educational organization. It met every Sunday afternoon, and at each meeting there was a speaker who would discuss some question of current interest. I always listened eagerly and continued to do so years later when I returned as the delegate of the New York Women's Trade Union League.

The only cloud in the picture was mother's attitude toward my becoming a trade unionist. She kept saying I'd never get married because I was so busy—a prophecy which came true. Of course, what she resented most of all was my being out of the house almost every evening. But for me it was the beginning of a period that molded all my subsequent life and opened wide many doors that might have remained closed to me. . . .

That June we decided to put our strength to the test. In the summer the men usually worked only half-day on Saturdays, which was pay day. But even when there was no work we women had to hang around until three or four o'clock before getting our pay. I headed a committee which informed Mr. Fox that we wanted to be paid at the same time as the men. Mr. Fox was a portly gentleman of German extraction, a rather handsome man with luminous brown eyes and a piercing look. After I presented our case he studied me with a grin and then said, "You want your pay, do you? Well, I'll see about it." He didn't say outright that he agreed; he wouldn't give us that much satisfaction. But on the first Saturday in July, when we went for our pay at twelve noon, there it was ready for us. . . .

Our convention that year, 1903, opened as usual on the first of May, always regarded as a kind of international workers' holiday. We took the day off on our own, receiving no pay. I was elected delegate from my union. We women rode in the parade in a wagon, for it was not considered ladylike to participate on foot. It was an exciting and heartwarming day and I enjoyed it tremendously.

After the next convention I participated in my first strike. To bypass the union, one of the employers had moved to New Jersey, so the officers of the union called a strike against the runaway employer in Bayonne. We gave all of our strength to the battle even though the number of workers involved was not large. We felt that if one employer was allowed to operate a nonunion shop, he could easily undersell union firms and they might be tempted to follow his example. . . .

A mass meeting of the strikers was scheduled. . . . On the way over to the meeting, Mikol asked me whether I would speak at it. I was scared stiff. What was I to say? It was a big hall and the meeting was well attended. But it was a cold night and there was absolutely no heat in the place. Everyone was chilled to the bone, including me. When I was called on to speak, my knees turned to putty. I doubt whether I lasted more than five minutes and I don't believe I deserved the enthusiastic applause they gave me. But even if it was undeserved, it felt good. The next day I came down with the grippe and had to stay in bed the rest of the week.

"Women on Strike" is the subject of the following excerpt from Louis Levine's pioneering work, The Women's Garment Workers.

LOUIS LEVINE

NUMEROUS STORIES were current at the time illustrating the pertinacity, the courage, and the self-sacrifice of the young women strikers. There was the story of Miss Reisen, who undertook to hold the hall of the Italian strikers. The Italian women joined the strike slowly and in small numbers. It was hard to approach them because they would come to and return from their shops escorted by their fathers and mothers or other members of their families. Those who did strike met in a hall on East Fourth Street. Almost daily someone among them would jump up and propose to return to work. Miss Reisen, who did not know the Italian language, would guess what was proposed, jump to the platform and plead vociferously until she would get the Italian women to remain with her in the hall. She had to put up at first with a lot of abuse, but gradually she won the hearts of the Italian strikers. And toward the end of the strike she could report to the strike committee that she "could almost understand what the Italians were talking about."

There was Esther Lobetkin, a recent arrival from Russia. She was in charge of one of the shops. Food or sleep did not seem to be part

Wrapper and kimono workers striking for a minimum wage of $10 a week, fifty hours of work and the abolishment of child labor, 1913.
JEWISH DAILY FORWARD

of her daily needs. All day long she kept strict watch of "her" strikers and then she would appear at headquarters to report and to attend the meetings till the wee hours of the morning. A sandwich at midnight and a casual hour of rest kept her on her feet. She was arrested time and again, and every time she would shout from the patrol wagon: "Do not lose courage. We'll win yet." And there were Bessie Switski, a member of the executive committee of Local 25, and her sister. Theirs was one of the hardest picketing jobs in front of a shop which was the storm center of the strike. According to eyewitnesses, the private detecives and guards placed in front of that shop were exceptionally notorious. They were called the "gorillas" and their faces were "terrifying." The young women of the shop were afraid to come near the place. But Bessie and her sister fought the "gorillas" day after day, until the employer tired of it and came to terms with the union. . . .

. . . One of the social workers described the "spirit of the strikers" as follows. "Into the foreground of this great moving picture comes the figure of one girl after another as her services are needed. With extraordinary simplicity and eloquence she will tell before any kind of audience, without any false shame and without self-glorification, the conditions of her work, her wages, and the pinching poverty of her home and the homes of her comrades. Then she withdraws into the background to undertake quietly the danger and humiliation of picket duty or to become a nameless sandwich girl selling papers on the street, no longer the center of interested attention but the butt of the most unspeakable abuse."

"We are collecting provisions for the striking tailors."
JUSTICE/ILGWU

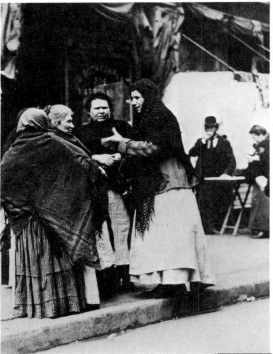

East Side women protesting meat prices.
Photograph by George Bain.
LIBRARY OF CONGRESS, BAIN COLLECTION

Members of a Brownsville Consumers
League, circa 1930.   JEWISH DAILY FORWARD

*The deeply ingrained conservatism of Jewish life with regard to
sexual mores, the place of women, and the relations between the
sexes had to break down in the American setting. There were the
temptations of school and college, which put a cluster of new
thoughts into the minds of young women. There were the styles of
the fashionable world, which they could follow in the English-
language papers. There were the values of modern intellectuality,
which an articulate minority took over with great seriousness.
There were the lures of romanticism and sexuality, no longer
repressed through traditional rituals and denials but now brought
into the open and stimulated by every aspect of popular culture.
Not many immigrant girls, or daughters of immigrants, could resist
all of these—why should they have? They too wanted a chance to
express themselves, to develop their personalities, to learn
something about the wide world, to find a place beyond kitchen
and bedroom.*

*As a result, there began to appear in the immigrant milieu a
generation of extraordinary women: torn, of course, between their
emotional attachment to parents and their hungers for new
experience, but determined somehow to make their own way. They
were brave, troubled, and heavily burdened. Some of them appear
in this section. Marie Ganz, who tells the seriocomic story of how
she almost assassinated a Rockefeller, was for a time a flaming
anarchist. Marie Syrkin, daughter of the theoretical founder of
Labor Zionism, would herself become a major figure in the
American Zionist milieu. Anzia Yezierska, born into a rigidly
Orthodox home, would write novels and stories about people like
herself, full of nervous discomforts and yearnings. Strong as they
were, these women formed part of a transitional generation,
necessarily ambivalent and sometimes confused in its values.
Perhaps that is what makes them so interesting to us.*

HUTCHINS HAPGOOD

THE . . . EDUCATED CLASS of ghetto women is, of
course, in a great minority; and this division includes the women
even the most slightly affected by modern ideas. Among the least
educated are a large number of women who would be entirely
ignorant were it not for the ideas which they have received through
the socialistic propaganda of the quarter. Like the men, who are
otherwise ignorant, they are trained to a certain familiarity with
economic ideas, read and think a good deal about labor and capital.
Many of these women, so long as they are unmarried, lead lives
thoroughly devoted to "the cause," and afterward become good
wives and fruitful mothers, and urge on their husbands and sons to
active work in the "movement." . . .

As we ascend in the scale of education in the ghetto we find women who derive their culture and ideas from a double source—from socialism and from advanced Russian ideals of literature and life. They have lost faith completely in the Orthodox religion, have substituted no other, know Russian better than Yiddish, read Tolstoy, Turgenev, and Chekhov, and often put into practice the most radical theories of the "new woman," particularly those which say that woman should be economically independent of man. There are successful female dentists, physicians, and even lawyers by the score in East Broadway who have attained financial independence through industry and intelligence. . . . Emotionally strong and attached by Russian tradition to a rebellious doctrine, they are deeply unconventional in theory and sometimes in practice; although the national morality of the Jewish race very definitely limits the extent to which they realize some of their ideas. The passionate feeling at the bottom of most of their "tendency" beliefs is that woman should stand on the same social basis as man, and should be weighed in the same scales. This ruling creed is held by all classes of the educated women of the ghetto, from the poor sweatshop worker, who has recently felt the influence of socialism, to the thoroughly trained "new woman" with her developed literary taste; and all its variations find expression in the literature of the quarter.

FORWARD, 1/7/'07

S H E W A S A M A I D and her husband was a rag peddler. Now she is rich and can keep up with the latest styles. Someone tells her that the women of the "400" smoke, so she starts to smoke as well. To be sure that she is doing it with proper style, she smokes in front of a mirror.

Everything is all right except for one thing—smoking makes her so dizzy that she is always about to faint. But she accepts this, the same way she accepts wearing a tight corset and high heels which ruin the feet: "If God is so good and allows one to be an *alrightnikeh*, one has to conduct oneself accordingly."

FORWARD, 7/25/'15

4 RULES FOR WOMEN

1. Don't say "I have nothing to worry about" just because you've already got a husband.

2. If your husband likes gefilte fish, don't shove fried fish down his throat and say: "You dope; you don't know what good is."

3. Don't neglect the cleanliness of your house and clothes just because your *nexdooreker* does it.

4. If you've been cursed with growths of hair on your throat, cheeks or upper lip . . . don't forget that makes a bad impression. Go immediately to your druggist and for one dollar buy Wonderstone.

For Marie Ganz there were no rules—only the rulers of an intolerably brutal and corrupt system.

MARIE GANZ

I M A D E M Y W A Y through the streets as if I were in a dream. I saw nothing, I heard nothing. . . .

In my hand was a crumpled newspaper. My eyes fell on the headlines over the latest report of killings in the mines, and I began to read it aloud to the crowd. It was easy to see that they were interested, and, encouraged by their close attention, I began a speech. I said a good deal more than I had intended to. At last I shouted out:

"One man in this city is guiltier than all others for what has been done out there in the West, and he must no longer live."

The crowd broke into cheers, and swept toward me in wild excitement. So close did they press that I was almost swept from the ledge. At that moment a hand reached out to me. It held a pistol. Not a word was spoken, and who it was that offered it, whether man or woman, I could not know, for the crowd surged round me, and the hand disappeared as quickly as it had come, leaving the weapon in my grasp. At last the hour had come. And I was ready for it.

"I am going down to Twenty-six Broadway to kill the guilty man," I shouted, "and his name is John D. Rockefeller, Jr."

Jumping down from the ledge, I ran down Park Row, and the crowd came roaring after me. The pistol was hidden under my dress, but even with that precaution I have never been able to understand why the police did not stop me at once, though I gave them not a thought at the time. . . .

As I ran into the corridor of the building the special policemen stationed outside brought to a halt those that had been following me, and I found myself almost alone. A waiting elevator stood near, and I stepped in and called out "Fourteenth floor." The Negro elevator man refused to start the car, and I jumped for the control lever, threatening to tear it from his grasp.

"You start this car, or I'll know the reason why," I shouted at him, and perhaps he saw the pistol peeping from my dress, for he slammed the door and we shot upward.

I walked very coolly to a door on which I saw the words Standard Oil Company, and opened it. A man stepped toward me, and I asked for Mr. Rockefeller. A card was handed to me, and I wrote my name on it, but as the man walked into the inner office with it I followed him. I entered the inner room just in time to see a man who looked very much like the pictures I have seen of the younger Mr. Rockefeller dive through a door in the rear and hastily slam it behind him. At the same moment my guide turned upon me.

"Mr. Rockefeller isn't in town," he said. "Can his secretary do anything for you?"

"I'll see the secretary," I answered.

A tall slender young man came out to me.

"What can I do for you?" he asked.

"If you're Mr. Rockefeller's secretary," I replied, "I want you to tell him that if he doesn't stop the killing of the workers in Colorado I'll shoot him down like a dog."

"I will deliver your message," returned the young man suavely, and bowed me out. . . .

Now that the excitement had passed away and I had only failure to show for all my furious enterprise, all my strength left me. . . . Already the newsboys were yelling extras that Marie Ganz had tried to shoot Rockefeller. Had tried! Bah! So this was the result of my dream of striking a blow for the cause that would startle the world!

ANZIA YEZIERSKA

. . . ALL THE YOUNG PEOPLE I had ever seen were shut up in factories. But here were young girls and young men enjoying life, free from the worry for a living. College to them was being out for a good time, like to us in the shop a Sunday picnic. But in our gayest Sunday picnics there was always the underfeeling that Monday meant back to the shop again. To these born-lucky ones joy seemed to stretch out forever.

What a sight I was in my gray pushcart clothes against the beautiful gay colors and the fine things those young girls wore. I had seen cheap, fancy style, five- and ten-cent-store finery. But never had I seen such plain beautifulness. The simple skirts and sweaters, the stockings and shoes to match. The neat finished quietness of their tailored suits. There was no show-off in their clothes, and yet how much more pulling to the eyes and all the senses than the Grand Street richness I knew.

And the spick-and-span cleanliness of these people! It smelled from them, the soap and the bathing. Their fingernails so white and pink. Their hands and necks white like milk. I wondered how did those girls get their hair so soft, so shiny, and so smooth about their heads. Even their black shoes had a clean look.

Never had I seen men so all shaved up with pink, clean skins. The richest storekeepers in Grand Street shined themselves up with diamonds like walking jewelry stores, but they weren't so hollering clean as these men. And they all had their hair clipped so short; they all had a shape to their heads. So ironed-out smooth and even they looked in their spotless, creaseless clothes, as if the dirty battle of life had never yet been on them.

I looked at these children of joy with a million eyes. I looked at them with my hands, my feet, with the thinnest nerves of my hair. By all their differences from me, their youth, their shiny freshness, their carefreeness, they pulled me out of my senses to them. And they didn't even know I was there.

As I entered the classroom, I saw young men and girls laughing and talking to one another without introductions. I looked for my seat. . . .

I turned to the girl on my other side. What a creature of sunshine.

"Is this the freshman class in geometry?" I asked her.

She nodded politely and smiled. But how quickly her eyes sized me up! It was not an unkind glance. And yet, it said more plainly than words, "From where do you come? How did you get in here?"

Sitting side by side with them through the whole hour, I felt stranger to them than if I had passed them in Hester Street. Wasn't there some secret something that would open us toward one another?

In one class after another, I kept asking myself, "What's the matter with me? Why do they look at me so when I talk to them?"

Maybe I'd have to change myself inside and out to be one of them. But how?

"'Mom, what does she know? She's old-fashioned!' But I'll tell you a big secret: My whole life I wanted to go away too, but with children a woman stays home. A fire burned in my heart too, but now it's too late. I'm no spring chicken. The clock goes and Bessie goes. Only my machinery can't be fixed."— Stella Adler portraying an American Jewish mother in Clifford Odets's Awake and Sing.

6

LABOR AND
SOCIALISM

Sweatshop

Those of us who come from immigrant Jewish families—which means mostly working-class families—may believe that we know how dreadful were the conditions in the sweatshops where our parents and grandparents had to work. We remember the stories we were told about these things during our childhood. But the truth, for once, is even more stark than the myth. When the editors of this book were working together preparing the material for World of Our Fathers, *we were repeatedly struck by the terribleness, the extreme suffering of the lives of the early Jewish immigrants. Wretched physical conditions, extreme exploitation, shamefully low wages, frequent humiliations, desperate strikes—all these were the lot of the early immigrants, men and women who deserve to be called pioneers just as much as those who settled the western states. The older American pioneers lived in log cabins, while the immigrant Jews piled into tenements; but such differences barely matter when one considers that both were establishing new ways of life, bringing with them cherished portions of a received culture while also opening themselves up to unknown possibilities. Of course, it may seem more romantic to celebrate hardy settlers and farmers than undernourished garment workers; but historical justice demands some righting of accounts.*

The testimony is overwhelming, and for each item telling of hardship and deprivation we could print another dozen. Among those who responded most sympathetically to the plight of the immigrants was a generation of young writers retaining something of the great tradition of nineteenth-century American idealism. One of these was Jacob Riis, whose book How the Other Half Lives *(1890), remains a valuable historical record; another was the journalist Ray Stannard Baker, a selection from whose work opens this section.*

RAY STANNARD BAKER

IT WAS NO UNCOMMON THING in these sweat-shops for men to sit bent over a sewing machine continuously from eleven to fifteen hours a day in July weather, operating a sewing machine by foot power, and often so driven that they could not stop for lunch. The seasonal character of the work meant demoralizing toil for a few months in the year and a not less demoralizing idleness for the remainder of the time. Consumption, the plague of the tenements and the especial plague of the garment industry, carried off many of these workers, poor nutrition and exhaustion many more.

They dared not stop working, knowing that there were plenty of other men ready instantly to take their places; and the contractor, himself the victim of frightful competition and the tool of the manufacturer, always playing upon their ready fears, always demanding a swifter pace, forced the price constantly downward. If, by chance, a man appeared who was so highly expert or so unusually robust that he could do a few more pieces in a day, the price went down, and the weaker ones were remorselessly spurred forward to keep pace with him, until they dropped out from exhaustion.

Nowhere was there, apparently, any relief for this ferocious waste of human life. These people were cast into the turmoil of the let-alone civilization of America; no one paid any attention to them, or cared what happened to them—with the result that many of them were literally worked to death.

JACOB A. RIIS

. . . F I V E   M E N   A N D   A   W O M A N, two young girls, not fifteen, and a boy who says unasked that he is fifteen, and lies in saying it, are at the machines sewing knee pants. . . . The floor is littered ankle-deep with half-sewn garments. . . . The faces, hands, and arms to the elbows of everyone in the room are black with the color of the cloth on which they are working. The boy and the woman alone look up at our entrance. The girls shoot sidelong glances, but at a warning look from the man with the bundle [the contractor] they tread their machines more energetically than ever. . . . They are "learners," all of them, says the woman, who proves to be the wife of the boss, and have "come over" only a few weeks ago. They turn out 120 dozen knee pants a week. They work no longer than to nine o'clock at night, from daybreak.

FOLKSTSEITUNG, 6/25/'86

C O M E   W I T H   M E to Hester Street, Number —. There lies an infant, three quarters of a year old, ailing, in a cradle. The cradle isn't so clean as the one in your home; it is surrounded by three sewing machines. The room is cold, dusty, and fumy. On a wooden chair next to the cradle sits a thirty-five-year-old woman whose face bespeaks onetime beauty and grace; it is now covered by pale death. With two dried-out hands she draws a shawl around her shoulders, blows on her hands to warm them, rocks the child and gazes at its face.

The infant is quiet but continually gasps, grimaces, and chokes. Nearby there's a long table; a tall thin man stands before it. His eyes, drawn deep into his forehead, show lack of sleep. His features are dark and worn. He's a Jew, one of our brothers. He looks like a Chinaman. The only difference is lack of a braid . . . his hair has fallen out from worry and pain.

"Avrohm," calls the woman, "I'm falling off my feet. Six nights have passed that my eyes have seen no sleep. Rock the child and I'll nap awhile. The baby's quiet; maybe it's resting easier."

"Nu, and who'll have the work ready by morning? The operators will show up six o'clock as usual."

"The devil with the bloodsucker. You can bring him the work a bit later."

Sewers and pressers working by gaslight. Dry-brush drawing by L. Kidlioski.
YIVO INSTITUTE FOR JEWISH RESEARCH

"You forget, Soreh, that if we don't work tomorrow we won't have anything to eat. If I don't give Mr. Leech his coats, I'll be without work—and then what?"

He grew still again. The woman rocked the baby as he went on with his work. The scissors snipped and there came an occasional gasp from the sick infant. Suddenly a scream tears out of the mother's mouth. "Help! Avrohm! The child's choking."

The man threw down the scissors, ran to the cradle. The child struggles, blinks its eyes, wants to catch its breath yet cannot. It gives out a terrible moan, two sighs, and then dies.

Father and mother scream. Four young children wake up. The wailing grows louder; everyone's crying, howling.

East Side immigrant Jews eating and working in a tenement sweatshop. The illustrations on this page first appeared in 1890 in Frank Leslie's Illustrated Newspaper. COURTESY OF LEON STEIN

Sewers, basters, pullers.
COURTESY OF LEON STEIN

SAM LIPTZIN

T H E   T A L L   M O I S H E H   was a Hungarian Jew with a big brown beard. . . . He appeared in the shop only when he brought the pushcart with the bundles of work. Then he used to march into the building in great tumult, as though he were in the process of rescuing humanity from a terrible catastrophe. Simultaneously, he would issue the order to the green apprentice boys, of whom I was one, to take the bundles up to the third floor. There was no elevator.

The Tall Moisheh's wife, Gutkeh, was always in the shop. She was the forelady, the manager, the bookkeeper—and the boss. She used to distribute the pay envelopes, an event that took place every Tuesday. She would pay us in single dollar bills to the following refrain: "See what a mountain of money you take away from us, you greenhorns!" My pay was all of eight dollars a week. . . .

In addition to her managerial activities in the "manufacturing" end of the business, she used to cook all her meals right in the shop. And she cooked not only for herself but for the watchman of the building, for several Hungarian *landsleit*, for a couple of apprentice boys, and for any worker who wanted a hot meal instead of a cold sandwich for supper. Because you must understand that after supper we had to go back to work again. . . .

In one of the three rooms of the shop stood a large oven which was already red hot. This was used not only for cooking Gutkeh's meals, but for heating the presser's irons. Gas or electricity was unheard of in a shop like this one. Even the sewing machines were an exhibit of primitive industrial inventions. [Until World War I] you could still find machines at The Tall Moisheh's with foot power, treadles, bicycle pedals, etc.

Inside a men's clothing factory.   JUSTICE/ILGWU

Morris Rosenfeld, one of the "sweatshop poets" whose work began to appear in the Yiddish press during the 1890s, was loved as an authentic, if sometimes melodramatic, voice of the Jewish working class. He sang of the travail of immigrants wasting their years in the shops, grown gray in their desolation.

MORRIS ROSENFELD

I work, and I work, without rhyme, without reason—
produce, and produce, and produce without end.
For what? and for whom? I don't know, I don't wonder
—since when can a whirling machine comprehend?

No feelings, no thoughts, not the least understanding;
this bitter, this murderous drudgery drains
the noblest, the finest, the best and the richest,
the deepest, the highest that living contains.

Away rush the seconds, the minutes and hours;
each day and each night like a wind-driven sail;
I drive the machine, as though eager to catch them,
I drive without reason—no hope, no avail.

The Yiddish writer Isaac Raboy shared the experiences of the immigrant generation; he wrote about it with a touching simplicity, even naïveté which still seems to bear the marks of truth. The following passage is translated from his novel Iz Gekumen a Yid (A Jew's Arrival).

ISAAC RABOY

MANNIS WAS HEARTSICK because there was no time to look into a *Sefer* [religious book]. It hurt him to watch himself gradually becoming vulgarized—outside and inside. What does he think about here in America? Very early, as soon as he gets up, he thinks that it's time to run to the shop. From morning to night he thinks that he has to keep moving. His neighbor, the redhead, also moves his hands very fast. At twelve noon Mannis thinks about taking a rest and about his stomach. After his dry lunch, sitting on a pile of rags, Mannis's eyes start to close. He would like to have a snooze. But that's impossible. The other workers play jokes on him—which are sometimes very unpleasant—and after lunch he keeps moving his hands very fast and runs and rushes until it gets dark. Then he rushes home and gulps his warm supper, and then he is so full that he sits like a dummy and can't move, and then he rushes to go to sleep.

He counts the hours and the minutes. Now it is nine; now it is half past nine, and by ten he is sprawled asleep on the soft bed.

All that takes care of the outside, the part you can see with your eyes. But what about the inside, the part you can't see with your eyes? All day he doesn't hear a single refined word. All day he doesn't hear a single soft word. The machines bore holes in his

Isaac Raboy (1882–1944), Yiddish novelist.

brain with their clatter, and the coarse shouts of Dave, the foreman, crush the spirit like lead. Day after day, this Dave is at war with the world. Nobody can please him—nobody ever does anything right. The feeling that you never do anything right twists your soul. Because you, too, have a soul, and you know that once in a while you do something wrong—but not everything you do can be wrong. And if the boss, Jacob, and his foreman keep watching you with such contempt, life loses its flavor and the very earth beneath your feet becomes abhorrent, and you feel like something useless. God, you say, I'm no worse than the horse in the stable; he gets beaten, but once in a while he gets a pat on the rump, too.

Some of the immigrants, though sparsely educated, turned out to possess natural gifts for social description. One of the best of these, I. Benequit, who wrote his memoirs in Yiddish, tells a typical story of working his way up from laborer to contractor—and the spiritual confusions that followed.

I. BENEQUIT

I S O O N S A W you become rich by becoming a manufacturer, not a little boss. But to become a manufacturer I'd need more capital, more experience, and more familiarity with the language. I observed that talent was even more necessary than money. I wanted to become a manufacturer, but through reading and thinking I concluded you don't get money for nothing—in other words, what the workingman loses, you gain. To become rich you have to be a boss. To become a boss you have to skim off the fat.

When I thought I'd become sufficiently acquainted with New York, I opened a shop to make shirts. Not like before, in my mother's house, but in a real shop with all the trimmings.

I went to Korn Brothers, the manufacturers, from whom I first received commissions.

The two brothers were *echt* German Jews. One had been forced to leave Germany for political activity. He'd been studious and an idealistic dreamer, but here, in business, his visions melted.

I bargained with him, explaining that from seven or eight machines I couldn't make anything.

"So," he laughed, "you want to get rich? You don't just want to make a living."

What does he care, I answered, so long as he doesn't pay higher prices? And why isn't *he* satisfied just to make a living. *I* should be the exception?

"Yes, someday you'll become my competitor."

"That should only come true. But my competition is not meant to damage you but to improve myself."

That pleased him.

We reached a price and two days later he sent me fifty dozen shirts. I also took on several workers and was not earning badly, but I was faced with the same problem as before. Not only did I work days, but also nights . . . and Saturday, peddling. Though Sunday I'd only work half a day—otherwise I'd have to give up lectures, my only spiritual pleasure.

Jews forsaking Moses to worship at the feet of Mammon. From the front page of The Big Stick, *an illustrated comic weekly published on the Lower East Side from 1909 to 1927.*

D U R I N G   T H E   T I M E   I had the shop the shirtmakers founded a union. My friends would needle me for considering myself a radical—an anarchist, yet—and not only do I not belong to the union, I've also gone the other way, hiring people. What came mildly from friends came as "enemy of the workers," "parasite," from strangers. They claimed I lived off others' labor, but I knew that I made no more than my workers, who earn more from me than elsewhere; and that I worked a lot harder. Nevertheless the words were painful and I debated with myself—am I a socialist? Do I believe in the anarchist ideal? Either I stay a contractor and give up my ideals or leave contracting and remain true.

The ideal won out. I left contracting and joined the shirtmakers union even though I wasn't working in a shop. I took another rest and supported myself from Saturday's peddling.

I read a lot, went to socialist meetings, studied English. I went to English lectures, to the theater.

After a while I remembered I'm a shirtmaker and took a job in one of the better shops where they made silk and flannel shirts, under a contractor, a certain Robinson.

I worked six weeks, made out well, but socialist agitation began against the long hours—7:00 to 6:30. . . . Under such conditions, just how long can workers sit around a shop without striking?

The ensuing strike lasted two to three weeks. I'll never forget the tragicomic scene of good husky union men who'd just joined two days earlier demanding strike benefits from the executive upon threat of scabbing; whereas longtime union members, men with large families, demanded nothing, comprehending that the union can't afford that. . . .

During the strike some sixty of the most prominent Social Democrats and anarchists got together, put in twenty-five dollars and a sewing machine each and started a cooperative steam-run factory. From each according to his abilities and to each union wages.

I was chosen treasurer and later, manager. I was almost the youngest but had more management experience and knew where to find work. . . . I was to be paid the wages of the highest paid worker; better for me I figured than working at a machine. But the first few weeks I had to work harder than anyone else, setting up the shop, arranging for steam and getting orders. . . . After I got enough orders at the right price, I awaited my well-earned wages, but my fellows reckoned that because no one else got anything while I was setting up shop, I shouldn't either. I swallowed this, as they say in America, "like a sport." Then there were silk shirts with French cuffs that the sleevemakers couldn't produce fast enough for the other workers not to lose time. This meant that the better workers worked less, were paid less, automatically reducing my wage. I swallowed this, too.

When there were fewer workdays for others my time wasn't lessened. Indeed, I'd have to work even harder running around for orders . . .

I decided to try founding a cooperative not with the intelligentsia, but with simple workingmen who could likely perform in harmony. . . . I began building castles in the air.

The problem lay largely in that the Jewish worker was no worker. Today he's a worker; tomorrow he opens a stand, later a little store; then a customer peddler; finally an agent. With this type it's impossible to build a cooperative.

Catching a breath of fresh air.
COURTESY OF LEON STEIN

Early Unions, Early Rebellion

The soaring new faith of the immigrant world was socialism—a vision of human fraternity that would bring to an end the exploitativeness, the inhumane competitiveness, the moral frigidity associated with capitalism. We're not inclined to go along with facile analogies between religious faith and secular politics; still, there does seem good reason to say that something of the messianic fervor of religious fathers was appropriated by radical sons and daughters. For Jewish socialism was far more than a politics—it was a gleaming faith, at once splendid and naïve in its dreams of perfection and brotherhood.

The Jewish socialists were stronger within their own neighborhoods than socialism ever was in America as a whole—indeed, that was a difficulty they could never overcome. Where they did their best work, making a permanent contribution to both Jewish life and American society, was in building the Jewish trade unions, mostly in the garment industries. For many years, these unions were models of militancy, warmth, decency—far more socially imaginative than most of the native American unions. In the garment unions the Jewish workers found not just a protector but a home, a cultural milieu. And over the decades, through strikes that were often bitter and through systematic organizational plugging, the garment unions—especially the International Ladies' Garment Workers Union and the Amalgamated Clothing Workers Union—helped to transform the lives of their members, bringing a bit of security and dignity.

The Jewish socialists also brought to the immigrant quarters a fierce intellectuality, a passion for cultural growth and acquisition, and in the earlier years, a less attractive spirit of sectarian narrowness.

In the years before the First World War, the Jewish unions, or at least many of their leaders, were often marred by a clumsy antagonism to both Zionism and religion, but with time even the more doctrinaire socialists came to see that it was possible for Jewish workers to believe in God and hope for a renewal of Zion while remaining devoted unionists and voting for Morris Hillquit, the major Jewish socialist figure.

Out of this ferment arose one of the most impressive types in the whole immigrant world: the self-educated Jewish worker, the man or woman aspiring not just to understand Marx but to read Tolstoy and, a bit later, Mark Twain or Theodore Dreiser; aspiring not only to organize unions and parties but also to gain something of the cultural heritage that oppression and prejudice had denied them. To our mind, the self-educated worker—that admirable poignant figure who would not let circumstances keep his or her mind from a life of activity and growth—constitutes perhaps the greatest achievement of the whole culture of Yiddish.

Here, in writings by Marcus Ravage, I. Benequit, Morris Hillquit (the last of whom was the most distinguished intellectual voice of Jewish socialism), and Rose Pastor Stokes, we gain a glimpse of that world of moral hope and intellectual aspiration.

161

MARCUS RAVAGE

Shorter Working
Hours Means:
Longer Seasons,
Higher Wages,
Longer Life.

. . . A TIME ARRIVED when I would start to the shop in the morning in hopes that I might find the power turned off and the boss explaining that work was "slow." On such days I would keep my coat and collar right on and take myself off to the nearest library, despite the boss's protests and assurance that he was expecting the bundles from the manufacturer to arrive any moment. There was so much for me to do. There were whole stacks of Norwegian dramatists, and Russian novelists, and Yiddish poets that I had as yet barely touched. In my room there was a collection of the Réclam editions of Zola and Maupassant, and an assortment of plays of all nations which had been suggested to me by Gordin's lectures which I had not yet found time to touch at all. . . .

With my mind so busy, then, it was not surprising that I should remain somewhat indifferent to what was going on in my soul. My ancient religion had, under American skies, vanished long ago; but I was scarcely aware that a burning new faith had taken its place with me, as it had done with thousands of others. I cannot now say whether I was taking it for granted or did not know it. I continually heard people in the shop, and in the quarter generally, referred to as "clodpates" and "intelligents," and I knew that an intelligent was a person who went to lectures and read books, and preferred tragedy to vaudeville, and looked upon America as a place which afforded one an opportunity to acquire and express ideas, while a clodpate cared more for dollars than for ideas, and worked hard so that someday he might have others work for him, and in the evening he went to a dance hall or to the Atlantic Garden or to Miner's or to a card party, and kept himself scrupulously respectable so that someday, when he could afford it, he might rise to be the president of the synagogue or the lodge, and read (when he read at all) the *Tageblatt* and the joke books. All this I knew, and, in addition, that I was already being classed as an intelligent among the hands at the shop.

It never occurred to me, however, to attach any ulterior meaning to the word. It was obvious enough; I could have seen it if I had only looked. But somehow I did not look—until one day the thing struck me and I had to look. It was an idle day at the shop. The boss had persuaded us to wait for the work, and we were lounging about on the machine tables and on the ends of cases. Some of us had been to a reading of Ibsen's symbolic drama *When We Dead Awaken* the night before, and were, of course, discussing it. I said that I liked it. Then the girl who had the year before put me on the intellectual track spoke up and asked me, in a tone of pained astonishment:

"Why, aren't you a radical?"

"Yes, of course," I said, a little uncertainly. "Who is not?"

"Who is not? The clodpates are not."

"But what has this got to do with literature?"

"Well," she answered, "it has this to do with it. This symbolism business is reactionary. It has always been. It's churchy."

Then I suddenly realized that everybody I knew was either a socialist or an anarchist. It came to me in a flash that this social idealism was the soul that stirred within everything that was going on about and within me. I remembered that all our meetings and lectures were colored by it. And I understood that every intelligent was an atheist partly because every clodpate was a believer and partly because the established creeds were cluttering the road to social and spiritual progress. When I asked myself why we studied the abstruse principles of physics, the answer was that it helped us to disprove the arguments of the religious. Our enthusiasm for evolution, I saw, was due to that doctrine's implied denial of the biblical story of creation. And if we loved the poets, it was because they seemed to us to be pervaded by a lofty discontent with the existing order of things. In short, I perceived that we were moved by a very vital religion of our own; although, of course, we would have scorned to call it by that hated name. . . .

Yes, our radicalism had all the nobility and all the weaknesses of a young faith. We were no mere parlor socialists, we toilers of the slums. Our atheism was no affectation; our anarchism was not a fad to make conversation with over the teacups. Nor were we concerned with the improvement of our own material condition merely. We were engaged in the regeneration of society, and we were prepared to take up arms in the great social revolution which we saw daily drawing nearer. We were all missionaries, and some of us were quite genuine bigots. On the Day of Atonement, when all the conservative people of the quarter fasted and repented and knelt in prayer, we ostentatiously went about with big cigars in our mouths and bags of food in our pockets; and in the afternoon we met in the public square and marched off in a body with flags and trumpets to the atheist picnic somewhere in Brooklyn. Similarly, during the Passover, we gave an entertainment and ball, where we consumed more forbidden food and drink than was good for us. No doubt this was foolish—perhaps it was even vulgar—but to us it was propaganda for our faith among the unconverted.

Longer Working Hours Means: Shorter Seasons, Smaller Wages, Shorter Life.

MORRIS HILLQUIT

IT WAS AN EAGER ASSEMBLAGE that foregathered there, mostly made up of young intellectuals, boys and girls ranging in age from eighteen to twenty-five, who had come here on the crest of the wave of mass immigration from Russia during the eighties of the last century. They were persons of high school or college education, who had been suddenly plucked from their studies and associations by persecutions and discriminations in their cruel native land and found themselves transplanted in new and strange soil. . . .

They felt unhappy and forlorn in their workshops, but at night on the roofs they again lived in a congenial atmosphere. Once more they were students among students, forgetting the miseries of their

In front of the socialist
Jewish Daily Forward.

hard and toilsome lives and enjoying the pleasures of freedom and companionship with the abandon and enthusiasm of youth.

Peals of gay laughter and voices of earnest and animated conversation would come from different groups on the roofs, while the melancholy and nostalgic strains of popular Russian folk songs would often resound in the still evening air. It was a slice of old Russian life that was thus transported to Cherry Street by the uprooted young immigrants.

But song and laughter were not the main pastime of the habitués of the roofs. Most of their evenings were spent in discussion. And what discussion! There was not a mooted question in science, philosophy, or politics that was not aired on the roofs in ardent, impassioned, and tumultuous debate. Politics was the favorite subject.

Some of these young people had received their political baptism in the underground revolutionary movement of Russia. All had definite social creeds and were ever ready to expound and defend them. . . .

In the United States the [socialist] movement was in its cradle. What there was of it was more like a foreign colony of Social Democracy in Germany than an indigenous American movement.

The socialists of that remote period were not practical politicians. They were idealists and propagandists, who clung to their social creed with religious zeal. They were few in number, misunderstood and railed at by the multitude, and felt more than a mere political kinship with each other. They were comrades in a personal and intimate sense.

Almost rivaling the socialists in numerical strength were the anarchists.

The anarchist movement was then at its zenith. The brutal suppression of socialist propaganda in most countries of continental Europe had weakened the faith of many in the efficacy of peaceful methods and embittered them. . . .

It was amusing to hear these mild-mannered and soft-spoken boys and girls talk glibly about blowing up buildings and killing tyrants. But it was all theory with them, and many a night did we spend in heated discussion of the respective merits of the bomb and the ballot as agencies of social salvation. In later years the anarchist movement gradually declined. . . .

The newsroom of the anarchist newspaper, the Freie Arbeiter Stimme.
YIVO INSTITUTE FOR JEWISH RESEARCH

. . . The fraternity on the roofs for a time was the main link between the idealism of my youth and the sordid realities of my new daily occupations. I relished the discussions of lofty problems and high themes which constituted the daily conversational fare of the roofs, the clashes of opinions and faiths, the ardor of controversy. . . .

At that period I already considered myself a socialist, but my socialism was largely emotional and sentimental. My notions about the philosophy and practical program of the movement were quite vague. I had had no opportunity to study its theory and history. Here at least the finer points of the creed were discussed, analyzed, compared, attacked, and defended, and while it would have been unsafe to accept the haphazard and extemporaneous roof discussions as authoritative expositions of the social sciences, they were a tolerably efficient seminar. . . .

Through some of my newly acquired friends on the roofs I got my first opportunity to make direct contacts with the organized socialist movement. Many of them were members of a newly founded society called the Russian Progressive Union. This was composed of adherents of all shades of radical and liberal thought. Its only practical activity consisted of organizing public lectures, which were

"First of May, Our Holiday"—Anarchist leader Alexander Berkman speaking at Union Square, 1908. Photograph by George Bain.
LIBRARY OF CONGRESS, BAIN COLLECTION

held every Sunday afternoon. The lectures were mostly in Russian but sometimes also in English or German. . . .

It did not take me long to choose between the rival social creeds that divided the constituency of Cherry Street roofs and the Russian Progressive Union. I allied myself with the Social Democrats almost immediately.

As I recall it, the Cherry Street roofs lasted only two or three seasons as the social center of the Russian radical youth. With the development of practical organizational activities among its habitués, the gatherings on the roofs lost their charm and died out.

I. BENEQUIT

D E B A T E S   B E T W E E N   Jewish Social Democrats and anarchists made a miserable impression on me. I'll never forget the speakers throwing about lofty words and phrases. . . .

A meeting was scheduled where the two bigwigs, Abe Cahan and R. Lewis, debated about majority versus minority. After the session little groups stood about and discussed:

"Let's see, who has more writers and speakers—we, the socialists, or you anarchists?"

"All right," the anarchist answered, "let's see." . . .

Such discussions were frequent, even from the big shots. At a serious debate on majority versus minority, a Social Democrat wishing to deal anarchism a deathblow shouted out with pathos: "What would an anarchist do if he'd see several persons drowning in one spot and one person drowning at another?" "Whom," the man dramatically cried, "would he save—the one or the many? Or, what would the minority do if the majority decided to dam up Niagara Falls? Would the anarchist minority form a new waterfall?"

. . . The Anarchist answered: "Regarding whom would I save, the group or the individual, my response is as follows. If I knew that in the group there were such jackasses like the questioner, and the individual was someone with sense, I'd save the individual. About the waterfall question—if there's a majority of people so idiotic as to dam up a treasure of nature that enriches the world, that proves the anarchist theory which does not believe in the majority is correct."

Another anarchist addressed himself to the same issues, setting forth the worth of an individual over a group of blockheads. To the second question he replied, "In many instances one should not rely on the majority . . . a case in point being that the minority lives in luxury and the overwhelming majority in poverty. The same holds true with legal justice: sometimes a law is unjust."

At one point, someone with radical leanings, but who was neither socialist nor anarchist, and already a bit of a Yankee, got up and said, "We Jews have to respect the laws of all countries, especially of a free land like America." Many laughed at him, and I believe Hillel Zolatoroff answered: "How dare governments demand that their people protect the law if the law does not protect the people?"

Jewish radicalism, like much else in the immigrant world, was often raw, untempered, lacking in nuance and sophistication. Leon Kobrin, the Yiddish writer and playwright, recalls here a conversation with the wife of a landsman, *an anarchist showing off her daughter's "knowledge."*

LEON KOBRIN

"SOPHIE, I WANT TO ASK YOU SOMETHING but answer me in Yiddish because the gentleman doesn't yet understand English."

"All right, mama," the child nods her blond head.

And then Rivkah winks to me and afterward there ensues between her and the child such a conversation that until today the impression remains fresh in my memory. . . .

"Sophie," Rivkah says to her, "do you believe in God?"

"No." Sophie shakes her blond curls.

"Why, Sophie?" Rivkah's eyes twinkle in wonder.

"Well, who created God? God has no papa-mama and without a papa-mama you can't create anyone," Sophie declares with a childlike, earnest attitude.

"And who believes in God, Sophie?" Rivkah inquires further.

"All the capitalists who want people to be stupid and they should believe in God."

"Why do capitalists want that, Sophie?"

"Because stupid people are afraid that God will punish them if they make a revolution against the capitalists."

"Right, and against whom else, child?"

"Against 'hypocrites.'"

"Right, and also against whom, Sophie?"

Sophie answers again in English and Rivkah translates: "Against status."

"You hear?" Rivkah cries out, inspired, and she beams.

"And what will you do, Sophie, when you grow up?" Rivkah afterward turns again to the little girl.

"I will make a revolution."

"For the good of humanity?" Rivkah cuts in with a beaming face.

"Yes, mama, and for the community."

"What sort of community, Sophie?"

"For the anarchist community, mama."

Rivkah grabs her on her lap and kisses her.

"That's how I raise my children," says the inspired Rivkah to me.

ROSE PASTOR STOKES

NAT TOLD US ABOUT A MAN by the name of Karl Marx—a name, he said, that was sacred to the working classes. Karl Marx would show the workers how to abolish poverty.

"Poverty, and misery, and insecurity," said Nat, "are not things that a cruel God put into the world to punish us for our sins. Poverty and all its evils can be abolished, and the workers will someday abolish them through socialism."

We need not suffer poverty! What a world-shattering idea. We—we the workers—will change it all someday. . . . The how or when we didn't know, but the seed was planted.

Rose Harriet Pastor (1879–1933), immigrant writer, Socialist and later wife of millionaire reformer and University Settlement worker J. G. Phelps Stokes.
COURTESY OF UNIVERSITY SETTLEMENT

The bristling colorful pages of the Commercial Advertiser, *probably the best English-language newspaper in New York around the turn of the century, were often opened to reports of Jewish workers on strike. As in 1898:*

COMMERCIAL ADVERTISER, 8/13/'98

A FOURTEEN-YEAR-OLD LEADER sprang up this morning among the East Side striking garment workers. His name is Harry Gladstone . . .

Harry is a machine tender in a sweatshop. The average machine tender, or "turner," gets from two to three dollars a week, and the strike was for an advance of wages. "What we want is one dollar per machine," said Harry. "While the operators are working on the jackets we must keep turning the sleeves and the flaps and the collars, and sometimes three or four operators start to yell at us. But the boss, he don't care. He pays us the same. That's why we want a dollar for each machine and no more than nine hours a day. It's enough, ain't it?"

As Harry talked on, dilating upon the grievances of the basting pullers, he warmed up to the subject. "At the next meeting of the union I'll tell them to stick together and to think about their poor fathers and mothers they have to support. I'll speak to them of the

169

schools and how they can't go there because they spend fourteen hours a day turning collars and sleeves and pulling bastings. 'You have not had time to grow up and get strength for work,' I'll tell them. 'Think of how your mothers shed tears over you because they see their children treated like slaves. Try to make a few dollars for them at least. Then you can come home and kiss your mamas and say, "Don't cry. I've brought you some money for rent."' The only way to get the bosses to pay us good wages is to stick together, so let us be true to our union."

COMMERCIAL ADVERTISER, 2/9/'98

A CROWD OF CADAVEROUS MEN, WOMEN, and children, a multitude of black eyes gleaming out of the uncouth, disheveled, weird mass, last night shouted and gesticulated about on the glossy dancing floor at the Pleasure Palace Hall, 63 Pitt Street. The gallery overhead was decorated with the Stars and Stripes and a red flag, and these were aflutter, as if struggling to break loose from their staffs to join in the excitement of the men and women below.

Workers parading in Union Square, 1887.   MUSEUM OF THE CITY OF NEW YORK

"And I say that you men are big slices of nothing and that's all," yelled a woman of thirty with the reddest hair and the stateliest figure in the crowd. "What's the use of calling yourselves men when you haven't sense enough to tie up the tail of a pig!"

Several of the young fellows fell silent, to listen to her, with sad, skeptical smiles.

"What would you do if you had everything your way?" somebody asked her.

"What? Why, if I were the union, the whole union, you understand, I should not have a strike every Monday and Thursday. I would teach the bosses such a lesson that they would never forget it and would rather pay decent wages than run the risk of violating the contract."

"She is right! She is right!" came from half a dozen voices. "What was the use of rejoicing when we are now just where we were before the previous strike. No sooner is the season over than the contract is broken and we are as badly off as ever."

"Even worse! Don't you have to work from thirteen to fourteen hours a day to earn seven or eight dollars a week?"

"Seven or eight? Why sometimes I am glad if I earn five. Let this be the last time! Let us get so organized that the bosses will be afraid to break our contracts, season or no season. We have nothing to lose anyhow. Rent is so high, one is obliged to keep boarders, and even at home we have no homes. We live from hand to mouth; the boss treats us like dogs. Is that what we came to America for? While we are standing here our children are crying for bread at home. Have we got any bread to give them? We work so hard, we put up with so much humiliation. I, for one, wish I had never been born at all."

The speaker was a woebegone man of twenty, and he uttered his extemporaneous speech with calm earnestness. Its effect upon the bevy of strikers was immediate and deep. Grave silence ensued, broken only by here and there a heavy sigh.

"But what's to be done? What's to be done?"

"Hold together," the young man answered. "Hold together and the bosses will be in our hands. Will they make the pants?"

One of the most admirable of the early figures in the Jewish trade union movement was a man named Bernard Weinstein. Absolutely devoted to his cause, he worked for many years to build the Jewish unions. Later in his life he wrote valuable memoirs in Yiddish, from which the two following selections are taken.

BERNARD WEINSTEIN

THE SYNAGOGUE WAS FILLED to capacity with middle-aged people. In front, near the *oren kodish*, the officers of the union were seated: old men with skullcaps on their heads, dressed in *kapotes* ("gabardines"). The president, short and stocky with a long beard and side curls, stood near a table on which lay a stone. In his hand he held a large gavel. The platform was in the middle of the room.

Suddenly, the chairman banged on the table three times and all present rose from their seats. This was done in our honor. The president introduced us and we were greeted with applause. Again the chairman stood up, again he banged with the gavel, and the pressers applauded loudly. Everybody was seated. The hall became absolutely still, contrary to the meetings with younger people where we had great difficulty in keeping them quiet.

The brother president smoothed out his *kapote*, looked around him and began his speech:

"Brothers," he began in a loud voice, "do you know who was the first walking delegate?"

Silence.

"The first walking delegate among the Jews," continued the chairman, "was Moses, and the *sanhedrin* was the first executive board."

The scholarly chairman went on with his speech, overflowing with wisdom from the Torah and the Talmud. His parables went straight to the hearts of his listeners. All comparisons led to the union. The people in the skullcaps became warmed up and signified their hearty approval by stamping their feet upon the ground. Again the chairman banged three times and quiet was restored.

A M O N G T H E U N I O N S that existed at the end of the past century were a few composed of old men, like the pressers, butchers, or ragpickers locals. One of these that we of the United Hebrew Trades helped organize in 1894 was a union of cleaners. Its members, who'd mainly been tailors in Europe, operated out of cellars and worked by hand. They'd take dirty old clothes, wash them with benzine, dye them with brushes like a painter, and then press them. Many a time their pails of kerosene would spill and cause fires in the tenements.

The union of these elderly cleaners had been started by one of its younger members, M. Segal of the Socialist Labor party, and their meetings turned out quite lively—they usually arranged to have representatives there of the United Hebrew Trades in order to settle the frequent fights that would break out: fights of joy!

We could not really complain about this uncomradely mode of celebration because the actual work life of these persons was quite bitter—old men, usually in *yarmulkahs*, standing twelve to fifteen hours per day by long tables in dirty cellars, cleaning dirty clothes.

One day two other Hebrew Trades people and I were invited to one of their meetings held on the top floor of a loft at 49 Henry Street. This time, as it turned out, there would be no fighting— apparently our presence shamed them out of this.

When we arrived everyone was gathered around a table facing the chairman; they all wore *yarmulkahs*, except a few younger members with hats. Most were dressed in long smocks resembling caftans. Everyone had a glass of beer in hand, and before him, a plate of herring and pieces of pumpernickel. The place was half dark from the smoke of pipes and cigarettes and one could have been deafened from the banging of beer glasses. A few fellows served as head waiters and would steadily set forth full glasses of beer with a "*L'chayim.*"

The chairman stood on a platform in the middle of the room. When he noticed our little delegation—we'd not known where to place ourselves among the hundred or so members—he summoned us to join the others at the table. As we drew nearer, everyone rose, and as the chairman recited our "pedigrees" we were resoundingly toasted with the clinkings of beer mugs.

Then we were seated and urged to participate in the eating and drinking, assured that "we wouldn't be working for nothing"—in the words of a long-bearded Jew with spectacles resting on his nose—"soon you'll have to make 'spitches.'"

The noise grew—someone began a *Simchas Torah* melody; glasses were continually filled from a nearby barrel; there were also pails of ice to keep the beer cold. Finally I asked my bearded neighbor: "What's the occasion?"

"I should know?" he answered. "It's just today? Every meeting is like this, or else we wouldn't show up. The men give a few dimes apiece and we have a *Simchas Torah.* That's how we are— sometimes we kiss each other from happiness, sometimes we fight."

The chairman announced each delegate of our committee, and at the end of each speech we cried out: "Long live the union!" as the Jews applauded and bumped glasses. Meanwhile a few of them moved the tables to the wall and began dancing to a Hasidic tune.

Later in our report to the Hebrew Trades, we called this group the "*Simchas Torah* Union."

The cleaners union indeed bettered its members' lives—through bargaining successfully for shorter hours and higher wages.

ARBEITER TSEITUNG, 5/8/'91

IN NEW YORK the grand parade began at 9:00 A.M. By 3:00 P.M. all Jewish unions were gathered at Rutgers Square, from which they marched onto East Broadway, from there to Worth Street, south Fifth Avenue, Fourth Street, Fourth Avenue, then Union Square. Before the unions came together each had marched individually through the main points of the Jewish quarter.

In all, 14,775 marched on Union Square. In addition to the unions there marched 200 pale and worn-out young boys, basters in the tailor shops. They carried a banner that read: We Want to Go to School, Not the Shops.

Other banners read:
We Make the Clothes, Yet Go Naked!
Americanization, Culture, and Organization!
Down with the Sweat System! Down with Capital!

Union demonstration on the Lower East
Side: The signs read, "We Demand
Bread and Freedom!" JUSTICE/ILGWU

Jewish socialism meant a remarkably wide range of interests and
activities—working in unions, campaigning in the streets, cultural
evenings, endless lectures, marching on May Day. To belong to a
Jewish socialist group signified not just a political commitment; it
made possible a new cultural ambience, a widening of horizons.
Sometimes, one suspects, immigrants became involved with
socialism less for political reasons than because they found in it an
avenue to the outer world of thought and culture. For the Jewish
immigrants, socialism served as a school of popularization and a
training ground preparing them for the larger American world. To
say this isn't, of course, to deny Jewish socialism its distinctive
world outlook and political program; but seen historically, with
some detachment, Jewish socialism has to be described as also
comprising a stage in the "Americanization" of the immigrants.

Here, in any case, is a group of pieces by a variety of Yiddish
writers providing a picture of the Jewish socialist milieu in the
1890s and a bit later.

BERNARD WEINSTEIN

OUR CAMPAIGN SHOULD HAVE BEEN in full swing because only a few weeks remained till the elections. We had a hard time finding comrades who in order to become candidates had to be both citizens and residents of the assembly district. We decided on an open-air meeting like the other political parties. . . .

On a Friday evening a committee from the Eighth Assembly District hired a wagon hooked up to a thin yellow horse. The candidates and our other Yiddish orators packed themselves into the wagon to which was attached a sign reading, Vote for the Socialist Candidates. Two comrades held two tin lamps on either side of the wagon.

The first stop was the corner of Hester and Allen streets. "Are you the chairman?" Comrade Spector, the Fourth District candidate, turned to me and asked.

"All right!" I answered and started shouting, "Citizens and workers!" As soon as I got out these few words, the wise guys standing around the truck began hooting: "Aha! The *tsitsilisten* are here." Religious Jews would call socialists missionaries. . . .

I kept on speaking; the interruptions didn't bother me. Then the stones began flying. The comrades didn't mind becoming martyrs, but the horse got scared and ran. The comrades were shaken and yelled to the driver: "Go to another corner." We had a choice?

The next stop was the intersection of Essex and Hester streets; there we had a worse experience than the earlier—from both Tammany politicians and members of the Johnny O'Brien Association (Republicans) who could not tolerate the novelty of *tsitsilisten* speaking in the street. We hardly got away alive. We rode around awhile and at last stopped at Rutgers Square. Then Comrade Abraham Cahan delivered an inspiring speech. We escaped with some bruises from the stones, but satisfied with the success of the first open-air socialist propaganda meeting.

The election result was not wonderful. Alexander Jonas, our mayoral candidate, received a bit less than three thousand votes. As a beginning for a new party whose members were entirely foreigners, this was not bad. Candidates in the Jewish districts received fewest votes. In the Fourth District our candidates received forty-six votes and in the Eighth, twenty-six votes. This was to be expected—socialist supporters in the Jewish districts had not yet been naturalized.

LEON KOBRIN

THE GREAT HALL of the German Labor Lyceum at Sixth and Brown was packed with women and men. Only the first few rows were unoccupied, held open for a few dozen *skebikhes* ("scabs") who'd been tricked into showing up at the hall and were meanwhile being detained in a side room until Cahan arrived. . . .

Impatience grew. "Will he get here?" was asked louder and

oftener. . . . Suddenly a few burning-cheeked young women and a few young men rushed in, out of breath. "He's here! He's here!"

Women's eyes sparkled and across their lips passed the womanly smile of adulation—one I'd later see so often in the theater whenever a godlike actor crossed the stage. The movement was still young, and so too the belief of all assembled in the idea for which Cahan stood as prophet. . . .

He takes a seat on the platform, in a black Prince Albert, his eyes turned wryly toward his public. . . . Cahan does not smile, not even to the chairman of the gathering, who keeps turning toward him with a flurry. . . .

Soon the chairman perched before the rostrum calls out in fiery tone: "Bring in the scabs."

Then complete quiet, as of a courtroom. The judge orders the accused led in.

Everyone looks at a side door. . . . A girl appears, her head drooped—then another girl and yet another. Soon, a few dozen, all through that door. They enter confused, unnerved. . . . They pass before thousands of eyes. . . . They're little more than children pale, trembling, drained.

Suddenly the "boos" begin—from women, from men: like one throat disgorging hate and scorn. . . .

The girls lower their heads even farther, grow more confused. (I found out that there were male scabs, too, but they'd not been fooled, as the girls had, into appearing.) The chairman banged on the table—"Order!"—and all was still.

The girls took their places before the platform. Cahan rose. He stood in front and scanned the scabs with hostile eyes. They feared to return his gaze. . . . His nostrils opened and shut from anger, opened and shut. . . . His eyes rested on a girl. He pointed a finger at her, spoke in cold anger: "A face! Take a look at it. Prettier ones than that have been laid in the ground for the worms." He stamped his feet and shouted . . . the nostrils working hysterically. . . .

The boss drains their blood, he told the young women . . . yet instead of tearing out his insides they scab against brother and sister. "Such girls should be thrown down, beat and flogged, their flesh torn piecemeal, strip by strip. Skinned alive."

The audience, of course, applauded and the girls looked like chickens before slaughter.

He told stories that made everyone laugh, the most successful of which was about the wagon driver who accustomed his horse to fewer oats. The animal ate less and less each day until it collapsed. In like manner, the boss wants to train the workers. . . .

Cahan ended his talk with a cheer for socialism and the words: "And a redeemer shall come unto the proletariat." . . .

After the talk, all the girls, the *skebikhes*, came forward to the chairman's table and signed up as union members.

It was all very well to be a socialist—but meanwhile a man had to feed his children, and sometimes he even discovered opportunities for working his way up in the world, becoming a contractor or accumulating some money. This led, inevitably, to severe conflicts of feeling between socialist persuasion and personal ambition. Many of the memoirs written by early immigrants speak movingly about these problems. One such worker, Sam Schaeffer, a pants maker in Boston, sent a letter to his union in 1902 after he had committed the sin of scabbing in a strike. What impresses one in such writings is the strength of moral impulse among these people even when circumstance and desire led them to violate it.

SAM SCHAEFFER

TO THE PANTS MAKERS UNION:

I appeal to you, president, and the members of the Pants Makers Union, I would feign call you brothers, but I know you will not take it in good faith. I know that you will say, "What think you of the boldness of this scab; he even calls us brothers?" I know that the brothers will be angry and make a motion to fine me with twenty-five dollars. An amendment will be made for fifty. Perhaps you will table my appeal altogether for several weeks.

Dear brothers, I beg you to have mercy on my children. If you would come in my house you would see how frozen my stove is, and how my children shiver terribly with cold—on empty little stomachs—just as I do. But I can only answer my dear little children with a sigh: "I was a scab, therefore must we starve from hunger and cold. I cannot justify myself against the union. I can do nothing."

Dear brothers, I hope that among you will be found men with feeling. I know that among you there are fathers who know that children ask for bread: How does it feel when you have nothing to give them?

Dear brothers, I will ask you something, but answer me feelingly. Are my children responsible for my being a scab? Are they to be blamed because their father is a tomfool? Answer me, are they to be blamed? I beg of you in the name of my little ones let me in the union; we are cold, we are hungry, you are men, have sympathy, have mercy, brothers. I am no scab, I am to be blamed, I committed a crime, I did take money from the union, all is true. I can no longer give it back, I will do it no more.

Brothers, men, men, brothers, we are hungry, we are cold, take me in the union, let me go to work. Brothers, if you do not take me in the union the blame will be upon you. I am doing my duty. I beg and keep begging you to take me in the union.

APPEAL!

TO ALL LADIES' WAIST MAKERS !

While all workers of other trades have succeeded in improving their condition, increasing their wages, shortening labor hours, and receiving better treatment by their bosses and contractors, but we the Ladies' Waist Makers are still in a miserable position.

We are still compelled to toil long hours for very small salaries.

We are those who create so much for others and enjoy nothing. Why? because we are disorganized and fight our battles singularly.

The way to better our condition is to UNITE and work in harmony. The bosses will treat us severely so long, as we will not have a strong Union to be always ready to defend our interest.

Come, LADIES' WAIST MAKERS, to the

MASS-MEETING

of our Union, which will be held on

Friday, August 2nd, 1907,

AT 8 P. M.

at 206 E. Broadway, 1st floor.

Prominent speakers will address the meeting and explain the importance of a strong Union in this trade.

COME AND HELP YOURSELVES.   ADMISSION FREE.

אויפרוף צו אלע ארבייטער ליידים וויסטם.

א ריזען מאסען פערזאמלונג

אינגערופען פון דיא

ליידים וויסט מייקערם יוניאן

יעדע אבענדהאלבען וועלען פרייטאג, דען 2-טען אוינוסט, אין א איהר אבענדס,

אין 206 איסט בראדוויי, 1-סטן פלאר.

דיא נעע. ב. פינענבוים און מ. פיין, וועלען פאזביבי רייעה

ליידיעם וויסט מייקערם! קומט אין מאססען יעצט, אור דא דער זיאן דארף זיך יעצט אנגאנגען, איז

דיא צים ארף צו נירען א שטארקן יוניאן וועלבע זאל אונז בעשיצען געגען אונזרע באסעס.

קומט אין מאסען. אינטערים פרייע נור פיר ליידים וויסט מייקערם.

Struggles and Victories

The rise of the Jewish trade unions, most of them in the garment industry, during the early decades of this century is a story of heroism and stumbling, partial victories and major setbacks, great sacrifice and organizational disintegration. It seemed as if no victory was ever final, as if each struggle had to be fought over and over again. It seemed as if each new generation of workers had to experience once again the traumas and lessons of the preceding one. Yet, gradually the Jewish unions consolidated and stabilized themselves, came to be accepted as an integral part of the industries in which they organized workers, and improved the conditions of their members, sometimes little by little, sometimes dramatically.

It would be foolish even to try to tell that story in this brief space, so we have decided just to present a few highlights, moments of triumph, moments of defeat. First comes a passage from World of Our Fathers *describing the great strike of the shirtwaist makers in 1909, a strike of young women and girls that sparked a whole series of other strikes in the garment industries. Next a piquant account by Jacob Panken, a fiery socialist orator, of his effort to organize a union against the opposition of thugs.*

IRVING HOWE

On November 22, 1909, twenty thousand shirtwaist makers, most of them girls in their teens or early twenties, and about two thirds of them Jewish, went on strike.

The manufacture of shirtwaists, or blouses, was a relatively new segment of the garment industry. Since 1900 it had been growing rapidly, its 1909 output in New York alone reaching fifty million dollars. Physical conditions in the shirtwaist shops tended to be better than in other parts of the industry, mostly because these shops were newer, cleaner, and more likely to use electrical power; but the girls were subject to many small tyrannies, sexual discrimination on top of class exploitation. "Inside subcontracting" was common in the shirtwaist shops, which meant that male employees would themselves employ several "girl helpers," who earned no more than three or four dollars a week. These doubly ill-used "learners," who sometimes kept "learning" long after there was nothing left to learn, formed 20 to 25 percent of the work force. Female workers were charged for needles, power, and supplies at a profit of 20 percent; taxed for the chairs on which they sat; made to pay for clothes lockers; fined if they came to work five minutes late. Sporadic efforts to organize them had failed, and the common view of the time was that because they were girls who hoped soon to marry they could not be unionized.

When the strike began, the shirtwaist makers union, Local 25 of the ILGWU, had slightly more than one hundred members and some four dollars in its treasury. Limited strikes had already been called against several firms, the Triangle Waist Company and the Leiserson Company, but these seemed on the edge of collapse because the employers, mostly east European Jews, had used strikebreakers and thugs to frighten the girls. In desperation, the leadership of Local 25 began to consider the total gamble of a "general strike" in the shirtwaist industry.

On November 22 it called a meeting of workers at Cooper Union. Thousands came, with crowds spilling over into other halls. Gompers spoke; so did Mary Dreier, head of the Women's Trade Union League; and, as usual at such meetings, Jacob Panken and Meyer London, the big guns of Jewish socialism. But no clear strategy had been worked out by the local's leadership, and the speakers, hesitating before the prospect of an ill-prepared general strike, could not quite decide between exhortation and caution. As the evening dragged along and speaker followed speaker, there suddenly raced up to the platform, from the depths of the hall, a frail teenage girl named Clara Lemlich, who had been picketing at the Leiserson plant day after day. She burst into a flow of passionate Yiddish which would remain engraved in thousands of memories: "I am a working girl, one of those striking against intolerable conditions. I am tired of listening to speakers who talk in generalities. What we are here for is to decide whether or not to strike. I offer a resolution that a general strike be declared—now."

A contagion of excitement swept the meeting, people screaming, stamping feet, waving handkerchiefs. The chairman, Benjamin Feigenbaum, stood on the platform trying to restore order, and when finally heard, asked for a second. Again pandemonium, the whole crowd shouting its second. Shaken by this outburst, Feigenbaum cried out: "Do you mean it in good faith? Will you take the old Jewish oath?" Thousands of hands went up: "If I turn traitor to the cause I now pledge, may this hand wither from the arm I raise!"

Week after week the strike went on. Most shops were closed, a few tried to use scabs. The Jewish socialists threw themselves into the day-to-day work. The Women's Trade Union League sent help to the picket lines, sharing blows and abuse with the Jewish and Italian girls. Lillian Wald and Mary Simkhovitch did publicity. Wealthy New York women such as Mrs. Oliver Belmont and Anne Morgan, sister of the banker, provided bail money. Wellesley students donated $1,000 to the strike fund. In the first month alone, 723 girls were arrested and 19 sent to the workhouse; the average daily bill for bail came to $2,500. Sentencing a striker, Magistrate Olmstead declared: "You are on strike against God and Nature, whose firm law is that man shall earn his bread in the sweat of his brow." About which Bernard Shaw, in reply to the Women's Trade Union League, wired: "Delightful. Medieval America always in the intimate personal confidence of the Almighty."

Nothing in the strike was as remarkable as the girls themselves. Some turned out to be natural leaders, fighting with great boldness, even ferocity. "Into the foreground," wrote an observer, "comes the figure of one girl after another as her services are needed. With

Young women on strike. Photograph by George Bain.
LIBRARY OF CONGRESS, BAIN COLLECTION

Lending support to striking salesgirls, 1916. Left to right: Mrs. J. Sargent Cram, Fannie Webber, Rose Stern, and Bertha Newman. UNITED PRESS INTERNATIONAL

extraordinary simplicity and eloquence, she will tell before any kind of audience, without any false shame and without self-glorification, the conditions of her work, her wages, and the pinching poverty of her home."

A young reporter for the *New York Sun*, McAlister Coleman, went down one morning to the garment center. It changed his sense of things forever,

> to watch a picket line form in front of a struck shirtwaist-factory.
>
> The girls, headed by teen-age Clara Lemlich, described by union organizers as a "pint of trouble for the bosses," began singing Italian and Russian working-class songs as they paced in twos before the factory door. Of a sudden, around the corner came a dozen tough-looking customers, for whom the union label "gorillas" seemed well-chosen.
>
> "Stand fast, girls," called Clara, and then the thugs rushed the line, knocking Clara to her knees, striking at the pickets, opening the way for a group of frightened scabs to slip through the broken line. Fancy ladies from the Allen Street red-light district climbed out of cabs to cheer on the gorillas. There was a confused melee of scratching, screaming girls and fist-swinging men and then a patrol wagon arrived. The thugs ran off as the cops pushed Clara and two other badly beaten girls into the wagon.
>
> I followed the rest of the retreating pickets to the union hall, a few blocks away. There a relief station had been set up where one bottle of milk and a loaf of bread were given to strikers with small children in their families. There, for the first time in my comfortably sheltered, Upper West Side life, I saw real hunger on the faces of my fellow Americans in the richest city in the world.

The strike dragged on until mid-February 1910, and was finally settled with improvements in working conditions but without the formal union recognition for which the ILGWU had held out. A victory or defeat? In the eyes of some intransigent leaders, probably a defeat; in retrospect, a liberating event for the Jewish workers. By the strike's end, Local 25 had grown to ten thousand members. In the immigrant world, the shirtwaist makers had created indescribable excitement: These were our daughters. The strike came to be called "the uprising of the twenty thousand," and the phrase should be taken as more than socialist or Jewish rhetoric, for it was indeed an uprising of people who discovered on the picket lines their sense of dignity and self. New emotions swept the East Side, new perceptions of what immigrants could do, even girls until yesterday mute. *"Unzere vunderbare farbrente meydlekh"* ("our wonderful fervent girls") an old-timer called them.

WHEN I GOT OFF THE TRAIN, I was met at the station by a committee of rough-looking men, two of whom carried sawed-off guns. The mobsters informed me that I would not be permitted to speak. I carefully explained that as an American citizen, my rights to speak were guaranteed by both the federal and state constitutions. My remarks were either not understood or were utterly and completely disregarded. They were determined that I was to remain silent. I was equally determined to conduct the meeting as planned. I walked about a mile and a half to the residence of the local judge. He listened attentively, and when I was all through telling him about my rights as a citizen, I was informed that I must wait until an overt act had been committed by the gangsters before he would interfere.

When I saw that I could get no legal assistance, I proceeded to the hall in which the meeting was scheduled to take place. Among the people who were standing around the front of the building, I recognized my friends with their sawed-off guns. Now instead of there being six, there were an even dozen. They were planted in front of the building and refused to permit anyone to enter the hall. None of the natives were courageous enough to brave the muzzles of those guns.

I was determined that I would speak in Spring Valley in spite of the unlawful and brutal steps that were taken to prevent it. I looked about and discovered a conveniently branched tree near the entrance of the hall. I climbed into the sheltering limbs and delivered my speech to the assembled listeners. Some told me afterward that I had been foolhardy and taken my life in my hands unnecessarily. I thought otherwise. I knew that gangsters were cowards.

Of course I did not succeed in organizing a branch of the union that night. Yet my speech, and the way it was delivered, heartened the workers who were present, and they served as self-appointed messengers to sing my praises and that of unionism. It was not long before a branch of the union was established in Spring Valley and a strike was called against Max Roth.

Abraham Rosenberg, an early president of the International Ladies' Garment Workers Union, wrote a stirring account in his Yiddish memoirs of the 1910 general strike of cloak makers.

ABRAHAM ROSENBERG

THE PRESS THROUGHOUT THE country carried long articles about the coming strike in New York. Only the New York cloak manufacturers maintained a front of innocent calm. They didn't believe workers would leave the shop for the union.

Our historic Madison Square Garden meeting was set for [Tuesday] June 28 at eight in the evening. But by three o'clock in the afternoon streets in the neighborhood of the Garden were flooded with thousands of workers. The committee was compelled to open the Garden doors at five o'clock. In fifteen minutes, the huge hall with its galleries was packed to choking.

The committee stationed eight trucks in the street from which speakers could address the masses. The next day the press reported the streets had been jammed by forty thousand workers unable to get into the hall. New York had never before seen such a demonstration.

The enthusiasm at the meeting defies description. Each one felt this was the start of a new era for the labor movement—of a new life for the cloak makers.

On Wednesday morning, the sixth of July, the committee of three met. They fixed the time for the general strike at exactly 2:00 P.M., Thursday, July 7.

The same day the committee wrote [a] strike call in English, Yiddish, and Italian. It directed that it be printed on blood-red paper. . . .

Shortly before two o'clock, members of the strike committee, along with many newspapermen, went into the cloak district to see how well the cloak and skirt makers would respond to their union's call to strike. When the clock showed ten minutes after two we could still not see a single soul. Cahan turned to one of our men and asked, "Well, so where are your strikers, already?" The other's heart sank.

But in that same minute, a wave of humanity began to form, coming from distances on all the side streets, turning into Fifth Avenue, heading downtown. With every minute, the mass grew larger, coalescing in one direction. By half past two, all the streets in New York from Thirty-eighth Street down, east and west, were crowded with thousands of workers. In many streets all cars and freight wagons were halted by the crush of the crowds.

I do not know if many people have ever before witnessed such a scene. Many of our devoted members wept tears of joy seeing their long years of work and sacrifice crowned with success. To me it seemed that such a spectacle had happened before only when the

Jews were led out of Egypt—and now, as then, even their riffraff marched in the exodus.

Thousands of marchers passing the union office on Tenth Street shouted slogans and greetings. The city was in turmoil. Workers in other trades left their shops to see the amazing sight. So did businessmen. In a word: The entire population of the city was out in the streets.

Nothing that ever happened in the Jewish immigrant world was more tragic, more terrible, than the 1911 fire at the Triangle Shirtwaist Company at the edge of Washington Square. In the eighteen minutes that it took to bring the fire under control, it was alleged that 175 workers, most of them young Jewish and Italian girls, were burned to death. Amid charges that the company management had been negligent, the nerves of the East Side broke. Nothing could quench the grief of the Jewish community. It broke into scenes of hysteria, demonstrations, mass meetings, as if its burdens were simply too much to bear.

FORWARD, 3/26/'11

MORGUE FILLED WITH OUR CASUALTIES!
175 Workers Lose Their Lives in a Burning Shirtwaist Factory.

The three top floors of a ten-story building on Washington Place, where the Triangle Waist Co. has its shops, destroyed by flames. Firemen with their ladders cannot reach the poor workers perched on windows trying to save themselves. Many holding on to the windows forced to jump as the fire reaches their hands and they fall from up high to their deaths. 141 dead in morgue. 56 bodies unidentifiable. Mothers and relatives weep and wail at site of tragedy.

175 workers—men, women and children—perished yesterday by fire that broke out at 33 Washington Place. Many were consumed by the fire, and many fell from the windows.

The fire broke out at 5:30 P.M. just after the quitting bell rang. The building is ten stories high. The top three are occupied by the "Triangle Waist Company," and the fire started in that factory.

The flames spread very fast. A stream of fire tore up through the elevator shaft and stairways to the upper floors. Fire instantly appeared at all windows, and tongues of flames crept higher and higher along the walls to where little groups of terrified girls, workers, stood in confusion.

The fire grew stronger, fiercer, bigger. The workers on the top floor could no longer tolerate the heat, and one after the other, jumped from the 8th, 9th, and 10th floors to the sidewalks where they piled up dead. And when a mound of dead had already accumulated the first fire truck arrived.

The firemen were helpless to deal with the fire. Ladders reached only to the 7th floor. The firemen stood about forlorn and stared as one woman after another fell from the burning building.

The first to jump were women. The men hung on longer.

And below, screaming and howling, thousands of laborers from surrounding factories. At the 8th floor window appears a young man and a young woman. He holds her tightly by the hand. Behind them, the red fire. The young man lets go. She springs. She hits the sidewalk hard.

The next instant he jumps and his body falls hard next to hers.

After the fire.
April 7, 1911.

IMUSEUM OF THE CITY
OF NEW YORK

"The Morgue Filled With Our Sacrifices . . . the Whole Jewish Community in Mourning."—Jewish Daily Forward, March 26, 1911.

Rose Schneiderman, by now one of the oustanding women trade unionists in the country, spoke at a memorial meeting for the victims of the Triangle fire. Here are a few of her words:

ROSE SCHNEIDERMAN

THE OLD INQUISITION had its rack and its thumb-screws and its instruments of torture with iron teeth. We know what these things are today: The iron teeth are our necessities, the thumbscrews are the high-powered and swift machinery close to which we must work, and the rack is here in the firetrap structures that will destroy us the minute they catch fire. . . .

This is not the first time girls have been burned alive in this city. Every week I must learn of the untimely death of one of my sister workers. Every year thousands of us are maimed. The life of men and women is so cheap and property is so sacred! . . .

I can't talk fellowship to you who are gathered here. Too much blood has been spilled. . . . It is up to the working people to save themselves.

188 *The history of Jewish socialism did not, of course, follow the hopes or predictions of its early leaders. Beginning as a mass movement in the early years of the century, it reached a climax with the election of Meyer London to Congress from the East Side in 1914 and the powerful campaign of Morris Hillquit for the mayoralty of New York City in 1917. The movement then came upon rocky times in the 1920s. Factionalism, prosperity, Communist rivalries, the gradual domestication of the Jewish trade unions—all led to socialist decline until, in the thirties, with the rise of the New Deal, the Jewish socialist movement largely dissolved itself into the larger stream of liberalism.*

On November 4, 1914, the day after the election, the Forward *ran an ecstatic account of Meyer London's victory, from which we take a few passages.*

FORWARD, 11/4/'14

ABOUT FIFTY THOUSAND PERSONS gathered yesterday in the park across from the *Forward* building. They'd started gathering toward evening, and the human sea grew from minute to minute. It is no exaggeration to say that most persons were primarily concerned about election returns in the Twelfth Congressional District. . . .

Returns from this district arrived late—only around 9:00 P.M. did the counting begin. . . .

When the first returns, from one polling district, appeared on the canvas on the *Forward* building, Meyer London was ahead of Goldfogle. The crowd of fifty thousand let out a thundering "Hurrah" that shook surrounding streets. . . . By 11:00 P.M. we just about knew that London was elected. . . .

Then the *Tageblatt* came out with a special edition announcing Goldfogle's victory. The crowd grew angry. They saw through the cheap bluff of the *yarmulkah* newspaper. . . .

By 2:00 A.M. there was no longer any doubt that London had been chosen. We announced this with an extra.

At that time over ten thousand were gathered at the *Forward* building. They took to singing and dancing for joy. They fell upon each other with kisses. People who didn't even know each other kissed. . . .

From the *Forward* office an orchestra appeared that, with the strains of the "Marseillaise," announced the joyous socialist news in the streets of the Jewish quarter.

The crowd outside waited for London to speak. Someone called out: "Abe Cahan is in the editorial room of the *Forward*. He should speak."

The crowd began calling for Cahan to give a speech.

When Cahan appeared at the windows of the first floor he was greeted with stormy applause that lasted minutes. Cahan spoke briefly. He said that the first socialist victory in New York will have tremendous significance. The first socialist congressman comes from the Jewish quarter of New York, from the very heart of the Jewish people of a metropolis. The initial victory will bring others.

Then a few comrades informed London that a crowd of ten thousand awaited him in front of the *Forward* building. London was quite tired, but he arrived by automobile. The crowd gave him a hearty ovation and made way for the automobile. But nearing the building he was surrounded and could go no farther. . . . Speaking from atop the car London thanked his comrades and the socialist press for their successful efforts. . . . He concluded: "My only wish is now that I should have enough spiritual and physical powers to carry on the great struggle for the liberation of the working class. Organize, friends. Build strong unions. Join the Socialist party and carry on the fight for freedom till the final victory.

Moving scenes took place before the *Forward* building until 8:00 A.M. From there the gigantic crowd dispersed to go to work in the shops.

"An Historic Evening in the Jewish Section . . . Meyer London, the First Jewish Socialist Elected to Congress"—Jewish Daily Forward, *November 5, 1914.*

And finally, a credo of Jewish socialism Morris Hillquit wrote in his autobiography toward the end of his life.

MORRIS HILLQUIT

I AM A SOCIALIST because I cannot be anything else. I cannot accept the ugly world of capitalism, with its brutal struggles and needless suffering, its archaic and irrational economic structure, its cruel social contrasts, its moral callousness and spiritual degradation.

If there were no organized socialist movement or socialist party, if I were alone, all alone in the whole country and the whole world, I could not help opposing capitalism and pleading for a better and saner order, pleading for socialism.

By violating my conscience, I might have made peace with the existing order of things and found a comfortable place among the beneficiaries of the system. I might have joined one of the political parties of power and plunder and perhaps attained to a position of influence and "honor." I might have devoted my life to the acquisition of wealth and possibly accumulated a large fortune. But my apparent success would have been dismal failure. I should have felt dissatisfied and mean. I should have been deprived of all the joys of life that only an inspiring social ideal can impart, of the pleasure and comradeship of the best minds and noblest hearts in all lands, and, above all, of my own self-respect.

Having chosen and followed the unpopular course of a socialist propagandist, I am entirely at peace with myself. I have nothing to regret, nothing to apologize for.

"3 Socialists in Congress"—Jewish Daily Forward, November 4, 1914.

7

EDUCATION

Learning English at the Cooper Union.

Educating the Immigrants

The hunger of the Jews for education is legendary. Its origins go back to the experience of an oppressed and scattered people trying to maintain its distinctiveness through a scholarship of sacred and recondite books. The encounter with America enabled large numbers of Jews, for the first time, to gain access to secular learning, an opportunity many jumped at for its own sake, out of a pure-spirited desire to "catch up" with Western thought and culture. Many more took advantage of this opportunity in a pragmatic spirit, seeing education as a stepladder to economic improvement.

But if the hunger of the Jews for education is legendary, we should also remember that for many immigrants it was impossible to satisfy that hunger. The truth is that few of the adult immigrants could manage to acquire much formal learning—that they usually had to leave to their children. What they picked up—smatterings and tatters, bits and pieces—they got from the Yiddish press, itself often half educated and not too reliable a source; from the innumerable lectures, wildly varying in quality, sponsored by Jewish political and cultural groups; and from occasional ventures into night schools, too often brief, erratic, and ill-conducted.

We begin this section with Abe Cahan of the Forward *exhorting his readers to learn English; then a* Forward *report on night school conditions; and finally two reminiscences of what it was like to teach and learn.*

FORWARD, 1/3/'10

THE FORWARD "MAILBOX" receives numerous letters from immigrants who have cut off their beards and forgotten the name of their birthplace in Russia but they are helpless because they still don't know English. It is understandable: when your stomach is empty and your head full of worry about making a living, you're not going to think about studying. But just as their muteness has a cause, it has results—they could get a better job if they knew English. Other immigrants, who do have a chance to study, keep procrastinating: tomorrow, next summer, next winter. Many Jews who have been here ten to fifteen years still don't have their first papers. Russian comrades who were active at home have not joined the party or a union here. . . . There are many intelligent people who spend their lives in a candy store on Ludlow Street, or a paper stand, wasting away. . . . This is unforgivable neglect. . . . A principal of an evening school told our reporter that at the beginning of the season there is heavy registration, but that after a while they begin to stay away. One misses an evening, another a whole week. By the end of the term only 50 percent are left.

FORWARD, 11/6/'09

WE HAVE RECEIVED A LETTER from a night school principal asking us to remind our readers that the new school season is beginning, and urging them to go to night school to learn English, arithmetic, etc.

Unfortunately, we cannot at this time exult over the vital institution of night schools, because until now they have just not been satisfactory. Only a small fraction of the tens of thousands of Jewish boys and girls who thirst after knowledge attend. Why? The board of education is not taking them seriously; when its budget decreases, it saves on night schools; many teachers are incompetent, and courses are not adapted to older students. Students of varying abilities are lumped together in a class. Day schools have homogeneous groups, such as the special classes for retarded. Night school students are varied: Some are highly educated and speak several European languages; others have never read a book.

Night school teachers are negligent because the board of education is negligent. They know that nobody will check on them; they are only held responsible for trivialities such as keeping an attendance record. The students, treated like children, are unhappy and frustrated.

The principal who wrote us the letter has his school on the corner of Forsythe and Hester streets. He has tried to better his school, and we wish him luck.

Our city fathers believe that greenhorns will be satisfied with any kind of schooling. But they forget that immigrant students, who are so eager to learn, cannot be fooled.

GREGORY WEINSTEIN

TO MEET MY OBLIGATIONS, I applied for the position of evening school teacher under the board of education. My labors in school were very interesting to me. My class would start with a register of sixty to seventy pupils. Quite a number would soon get tired of sitting on the windowsills or on the radiators and would drop out. I had no problem in keeping order, but I found it hard to keep some of them awake, because nearly all came to school tired out after a hard day's work. But they were keen to learn and they did make rapid progress in spelling and reading. The flexibility of the English tongue and its idiosyncrasies were a wonder to them. Such expressions as "Post No Bills," "Watch Your Pocket," or "Pocket Your Watch," were puzzling to them, as they had been to me in my first years.

I had one amusing incident in my class. The principal once dropped into my classroom with a cheery "Good evening, gentlemen." All arose and responded, "Good evening, Mr. Principal." He then asked the pupils, "Are you making any headway?" Almost with one accord they answered, "No, sir." The principal looked at me quizzically, and wrote the question on the blackboard. "Now," he asked, "translate the word headway." *"Kopfweh"* ("headache"), they answered. The principal smilingly said, "I now understand why you are making no headway."

Teaching night school after a day's work was rather tiring for me, but the respectful attitude toward the teacher which my pupils had brought over from abroad and their appreciation of the teacher's efforts were compensating elements. I kept on teaching for five years and resigned only because the school work deprived me of all other social contacts.

ABRAHAM CAHAN

I ENROLLED in a public evening school. I threw myself into my new studies with unbounded enthusiasm . . . the teacher, a young East Side dude . . . was of German descent. He would either address us wholly in [English] or intersperse it with interpretations in labored German which, thanks to my native Yiddish, I had no difficulty in understanding . . . At first I did not like him. Yet I would hang on his lips, watching intently, not only his enunciation but also his gestures, manners, and mannerisms, and accepting it all as part and parcel of the American way of speaking.

. . . One can tell the nationality of a stranger by his gestures as readily as by his language. In a vague, general way I had become aware of this, probably from contact with some American-born Jews whose gesticulations, when they spoke Yiddish, impressed me as utterly un-Yiddish. And so I studied [the evening school teacher's] gestures almost as closely as I did his words. . . . One of the things I discovered was the unsmiling smile. I often saw it on the principal of the school, for instance, who was an Anglo-Saxon. In Russia, among the people I knew at least, one either smiled or not. Here I found a peculiar kind of smile that was not a smile. "They laugh with their teeth only," I would say to myself. . . .

Studying after work. Drawing by B. Rivkin for **The Big Stick.**
YIVO INSTITUTE FOR JEWISH RESEARCH

ONE EVENING I asked my evening school teacher to tell me the "real difference" between "I wrote" and "I have written." He had explained it to me once or twice before, but I was none the wiser for it.

"What do you mean by *real* difference?" he demanded. "I have told you, haven't I, that 'I wrote' is the perfect tense, while 'I have written' is the imperfect tense." This was in accordance with the grammatical terminology of those days.

"I know," I replied in my wretched English, "but what is the difference between these two tenses? That's just what bothers me."

"Well," he said grandly, "the perfect refers to what *was*, while the imperfect means something that *has* been."

"But when do you say 'was' and when do you say 'has been'?"

"You're a nuisance," was his final retort.

I was tempted to say, "And you are a blockhead." But I did not, of course.

We come to a subject almost mythical—the unquenchable and all-but-universal passion of the immigrants to provide their children with education. In thousands of Yiddish-speaking homes the word lernin *("to learn") was spoken with tones of reverence. Enormous sacrifices were made to send children to high school and college— in later years, to graduate school. Religious Jews, secular Jews, and Jews both a little religious and a little secular—all shared this worship of the possibilities of mind.*

What, one wonders, did immigrant parents make of it all? Obviously it wasn't always pure spirited; surely at times it was entangled with worldly ambitions for social success. After a time, the mystique of education seemed to take on a life of its own, something that had seized the imagination of the Jews and would not let go. Only analytically, in talking about it, can one distinguish among their motives; in actual life, things were so complicated, desires so interwoven, that no such distinctions could readily be made. Love for the workings of thought ran deeply through the Jewish tradition, and while the bulk of the immigrants were skimpily educated, still, they respected those who were and wanted their children to become so.

SAMUEL CHOTZINOFF

IT WAS OUT OF THE QUESTION for me to begin school without a pencil box and some other less important "supplies" that beckoned through the window of the candy store on our block. Those others ranged from plain and colored blotters to school bags in the shape of knapsacks. Though I pleaded hard for a two-storied pencil box costing a quarter, my mother bought me a plain, oblong casket with a sliding top for ten cents. When our shopping was done, my supplies consisted of the pencil box, four writing pads at a penny each, and a set of colored blotters costing a nickel, the last wrung from my reluctant parent after I had conjured up a classroom crisis in which the teacher would call for a show of blotters and I would be the only pupil unable to produce any. My mother had a horror of nonconformity, a failing I early spotted and often exploited.

On the first Monday in September my mother took me and my scanty supplies to school, where I was enrolled, and given a desk and a seat in a large classroom. The teacher, a gray-haired, middle-aged lady, told us to call her Miss Murphy. I wondered if she meant to imply that this was to be her name in class and that at home she was called something else. The name sounded alien and therefore forbidding, and might have been chosen to emphasize the natural barrier between teacher and pupil. She was obviously a pagan—a *creetch*—our name for any non-Jew. Miss Murphy read out our last names from a long paper in front of her, and we raised our hands to signify our presence. She was severely distant, and her impersonal attitude, added to the formality of being called by our last names, cast a chill on the classroom. Soon one began to long for the sound of one's first name as for an endearment that would, at a stroke, establish a human relationship between oneself and Miss Murphy. But it was not to be. By the following morning Miss Murphy, having already memorized the surnames of her entire class, called the roll without once referring to her paper.

She then went to the blackboard and in beautiful script wrote *"Catt"* and, looking over the sea of heads in front of her, said: "Something is wrong with the spelling of this word. Katzenelenbogen, stand up and tell me what is wrong." A small skinny boy rose in the back of the room and said something in an indistinct voice. "Speak up, Katzenelenbogen!" Miss Murphy sharply commanded. My heart went out to Katzenelenbogen in his ordeal. I was conscious of the disparity between the long and important-sounding name and the frailty and insignificance of its possessor. Miss Murphy, however, could not be blamed for adhering to a long-established practice in all public schools. . . .

Miss Murphy lived in Brooklyn, an hour's journey by the Grand Street horsecar to the East River, the ferry to cross it, and another horsecar on the other side. She therefore always brought her lunch with her. This consisted, much to our surprise, of one sandwich of jam, the bread remarkably white and of the texture of cotton, and

Girls on their way to P.S. 4, Pitt and Rivington streets.
COURTESY OF COMMUNITY SERVICE SOCIETY OF NEW YORK

one thin slice of sponge cake, each wrapped in tissue paper, and both done up in brown wrapping paper and tied with cord. It seemed to all of us rather meager nourishment for a strong-minded, powerful woman. But I had heard it said that Christians in general ate sparingly, the women especially showing a marked distaste for food. The men, on the other hand, were partial to drink, as could be verified by visiting the Bowery around the corner from the street I lived on. When she dismissed her class at noon, Miss Murphy would ask one of her pupils to run out and buy her a bottle of milk, and we soon began to regard this errand as a privilege and a special mark of favor. Yet she was careful to rotate us, and by the end of the term every boy in the class had bought her a bottle of milk. She had a way of saying: "Would you hand me my *puhss?*" which we thought elegant. When the pocketbook was handed to her, she would extract a coin from it delicately with her thumb and forefinger, the little finger stretched out as if she was about to bring forth something precious or highly dangerous. She ate her lunch privately, seated at her desk. Even with no one to see her, one could be sure that she ate her jam sandwich with the decorum of Chaucer's "Nonne, a Prioresse," and "let no morsel from her lippes falle."

FORWARD, 9/27/'10

A TEACHER HAD PROBLEMS with a boy in her class who did not follow instructions, such as putting away pencils and opening readers. He was a quiet, good boy and did his homework. After trying all methods, she resorted to whipping him. She did it every day, to no avail. When he was promoted to the higher grade, she told the new teacher about her problem. The new teacher decided to call his mother, and found out he was a little deaf, and simply did not hear what was said to him.

The mother herself didn't have the brains to tell the school about her child's condition, and the boy had to suffer every day.

Jewish mothers on the whole never come to school to talk to the teachers, and this is very wrong. The board of education is waging a campaign to get mothers to come to school, but is not successful in the Jewish districts. Many mothers are afraid to come to school; they think the teachers call them in order to punish them. A mother knows her child better than the teacher, and can help him a lot. . . .

JEWISH WOMEN REGARD the schools as strange institutions; if they don't know English they are ashamed to come, afraid they will be laughed at. These women shouldn't care even if they are laughed at; the fate of their children is more important. Furthermore, teachers are refined and treat everybody courteously. Most teachers are Jewish girls anyway, whose parents don't know English. These teachers will talk to you in Yiddish.

Honor to whom honor is due—a citizen's dinner for Joseph Barondess (1863–1928), immigrant Jewish socialist and East Side community leader.

YIVO INSTITUTE FOR JEWISH RESEARCH

FORWARD, 5/6/'02

A HIGH SCHOOL TEACHER had the following talk with your editor about Jewish children in New York schools. "All the teachers are amazed by their ability," he said. "The best minds in each class are Jewish. The children show the greatest interest in their studies. Jewish boys, however, are disrespectful and untidy; non-Jewish boys conduct themselves better."

The teacher cited the children's behavior during Passover. Many of them brought *matzo* and onions for lunch. When they finished, the floor was covered with onions and crumbs that greeted teachers

199

East Side Arbor Day orator, Leon Berman, May 1908. Photograph by George Bain. LIBRARY OF CONGRESS, BAIN COLLECTION

of the next class. Our guest said a German, American, or even an Irish boy would never do that.

Children of Jewish immigrants have ways, he went on, that are inappropriate to cultivated students. They gesticulate with hands and eyes, speak in talmudic singsong, and sway prayerfully. When teachers call on them they respond with noises, gestures, and uncontrollable laughter. He described wonderful pupils who recite their lessons with *yeshiva*-style outcries. "Too bad," he commented. "These children with manners would be gems."

Here in a 1910 Forward *piece by the Yiddish poet Morris Rosenfeld, a different problem is touched on: Jewish sensibilities at the time of Christian holidays. And then another* Forward *piece, from 1906, about difficulties in a Hester Street school: the more things change . . .*

FORWARD, 12/14/'10

FOR JEWISH CHILDREN Christmas is a sad season. Their heads droop. As their friends rejoice they must remain blind to the store windows winking their lights at every passerby.

. . . In America, where the wall between Christian and Jew is not so high, the Jewish child is exposed to Christmas more than anywhere else. Children attend the same schools under the same teachers and sing the same carols. . . .

If a child doesn't know why he's a Jew and not a Christian, at this time of year he feels like a blunderer in the wrong place, a stranger among friends with no world of his own. No spheres or spiritual firmament with stars and galaxies to light up his cosmic loneliness.

"Papa, what are we?"

"Jews."

"Why are we Jews?"

"Because we're not *goyim*."
"Why aren't we *goyim?*"
"Don't bother me."

No! No! No! That's no answer. Your "Don't bother me" pains the child more than before. Now he really has a claim to a Christmas tree! If your child doesn't know why he's a Jew, he has a right to know at least why he's not a *goy*. You must explain.

FORWARD, 1/16/'06

THE *FORWARD* HAS RECEIVED conflicting letters about conditions in the new Hester Street school. Some mothers are satisfied, others are not. . . .

Ostensibly the schools are for all children, and offer the same advantages and equipment. But as it turns out, the children who live in spacious apartments also have comfortable, roomy schools. The poor children, who live in congested homes, are packed like sardines in a box. The poorest neighborhoods, where the workers live, have the worst conditions.

In the Henry Street school (near Pike) there are eighty children in a classroom built for forty. One of the classrooms is dark and dingy; seventy children are packed in; the teacher is twenty years old, herself practically still a child. In Brownsville, Schools 147 and 43 on Siegel Street, there are seventy-five classes in a building equipped with thirty classrooms.

A teacher is so busy keeping order that she has no time to teach. The main subject is *Discipline*; obviously school authorities believe that poor children are incapable of becoming anything but clerks, so they must be taught to obey, not to think.

Education took place not only in schools—there were also libraries. In a library you were on your own; you could look with awe at the vast piles of books; you could venture into the forbidden; you could taste pleasures and excitements that you knew were more appropriate for later years. The library was a hangout, a social center, away from home, away from teachers. And many of those librarians were very nice—gentle, quiet, sympathetic.

SAMUEL TENENBAUM

IN OTHER NEIGHBORHOODS, the ice cream parlor, the poolroom, the dance hall were the favorite gathering places. In Brownsville, it was the library on Glenmore and Watkins avenues. There we got to know one another, there we argued about books and writers, there we made intellectual discoveries. We were first-generation ghetto immigrants. Our taste in literature did not come to us by family tradition; we ran across books and authors by chance, mostly by hit-and-miss. Hence, our password: "Do you know of a good book?" I "discovered" Jack London, Upton Sinclair,

Receiving books from the Brooklyn Public Library.
BROOKLYN PUBLIC LIBRARY,
BROOKLYN COLLECTION

Oscar Wilde, Bernard Shaw, H.G. Wells; and I am indebted to a friend, my high school teacher, who introduced me to Balzac, Romain Rolland, Zola, Anatole France, Maupassant.

A book such as *Jean Christophe* was kept hidden in a special alcove, carefully guarded by a vinegary librarian. I remember how she scrutinized me to see if I came up to specifications, whether I was of the right age and maturity. Never have I seen anyone—before or since—hand out a book more unwillingly and disapprovingly, as if she herself had somehow become an unwilling accomplice in a plot to undermine public morals. If the truth be told, many of my books seemed to come from that forbidden section, so that the librarian, even when I didn't ask her for a book, developed a special disapproving eye for me.

The library was something more than a place where one went for books. Here one met and made friends, those from high school, but even more important, those men and women who had little formal schooling, who worked in factories and were socialists, anarchists, Zionists, Macfaddenites, chiropractors, atheists, food faddists, sun worshipers, Buddhists; men and women who wanted so much from life: to be great writers, to be great humanitarian leaders, to be innovators of world-shaking importance.

In the files of the library, one can find today the reminiscences of a Brownsville librarian, which he published in a professional journal about forty years ago. Excerpts follow:

> . . . you are constantly beseeched for more books on sociology and for the best of the continental literature. Your reading room is full of young men preparing themselves for civil service and college-entrance examinations. Your reference desk is overtaxed with demands for material for debate on

every conceivable public question, from "equal pay for women" to the comparative merits of the library and the gymnasium. And there are more youngsters awaiting help in looking up every single allusion in their text-books than the assistants can serve . . . and what is better still, you have to be conservative and ever on your guard lest your reading public increase three times as fast as the library's resources. . . .

Their reading is an odd mixture of the serious and the childish. Their race tragedy often sobers them in appearance and taste early, and as is well known, they are very precocious. Sometimes a little toddler will come in whose head just reaches up to the registration desk and to the surprise of all . . . will read right off some paragraph given as a test. . . . Toward those books whose use some libraries restrict, the attitude of the adults is very liberal. No explanation completely satisfies them and their indignation rises high when they learn that libraries occasionally see fit to withhold certain volumes of Tolstoy, of Zola, or of Shaw.

Reading room at the Seward Park Library, across the street from the Educational Alliance. NEW YORK PUBLIC LIBRARY, SEWARD PARK BRANCH

KEHILLA, LIBRARY REPORT, 1913-14

MISS S. P. KENT, head librarian of the Rivington Street Branch, claims that for the year 1911, 265,405 volumes were taken out, 60 percent of which were drawn by children, 40 percent by adults. In point of numbers the order in which books were read was: fiction, first; sciences, second; literature, third. The percentages of foreign books taken out was 12 percent. Books on civics, American history in general, and local history pertained to city and state cannot be furnished quickly enough to satisfy the demands of the readers. This library, as well as others in this district, make it a point to keep in close contact with the evening and day schools, as well as with the several social centers in the neighborhood, and in that way the library is made known to those who frequent these centers. Miss Kent emphasized the fact that the books drawn were largely of a utilitarian character.

FORWARD, 5/7/'04

A THIRTEEN-YEAR-OLD GIRL returned two books and asked for others—a novel and something else. The novel must be a good one.

"Do you want Dickens's *Dombey and Sons?*" asked the librarian.

"I've read it," said the girl.

"Have you read Thackeray's *Adventures of Philip?*"

"Yes."

The librarian mentioned several other novels by first-rate authors, but the girl had read them all. When she suggested a novel by F. Marion Crawford, the girl was insulted. "That's not for me! I won't read that!"

Crawford is the most popular novelist in America today.

The thirteen-year-old is not an exception. Stand by the takeout desk and you will be amazed at the good taste of the young readers.

FORWARD, 10/4/'03

THE MANHATTAN PREPARATORY SCHOOL
201 East Broadway.
Evening classes from 7:00 to 10:30

Courses include: civics; economics; algebra B; German through 3rd year; United States history; French, 1st and 2nd year; advanced English and English composition; arithmetic, business arithmetic; Latin; physics, advanced physics; geometry; elementary English.

Sign painting studio, Baron de Hirsch Trade School, New York.   AMERICAN JEWISH HISTORICAL SOCIETY

MARCUS RAVAGE

THERE HAD LATELY BEGUN TO APPEAR a whole crop of evening preparatory schools on East Broadway. They were usually owned and manned by young East Siders who had recently graduated from the City College. I entered one of them simply in order to study English; but, once there, my ambitions expanded. I recalled my father's professional hopes for me, and conferred with my teachers about the possibility of preparing for a medical college. They encouraged me, and I agreed to pay fifty dollars for the forty-eight-point Regents course in monthly installments of five dollars each.

The institution occupied the remodeled top flats of two buildings on both sides of the street. The ground floor of one of them was occupied by a secondhand bookstore, and the basement of the other housed a butcher shop. The classrooms themselves were on off nights the meeting places of lodges and societies.

I used to travel across the street from algebra to English, and back again for German. The stoops and the halls and the stairways were always crowded with students, and during change of classes it was almost impossible to break through. I often wondered what would happen if there were a fire. At last the management rented a flat in a third building and turned it into a waiting room and study hall. The classes were overcrowded, so that, even with the best instructors, anything like a recitation was a practical impossibility.

The evening was divided into four periods, beginning at seven fifteen and ending at eleven o'clock. As there were four Regents examinations annually, our school year was arranged into four corresponding terms. Every course ran through a term. For instance, I took algebra three times a week for ten weeks and then went up to the Grand Central Palace and passed the examination along with high school pupils who had had the work five times a week for a year. I cannot tell you how we did it. I only remember that I would sit and puzzle over x's and y's from the time I got home at eleven o'clock until my eyes would give out; and at seven in the morning I would be back at the machine sewing shirts. I had registered late, and had missed the first two or three lessons. For a time the idea of algebra simply would not get through my head.

But even algebra was as nothing beside English. We were trying to cover the prescribed Regents requirements, in spite of the fact that the majority of us could hardly speak a straight English sentence. The formal grammar, which was the bugbear of nearly everybody in the class, did not worry me. The terms were the same as in Rumanian, and I had been well trained at home. But the classics! The nights and Sundays I spent on *L'Allegro* and *Il Penseroso*, looking up words and classical allusions, if I had devoted them as earnestly to shirtmaking, would have made me rich. And then I would go to class and the teacher would ask me whether I thought there were two separate persons in the poems, or just one person in two different moods. Bless my soul! I had not thought there were any persons in it at all.

Sewing Department of the Jewish Manual Training School, Chicago, 1892.
AMERICAN JEWISH HISTORICAL SOCIETY

For a small minority of Jewish boys, immigrants or the children of immigrants—by the 1930s, for a much larger number—City College was a mecca of intellect, the place to reach fulfillment, knowledge, success, perhaps even wisdom. In this experience of learning, no one was more important than Morris Raphael Cohen, the philosopher who for many years taught at City College and was regarded with a mixture of awe, fright, and admiration by generations of students.

Here Cohen and others remember their days at City College.

MORRIS RAPHAEL COHEN

... THE IDEA OF ADAPTING higher education to the needs of the great multitude who have to go to work relatively early in life—this made teaching at City College a challenge. Here was the front line of the struggle to liberalize education in a democracy. To make available to the poorest member of society the highest experiences of the human mind had been the driving objective of my early socialist dreams. Now, at last, I was privileged to play a significant role in that process.

That role I did not find an easy one. When I started to teach philosophy in City College I found myself devoid of the gift of verbal fluency, and so I naturally resorted to the use of the Socratic method: teaching by means of searching and provoking questions. The head of the department, who was not similarly handicapped— in fact he was exceptionally gifted as a lecturer—at first demurred.

"What do you do to make your students into fine fellows?" he once asked.

To which I replied, "I'm not a fine fellow myself, at least not so much better than my students that I can venture to impose my own standard on them."

And this I meant not by way of irony or false modesty but in all sincerity. As a son of immigrant parents I shared with my students their background, their interests, and their limitations. My students were, on the whole, relatively emancipated in social matters and politics as well as in religion. They did not share the Orthodoxy of their parents. And breaking away from it left them ready and eager to adopt all sorts of substitutes. Though many of their parents were highly learned, as was not uncommon among Russian Jews, my students had gone to American public schools, and the learning of their parents, being permeated so deeply with the talmudic tradition, was in the main foreign to them. City College offered a rich variety of courses in languages, literature, and science, but the curriculum allowed few courses in philosophy itself. I therefore saw no adequate opportunity for teaching philosophy along traditional lines. Instead I had to give courses primarily in related subjects, hoping to bring philosophic insight to my students through courses on the nature of civilization, the philosophy of law, and the topics covered by Santayana in the last four volumes of his *Life of Reason*.

Even when I essayed, in later years, to give more technical courses in philosophy, as in metaphysics and advanced logic, what gave life to the give-and-take of classroom discussions was the fact that these courses afforded an opportunity to press a thoroughgoing analysis of living ideas beyond the points where polite conversation generally stops. In later years when I faced more placid Western students who were less interested in bringing to light their own first principles, I came to realize more clearly how much student attitudes at the City College had contributed to the form of my teaching and of my thought.

Never having discovered for myself any royal road up the rocky and dangerous steep of philosophy, I did not conceive it to be part of my function as a teacher to show my students such a road. The only help I could offer them was to convince them that they must climb for themselves or else sink in the mire of conventional error. All I could do to make the climbing easier was to relieve them of needless customary baggage. This exposed me to the charge of being merely critical, negative, or destructive. I have always been ready to plead guilty to that charge.

It seemed to me that one must clear the ground of useless rubbish before one can begin to build. I once said to a student who reproached me for my destructive criticism: "You have heard the story of how Hercules cleaned the Augean stables. He took all the dirt and manure out and left them clean. You ask me, 'What did he leave in their stead?' I answer, 'Isn't it enough to have cleaned the stables?'"

Knocking logical errors and comfortable illusions out of young people's heads is not a pleasant occupation. It is much pleasanter to preach one's own convictions. But how could I hope, in a few weeks of contact with my students, to build up a coherent world view that should endure throughout their subsequent lives? And even if I had had the time, respect for the individual personality of the student before me would still have kept me from trying to impose my own world view on those whose temperament, tastes, and experiences were different from mine. Davidson had long ago cured me of the natural urge which so many men and women never outgrow to remake God and the universe in our own images. . . .

Judging by the unprecedented attendance and the eager response I received from my students, I seemed to have aroused genuine interest in philosophy not as a body of doctrine but as a liberation from superstitions, new as well as old. By challenging the opinions current among young people at the time—such as the uncritical acceptance of psychoanalysis, economic and other forms of materialist determinism, the complacent cult of progress, and other myths which parade as modern "science"—I think I succeeded in bringing to some of my students the realization that the problems of philosophy are matters of such vital importance that they have to be faced most seriously in every realm under penalty of otherwise falling into grievous and devastating error.

The new City College campus, circa 1910.

Whatever my failings as a teacher, I tried to tell my students what I thought they ought to hear, rather than what I thought they would like to hear. The process of demolishing youthful illusions would have hurt sensitive students keenly even if I had been more circumspect than I knew how to be in salving tender feelings. Actually I found the method of treatment by shock the most effective way of leading students to appreciate the nature and dimensions of ignorance. Though I had deep respect for the personality of the individual student, I lacked, except on rare occasions of good health, the courtesy of Socrates.

Joe Davidoff, City College Cager, 1931.
COURTESY OF THE ARCHIVES OF THE MORRIS RAPHAEL COHEN LIBRARY, CITY COLLEGE OF NEW YORK

STEVEN DUGGAN

... N O T E A C H E R C O U L D H A V E had a finer student body to work with. They were studious, keen and forthright. They did not hesitate to analyze any subject to its fundamentals regardless of tradition or age. The reverence paid to the Constitution did not prevent them from questioning the continuance of the anomaly of New York and Nevada each having two senators despite their enormous disparity in population, or whether the Supreme Court was a better judge of the "general welfare" than Congress, e.g., in deciding the first federal income tax unconstitutional. I allowed the freest discussion in my classroom and placed no restrictions upon a student putting forward views that were radical or unpopular. I did this from preference but I also discovered that untenable views were frequently demolished by the students themselves. I usually closed the discussion by presenting my own attitude on the subject, which ordinarily carried weight possibly because of the greater experience behind it. I do not hesitate to say that I learned a great deal as the result of the keen questioning of these young men. It was fatal to evade; one had always to be on the *qui vive*.

DAVID STEINMAN

T H E R E W E R E A T H O U S A N D in my class in 1900 when we started in Sub-Freshman B, and only 140 of us remained to graduate six years later.

My parents gave me five cents a day for lunch and all other expenses. Like many of my fellow students, I walked over a mile each way in going to college. I spent three cents a day for my lunch, and saved the rest for my dues in the Phrenocosmia Literary Society.

The course in metal work included forge work as well as machine shop work on the engine lathes. Many of my classmates were naturally more adept at these tasks, which taxed my puny strength. To make up for my shortcomings I worked many extra hours through long afternoons at the forge, grimly determined to succeed in the seemingly baffling task of accomplishing a successful weld. Mr. De Groodt later told me that this persistence and determination despite my handicap had won me the prize.

Norman Thomas
and four City College
disciples.

In my Junior year we had Professor Legras in differential
equations and in advanced theory of equations. It seemed decreed
that I was to carry off the prize, as month after month my marks
were regularly 100 percent. But one day, when Legras was reading
off the monthly marks, he paused at my name and announced a
mark of 99-3/4 percent. The class gasped. The professor then
launched into a lengthy disquisition, explaining that 100 percent
meant perfection and that there was a greater difference between
99-3/4 and 100 percent than there was between 90 and 99 percent.

I was obviously Legras's favorite. One day, as I was working out
an assigned problem at the blackboard, I noticed that my classmate
Elliot Noska at the neighboring blackboard was in distress. I
scribbled some equations on my board to help him. Legras detected
it and called Noska to his seat, giving him a zero. That mark would
have meant disaster for Noska, but a zero for me would mean
merely losing the Mathematics prize for the year. So a sacrifice play
was indicated. At the end of the period I went up to Professor Legras
and told him it was all my fault and pleaded with him to transfer the
zero to me. Legras could not bear to see me lose the prize, so he
excused both of us and Noska was saved.

I was growing not only in the affection of my classmates and the
friendship of my teachers, but also in physical stature. I had shot up
in height and taken on weight. One day—it was in my Junior
year—I came to college wearing long trousers. My classmates staged
a celebration.

Meyer Liben was one of the more gifted American Jewish writers who, in his stories about the life of his time, managed to avoid both sentimentalism and nastiness. His memoir of his days at City College, from which some excerpts follow, captures the excitements and yearnings of several generations of Jewish students.

MEYER LIBEN

. . . [O U R C I T Y C O L L E G E] alcoves were alive with lost causes—all that activism, fanatical intelligence, emotional invest-ment, never paid off in the great world. Power was not seized, society was not being transformed (except for the worse), the dream of justice (practical or millennial) was not being realized. The unemployment figures mounted, the Scottsboro boys stayed in jail, the New Deal hadn't come to power, international fascism was on the march, the heartland of America was not deeply impressed by the cries of the students; the country was not moving in the direction of peace, harmony, and justice, and resisted the analysis of Marx the way other lands in other times had resisted the thunderous anguish of Isaiah. Something stubborn, intractable, stood in the way, and that led to the problem of human nature. *There* was the great enemy to human progress. But human nature was created by its social surroundings. Change society and human nature would be changed. But societies *had* changed, and human nature remained the same—aggressive, murderous, selfish (present company ex-cluded). So ran another of the interminable arguments. It was before the flowering of Freudo/Marxism.

There is nothing so pure as a lost cause which has no power connection. In that way the Communists, heady with ideology, though making little headway, were not lost causers, because of the Soviet power base. The socialists were quite genuine lost causers, for their dream of a cooperative commonwealth had rough going in a land so recently seized from its native inhabitants and among a people so property-oriented, so money-oriented, so power-oriented (even the cooperative elements—unions, fraternal organizations, manufacturers' associations, teams, and groups of friends, cooperate in a competitive way). But the Art of the Possible had its adherents; voices were raised asking the students to pay some mind to the less glamorous intramural matters—to the college curriculum, for example! The radicals either disregarded such matters, or pinned on the label of Escapism, for preoccupation with curriculum, better teaching, a clean lunchroom, meant that you did not comprehend that the college was caught up in the world struggle, that you could not isolate one kind of problem from the other, and if you persisted, why then you were "confused," a common, if mild epithet. Undue preoccupation with curriculum, etc., was escapist, but taking sides, "involvement," in the Manchurian War was for real. . . .

The socialist struggle for a cooperative commonwealth, the Communist demand for a Soviet America (the Trotskyists had to transform both the Soviets *and* America), the hope and struggle of the liberals for a transformation of capitalism, spreading the benefits, strengthening civil liberties and minority rights—well, the situation was not hopeful, was not "ripe," in the Marxist way of putting it. America was a stony ground, there waved the banner of the Lost Cause (a curiously pessimistic phrase which assumes a future condition, rules out, with a crushing finality, the possibility of a victorious outcome). Most everyone was interested in the cause and cure of the surrounding social horrors, but few were deeply involved.

City College lunchroom alcoves.
CITY COLLEGE OF NEW YORK

M O R R I S   C O H E N—I summon up this man (about five foot seven), with his great head and brow, jutting chin, and his dancing eyes, which moved in the way of severity or approbation, as though to ask: "What do you *mean* by this?" or, as though to say: "Good, good, all will be well, continue the struggle, the truth will prevail."
. . . One recalls his famous probing, combative style—a kind of smiling struggle to the death. The room was electrified, we jumped to the defense of our fellow student, but our teacher took us all on, in a razzle-dazzle of knowledge, of analytic power, of fighting intellect. But truth was the quarry, and we were really fellow participants in the hunt. There was another style, a kind of entrancement—he stood at his ease, his eyes looked off, away from us; we recognized his mood in an instant, the timid ones straightened up, for he was not seeking us out, our ignorance was safe for the moment, he was bemused, following some wraith of

thought into the caverns of history and mind, as though he were alone, but for our sakes nevertheless.

THE MAIN THING ABOUT City College as I lived it is that it was a place where young people were learning, and where the process of learning had a certain excitement, and led to further learning, further growth. The particularities of a given time are less important than this process, which nevertheless lends the weight and drama which always makes the contemporary the most interesting. We learned from one another, we learned from our teachers, we learned from the world outside, we learned from our books and from ourselves. We did not all learn at the same rate, some were less interested than others, some were hardly interested at all. But for those who wanted it and were drawn to it, the world of knowledge and meaning and commitment and process was there for us to explore, and if you do not explore that world when young, you will never learn to explore it at all.

Night school in the Bronx.
TEACHERS COLLEGE LIBRARY,
BOARD OF EDUCATION PHOTOGRAPH COLLECTION

8

POLITICS

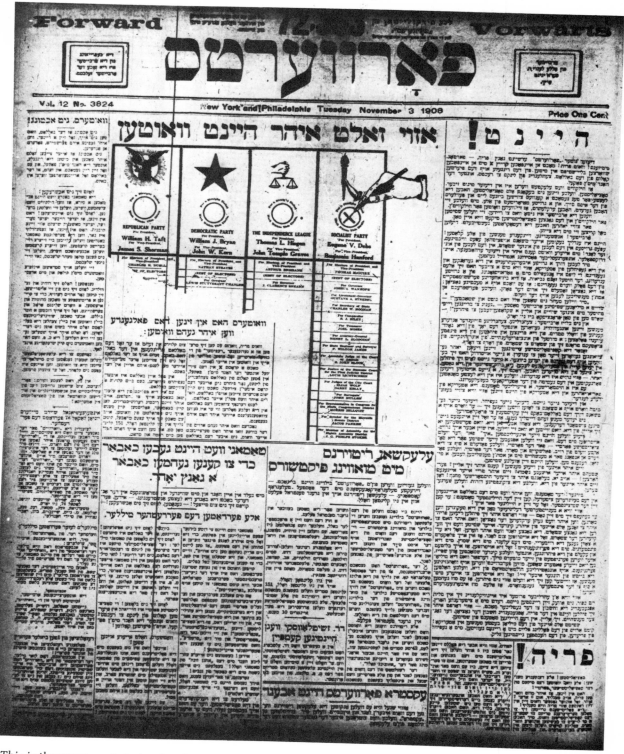

"This is the way to vote today."—election day edition of the Jewish Daily Forward.

JEWISH DAILY FORWARD

Tammany and the Jews

*The entry into American politics of the east European Jewish
immigrants was slow and awkward. They came to America at a
time—the last two decades of the nineteenth century, especially—
when our politics was marked by corruption, low morals, cynicism.
They had had little political experience in eastern Europe, certainly
nothing that would prepare them for the hurly-burly of American
democratic life. They were suspicious—and their history gave them
plenty of reason to be suspicious—of all governments. Some of
them, especially the religiously Orthodox, tended to look upon
politics as something that Jews should stay away from: something
dangerous, soiling, a prerogative of the Gentiles. Others, especially
the active minority of Yiddish-speaking socialists, regarded
American politics as vulgar, devoid of seriousness and ideas, a mere
device for manipulating the masses.*

*Still, the needs and opportunities of immigrant life soon tempted
the immigrants to venture into politics. Most were drawn to the
Democrats, while an articulate minority went to the burgeoning
socialist movement. It took several decades before the immigrants
could learn their way through, and around, the intricacies of ward
politics, the strange customs of Tammany Hall (part corruption,
part social services), the frigid structures of patrician reform.*

*We start with the voice of Abraham Cahan, the Yiddish writer
and editor, as in his memoirs he describes the 1884 national
election—the first one that the early immigrants from eastern
Europe witnessed. It is an account as notable for its innocence as
its shrewdness: the hubbub of American politics seen by a bright
but distant young radical from Vilna. Next comes an item from the
Commercial Advertiser detailing the half-comic carryings-on of
East Side politicians and hacks. And then parts of a memoir from
an old-timer, S.L. Blumenson, far less indignant than Abraham
Cahan, indeed, mostly amused in describing the sordid antics of
Tammany Hall as it tried to gain a foothold in the Jewish quarter.*

ABRAHAM CAHAN

I SPENT ALMOST MY ENTIRE first presidential election day walking the streets and watching the politicians operating and the people voting. There was as yet no secret ballot. The names of candidates were listed on printed sheets which were distributed not by officials sitting at the ballot boxes but by politicians who had posted themselves outside the polling places.

Each party printed its ballots or listed its candidates, and then friends of the candidates descended on citizens on their way to the voting places. With the same vigor that "pullers" of clothing stores on Canal Street show toward passing customers they persuaded them to vote for their candidates.

Votes were bought and sold in the streets. There was haggling in open view, as if it were fish and not votes that were being sold. Politicians posted themselves at the street corners and flashed bundles of dollars. I had seen this happening on a small scale during the 1882 and 1883 election days. Now the stakes were much greater and so too was the haggling.

I was pained by the ease with which corrupt politicians were able to persuade our uneducated Jews to sell their votes. There were no elections in the country from which we had fled. The ballot box and all it represented was the sacred hope for which many of our socialist comrades in Russia had martyred their lives.

COMMERCIAL ADVERTISER, 11/3/'98

WHILE H. J. GOLDSMITH, a lawyer, was making a speech last night from a wagon at the corner of Canal and Forsythe streets, he asked who was to be the next assemblyman from the district. Joseph Oppenheimer yelled back, "Charlie Adler!" Several others echoed the answer. As Goldsmith had expected to hear the name of Louis Jaffey, the Tammany candidate, this interruption created some confusion. Benjamin Sanftman and Frederick Paul, Tammany Hall men, grabbed Oppenheimer and led him toward the police station. On the way they met Samuel Pellman, a cloth dealer, 96 Canal Street, who remonstrated with the men for arresting his clerk, Oppenheimer. Sanftman and Paul let go of Oppenheimer and grabbed Pellman, who showed fight. In the scrimmage Sanftman was cut over the right eye.

Pellman was arraigned before Magistrate Flammer in the Essex Market Police Court this morning. When the magistrate learned that Pellman was arrested by Sanftman and Paul he discharged Pellman, saying that they had no right to arrest Pellman, not being officers of the law.

S. L. BLUMENSON

IT WAS UP TO MAX HOCHSTIM to keep the Tammany voters in line. He depended on the election district captains, all city employees, to deliver the vote—by hook or by crook. Their livelihoods were at stake. . . .

Hochstim spoke the language of the district, not the high-falutin English of the Fusion agitators who came downtown to address outdoor meetings. "Boys," said he, "we're in trouble. If we lose the election we lose our jobs. And jobs, you know, are hard to get right now." This was language the assembled could understand. "Them reformers have given us a bad name." Max had no use for reformers, nor was he afraid of them. (He had stepped down from the witness stand at the Lexow Committee hearings and tried to punch interrogator Frank Moss in the nose.) "We have to elect our aldermen to hold our jobs, or we don't eat."

GRAND   *ANNUAL*

OUTING

OF THE

MAX HOCHSTIM ASSOCIATION,

TO

DONNELLY'S BOULEVARD HOTEL,

COLLÉGE POINT, LONG ISLAND,

MONDAY, AUGUST 6th, 1894.

Steamer leaves foot of Broome St., East River, at Nine O'Clock, A. M., sharp.

TICKETS,   FIVE DOLLARS.

Max stopped to drink a glass of water, letting his comments sink in. Then he resumed: "We need an issue and we need a slogan that will give us the aldermen. The Second Assembly has come up with the slogan, 'A glass of beer on Sunday for the workingman.' This is all right for the Irish. It is not a slogan for Jews. We need a good issue, a good slogan to get out the Jewish vote. Anyone got ideas?"

The "counselor," Julius Melkin, arose in all his diminutive dignity. He pushed his pearl-gray derby to the back of his head (it wasn't safe to leave your hat lying about) and, addressing the visiting statesmen as "your honors," he cleared his voice and said: "I have a slogan. Jews have not been getting political jobs. Everything goes to the Irish. Where do you see a Jewish copper, a Jewish fireman, a Jewish street cleaner, a horsecar driver or conductor? To get out the vote we must demand our rights. What kind of blokes are we to keep taking it on the chin? I have the slogan which will get out the vote for Tammany: 'Jobs for Jews.'"

Everyone applauded. Julius was encouraged to proceed. "Why," he shouted . . . "we could even get Yussel Tunick next door to go along with us and get the radical vote. I have already discussed this with Mr. Chaim Rabinovitz and he agreed to help. You all know what the name of Chaim Rabinovitz means among the Orthodox voters. He is a good friend of Kathriel Sarahssohn, the owner of the *Tageblatt*, and you all know what influence the *Tageblatt* has among conservative voters. With the slogan 'Jobs for Jews—A Glass of Beer on Sunday,' the voters will flock to Tammany. *Subpoena duces tecum*—it can't fail."

Prolonged applause. Mr. Hochstim shook hands with Julius and congratulated him. Said Max: "Counselor, you are an asset to the party. We won't forget you." And then Max delivered the famous line which won the municipal elections for Tammany three years later.

"Boys," said Max, "we will beat them uptown bums yet. Get busy, go out and scratch. To *hell with Reform!*"

For a long time, the well-entrenched Irish machine of Tammany Hall retained its power on the East Side of Manhattan, even though the district was overwhelmingly Jewish. Shrewd and quick to adapt to new circumstances, the Irish party bosses began to share a modest portion of the spoils, but very little of the power, with Jewish mouthpieces, assistants, and errand boys. Not until the late twenties and early thirties did Jews begin to replace the Irish bosses in their own neighborhoods.

In 1908 a young Jewish lawyer, Henry Schimmel, walked into a Tammany "clubhouse" on 209 East Broadway and became a member of the John F. Ahearn Association. Schimmel worked first for Mr. Ahearn and later for his son Eddie. In 1973, looking back on the old days, Schimmel talked freely about the knack of the Ahearns for staying in power.

HENRY SCHIMMEL

MR. AHEARN KNEW WHAT TO DO to keep the Jews on his side. When the chief rabbi of New York died in 1902 and a mob of Irish factory workers began throwing bricks at the Jewish mourners, Mr. Ahearn instructed his men to move in and break their heads. When a peddler received a summons to pay a fine for violating a city ordinance, someone from the clubhouse was sent to court to straighten things out. When a widow with orphans needed coal in the winter or ice in the summer, Ahearn's men were there before anyone else.

All Democrats elected from the district were nominated by the Ahearns, and a Democratic nomination from the Fourth A.D. usually meant election. After I was elected to the state assembly in 1918, I was expected to show up regularly at the clubhouse and make myself available to the voters.

The Ahearns did a lot of good. John Ahearn was the first district leader in New York City to nominate an East Side Jew to run for municipal court judge. His son Eddie could always be counted on to get Jimmy Walker to do one of us a favor. They did for Jews what no Jew could do—until we grew stronger and finally replaced them.

"Big Tim" Sullivan, East Side Tammany boss and "friend" to the Jews.

Here is a description of the gradual absorption of Jews into American political life, taken from the Yiddish memoirs of Bernard Weinstein, a pioneer of the Jewish labor movement in America, who recalls the tensions between old party figures and the young Yiddish-speaking socialists.

BERNARD WEINSTEIN

WHEN TAMMANY and the Republicans on the East Side first saw the *tsitsilisten* coming into the streets to hold campaign meetings they went wild. Their toughs greeted socialist speakers with stones, blows and tin can music. When that didn't work pails of dirty water would be hurled from windows onto the socialist orators. . . .

The politicians of the two older parties on the East Side did not understand us socialists; yet they perceived us as a growing threat. They found out that we were starting unions. Their only consolation was that the Jewish workers were not yet citizens and were not allowed to vote. But they could become citizens, the politicians reasoned; something has to be done. Their attacks did not frighten us off; with each campaign we grew. Some of the older politicians offered a plan to appear as the true "friends of the workingman." If Jewish unions struck and workers were arrested, the politicians would use their pull to free them. . . .

By 1896 when the SLP head Daniel DeLeon was candidate for assemblyman in the Sixteenth District, conditions had changed. The socialist candidate with 2,300 votes almost won. . . . Christians and Jews all over the city showed great enthusiasm for socialist candidates. . . . The younger generation took to sympathizing with the socialists. We gained new forces, young children as campaigners, and that, as they say in America, takes the cake.

But it was still impossible to elect socialist candidates because . . . there were still too few Jewish workers who were citizens.

Inside and Outside

In 1893 Tammany Hall started to publish a small weekly, the Tammany Times, *which was distributed to the faithful at party headquarters, barbershops, etc. Despite its rather limited powers of expression, this weekly is an enormously revealing source for gathering a realistic picture of how Tammany hacks looked at Jews, blacks, socialists, and other sources of disturbance. Here are a few Tammany gems taken from the* Tammany Times, *1893 and 1894.*

TAMMANY TIMES, 8/27/'93

E A S T S I D E D I S T U R B A N C E S B E G A N last week in an attempt to wreck Walhalla Hall on Orchard Street, because its proprietor would not give it, rent-free, to a mob of socialistic and anarchistic Russian Jews who desired to hold a meeting in which to denounce capital and the "Capitalistic Press." . . . Every day the same restless and un-American element, which desires nothing better than to overthrow law and order, held dozens of meetings, which were harrangued and incited to violence by rabid anarchists of the Emma Goldman stripe. Police vacations were stopped and the police department took all necessary measures to strangle active anarchy at its first overt act. Never has the crowded East Side been so well policed. The biggest men, physically, of the entire force, were detailed on duty here, and their great size undoubtedly had a soothing effect on the undersized and puny rioters who were at the bottom of the trouble.

The Democratic Weekly of New York.

THE TAMMANY TIMES

Copyrighted 1891

Vol. III. No. 23.   New York, October 13, 1894.   Price, 10 Cents.

NATHAN STRAUS,
Democratic Candidate for Mayor of New York.

The front page of The Tammany Times featuring Nathan Straus, Tammany's first Jewish mayoral candidate. Embarrassed by anti-Tammany attacks, Straus eventually withdrew from the race.

TAMMANY TIMES, 9/24/'93

"REPECCA, YOU SHALL NOD SHPEAK mit dot Schake Silverstone vonce more," said Mose Schaumburg to his daughter.

"Oh, fodder, you preak mine heart. Ve vas almost engaged already. Vy shall I not shpeak mit Schake?" sobbed Rebecca.

"He have sheated me. He have sold me a paste diamont for a genuine stone."

"Oh, fodder, dot should recommend him to you as a son-in-law. If he can fool a vize man like you, tink vat a fortune he vill have in ter chewelry pishness."

"Vel, Repecca, you vas schmarder as I thought. Get married ven you like. I am anxchious to go in partnership mit mine son-in-law."

TAMMANY TIMES, 9/30/'93

THE AHEARN CLAN does not mind a little thing like a damp day, so when last Monday dawned muggy and misty, there was no postponement of the scheduled outing. By nine o'clock the clubhouse at No. 290 East Broadway was crowded, and when the march to the river began, there were at least two hundred braves in line. On arriving at the foot of Gouverneur Street, the steamer *Sirius* was found waiting, and in a few minutes the big boat was bearing up bravely, under its huge load of statesmen. . . . On the return to the city, in the evening, the association was met by the blare of tin horns and the glare of fire works; the streets back to the club were lined with people and enthusiasm.

DE LAWD BE PRAISED dat dar am no nigger wot am known by de kognomin ob Debs. Hit am de name wot hab hits offspring from his satinik majesty hisself. Debs am short for debbil, an' it am de human debbil wot is called Debs. Wot does he do? He ups an' proklaims de poah workin' man ter frow up his job an' strike! Dats wot he do.

To go from the Tammany Times *to the* Forward *is a dizzying leap, yet it spans the political experiences and attitudes of the immigrant Jews during the early decades of life in America. With its flair for ironic judgments of American politicians, indeed of America in general, the* Forward *kept hammering away at hypocrisies, deceits, lies, broken promises.*

FORWARD, 7/30/'02

JEWISH STREETS RESOUNDED yesterday with Tammany and Republican windbags bemoaning the fate of Jews insulted and beaten during the bloody pogrom precipitated by the funeral of Chief Rabbi Joseph yesterday. But during election time these same politicians work with all their might convincing the Jew to cast his vote for the two parties who "educate" the police to break the heads of the workers during a strike.

The Essex Market Police Court between Grand and Broome Streets, circa 1892. During the day the Tammany-appointed judge doled out justice; at night lodge brothers met upstairs.

NEW-YORK HISTORICAL SOCIETY

Dignitaries and a band opening the Rivington Street Public Bath, October 29, 1917.
MUSEUM OF THE CITY OF NEW YORK

FORWARD, 10/23/'03

LAST SATURDAY THE REFORMERS celebrated the opening of Seward Park with a big show—a rabbi and a priest; a mass of flags and policemen; uptown millionaires speaking and proletarian children parading. But disbelievers ask:

Why not in midsummer when the park opened?

Answer: The baths weren't completed.

Question: Why weren't the baths completed during the hot months?

Answer: Because of the strike by the building trades.

Question: Why didn't the City force its contractors to comply?

Answer: No answer.

FORWARD, 7/14/'04

AS IT IS, pushcart peddlers hate Commissioner Woodbury. Whenever he rides by in his red auto, they shake with fear. Now Woodbury is threatening to make every pushcart display a photograph of its owner just as though he were a criminal. The four associations of pushcart peddlers have decided to protest. The United Citizens Peddlers Association of Greater New York met at

85 Forsythe Street, where Sigmund Schwartz, the president, suggested that they march to city hall to protest against Woodbury. At city hall the mayor informed a delegation of ten that he is opposed to the photograph edict and has no intention of carrying it out. But Commissioner Woodbury threatens now to drive the pushcart peddlers off the streets: everything is to be sold under the bridge to make space for the firemen.

FORWARD, 7/24/'07

POLICE IN THE JEWISH QUARTER of New York are the most savage in America. It is not anti-Semitism; the policeman is taking advantage of a weakling, and nothing more. A loafer in uniform, the policeman is bored with doing nothing. Impatient waving his club without results, he wants to get his hands on human flesh.

HOUSEWIVES RIOT
OVER HIGH PRICES
Yesterday . . . four hundred women held a meeting in Rutgers Square and then went to City Hall to demand that the Mayor take action over high prices. Police dispersed the crowd. Some women were arrested and fined $1. Jewish Daily Forward, 2/21/17.

NATIONAL ARCHIVES,
U.S. WAR DEPARTMENT PHOTO

Reform and the Jews

*For the political reformers who kept appearing and reappearing in
American society, the Jewish immigrant community was a natural
object of interest. The reformers, mostly patrician Gentiles, though
with a smattering of well-to-do German Jews, were attracted by the
moral idealism, the social imaginativeness they found among the
immigrant Jews. Though not themselves socialists, the reformers
thought they might be able to strike up relations with the Jewish
socialists in behalf of immediate ends. But not until the thirties,
when Franklin Roosevelt gained the support of most Jewish
socialists for his welfare measures and social reforms, was such an
alliance possible. Before then, there were clashes of ideology,
temperament, and style. Those Jewish socialists who were practical-
minded trade unionists found that in their day-to-day work, if only
to protect the unions, they sometimes had to establish relations
with the dominant Tammany power in New York politics. The
more ideological among the Jewish socialists looked with scorn
upon the reformers as people who simply wanted to pretty up an
unjust social system. In turn, the uptown reformers could not
adjust themselves to the turmoil, the noise, the rhetoric, the
passion of the immigrant Jews. Most of the reformers tended to be
refined gentlemen appalled by the roughhouse methods and
amiable corruption of Tammany Hall. But in some ways Tammany
could speak to the Jewish immigrants as the WASP reformers could
not. For, whatever else, Tammany was utterly plebeian; its leaders
understood the needs of poor people and used a little of what they
gained while in office to provide some help—social services, we
would later call them—for those who had voted them into office.
Tammany ward captains made it a point to attend weddings and
Bar Mitzvas; they usually lived in or near the Jewish
neighborhoods; while the reformers were hopelessly "uptown,"
well-intentioned but chilly, earnest but distant.*

*One of the more effective, because combative, reformers was
Lawrence Veiller, who campaigned for decent living conditions in
the Jewish quarter. He recalls below an effort at reform.*

LAWRENCE VEILLER

WITH THE BACKING of the Charity Organization Society, I presented recommendations for new tenement laws to the
committee of the board of aldermen, but they did not take me
seriously, knowing as they did how firmly entrenched the building
ring was in the government at that time. Embarking upon a plan to
educate the people of New York City as to the evils of tenement life,
I rented space in the Sherry Building on Thirty-eighth Street and
Fifth Avenue and mounted an elaborate exhibition which included
a series of poverty and disease maps. It was these maps which "got"
Governor Theodore Roosevelt, who opened the exhibition for us,
and who afterward said to us, "Tell me what you want from Albany
and I will do everything I can to help you get it."

WE BELIEVED THAT COURT BUILDINGS should be dignified and fitting halls of Justice. A shocking situation in this regard existed in the Third District Court in Manhattan, known as the Essex Market Court. Located in the center of a public market where the chief industry was the slaughter of live chickens and their sale, it was a place of filth, disorder, street congestion. The Tammany leader of that district was the notorious Martin Engel, who, with his brother, was the king of the *kosher* chicken racket. His connections with the police and other branches of municipal government were intimate and corrupt. After persistent attempts on our part, the court at Essex Street was finally abandoned in 1911 and moved to Second Street and Second Avenue.

AT MY REQUEST the Charity Organization Society in 1902 instituted a committee to study the TB problem. The committee even went so far as to print brief advice about TB on the back of streetcar transfers. We developed strong cooperative relationships with leading labor unions in the city and sought to enlist them in this campaign. We set up a traveling exhibition and used the facilities of social settlements, churches, synagogues, public libraries—even vacant stores. Thousands of public school children, accompanied by their teachers, received a careful explanation of the exhibition. During 1908 we sponsored 224 public lectures given by physicians in English, Yiddish, Italian, Bohemian, Swedish, French, and German. In 1910 our committee instituted fresh-air classes in the public schools to prevent sick-looking children from getting TB. By 1917 there were 98 of these fresh-air classes as well as a school textbook on TB prepared by our committee. In 1919 the New York Tuberculosis Association was formed and my connection with this work came to an end.

Reform candidate Henry George campaigning for mayor on the Lower East Side, 1886. George lost the election to Abram Hewett, the Democratic candidate; however, the Lower East Side gave him almost the largest plurality of any district.   MUSEUM OF THE CITY OF NEW YORK

דיא פאקטען איבער
דעם קאנדידאם

בייא
ביראן אנדראום
סערפאסעד פון איסטערן קאו-
פליקט , „רייף אף לאכא,
„איצעד פו פאלק,
און 'וו. אז' וו.
איל' זסמריל'ם ביי א. דש. קלאפף
איבערזעצט פון
הרב שמעון בן מה' הרב חיים פרי-
פאבלישעד ביי סיעם פטען, שיקאגא
19.4

"The Facts About the Candidates," a 1904 Roosevelt for President campaign pamphlet sponsored by New York's Yiddish-speaking leaders.

Immigrant Jewish socialists like Morris Hillquit supported many of the same measures championed by uptown reformers. In 1906 and again in 1908 Hillquit ran unsuccessfully for Congress on a platform that urged protection for pushcart peddlers, sanitary tenements, clean streets, and better factory conditions. Here Hillquit describes what it was like to campaign for socialist reform on the Lower East Side.

MORRIS HILLQUIT

THE [1 9 0 6] CAMPAIGN KINDLED an indescribable fire of enthusiasm on the East Side. The Socialist party had already gained a political foothold in the district. In the preceding campaign Joseph Barondess, the popular leader of the cloak makers, running on the Socialist ticket, had polled over 3,000 votes, about 20 percent of the total. In 1906 the prospects seemed to be particularly promising because the district faced a four-cornered fight. In addition to the three parties who had contested the congressional election in 1904, William R. Hearst's Independence League entered the arena with a full ticket of its own. Hearst had proved very popular on the East Side in the mayoralty campaign of the preceding year, and it was confidently expected that his candidate would seriously cut down the normal Democratic vote.

My chances of election were considered excellent, and the whole working East Side threw itself into the campaign with almost religious fervor. The trade unions organized a demonstration in the form of a street parade, which the newspapers described as "the largest ever staged by the socialists in this city, if not in the country." The women, then not yet entitled to vote, organized a committee of three hundred to help in the campaign. Young boys and girls between the ages of thirteen and seventeen constituted themselves into a Juvenile Workers' League. Doctors, dentists, and lawyers formed a Professional League in support of the Socialist ticket. . . .

229

Street meetings were held by the score every night. Campaign literature was distributed by hundreds of volunteers. Our headquarters hummed with activity. It was, in the unanimous testimony of neutral newspaper observers, "the liveliest thing" in the campaign of 1906.

My election was practically conceded at the height of the campaign, and I did in fact poll a larger number of votes than any other congressional candidate in the district on any party ticket, but I was beaten by an unexpected eleventh-hour combination. . . .

Disappointed but not discouraged, I returned to the charge two years later, when the situation and prospects appeared even brighter. Hordes of young intellectuals came down daily to speak at street corners, distribute campaign literature, canvass voters, and make themselves generally useful at headquarters.

דער קאמפף פאר'ן שטול

Presidential contenders William Jennings Bryan and William Howard Taft fighting for the same seat in a 1908 cartoon from The Big Stick. *In spite of their respect for Theodore Roosevelt and other "new style" politicians, immigrant Jews remained contemptuous of major party politics.*

YIVO INSTITUTE FOR JEWISH RESEARCH

Support of the socialist candidates in the district came from persons in high places in the literary and academic worlds. We were particularly proud of the endorsement of William D. Howells, the dean of American letters, then in his seventy-ninth year, who sent us a warm letter of encouragement with a campaign contribution.

The red-letter day of the campaign was when Eugene V. Debs appeared in the district. The whole East Side seemed to be on its feet as the socialist presidential candidate, seated in an open car, made laborious progress from one speaking place to another through the dense, cheering, and excited crowds.

. . . In the closing days of the campaign the Democratic camp became thoroughly panicky. A deal was speedily made with the local Republican machine, which openly urged its supporters to vote for Henry M. Goldfogle. In spite of the fact that the year was one of a presidential election, with William Howard Taft running against William Jennings Bryan, the Republican candidate polled a purely nominal vote. Mr. Goldfogle received all the votes of the Democratic party and the Independence League and most of the Republican votes.

This was the last of my campaigns on the Lower East Side.

Millionaire settlement house worker J. G. Phelps Stokes campaigning on the Lower East Side, 1908. Stokes ran unsuccessfully for the state assembly on the Socialist ticket.

MUSEUM OF THE CITY OF NEW YORK

A 1908 campaign poster supporting Henry M. Goldfogle for Congress. Goldfogle won over Socialist Morris Hillquit by making a deal with the local Republican machine.

TAMIMENT COLLECTION, NEW YORK UNIVERSITY

The popular comedian Eddie Cantor began his life as a kid in the Jewish streets of the East Side. To earn a few pennies or gain some attention, he would do almost anything—sing and dance at street corners, perform at social clubs. Eddie went to work for a time campaigning in behalf of Al Smith, the brilliant plebeian politician. Smith worked with and for Tammany Hall, yet also had a larger social vision and upon becoming governor of New York introduced some valuable social legislation.

EDDIE CANTOR

ONE OF MY FIRST ASSIGNMENTS was to speak for a young assemblyman running at the time, known as Alfred E. Smith. I decided to make a great speech because this was the first candidate I really knew personally. For young Mr. Al was a popular and lovable figure on the East Side. When I lived on Henry Street, Alfred Smith lived on Oliver Street, two blocks away. From the poolroom around the corner where the other boys and I spent edifying hours, Mr. Smith would call the whole crowd over to Bassler's saloon and blow us to drinks. But Al always picked the youngsters out of the crowd, separating them from the rest, and he would order nothing but sarsaparilla for the kids and schooners for the young men.

He would lead us in song, protect the weaklings from the bullies, and add that bit of kindliness and sunshine to the dingy gloom of our lives which would be reflected on our faces for many days.

When tough, heavy-set men of the alleys, with big, square jaws and shifty eyes, would throw a rock at an old peddler merely because he had a beard, Al Smith would come to the old man's aid and put his arm around him like a brother. It was the downright, simple heroics of the thing that struck the slum boys with wonder, and I can never forget the picture of this young and handsome Mr. Al coming among the ragged, hairy, bearded people of the abyss, extending a hand of welcome and friendship to all of them, as if the lady of the Statue of Liberty had sent her own son to receive these poor, bewildered immigrants on her behalf. So when I took the stump, my first words were, "This man who is running for assembly now will some day sit in the White House, and the present assemblyman is the future president, Alfred E. Smith!"

After words like these I felt I had suddenly become a man, and I secretly resolved that the next time Al Smith invited the boys to Bassler's saloon I would refuse the sarsaparilla and insist on the schooner. Al Smith, however, told me, "Kid, you may be old enough to prophesy, but you're too young to drink beer."

JONAH GOLDSTEIN

AS LONG AS I KNEW HIM, Al Smith was not ashamed to say, "Let's see if I understand you." That was one of the secrets of his greatness.

An earnest young reformer who had worked with Theodore Roosevelt's Progressive party and later with Al Smith, Henry Moskowitz had keen perceptions on the relationship between old-line and new-style politics, ward heelers, and reformers.

HENRY MOSKOWITZ

SOCIALIST OFFICEHOLDERS lack the *bonhomie* of the Tammany officials. They appeal less to surface emotions and more to what they regard as fundamental economic causes and to the general social passion for a new order of things. Indoctrinated with socialist dogmas, they plunge into the details of their jobs with grim earnestness and with the concentration of the student mind. This minority group is performing the function of stimulating criticism, and incidentally it is educating the old-timer with a lingo the sound of which is unfamiliar to the old walls of the board of aldermen's room.

Immediately upon taking office this group submitted resolutions pertaining to municipal purchase and sale of food. It submitted other socialist proposals, including the taking over by the city of the Brooklyn Rapid Transit, the establishment of a bureau of school feeding to provide the poor children of the public schools with hot and nourishing lunches, and an inquiry into the conditions of labor in the street cleaning department.

From now on municipal reform will be measured not by form but by social content. The emergence of the socialist as a factor in municipal government will result in interesting political history. The citizen will demand more radical measures. Tammany will give the city considerably less administrative efficiency, but it will be goaded on by its instinct for self-preservation "to beat the radicals and socialists to it," and become in some measure an instrument of progress.

We are on the eve of a fundamental change in our municipal policies. Tammany will try to get away with it by a program of just enough radicalism in response to the tingling of its East Side nerves.

Meeting in 1903 to maintain New York's hard-won tenement house reform laws.
AMERICAN JEWISH ARCHIVES ON THE CINCINNATI CAMPUS OF THE HEBREW UNION COLLEGE, JEWISH INSTITUTE OF RELIGION

Jacob Panken was one of the most effective soapboxers in the Jewish socialist movement—a clear ringing voice, sharp wit, bursts of indignation. In his final years he became a municipal judge. Here are some of his unpublished notes from one of his innumerable and unsuccessful political campaigns.

JACOB PANKEN

SEVEN HUNDRED THOUSAND consumptives in America, most of them workers who have contracted the disease either in the factory on in the dingy homes that they live in.

Sixty thousand are added annually to this army of the white plague.

MILLIONS ARE SPENT for improving and maintaining the avenues of the rich. The streets in which the poor live are not even flushed or properly cleaned, the excuse always being by the business administrations of the city of New York that there aren't sufficient funds.

Filth, dinginess, causes the spread of consumption.

WHEN THE WAR COMMISSIONS came from England, Italy, Russia, and France, the city had sufficient money to wine and dine them at $140.00 a person and to spend hundreds of thousands of dollars in decorating the city.

No funds to enable the people of the city to buy their food cheap enough to feed their children, but sufficient funds to wine and dine a lot of possible unwelcome guests.

FIVE HUNDRED THOUSAND WORKERS are killed and wounded each year in the United States. That is the number of victims that industry claims annually.

Five million were killed and wounded by industry in the United States during the last ten years.

IT IS BECAUSE of the private ownership of industries/the private management of public utilities, that they are managed for profit.

Socialist Jacob Panken (1879–1968) addressing a New York audience in one of his many unsuccessful campaigns.
JEWISH DAILY FORWARD

Therein lies the reason for the increase in the cost of living. The resultant tremendous profit to the owners of these public industries.

Therein lies the cause for the annual killing and maiming of hundreds of thousands in industry.

Public utilities, industries as a whole, if cooperatively and democratically managed, will be for use and service only.

Installment of safety appliances will reduce profits but they will save life and limb.

The former will not be exploited and the worker will not be robbed.

The remedy for these evils is socialism—Industrial Democracy.

We conclude this section with a profile of Tammany reformer William I. Sirovich, who represented the Lower East Side in Congress during the depression years.

RICHARD O. BOYER

DR. WILLIAM I. SIROVICH, the Democrat who represents New York's Fourteenth District in Congress, maintains that a day spent in his office on the Lower East Side would give a visitor some insight into the complexities of the problems facing the modern statesman. His office is actually a room of a house on East Sixth Street, which he has occupied for seventeen years. There, when he is not in Washington, he devotes much of his time to receiving his constituents. The morning began with the case of a Mr. Katz. "Here," Dr. Sirovich said, for the benefit of an admirer who was in the office at the time, "is a World War veteran who lost his job as a postal clerk. And what do I do? I go clean up to the postmaster general! And what do I find? Not a wrong charge against this man's record. 'Mr. Postmaster General,' I say, 'here is a man who has bared his breast to the shot and shell of the enemy. . . .' It was such an eloquent plea that he was reinstated on the spot."

Mr. Katz cleared his throat. "But I ain't been reinstated," he said. "Or if I have been, I ain't been taken back to work."

"Take a letter," said Dr. Sirovich to his secretary. "My dear Jim: When you were kind enough to reinstate Mr. Katz, that veteran who bared his breast to shot and shell, you were kind enough to express your indignation. Mr. Katz, however, says that through some oversight he has not been reinstated and so I will appreciate your taking care of this horrible miscarriage. With every kind and good wish, I remain, et cetera, et cetera.' There. Does this kind of work require a man like me?"

On such a day, Mr. Richey, a Democratic district captain of the neighborhood, is almost certain to appear. Dr. Sirovich sometimes greets him with a tribute which starts, "This man controls two thousand Italian votes." Mr. Richey, who usually chews the stub of a cigar and wears his hat on the back of his head, says complacently, "Sure, they vote the way I want them to." This beginning often results in reminiscence. "Remember the time," said the congressman to Mr. Richey, "that I helped you and Father Zolan about the woman in Albany killed her husband for insurance?"

"Yeh," said Mr. Richey, "but you couldn't do anything."

"Couldn't do anything! Why, I stopped that electrocution for three months!" . . .

When Sirovich was first elected to Congress in 1926, he introduced bills that were before their time by about a decade. ("They laughed at me," says Sirovich sadly, "when I urged old-age pensions.") In his first session of Congress he introduced bills providing for unemployment insurance, old-age pensions, and child welfare, and the principles of these bills are now embodied in the Social Security Act. ("I regard Congress," says Dr. Sirovich, "as the uterus and myself as the fertilizer preparing it for pioneer measures yet to be born.") He has been reelected without interruption by successively larger majorities and has fought for civil service reform, the creation of a federal Department of Science, Art, and Literature, slum clearance, safety-at-sea legislation, the Wagner Labor Act, the liberalization of copyright and patent laws, the repeal of prohibition, the strengthening of pure-food measures, the enforcement of narcotic laws, and the establishment of a National Institute of Public Health. Dr. Sirovich is an ardent New Dealer and his loyalty is such that he has backed every Presidential proposal.

Whenever the gentleman from New York rises to say, with that solemn courtliness of the born orator, "Mr. Speak-ah, lay-dees, and gen-tul-men of the House," there is a rush from, not to, the cloakrooms. Almost the last representative of old-fashioned down-the-line oratory is about to use all the stops, and that is the kind of oratory congressmen like to listen to. Dr. Sirovich always pauses after these opening words and looks slowly right and left, his features noble and composed. His shorter speeches last an hour. He does not write them down beforehand, for apparently when he is speaking he can recall to mind anything he has read once. He does draft a short outline. A typical one reads as follows:

> Hobbes—*Homo homini lupus.* Man is a wolf to his fellow man.
>
> (a) Man is radically bad and needs the state, his highest authority, to curb him.
>
> (b) The theory of social pessimism justifying dictatorship.
>
> (c) The state is the Leviathan to the individuals, first swallowing them & then swallowing other states.

Such an outline is deceptively brief. That speech lasted for fifty-five minutes.

9

THEATER

Libretto cover for Shmendrik by Abraham Goldfaden
(1840–1908), playwright and a founder of the Yiddish theater.

Early Years

The history of the Yiddish theater is brief, stormy, vivid, and ambiguous. It is a history rich in achievement and trash, the two sometimes so interwoven as to be almost indistinguishable. It begins about the middle of the nineteenth century—a hundred or so years ago—and by now, as we creep toward the end of the twentieth century, it is all but over.

In eastern Europe Yiddish theater begins with ragged groups of minstrels, acrobats, and singers wandering from shtetl to shtetl, the enjoyable but neglected ragamuffins of a culture. After a while, they start improvising little skits as fillers between songs and dances. And then, from all this, there emerge impoverished companies, patching together scripts, picking up actors on the run, performing in wine cellars, and suffering harassment from both czarist government officials and Jewish Orthodoxy. No sooner do larger numbers of Jews start coming to America than the Yiddish theater, though still in its swaggering infancy, comes along.

Here, starting in the early 1880s, theatrical companies lead a catch-as-catch-can existence. They put on plays that yoke, improbably, tragic event, comic buffoonery, song and dance, national exhortation, splendiferous tableaux. The early immigrant audiences, without esthetic training or experience but with wonderfully avid hungers, have little taste for realism—there is enough "realism" in their lives. What they want is bang-up spectacle, florid declamation, turbulent melodrama. The Yiddish theater becomes a passion among these immigrants, indeed their first major outlet for communal emotion. In piercing historical plays and grinding social melodramas, the immigrants find a mirror not so much to their daily experiences as to their frustrated aspirations, their cramped emotions, their burgeoning fantasies. This theater overflows, in the 1880s and 1890s, with vivid junk and raw talent, largely innocent of art, skipping rapidly past the problems of immigrant life, and appealing to rich new appetites for spectacle and high gesture. It is a theater superbly alive and full of claptrap.

One of its major figures, the actor David Kessler, has left an unpublished memoir, and we start with a few pages of his recollections about the early days.

DAVID KESSLER

OUR THEATER ALWAYS WAS some rented loft that was standing vacant at the time. Our stage consisted of some boards which we had banged together, with a sheet of some sort serving as our curtain. Without any food, we used to drag ourselves around, performing, encouraging one another, arguing, quarreling, and complaining. The poverty of our troupe was so acute that we simply did not have any clothes which we could use in public. Costumes and theatrical clothes were out of the question. I had only one costume. Occasionally we would run across some good-hearted enthusiast of the Yiddish theater, who would give us some sort of support. For instance, a certain wealthy tie manufacturer took us into his home, supplied us with all necessaries and even lent us a few hundred rubles. In another place we all barged in on an uncle of mine. But if there was no such opportunity, then we would go hungry. . . .

Lack of funds prevented our traveling around with our own orchestras. In the cities where we used to stop, particularly the small towns, we used to get the military bands made up of soldiers who were then dispersed about Rumania. Our choir consisted of the wives of all the actors in the troupe, with Mrs. Finkel as the prima donna. . . .

When we came to Galatz for the second time on the tour, it occurred to us that to play over the same repertoire would not be making a very good impression. But where does one get new operettas? Where should we get new music? You can understand the difficulty of obtaining these commodities in Rumania at that time. We began to dig into our books, and picked out an old Russian operetta. Mogulesco became the playwright, and we did over the operetta. We gave the leading role to Mogulesco in reward, even though his voice did not exactly fit the part. . . .

For the first few days after our arrival [in New York] nobody said a word about acting. Our group was divided into various quarters of the city. We were all busy resting, and getting used to our new surroundings. On the third day, Mogulesco called us all together, and introduced us to our benefactor, the then-time Yiddish theater boss, Yechiel Schreiber. Schreiber owned a saloon at the corner of Canal and Orchard streets. He was one of the most prominent people in the Yiddish theater world in New York. We were told that

Immigrant Jewish actors in the 1890s: (front, left to right) David Kessler, Rudolf Marx, Zigmund Mogulesco, Jacob P. Adler; (rear) I. Kratoshinsky, Zigmund Feinman.
YIVO INSTITUTE FOR JEWISH RESEARCH

The Bernardi family in a touring company production of King Solomon. Chicago, 1915.

he too was a president, and I must say that we were puzzled at the fact that America had so many presidents, and that all of them spoke Yiddish fluently. There, in Schreiber's saloon, we began to talk "business." Mogulesco "explained" whatever we didn't understand too well. He spoke an Anglicized Yiddish. From there we all went to Schreiber's house. He lived on Henry Street. Schreiber and Mogulesco already had a package of papers prepared, which we were given to sign. We all signed, were given five dollars apiece by Schreiber, and our first meeting was ended. . . .

It was around this time that we met Professor Ish Hurwitz, who later became our close friend and fellow actor. The professor (a title self-bestowed) was a shrewd fellow who had been a Hebrew teacher in Jassy, but had seized an opportunity for advancement, and posed as (or actually became) a Christian. He spoke Yiddish very poorly. The professor also wrote plays. We did one based on the infamous ritual murder accusation of that time. . . .

Professor Hurwitz's newest operetta, *King Solomon*, was an extravaganza. In honor of that play, we bought a whole new wardrobe, including new stage settings, from a lodge of Shriners. When we had finished the first act, to a packed house, we saw that it would take at least a half hour to change all the props. It was already eleven o'clock, and we had no less than four acts. The audience began to stamp their feet. Behind the stage, Mogulesco and Edelstein were running around nervously, cursing and yelling. Finkel, our stage manager, was going from one person to another asking what is to be done, until finally one of us hit upon a plan. The plan was a simple one: Fool the people. Since we had already

241

performed one operetta in two parts, one part each evening, we decided that we would go out to the audience, and tell them that an error had been made, and that instead of four acts, three acts should have been announced. Also, that these three acts would be shown in two parts, the first one tonight, the second part tomorrow night. It was ostensibly a good idea, but the audience had something to say about it as well. They were not happy with the plan. The end was that we finished the whole play at 4:00 A.M. And through that whole time, the audience sat quietly, and patiently, hearing us out till the end. . . .

Professor Hurwitz proved himself to be a very useful member of our "family." He was able to edit the various pieces in our repertoire so that we weren't continually chasing scriptwriters for new scripts, as is necessary even today. For example, one of our best plays of that season was an adaptation of Schiller's play *Two Sergeants*. I had first seen that play on the Rumanian stage. It is about two friends ready to die for each other. The script was originally in French. Hurwitz did a fine job of Yiddishizing the play, giving the leading characters Jewish names. And the play was actually performed under the name *Judah and Israel*. The New York audience was thrilled with it.

FORWARD, 7/6/'99

Important Notice:
We announce to the honorable public that we, the undersigned Jewish artists: Mr. David Kessler, Mr. Zigmund Mogulesco and Mr. Zigmund Feinman, have rented the big Thalia Theater for the next three years. Ten thousand dollars will be spent to fix up the theater, so that it will be one of the most noble theaters in New

The Thalia Theater, 46 Bowery, where Jacob P. Adler and Bertha Kalisch starred in plays by Jacob Gordin.
COURTESY OF COMMUNITY SERVICE SOCIETY OF NEW YORK

York. The greatest Yiddish artists are connected with us. We will provide a double union choir, a union orchestra and the best plays by the most important Yiddish playwrights. For the first time we will show the honorable public an example how a theater has to be managed, and we expect your sympathy.

Our Policy Is Honesty.

Our books are open and we are ready to sell benefits for the cheapest prices. Lodges and societies should apply to the office of the Thalia Theater, every day from ten till two and from eight till one at night.

Faithfully,

L. Spachner, Bus. manager.

NEW YORK WORLD, 11/1/'91

THE EAST SIDE HEBREWS IN GENERAL, and the Russian Hebrew colony in particular, have been thoroughly stirred during the past few weeks by a series of performances given at the Rumania Opera House, where a four-act play called *The Persecution in Russia* has been presented to large audiences of exiled Russian Hebrews recently driven from the czar's domains. They have swarmed to the little playhouse in such force that standing room has been at a premium each evening.

Of the play itself it is somewhat difficult to find a title by which to fittingly describe it. The author, one Joseph Lateiner, calls it simply "a drama," but were it given in one of the regular theaters it would probably be billed as "a tragical-musical melodrama" or some equally comprehensive title, for in its four acts and ten scenes one finds a mingling of music, mirth, comedy, tragedy and realism. Prison courtyards, nihilistic secret meeting places, dungeons, palaces, and other interesting places are made the scenes of such hair-raising happenings as terrible hand-to-hand battles, single combats and mysterious trials. Soldiers, priests, nihilists, detectives, lovely conspirators in red silk skirts, who sing patriotic songs and revile the czar (amid tremendous applause from the audience), and a wide variety of other interesting persons are ever providing excitement and mirth. At last in a great prison scene all come to violent deaths after a terrific ten minutes of active work with pistols, swords, and deadly poison. This absolutely horrifying climax is promptly followed by a parade of New York's foreign citizens, all in red, white and blue regalia and red flannel yachting caps, who are headed by a brass band playing "The Star-Spangled Banner." At the end of the procession comes a big pushcart in which are seated eight children, who are looking most pleased and most of whom are devouring bananas and buns. Then a tableau is formed: the Stars and Stripes wave side by side with the scarlet socialistic banners, red fire is burned at the wings and the curtain comes down amid a whirlwind of applause.

Much of what we know about the early days of the Yiddish theater comes from the Yiddish historian, B. Gorin, who in 1918 published a historical account. Here in an article written for the Forward *in 1903 he talks about the caricaturing of Gentiles in the Yiddish theater.*

FORWARD, 4/25/'03

JEWS ARE RESENTFUL when a Gentile writer caricatures them, and when the English stage depicts Jews in a bad light. There was much tumult over Shylock, who was not really anti-Semitic. One would think that Jews would try to be tolerant to Gentiles in Yiddish plays. But it is not so. In all Yiddish historical plays the Gentiles have major roles; they are always the embodiment of evil, and commit every crime in the book. The priest is never pious, he is a drunkard and has a red nose. Kings and servants are treated with more respect, because playwrights remember from their childhood that kings have influence in heaven, and when a king dies you never say he "kicked off" like an ordinary *goy*. Servants are played by comedians, so their roles are more sympathetically written, and they are loved by the audience.

Thank God the *goyim* never come to the Yiddish theater. But it does not mean we should divest *goyim* of their human qualities. Jews have been persecuted and tormented, but turning all *goyim* into beasts is petty revenge. We dare not demand tolerance toward ourselves when we have none for others.

Here is another item about the rough-and-tumble early Yiddish theater in the years before 1900—a review by Norman Hapgood of a Yiddish play.

COMMERCIAL ADVERTISER, 3/14/'99

THERE ARE LIGHTS AND SHADES in the acting at the Windsor. The less luminous elements of the company are prominent in a parody on *Hamlet*, a kind of seriocomic play, with occasional music. The dominant quality of it is comic, intentional or unintentional. The author of the play is Isidor Solotorofsky, and the character of Hamlet is enacted by Boris Tomashevsky, the

Boris Thomashefsky (1866–1939) as a zaftig Hamlet.

"Jewish Hamlet." Mr. Tomashevsky also plays a serious version of *Hamlet*—an almost literal translation from Shakespeare's play. He treats the two with fairness, playing them much alike.

In the burlesque the first act represents the wedding feast of Hamlet's mother and uncle. But in this case the uncle is a rabbi in a small village in Russia. He did not poison Hamlet's father, but broke his heart by wooing and winning his queen. Hamlet is off somewhere getting educated as a rabbi. While he is gone his father dies. Six weeks afterward he returns in the midst of the wedding feast. He is told that his father is dead, then that his mother is about to marry, and he turns the feast into a funeral. He finds a letter written by his father, telling him to revenge him on his uncle, but to spare his mother. Scenes of rant follow between mother and son, Ophelia and Hamlet, interspersed with jokes and sneers at the sect of rabbis who think they communicate with the angels. The wicked rabbi conspires against Hamlet, trying to make him out a nihilist. The mob nearly kill the young man. His mother, who is repentant, tries to save him, but is murdered. The plot is discovered and the wicked rabbi is sent off to Siberia. The last act is the graveyard scene. It is snowing violently. The grave is near a huge windmill which revolves. Ophelia is brought in on the bier. Hamlet mourns by her side, and is married, according to the Jewish custom obtaining between betrothed persons, to the dead woman. Then he dies of a broken heart.

Through the years there were a number of serious theater critics reviewing Yiddish plays and writing about the Yiddish theater in general. One of them, Jacob Mestel, comments on the role of the prompter in the early Yiddish theater.

JACOB MESTEL

THE PROMPTER (or stage manager) would note down scenes that were impulsively created during rehearsal or after several performances. He was a "qualified" person, who hung around the theater, could read and write, and was made a prompter. He served as artistic adviser and assistant director; improved on language, gave advice on Jewish customs and often decided on the choice of

From a program cover
of the People's Theatre
on the Bowery.

L. LIPSHITZ,
Steam printer & publisher
180 Grand St. N.Y.

Adler, Edelstein & Thomashefsky, Lessees and Managers. · · · · Joseph Latelner, Author.

repertory. Prompters carried over into the twentieth century, often steering the theater into the past. His influence was strong. Many playwrights emerged from the prompter's box.

LETTER TO THE DAY, 11/11/'15

. . . I WENT TO THE ENGLISH THEATER. The play is passable, but the theater! It is not like our Jewish theater. First of all I found it so quiet there . . . that I could not hear a sound! There were no cries of "Sha!" "Shut up!" or "Order!" and no babies cried—as if it were no theater at all! . . .

And then, there is a total lack of apples, candy, or soda, just like in a desert.

There are some Gentile girls who go around among the audience handing out glasses of water, but this I can get at home, too.

For the Forward—*both because of its socialist slant and the passion for realism of its editor, Abraham Cahan—Yiddish theater mattered most as a medium for stimulating social self-awareness among the immigrants. In 1903 it invited its readers to discuss what they liked, or didn't like, in the theater.*

Character actress Bina Abramowitz.   JEWISH DAILY FORWARD

FORWARD, 1/'03

THE FORWARD INVITES ITS READERS TO WRITE ABOUT YIDDISH THEATER:

The radical press has educated the masses to understand good theater and to discriminate between good and bad. We feel it is time to let the people express their opinion about various stage productions. In his own words let the reader discuss:

(1) opinion of Yiddish theater; (2) what makes a play good; (3) what makes it bad; (4) which plays are real life, which historical, and why; (5) what he looks for in a play and why; (6) what is good acting

Do not write too long. Write on one side of the paper. Do not mention actors' names.

L. GOLDBLATT WRITES: "I want entertainment, not education. The critic condemned the play *Aygene Blut* with "scientific arguments" proving it was not modern, not moral, etc. But there are long lines at the box office. I was deeply moved in the first act when Lydia sang *Kol Nidre* to prove she was a Jewess. The second act was entertaining from beginning to end. In the third act the sick mother was good; when she discovered who Lydia really was I got chills down my spine."

HARRIS COHEN WRITES: "A play should teach us how to behave toward our wives, sweethearts, parents, etc. The *Kreutzer Sonata* can teach young children; *King Lear* can teach older children; *The Wild Man*—stepmothers. A play should not be tampered with by an actor or actress; it is like a clock—you touch one screw and it is spoiled. An actor should remember that the audience comes to see the role he is playing, not him personally."

L. R H E I N G O L D   W R I T E S: "Theater can teach good manners, speech, appreciation of music, etc. Yiddish theater tries to compete with world theater not among the actors but externally, for audience. Yiddish theaters are a potpourri of opera, vaudeville, drama, etc., and don't satisfy those who want specific kinds of entertainment. It must reform. Each theater must devote itself to one kind of show. A play should have action, and no miracles. Also psychological study of good and bad characters."

How should we describe the early Yiddish plays? Crude, melodramatic, wildly implausible, yet sometimes revealing the inner emotions of the immigrants who flocked to them. The long-suppressed emotions, the turbulnt romanticism, the inner and sometimes wild yearnings of these people were caught in these brilliantly trashy plays and acted out on the stage. A group of reviews from the Commercial Advertiser, *written around the turn of the century, captures the quality of these early scripts.*

T H E   J E W E S S is a story, adapted from Halévy's *La Juive*, of how the daughter of a cardinal is lost in early childhood and adopted by a Jew. A Christian prince falls in love with her, for which crime father, daughter, and prince are condemned to death at the stake by the Christian cardinal. The last scene is at the stake. The Jew and his daughter are to be burned alive. The cardinal, in rich robes, is there. There is a touching scene of farewell between father and daughter. Then the girl is torn away and led to the burning pile.

"Where is my daughter?" asks the cardinal for the last time. "I will save your life if you tell me."

A moment later the girl is precipitated into the flames.

"There," shouts the Jew. "There she is!"

T H E   B E L A T E D   W E D D I N G by Libin is simple, direct transcript from the life of the people. A girl has a good honest workman for a lover. But a medical student comes to her house to board, and dazzles her by his learning and swelldom. So she leaves her honest lover and goes with the student.

The next act is in the poor quarters of the couple, a sordid, miserable scene. The girl is sick in bed, but the brutal student forces her to get up and work in a factory in order to support him. She drags herself off to her task.

Years pass and the student is rich and they are married. Now, however, a new trial is in store for the poor woman. He is ashamed of her for her simple manners and her lack of education, and is miserably rude and brutal to her. Her old lover, the honest workman, comforts her. Her coarse husband has a mistress and in every way expresses his contempt for his wife. . . .

UNCLE TOM'S CABIN: It is interesting to see that the Yiddish actors can present a distinctively American play so competently as they did last night at the People's. They were weakest in the melodramatic and comic places, but strong in the character sketching. Topsy was well done by Mrs. Thomashevsky, and Uncle Tom received an uncommonly conscientious and unexaggerated interpretation by Mr. Thomashevsky, who was also made up realistically.

DIE GREENERS is a Yiddish comedy containing decided satire of certain ghetto conditions. Two "greenhorns," mother and daughter, arrive in New York. They wear wigs and are very pious. The man, whose dead wife was the sister of the girl's mother, makes love to the girl. She hates him because he is a cruel "boss." He mistreats his workers and is determined to get rich, which is a great sin in Yiddish drama. The girl loves his secretary, who is in reality an escaped criminal from Siberia. An old workingman, driven by the starvation of himself and family, steals some money from the boss. At this point the audience applauded. Why shouldn't he take the money he needed from a rich man? The boss is about to identify him as the thief, when the girl interferes. His heart is softened and his reward is ultimately that he marries the girl.

No matter what the play—serious or comic, historical or topical, universal or parochial—Yiddish audiences insisted upon singing. They loved the voices, even if sometimes screeching and bellowing. They weren't purists about genre: So what if different kinds of dramatic action got mixed up? Here, in both Yiddish original and English translation, is a once-popular theatrical song.

YANKELE'S LID	YANKELE'S SONG

Zintik, ven di zin shaynt
Hob ikh shtark faynt,
Tsi geyn in dem finstern
  kheyder,
Tsi kvetshn di bank keseyder.
	Sunday, when the sun shines
	That's when I really hate
	To go to that gloomy
	  schoolroom
	To squat on that bench
	  endlessly.

Ikh loyf—kh'fil zikh zeyr mid, In sing zikh Yankele's lid.	I run about, I feel very tired, And I sing me Yankele's Song.

Refrain:
Oy—Vet mikh der rebbe
  shyaysn!
Mayne peyelekh vet er fin mir
  oysraysn!
Vay'hi erev, vay'hi voyker—
  yom ekhod.
	Refrain:
	Oh, how the *rebbe* will smack
	  me!
	My little ear curls he'll tear out
	  altogether!
	"And it was morning, and it
	  was evening the first day."

Montik vel ikh nisht fargesn.
S'iz nisht geven in shtib vos tsu esn.
Di mame hot gegosn mit trern.

Ober shtil, der tate zol nisht hern.
Der tate shrayt vi a meshiginer Yid.
In ikh zing zikh Yankele's lid.

Monday—I won't forget it.
There wasn't a bite of food in the house.
My mother was crying her eyes out,
But silently, so my father wouldn't hear.
My father shouted like a crazed Jew.
And I sang Yankele's Song to myself.

Refrain:
. . .yom sheyni.

Refrain:
". . .the second day."

Dinstik hob ikh dem kigl oyfgegesn.
Vos men hot fin letste vokh fargesn.
Kh'bin gevorn grin in geyl.
Hot men mir gegeben ritsn eyl.
Oy, ikh loyf—kh'fil zikh zeyr mid,
In zing zikh Yankele's lid.

Tuesday I ate up the pudding
That had been forgotten since last week.
I turned green and yellow.
They gave me castor oil.
Oh—I run, I feel very tired

And I sing Yankele's song to myself.

Refrain:
. . . yom shlishi.

Refrain:
". . . the third day."

Mitvokh veyst a yeydr
Geyt men take nisht in cheder.

Hertshet oyf patshen glaykh.

Der rebbe patsht genig far aykh.
Hot rakhmones—ikh bin mid—
In singt mit Yankele dos lid.

Wednesday as everybody knows
One certainly doesn't go to *cheder*
Stop smacking your hands together right now.
The *rebbe* smacks us quite enough!
Have mercy—I'm tired—

And sing along with Yankele his song.

Refrain:
. . . yom reviyee

Refrain:
". . . the fourth day"

Shoyn!

Enough!

Here's a recollection of the comic Zigmund Mogulesco as remembered by novelist and playwright Leon Kobrin.

LEON KOBRIN

I SAW MOGULESCO the first time in *Mishka & Moshka* by Professor Hurwitz. Among the other actors on the stage was an old emaciated woman, with a wrinkled face, who looked as though she had mistakenly wandered in from the street and the actors were making fun of her. The action took place on an immigrant ship en route to America. She had to be vaccinated before disembarking, and put out a skinny, trembling arm; her whole body quivered; every wrinkle in her bewildered face fluttered, and her voice was quavering and pathetic.

The curtain fell and the audience applauded: "Mogulesco!" The old woman appeared, smiled charmingly and bowed.

I could hardly believe this was an actress; and certainly she could not be an actor!

After the performance I went backstage and was introduced to Mogulesco: He was slim and elegant; with broad shoulders, a graceful neck; a sensitive, cheerful face. There wasn't a sign of the exhausted, tormented old woman.

Maurice Moscowitz, Mogulesco, and I went to a café on Canal Street; and over a glass of tea Mogulesco, with his wonderful smile, talked with childlike excitement not about his acting, but about the songs he wrote. He sang some of them to me, quietly. The music was melodic, warm and Jewish, but the words—my God—when he sang them with that sunny smile of his it was as though a fountain of sunbeams had suddenly begun to spew filth and mud.

When I told him that he was degrading his talent by singing such songs he looked at me with amazement:

"You should hear the audience reaction. They practically break down the walls. I have to sing again and again."

Later Moscowitz said to me: "It's a psychological enigma. An artist of such caliber who should be proud of what makes him great, is proud of what makes him small and silly." . . .

During the illness which killed him and which destroyed his voice, he still sang on stage; and what his hoarse voice could not express, he said with his eyes, his face, his limbs and movements, so that the audience *felt* his singing.

In his last role, in Lateiner's *Yiddishe Hartz*, he had no voice and was very weak. He played a Jew who was afraid of his wife. His son-in-law convinced him to prove, by stamping his leg, that he was the boss. But when he saw his wife, the leg gave such a diffident and fearful shake and bend, that one saw the entire timid soul of the little Jew crouching and hiding in his leg.

When illness conquered his voice, he laughed with his eyes and face, and finally with a leg. He was fifty-six years old when he died.

The great Yiddish comic Zigmund Mogulesco. "When he danced, the audience, mesmerized by his exuberance, was aware only of him."—Leon Kobrin.

SAMUEL CHOTZINOFF

SEMIDARKNESS LAY LIKE A PALL on a structure whose like I had never before seen. Dim personages in capes brandished swords and spoke oratorically in words I could not quite understand. Yet I felt certain that momentous events were about to take place, and I braced myself for the shock of a revelation that could not long be withheld. And then the event that I both dreaded and longed to see suddenly took shape as a faint, sickly yellow light pierced the surrounding gloom and disclosed an eerie figure clad in diaphanous armor. I knew only too well that I was looking at a ghost—strangely attired, but beyond a certainty a ghost. "Gamlet," it said distinctly, in Yiddish, "I am your father's ghost." And with Hamlet I listened, with mounting horror, to the piteous tale of fratricide. But how incredibly brave of Hamlet to confront alone a ghost, no matter how closely related, bathed in unnatural light, at dead of night! I now began to surmise the intention of the plot, and could hardly wait for the scene that would put everything to rights. But the author seemed most reluctant to bring to a head the conflict he had set in motion at the beginning of the play. I was mystified and annoyed by soliloquies that brought matters no nearer to a solution. What *was* wrong with Hamlet? Why did he put off, scene after scene, the execution of the revenge he had at the outset resolved to take? Why was he so cruel to Miss Kalisch, his sweetheart, whose air of innocent bewilderment broke my heart.

A change of scene now disclosed a cemetery and two men digging a grave. I had never before seen a cemetery or a grave, but I knew what they were, and they were as horrifying to behold as a ghost. And now, at last, Hamlet assumed again the boldness he had shown at his first encounter with the ghost. He fondled and apostrophized a horrible skull. And when he heard the shocking news—shocking to me, too—that the grave was being dug for the corpse of Miss Kalisch, he leaped into the pit with no signs of fear at all. From that point on, the author, abandoning his former delaying tactics, moved swiftly to the denouement, and in the final scene of revenge and universal carnage he more than atoned for the inexplicable hesitations that had marred the greater portion of the play.

That night I could hardly sleep, for when I shut my eyes, the ghost stood before me and beckoned me to follow him; and to rid myself of his presence I quickly opened my eyes on the reassuring, dim outlines of the kitchen where I slept. In the daytime I could dwell on the ghost without fear, but on coming home from play at night I would run up the three flights of stairs with a beating heart and burst into the house like one pursued by a fiend, as indeed I was. A tiny gas jet burned on the wall of each landing, and the faint yellow light it feebly spread was the *same* that had enveloped the ghost of Hamlet's father!

FORWARD, 8/27/'16

THIS YEAR THE FASHION will be . . .

Every season the "styles" change. If one theater is successful, the others follow. At one time the pious Jew was the subject of mockery; a *Hasidic* rabbi was always prejudiced and when the curtain fell he had come to a bad end, to the delight of the public. With enlightenment, the pious Jew was treated sympathetically—after all, they were our fathers and grandfathers. Then came bosses and landlords. When a landlord appeared on the stage, the comedian tripped him and he fell. When the public realized that it was not the individual landlord or boss, but the system that threatened them, the new topic was love and treachery. Love used to be a secondary theme, but today it has the star role and the Jew with the *yarmulkah* is the comic who sings and dances. . . .

Will this year's "style" be successful? It remains to be seen.

The Adler Period

The high point of Yiddish theater—perhaps not artistic, but certainly as a vital institution of immigrant Jewish life—comes during the years (roughly from the late 1890s to the First World War) in which Jacob Adler is the dominant actor and Jacob Gordin the major playwright. It is a period of extraordinary boldness in adapting classical masterworks to the needs of the immigrant culture; extraordinary boldness in developing a high, flamboyant style of acting, so that what the cast does on the stage is always more important than the lines given it to read. The Yiddish theater becomes a central cultural institution, in which all the problems, aspirations, fantasies, and complaints of the immigrant Jews are discussed, presented, elevated, vulgarized.

A group of young Gentile writers and intellectuals followed Yiddish theater with wide-eyed fascination. Among them were Norman Hapgood, for a time theater critic of the Commercial Advertiser, *and his brother, Hutchins Hapgood, who also wrote for that paper. Here Hutchins Hapgood describes a high point of the theater of Gordin and Adler.*

HUTCHINS HAPGOOD

JACOB GORDIN HAS ADAPTED Shakespeare's play to popular Jewish needs. A patriarchal old Jew, very religious, wants to spend his last days in Jerusalem. So he gives away his money to his oldest daughter and her husband. His youngest daughter is a "new woman" who has ideas and wants to be learned, and her lover is also a student. The King Lear of the Yiddish play turns against his best daughter and goes off to Jerusalem, but his unnatural children send him no money, for sweet economy's sake. In the first part of the second act the poor old patriarch is back . . . to beg a little food. When he becomes fully aware that his children wish to drive him and his wife away, he rises to a great height of scorn and anger. Leaving his ignoble children, the old man and his wife totter out into the street to beg, with old Kent by their side. After years they return, the old man blind, his face thinner, the color of the dead. They come on to the stage and tell their woes. The good daughter, unseen, hears and weeps. Her father recognizes her voice and soon they are in each other's arms . . . the whole emotion of suffering and exhausted man expressing itself in the refuge of affection. . . .

Mr. Adler as the Jewish King Lear stood out alone and significant. It is a great impersonation, original, too, and would be enjoyed even by those who understand no word of Yiddish. For great acting is great pantomime, and Mr. Adler, being an actor, knows how to use his whole body, rather than merely his voice, to express what is going on in his soul.

Jacob P. Adler (1855–1926) as a Yiddish-speaking Shylock in an English-language production of The Merchant of Venice, *1903.*

The Yiddish actors of this time were extraordinary people—extraordinary in their artistic intuitions, despite (or because of?) their paucity of formal education; extraordinary in the quickness and eagerness with which they grasped some of the skills and achievements of both European and American theater; extraordinary, too, in their deep emotional kinship with the audiences for whom they performed. Here is a passage from Jacob Adler, as quoted in a 1901 issue of Theatre Magazine; *it seems likely that not every word here is Adler's own, but the sentiments certainly are. A vivid portrait of Adler follows, written by Harold Clurman, the distinguished theater critic who grew up on the Lower East Side and as a child often went to the Yiddish theater.*

JACOB ADLER

SHYLOCK IS ONE OF THE FEW among my roles that I have seen played by other actors. . . . Suppose that—always keeping scrupulously to the letter of Shakespeare—we reverse the traditional relative presentments of Shylock and Antonio, the Merchant. Shylock, who is rich enough to lend three thousand ducats to his Christian enemy in mere gratification of scornful pride, forgoing interest on the remote chance of the "pound of flesh" forfeiture, and later sacrificing the principal itself, and the proffer of double its amount, just for the moral satisfaction of his revenge—such a Shylock, I say, should be shown well dressed and proud of mien, instead of the poor and cringing figure which custom has made familiar. Antonio, on the other hand, is in reality far from being the chivalrous gentleman that he is made to appear in the ordinary acting of the play.

He has wantonly insulted and spit upon the Jew, yet comes with the hypocritical politeness to borrow money from him, and readily consents, in lieu of paying interest, to bind himself to a preposterous forfeit, which obviously he never expects to be called upon to pay. These two men, the Christian and the Jew, are finally confronted in an alleged court of justice, packed with Antonio's friends, where the judge is openly committed to condemning Shylock, by hook or by crook; where the prosecuting attorney, so to speak, is a masquerading girl, the affianced wife of Antonio's bosom comrade; and where Shylock stands alone against them all, without counsel, advocate, or friend, with nothing but the law on his side!

That such a court will interpret the law in his favor, the ironical Jew is not for one instant fatuous enough to suppose. But the opportunity is his for one moment of ineffable triumph and scorn, holding in his hands the very life of his former insolent persecutor. The real revenge that Shylock contemplates is *not* to take the pound of flesh which is legally forfeit to him, but to show the world that his despised ducats have actually bought and paid for it. His whetting the knife on his sole is a hyperbolical menace: his sardonic smile, accompanying this action, is the only sharp edge that shall cut the self-humiliated Merchant. Then a quibble reverses the case, the court and Antonio divide the spoils between themselves, and—"Exit Shylock"! That is the last of him, so far as Shakespeare's stage direction goes. But, having purchased so dearly the right to his contemptuous opinion of his Christian fellow townsmen, is it not certain that he will consummate his brief triumph by walking out of that court with head erect, the very apotheosis of defiant hatred and scorn?

HAROLD CLURMAN

. . . THE BRIGHTEST LUMINARY of them all was Jacob Adler. He was extraordinary in every way. His height and bodily strength, his hair, snow white even in his youth, his large eyes and penetrating gaze, his reverberant voice and regal stance were themselves sufficient to rivet one's attention to the point of fascination, and he evoked in his audience something akin to worship. Everything about him breathed a masculine fullness which commanded the admiration of both sexes. With this there dwelled within him a sensibility which one might (even today!) call "feminine." One felt him capable of cruelty abated by an overwhelming sensual tenderness. He had the air of a prophet with a touch of humorous cynicism and not without a remainder of naïveté! His skeptical smile was infectious, reflecting an understanding of the treacherous weaknesses which beset humankind. This gave rise to a forbearance due to a sense of his own sinful vulnerability.

His mode of living was lavish, and there was something larger than life in all his behavior. This gave the roles he played, for all their verisimilitude, a romantic aura that we often term "theatricality." His charm was captivating, his dignity awesome, his wrath terrifying. When he towered as the vengeful patriarch Shylock, or as Uriel Acosta raised the torch of free thought in epic loftiness, or teased as the shrewdly humorous ragpicker of *The Beggar of Odessa*, I was transported and a little frightened by him. The man's *size*—I do not refer to his physique—imposed a sense of peril. Grandeur always inspires a certain shudder at life's immeasurable might and mystery. When Jacob Adler died, two hundred thousand people came to his funeral. The image he created has never been forgotten. It has remained in the consciousness of a people, emblem of the stature of a human being, the overwhelming meaning of what it is to be a man.

Jacob P. Adler.

The Grand Theater in 1904—when it was still owned and operated by Jacob P. Adler.

Many of Jacob Adler's successes were in plays written by Jacob Gordin, the dominant playwright of that period. Gordin's plays now seem rather "heavy" and didactic, but they deeply touched the minds and hearts of his audiences. A keen description of him is provided by Melech Epstein, a veteran of the Yiddish cultural world, and is followed by a passage from the historian Ronald Sanders, about Gordin's role in the immigrant milieu.

MELECH EPSTEIN

GORDIN MADE FREQUENT USE of his cane to keep the actors to their lines. Every performance found him sitting in the first loge, his famous silver cane in his hand. If an actor, in his enthusiasm, tried to improvise his lines, he would bang on the rail with his cane, interrupting the performance, to scold him. One of them, Sigmund Feinman, who persisted in his ad libbing, was slapped in the face. The actors respected and feared him. Their respect was heightened by Gordin's aloofness from the opposite sex in the theater. A man of undeniable passion, the playwright, dedicated to his new calling, steered clear of becoming involved in affairs with the young attractive actresses whom he helped to stardom.

Gordin regarded himself not as an artist but primarily as an enlightener, an uplifter. The stage was to him a tribune for education. His victory over the *shund* theater was to him largely a social-political accomplishment. The radical *maskil* was still strong in him. It is quite possible that in his heart he thought of pure art, but the preacher won out.

The moralist in him was becoming alarmed by the rush for individual success which became noticeable in the socialist movement. In a lecture, he complained: "The race of radicals for money and career is the cause of the vulgarization of socialism and art, and consequently leads to the victory of the parvenu in elections and in the theater."

Yiddish dramatist Jacob Gordin (1853–1909). Drawing by Bernar Gussow.

RONALD SANDERS

Mirele Efros completed Gordin's rise to the cultural high priesthood of the Lower East Side. Although the plays of Horowitz and Lateiner still drew the larger crowds, Gordin's works were nonetheless commercially successful, and no other Yiddish writer in New York could rival his claims as a creator of serious literature. He bestrode the Jewish quarter like a colossus. Physically a great bear of a man, with a large black Assyrian beard and an air of flamboyant yet aristocratic Bohemianism that was often characteristic of Russian artists, he made a legend-provoking impression upon the public imagination. "I still see him walking through the streets," wrote one of his fellow Yiddish playwrights, Leon Kobrin, years after his death, "straight as a palm, his princely beard solemnly covering his broad chest, his eyes like two points of fire, sharp as daggers. In his right hand he carries a cane; in his left one of his plays. He is going to the theater to read it to the actors. People who know him say, 'That is Jacob Gordin.' Those who do not know him stop and remark, 'What a fine man!'"

The extreme touting of Gordin that was going on among some Lower East Side commentators, who often did not blush at comparing him to Ibsen, Chekhov, and Shakespeare, was too much for Abraham Cahan, editor of the *Jewish Daily Forward*. Cahan's objections to some of the shortcomings of Gordin's writing had even led to a personal rivalry between the two men. This had broken out in 1895, during the run of one of Gordin's first plays about life in the New World, *The Russian Jew in America*. The play was a scathing comment about the state of the human soul in America, and it presented a large portrait gallery of corrupt and opportunistic types. Among these was a Jewish labor leader named Huzdak, a man who was perfectly willing to compromise abstract socialist principles in order to obtain concrete gains for his union. Throughout the play, Huzdak kept repeating the line, "What do I need brains for when I've got a Constitution?" Upon first hearing this, Cahan leaped up from his seat and cried out in Russian, "That's a lie!" In the ensuing weeks, there was an angry exchange between Gordin and Cahan on the pages of the *Arbeiter Zeitung*.

It is difficult to get a satisfactory picture of these Yiddish actors. A few silent films survive, none very good. So we have to depend on the testimony of qualified observers, checking the dispassionate notices of distant non-Yiddish writers against the enthusiasms of Yiddish devotees. Of one thing we are certain: the style of the great Yiddish actors during the Adler-Gordin period was more flamboyant than has been customary in American acting during the last several decades. Working often with mediocre or rudimentary scripts, and sometimes not paying very close attention to those scripts, the Yiddish actors relied on their expressive powers: the shout and the whisper, the groan and the gag, the whole repertoire of gesture. For a culture breaking loose, enjoying the release of free expression, and indulging its inner emotions, actions had to be broad and underlined.

Here is an interview that Hutchins Hapgood held in 1904 with the brilliant actress Bertha Kalisch.

HUTCHINS HAPGOOD

MRS. BERTHA KALISCH . . . unites more tendencies and ideals than any other Yiddish actress. This is partly due to the fact that she is the youngest of the prominent ones, and that she is consequently not so steeped in Russian and Yiddish traditions. Those traditions affect her, of course, but she has experienced other influences, and therefore has in a way a broader point of view than any one of the others.

The older actors and actresses of the ghetto belonged for many years, before coming to New York, to wandering bands in Europe.

Sarah Adler (1858–1953), queen of the
Yiddish theater. JEWISH DAILY FORWARD

Bertha Kalisch (1875–1939), celebrated
actress on both the Yiddish- and En-
glish-speaking stage.
NEW YORK PUBLIC LIBRARY AT LINCOLN CENTER,
THEATER COLLECTION

They were subject to oppression and privation, and their *Yiddishkeit* was strongly rubbed into them.

The best of them, even today, interesting and strong as some of them are, remain purely Yiddish and Russian in their ideals and artistic habits.

Mrs. Kalisch, however, has never done much wandering.

"I played Juliet in 1896, and then for the first time I began to feel the difference between Sardou and Shakespeare—one all artifice, the other all natural art. Yet *Fedora* is magnificent theatrically. The part gives an actress a beautiful chance to portray the woman of the world. Juliet, on the other hand, is poetic, innocent, a beautiful thing. She lives in literature, while the actress must create Fedora.

"My next great dramatic experience was in faithful, realistic plays. I began this kind of thing with Libin's dramas—with *The Delayed Wedding* and *David and His Daughter*. They are both plays based on life in New York. Libin, as you know, was a sweatshop worker, and all his subjects are taken from sweatshop and pushcart life. His range is very narrow, but within those limits he is faithful and true.

"What a change from the sweeping, emotional unreality of Sardou, the large and poetical imagination of Shakespeare, to the simple truth of Libin! Here was another school altogether, one based upon Russian ideals of art. In his plays I was a simple shop girl.

"In his parts I never wanted to overdress, overfeel or overact. I just wanted to be the real thing, so to speak."

Here I am constrained to interrupt Mrs. Kalisch for a moment to explain that the Libin phase she describes is typical of what is really best in ghetto dramatic art. It is the kind of thing supported by the socialists, the "intellectuals" generally, and is a direct result of the influence of Russian literature.

> Here, Yiddish critic A. Mukdoyni describes an interesting development in the Yiddish theater—the evolution of the Shlimazl into a happy-go-lucky molodyetz.

A. MUKDOYNI

IN THE EARLY YEARS of Jewish operetta the dancing comedian was always a *shlimazl* with sidelocks and a long *kapots*. Usually he was called Shmayeh, Grunem, or Todress. He was a small-town ne'er-do-well. Clad in their skullcaps and short prayer shawls these good-for-nothings sang lewd songs accompanied by indecent gestures.

Then a new type of Jewish lad appeared in the Russian-Jewish milieu. He spoke half Russian and half Yiddish. He was a mixture of Russian munificence and good nature with Jewish cleverness and agility. He was a lad with a Russian shock of hair, polished boots, an embroidered shirt and a cap that sat jauntily and cockily on his head.

He had become aware that there are bourgeoisie and proletarians in the world, and he was with the latter. His name was not Shmayeh, but Liovke, or Yoshke.

He appeared first in real life, out of the ranks of the BUND and other Jewish socialist parties, who adored these vital, courageous folk children of theirs. During the revolution Liovke went into battle. In peacetime he sang and danced and laughed.

And then the *molodyetz* appeared on the stage, where the young *shlimazls* were still capering about.

An agile dancer, with a quick tongue, he will beat up anyone who insults him; he will fight for a girl, for the revolution, for a comrade. He is not comical. He is not a *yold* like the bourgeois sons and daughters. He is full of joy.

The Adlers were an extraordinary family, indeed, the "royal family" of the Yiddish theater—with some of them, like Stella and Luther, finding their way to prominence on the American stage in later years. Celia Adler, a daughter of Jacob, became a brilliant star of the Yiddish theater, as well as a chronicler of its history. She discusses here the star system.

CELIA ADLER

RARELY DOES ONE GENERATION spawn more than one actor of genius. But in the first generation our Yiddish stage was blessed with many geniuses. Their brilliance concealed their lack of knowledge in theater art and general culture.

They were spiritually impoverished, and did not grasp their historical responsibility; did not see that they were the builders of a cultural institution—a legacy for the future. They were careless—impure and unpolished in their execution. They could not resist temptation—the enticements that led to the birth of the star system.

However, their dramatic institution led them to the pinnacle of their art, even in roles which were unsuited to their figures, appearance, age, and individual genre. Thus David Kessler created one of his major roles—Hershele Dubrovner in Gordin's *Got, Mentsh un Tayvl*—although the sensitive, delicately formed scribe was the opposite of Kessler's brawny figure, strident voice, and sharp movements. When Kessler was already well along in years he played the young lover in Gordin's *Sappho*, and the eighteen-year-old Yosele in *Mirele Efros*.

When my father, Jacob Adler, was in his late fifties, he immortalized himself as the twenty-year-old Ben Zion in Gordin's *Madman*, and the still younger Lemakh in Gordin's *The Wild Man*.

Under the star system, the stars played the main roles even when they were unsuited for them.

In Yiddish cultural circles there was endless discussion of how to "improve" the Yiddish theater. Given its abundance of talent—if not among playwrights, then among actors—why could not a more refined and serious theater emerge? Why always this flamboyance, this outflow of theatricality, this mixing of genres, this lack of restraint? At least some of these discussions, we are now inclined to think, were misdirected—as if it made sense, culturally, to expect the Yiddish theater to conform to the standards of avant-garde European or American theater; as if efforts to repress and refine Yiddish theater might not lead to a loss of vitality without any compensating gain in depth! Still, the discussions went on and on, year after year. Here is a symposium from the Forward, *1909, in which some distinguished Yiddish actors discuss what, if anything, can be done to improve their theater.*

FORWARD, 12/25/'09

THE *FORWARD* asked the star managers: "We understand that you are interested in doing business; if cheap vaudeville in four acts brings in the money, it is natural that you should concentrate on it. But what about better plays? What can be done to stage better plays?"

Jacob P. Adler: "It does pay to produce four-act sketches with singing and dances because the public has always wanted it. Whose fault is it? The actors and the press. The theater grew up on this trash, and made actors and others rich. Until better-class writers and audience protested; by accident they got together with the critics and influenced the gullible audience. When *shund* was king the actors themselves used to make fun of their roles and of the plays. Many called themselves *Gordinists*. But when good plays and good writers began to fall off, *shund* and opera triumphed again.

"What to do? Write good plays; win over the better audience; give lectures on the subject. Although I have given away my theater and am free-lancing, I will rebuild, with the aid of good people. If not I, others will do it. . . ."

Kenny Liptzin: "Jewish drama is sinking lower and lower. There is nobody to take Gordin's place yet, perhaps because new dramatists are in too much of a hurry to create; they do not touch the hearts of the public, and let me tell you, I believe in the intelligence of the Jewish theater-going public. I believe the Jewish audience is ripe for better plays; but it has not reached the stage where it can express its appreciation or condemnation in an effective way, by patronizing only better theater.

"*Shund* is successful because the post-Gordin dramatists are weak, and the managers are afraid of literary drama. Even when it is a money-maker, they find other reasons for its success. They are simply afraid that good plays will frighten the public. Thirdly, the press, which should educate the public, is supporting and encouraging *shund*, and by default, not condemning it. Their critics are not honest and too insulting; they use language suitable for fish-

Celia Adler (1889–1979) in a 1919 production of Peretz Hirshbein's The Hidden Nook.

wives. . . . I have faith, and believe the Jewish drama will flourish again in the spirit of Gordin; and I believe the press will encourage good writers and actors by writing good critique—tactful and sincere, and showing how an artistic work should be played. Our critics ignore our better efforts and this is discouraging."

David Kessler: "*Shund* is more profitable; I must offer plays that attract the public, if I want to pay my rent. But as an actor I prefer good plays. *When I play trash it's like drinking castor oil.* My actors will tell you I would prefer to drink poison. But what can I do if a good play brings in only half the revenue? What to do? We need an audience that wants good plays. . . . Today's audience is more sophisticated, and must be developed, but it cannot be done by a private theater. The people should build a theater . . . at first it will not be successful, but will influence others."

Often enough, the better Yiddish actors felt dismay, even shame, at the misuse of their talents. Serious plays were presented during the early decades of this century, but also a great deal of shund, *or trash; worse still, the serious plays would often be interlaced with elements of* shund *in order to make them palatable to audiences. David Kessler, judged by many the equal of Jacob Adler as a virtuoso Yiddish actor, felt especially strongly, often bitterly, about this artistic corruption.*

DAVID KESSLER

I HAVE SEEN THE PEOPLE applaud an actor who ranted like the player whom Hamlet reproved. It made my teeth tremble. It was as bad as if "To be or not to be" had been bawled out by an idiotic rather than a crazy Hamlet.

I had a most heartrending experience myself in this same direction when I first came to New York. I was playing in *The Ironmaster*, and was talking to my wife, in what, you will remember, should be a dignified and restrained way. . . . Suddenly I heard a hiss, then laughter, and then more hisses. I could not go on. I was struck dumb. I knew that I ought to continue, but I was absolutely unable to do so. I turned to the audience and asked them what was the matter. Was there a rip in my clothes? Had I forgotten to button my doublet? Was there something the matter with the acting, into which I was putting all my intelligence and all my nerves? I was very angry, and I spoke with passion, and the crowd became silent, but the play did not continue. The next night I changed my manner of playing the part. I made a burlesque of it. I did not play it with truthfulness. I waved my arms and stamped my feet, and I was recalled eight times. And then I had a great contempt for the audience. Now I know when to act badly. It is useless to act well with some people. Realism, which I love, cannot always be realized.

The Broken Violin—*written, produced, directed and starring Boris Thomashefsky at the height of his career. In later years Thomashefsky performed at an Allen Street restaurant bearing his name.*

By the early 1920s Yiddish theater in America entered its second
distinguished period. Where the years of the two Jacobs, Adler and
Gordin, had been marked by overflowing energies, extravagant
styles, and indigenous themes, the more sophisticated and
cosmopolitan "art" theater starting after the First World War
absorbed a good deal of the experimentalism and boldness of
thought marking the best European theater. The Yiddish "art"
theaters, especially those in which Jacob Ben Ami was a dominant
figure, still retained strong ties with traditional Jewish sensibility
and concerns; but there was a new seriousness about literary form,
acting technique, and theatrical coherence. Ben Ami was perhaps
the purest of the new Yiddish theater people; the better-known
Maurice Schwartz combined something of the new seriousness with
something of the old exuberance; and the Communist-inspired
Artef theater would try in the thirties to blend propaganda with
modernist devices.

The work done in the ten or fifteen years after the First World
War was often on a high level. One mark of this is the frequency
with which actors and directors from the English-language theater
would visit the Yiddish theater and express their admiration;
another is the tendency of the English-language stage to take over
some of the best Yiddish actors—Jacob Ben Ami, Paul Muni.
Some of the most interesting work in the American theater during
the thirties, especially that of the fine repertory company calling
itself the Group Theater, showed the influence of Yiddish styles of
performance. But the tragedy of it all was that as the Yiddish
theater reached its high point, there occurred that gradual loss of
audience that would soon doom it to disintegration. The children
of the immigrants who cultivated esthetic tastes turned to English
literature and the American theater. The aging Yiddish audiences
became too small in size and limited in interest to sustain a serious
theater.

Still, for a brief period there was a genuine flourishing, and one
of the ways we know this is that the best dramatic critics of the
time, figures like Stark Young, Ludwig Lewisohn, and James
Agate, wrote glowingly about the Yiddish productions they saw.

LUDWIG LEWISOHN

IN ITS IDEAS AND INTENTION [the Yiddish Art
Theater] is the noblest theatrical enterprise now existing among us.
It stands aloof from all the pressures of commerce and popularity; it
has an audience that will respond to high passion and grasp the
force of tragic events; it has as its director Emanuel Reicher, one of
the great actors of our time, the original creator of many of the chief
roles in the works of Ibsen, Hauptmann, and Schnitzler. . . .
Naturalistic Jewish parts, whether grave or humorous, are done with
a skill and completeness rare among us. Nothing could have been

better of its kind—and it is by far the most important kind in any modern theater—than the *Ch'yenne* of Binah Abramowitz or the grandfather of Gershon Rubin in Peretz Hirshbein's *The Idle Inn.* The group scenes are incomparably good. . . . Compare the blank-looking supers of Broadway with these spontaneously tragic and comic masks which the ages themselves seem to have modeled.

SAMUEL GROSSMAN

IN THE FALL of 1918 Maurice Schwartz, an ambitious young actor from an older Jewish company, became insurgent and organized a new troupe at the Irving Place Theater. Vaguely he felt the urge for something better than the old Yiddish Theater offered, but his standards at the time were neither very definite nor very high. He, however, took every precaution to surround himself with sympathetic coworkers, so that when the "Modern Yiddish Theater" was launched, Ben Ami, Celia Adler, Ludwig Satz, and others of the old theater's youth were in the company.

Schwartz cut loose absolutely from the traditions of the old Yiddish theater in everything, from that date to this. Then came a series of standard Yiddish *and* translated plays, which as an acted repertory has not been equaled, either in standard or in number, by any theatrical organization in America, except perhaps the Jewett Players in Boston.

The famed Vilna Troupe in a 1925 American production of Peretz Hirschbein's Green Fields.
MUSEUM OF THE CITY OF NEW YORK, THEATER AND MUSIC COLLECTION

SCHWARTZ IS EBULLIENT with vitality and energy; in action he is a typical American executive "go-getter." As a youth he worked in a tailor shop; he became an actor by the sheer force of ambition and talent. With his native shrewdness and mimetic faculties he has grasped much that passes as a cultured man's equipment, although his training has been limited to the reading of classic plays and contact with cultured theatergoers who have visited him at his theater.

As an actor he is protean; a realist, he has a positive genius for finding bits of stage "business," things—*to do*—to characterize the role he is playing. He has a muscular feel, an intuitive motor sense for impersonations. As a mimic, as a simulator of human forms, and as a graphic physical portrayer of persons, he is preeminent. In these faculties he surpasses Ben Ami and indeed he is far ahead of most American stars. But in the inward light which shines through and beyond makeup, he is not as luminous as his younger contemporary.

THE JEWISH ART THEATER is the only repertory company of artistic pretensions in America. . . . Here is a company of artists engaged by the season and constantly employed in the production of new plays, irrespective of the material success with which established productions have met. On the contrary, the more profitable a new play proves, the sooner does the repertory company begin rehearsals of a new play—perhaps of a play that is regarded as a doubtful box office attraction.

The Jewish Art Theater, then, by the very mechanics of its organization, has had the opportunity of presenting a greater variety and quantity of plays than any other legitimate producer in America. In less than five years seventy-odd productions have been given: nearly all have been American premières and more than half the number were presented for the first time on any stage. The dramatists ranged from established playwrights like Andreyev, Asch, Gorky, Hauptmann, Hirshbein, Ibsen, Pinski, Shakespeare, Shaw, Schnitzler, Sholom Aleichem, and Tolstoi, to a newcomers' list which included the poet Leivick *(Rags)*, the folklorist Ansky *(Dybbuk)*, the psychologist Rosenfeld *(Rivals)* and the dramatic-balladist Sackler *(Yizkor)*.

STARK YOUNG

IF YOU GO TO THE PEOPLE'S THEATER and then to the Royal a block away on the Bowery you will discover a happy kinship in the world of men and art. The Yiddish actors are at one theater, the Sicilian at the other; and at both places the actor and audience are children of the Mediterranean. The Jews draw further back in time from Asia Minor; the south Italians have blood in them from the Greeks and Romans, the Africans, Saracens, Normans, Spanish, French and the first island tribes, whoever they

A 1925 production of Ossip Dymov's
Bronx Express. The sets are by Boris
Aronson.

were; and are no more like the Florentines today than they are like
the Danes or the Belgians. Both of these are folk theaters, and for
that reason the elements to be observed in them are perhaps more
fundamental; and the two of them together supply one of those cases
of repetition and variation within our microcosm that can teach us
so much about art.

There is no actor at the Jewish theater, of course, to compare
with Grasso; though among its company I have seen Miss Gerstn
exhibit a power and a terrible sincerity hardly surpassed in all New
York. But in both these theaters there is the same atmosphere of
animation, intense interest, response. In both the same tide flows
between actors and audiences; both audiences give themselves to the
play; the plays at both are melodramas and the story is the thing;
there is the same hum of comment and easy judging, like wonderful
children together. Among the actors there is the same vividness, the
same expressiveness of eyes and hands and shoulders. And you get
the same sense of tremendous and inexhaustible vitality on the
stage, and in the house, the capacity for strong food, strong bodies,
strong emotions and crises of living.

The Yiddish acting is more complex, and in that sense, at least,

269

more modern. It has the realism of intense feeling, and a deep respect for that feeling. Its best effects come from a compulsive rendering of that intensity; and the beauty of these effects is a spiritual beauty, almost without appeal to the eye. In its best moments it sacrifices everything to this spiritual truth; and beyond that its interest in beauty seems comparatively slight, whether beauty of manner, style or appearance; whereas the Sicilian art is more beautiful to the eye, with more grace, more flowing and flexible lines, more brightness and color in the voice and gestures, more abundance, as that lovely country has from which it comes. Compared to the Sicilian this Jewish art has infinities of mood; it has, too, more biting pain, more sentiment; and has a deep tenderness where the Sicilian has only the tenderness of simple affection or erotic impulse, nothing poignant, searching, understanding or profound. When we come to the other side of the picture, the defect of this excellence, we find that this art on its poorer side sinks into sentimentality, the mawkish, theatrical, insincere, tricky and false. And it is often at the same time vulgar. The Sicilian realism is more open, more easily copied after the current of life. In this sense it is supremely natural, the most natural in any theater. Its best effects are this naturalness in the display of terrific passions.

An expressionistic setting for S. Ansky's
The Dybbuk.

With the story [of *The Dybbuk*, its author S. Ansky] has interwoven the ecstasy of a race, all the shadowy origin of its passion, its faith, its primitive mysticism, and confusion and strength.

This deep racial element takes *The Dybbuk* far away from me. I feel the presence of a terrific force and fire and tenderness, but much of it is foreign to me; it seems to draw from remote ages and from places far away in the deserts of Asia. In our Western culture, men strove to create an outer form whose beauty would embody or represent the beauty of the idea within; a result that to their minds made for health and balance, in content and external fact, in impulse and release. But these expressive forms in the sacred objects, dances and rites, that I see in *The Dybbuk*, take their power from what they mean to their worshipers. They are pure symbols, all idea, rapture, fanaticism, fear, strength; pure symbols have no outer claim to representative beauty or expressiveness in themselves. Their beauty is inward, they live in men's minds. This passionate inwardness fulfills all parts of the Habima production of *The Dybbuk* and leads it to its summit.

STARK YOUNG

FROM THE START Ben Ami has the advantage of being free from the actor's faults. Every art makes pets of its faults, but the stage has made idols of them. The exaggeration, forcing, ranting, the empty gestures, the extravagant repose, and all the rest of that whole false world set up as theater, Ben Ami has none of them. Whatever faults he may have are at least his own; they are personal if anything, and are not actors' faults. In the art of acting this sort of omission is a distinction in itself.

What makes Ben Ami's acting so good is that it is so complete. Where most actors come to life only in spots, he is continuous. You feel behind the acting a cultivated and independent mind and a nature released and fluid, and exerting a mode of truth that is like Chekhov's. Chekhov hurries together and sets going a succession of impulsive incongruities and thoughts and emotions with a secure and unavoidably true result arising out of them; in the same way, exactly, Ben Ami works. He has also Chekhov's assurance of his own truth, without fear of what has been agreed upon as dignified, natural, causal, or rational, or capable of demonstration. He has Chekhov's careful leisure. His acting of Peter in Sven Lange's play *Samson and Delilah* was the first creative acting of a poet—in the sense that Romain Rolland's Jean Christophe creates the artist—that I had ever seen. The stage poet is always quaint, romantic, Chopinesque, or grandiose and tragic; his creator always takes pains that we shall be easy with him, that we can adopt him or pity him or make sentimental allowances for him. That takes the sting out of the poet's mystery and power and difference from us. We understand his case and in our own way are superior to him, and so feel at

Lazer Fried (left) and Jacob Ben Ami in Peretz Hirschbein's Green Fields.
YIVO INSTITUTE
FOR JEWISH RESEARCH

home with him. Whatever else we felt, we were not at home with Ben Ami's portrait; it was erotic, weak, swift, clairvoyant, violent, tender, but it was sure, unmanageable; and it was always a little strange, as the truth must always be.

In the first act of *Samson and Delilah* you watch Ben Ami eating, talking, moving about; it is the truth, you can see that; and you wonder what it all comes to. A little later you see him suddenly drop his head on his wife's breast and then down to the bend of her arm and stay there, and you get the first certainty of great acting. You begin to feel the life emerging naked from this suffering creature. You see a man bound to life by the depths of his own nature; and begin to understand what circumstances are doing to this being who is so capable of commanding and creating life and being destroyed by it as well.

JAMES AGATE

SOMETIMES ONE FEELS that praise may be taken a trifle perfunctorily. It is not an uncommon experience for a critic to find himself slapped on the back and challenged: "Of course I saw what you wrote about such and such a play. Now, tell me, what is it really like?" I want readers of the Sunday *Times* to take me at my word when I say deliberately, and weighing every syllable, that the performance of *The Seven Who Were Hanged* by these Yiddish players contains more great acting than I have ever seen on any stage in any one piece. The drama, in itself, is a great emotional and spiritual experience. One of the tests of a masterpiece is the inability to shake off experience; since Monday evening last I have spent my waking hours in Russia, in prison with these pitiful wretches. But I ask even more than that readers should take me at my word. I ask that they shall go and judge for themselves. The piece will be played again . . . and it is the duty of every person who takes an intelligent interest in the theater to witness this extraordinarily fine play with its magnificent presentation. A complete

Maurice Schwartz (1888–1960) starring in a 1926 Jewish Art Theater production of Abraham Goldfaden's The Tenth Commandment. *The settings and costumes by Boris Aronson were praised by critics of the day for their striking originality.*
NEW YORK PUBLIC LIBRARY AT LINCOLN CENTER, THEATER COLLECTION

ignorance of the language need not be a deterrent; the program contains an elaborate synopsis, and the scope of the play puts it above words. . . . There was no flamboyance. But not Duse could have launched you upon seas of diviner pity, nor Bernhardt have moved you to a greater quickening of the spirit. There are eighteen actors in this piece, and it is impossible to make distinctions. But if I must call special attention to any individual performances it would be to that of the cabinet minister, Mr. Isidor Cachier, who is to be compared with Lucien Guitry and none other, and to the father, mother, and son of Muni Weisenfreund, Anna Appel, and Alex Tenenholtz.

One of the most interesting Yiddish actors was Ludwig Satz, a great comedian, wonderfully resourceful on the stage, who was driven by financial need to act in plays that he regarded as cheap and coarse. For a time Satz acted on the English-language stage, doing the popular Potash and Perlmutter *in 1926. He wrote a short piece for the* New York Times, *comparing the problems of Yiddish with American theater, from which we take a section.*

Self-portrait of Yiddish star Ludwig Satz (1895–1944).
JEWISH DAILY FORWARD

LUDWIG SATZ

IN THE FEW WEEKS I have been playing Abe Potash at the Ritz Theater I have noted emphatic differences. Your American audience is receptive; your Yiddish playgoers are determined. Your American audience has not definitely made up its mind as to what it likes and what it doesn't like, but is willing to be shown what you have and to enjoy it if it is enjoyable. It has not decided and unchangeable views on acting, realism, romance, comedy and tragedy. If what you offer them amuses them they are more than satisfied.

The Yiddish audience, on the contrary, knows exactly what it goes to the theater to buy. It is as intense about the play and its performance as the playwright and the actor. It is a hearty, zestful, passionate collaborator. It is a homogeneous audience and it knows the life that its theater portrays. You cannot fool its members with false types and with false interpretations. Their drama may not be great—it is great as seldom as any other theater—but it must be true. They have your fingerprints, as it were, in advance, and you can't fool them. Hence, if you make the mistake of giving them something that they don't identify, no matter how basically good the things you give them may be, God forgive you.

But if you are what they want and if you do fit their prejudices and their understanding, no people in the world reward you with such enthusiasm. You may become anything from a hero to a savior. You not only become a figure of the stage, you become a figure in the race. And you feel that you have earned your reward, because you realize they know and are the character you are playing. He is in the audience by the hundred. You are a glass for many faces.

The Yiddish actor Muni Weisenfreund before he became Paul Muni.
MUSEUM OF THE CITY OF NEW YORK, THEATER COLLECTION

אַרויסגעגעבן פֿון
אַרבעטער מעאַטער פֿאַרבאַנד
פֿון (גרינוב גרינוב
אידישן אַרבעטער מעאַטער

ערשטער סעזאָן
1928—1929

A 1928 Artef program cover drawn by William Gropper. Founded in 1925 under the auspices of the Freiheit, a communist newspaper, Artef achieved its greatest successes in the Thirties with expressionistic adaptations of the plays of Sholom Aleichem.
AMERICAN JEWISH HISTORICAL SOCIETY

Seen now from the vantage point of historical distance, the decline of the Yiddish theater in America was all but inevitable. Once the children of the immigrants became Americanized, they turned away from—some hardly knew any—Yiddish. Each year the Yiddish theater had a smaller and smaller, an older and older audience. The stopping of immigration from Europe in the 1920s meant there were fewer and fewer recruits to the ranks of the Yiddish-speaking world. And by the 1930s the number of Yiddish playwrights and actors had seriously declined, so that the remaining theaters had to make do with old plays slightly reworked—and sometimes not reworked at all.

Still, the Yiddish theater hung on. Its partisans were astonishingly dedicated and tenacious. Despite the depression, there were during the early thirties somewhere between ten and fifteen Yiddish theaters intermittently open (and frequently closing) in New York City alone. The actors often experienced extreme hardships in their effort to keep the theaters alive. Maurice Schwartz would take his Yiddish Art Theater on tours of Europe and South America in order to make up deficits accumulated in New York. Some Yiddish actors, particularly talented or just lucky, found their way onto the American stage or the movies. But while the trend toward decline could be slowed, it could not be stopped. By the late 1970s Yiddish theater had become mostly a memory, cherished by those who could still recall its largeness of gesture, its closeness to the folk, its talented and large-spirited actors.

Her Last Dance as performed at Brooklyn's Hopkinson Theater.

10

CULTURE

A Plebeian Yearning

"The sweatshop was my first university"—so begins the first item in this section, taken from Marcus Ravage's eloquent memoir of his youth in the immigrant world. What he writes was true for many others. The Jewish immigrants came here with an enormous cultural hunger, a yearning for the ideas and achievements of Western culture which they had begun to learn about in the old country but only now, in the New World, could reach. Some of these immigrants had been profoundly affected by Russian culture at its best: the nineteenth century traditions of Tolstoy, Turgenev, Gogol and Chekhov. Others retained the deeply ingrained, traditional Jewish respect for learning, which they transferred from sacred to secular objects. Still others were stirred to consciousness by the ideals of the Jewish socialist movement. And some found the New World open and receptive, with its literature of democratic humanism and its doctrine of free-and-easy fraternity.

One result of these criss-crossing influences was the appearance in the immigrant Jewish world of its most impressive and moving figure—the self-educated worker, the man or woman who had no choice but to spend his or her days in the shops, yet tried to read, to learn, to appreciate. It was for this figure, above all, that Yiddish culture in America, during its all-too-brief period of glory, was dedicated. Yiddish poetry and fiction, the Yiddish theater, the best of the Yiddish press: all spoke to the self-educated worker, all gave him nutriment and stimulation.

We start this section with a few pieces of writing by those who were stirred into the pleasures of awareness by Yiddish culture.

MARCUS RAVAGE

THE SWEATSHOP was my first university. I was not long there before I discovered that there were better things I could do with my free evenings than to frequent the cozy hang-outs of my fellow-countrymen. When I overheard a dispute between the young buttonhole maker and the cadaverous, curly-haired closer, on the respective merits of the stories of Chekhov and Maupassant; and when, another day, the little black-eyed Russian girl who was receiving two cents per dozen shirts as a finisher boldly asserted that evolution pointed the way to anarchism and not to socialism, and cited the fact that Spencer himself was an anarchist, my eyes were opened and I felt ashamed of my ignorance. I had been rather inclined hitherto to feel superior to my surroundings, and to regard the shop and the whole East Side as but a temporary halt in my progress. With my career looming on the horizon, and my inherited tendency to look down upon mechanical trades, I had at first barely given a tolerant eye to the sordid men and girls who worked beside me. I had not realized that this grimy, toil-worn,

Shakespeare at Cooper Union. Drawing by Jay Hambidge.

279

airless ghetto had a soul and a mind under its shabby exterior. It knew everything and talked about everything. Nothing in the way of thought-interest was too big or too heavy for this intelligentsia of the slums.

I made an effort to listen attentively in the hope that I might get some hint as to where my fellow operatives got all their knowledge. I observed that nearly all of them brought books with them to work—Yiddish, Russian, German, and even English books. During the lunch hour, if the disputatious mood was not on them, the entire lot of them had their heads buried in their volumes or their papers, so that the littered, unswept loft had the air of having been miraculously turned into a library. While waiting for my next bundle of shirts, or just before leaving the shop, I would stealthily glance at a title, or open a pamphlet and snatch a word or two. I was too timid to inquire openly. Once a girl caught me by the wardrobe examining her book, and asked me whether I liked books and whether I went to the lectures. I became confused and murmured a negative. "You know," she said, "Gorky is going to speak tonight," and held out a newspaper to show me the announcement.

So they were going to lectures! I began to buy newspapers and watch for the notices. I took to reading books and attending meetings and theaters. There were scores of lectures every week, I found, and I went to as many as I could. One night it was Darwin, and the next it might be the principles of air pressure. On a Saturday night there were sometimes two meetings so arranged that both could be attended by the same audience. I remember going once to a meeting at Cooper Union to protest against the use of the militia in breaking a strike somewhere in the West, and then retiring with a crowd of others to the anarchist reading-room on Eldridge Street to hear an informal discussion on "Hamlet *versus* Don Quixote." It did not matter to us what the subject was. There was a peculiar, intoxicating joy in just sitting there and drinking in the words of the speakers, which to us were echoes from a higher world than ours. Quite likely most of us could not have passed an examination in any of the subjects we heard discussed. It was something more valuable than the information that we were after. Our poor, cramped souls were yearning to be inspired and uplifted. Never in all my experience since, though I have been in colleges and learned societies, have I seen such earnest, responsive audiences as were those collarless men and hatless girls of the sweatshops.

Self-portrait of immigrant Jewish artist Abraham Walkowitz, 1902.
COURTESY OF ZABRISKIE GALLERY

GREGORY WEINSTEIN

WHENEVER I PASS the present HIAS building on Lafayette Street near Astor Place, I cannot help regretting that the fine Astor Library, which was formerly housed in that building, is no more. Many are the hours of the day and night which I spent in that beautiful, majestically columned building. It was indeed a haven of rest and a home for self-education for many generations. Whenever I was out of work, I would hie myself to its warm, high-ceilinged rooms, pick out my favorite books and forget myself until the bell rang. There was not much red tape there. The private alcoves were inviting, but these were not for dilettantes like me; they were occupied by bespectacled college men engaged in research work.

On the way out, I would linger in the lower hall and look at the statuary of the old Greeks and Romans—Sophocles, Socrates, Demosthenes, Julius Caesar, and others. They must have since been sold to second-hand antique dealers, for I still see the ancient figures standing in front of some junk shops on Twenty-eighth Street. They look rather forlorn and badly chipped.

What a pity that this landmark of our city when Astor Place was uptown is now gone forever!

When the Lenox, Astor and Tilden libraries were consolidated and their books moved to the New York Public Library, the Astor Library was closed and then turned into an immigrant house—a splendid institution but not a fit successor to our old place of book reading, the Astor Library.

The higher reaches of the immigrant Jewish culture are charmingly summoned in a memoir of Nachman Syrkin, an intellectual founder of Labor Zionism, by his daughter, Marie Syrkin, herself a significant figure in the Zionist movement. Though a Hebraist in principle, Syrkin welcomed to his poverty-stricken home in the Bronx distinguished representatives of all strands of Jewish opinion, and there, in a clamor of Yiddish and Hebrew, the affairs of the world, the fate of the Jews, were warmly rehearsed.

MARIE SYRKIN

MANY COMRADES from the Berlin or Vilna days arriving in America found their way to our house. And periodically I would sleep on an improvised bed made of four chairs while the impecunious comrade searched for living quarters. Just as in other circles it was taken for granted that relatives or *landsmen* should be housed by those who had preceded them to America, in our midst the bond was ideology. I always knew that the four chairs meant a night of long talk, much tea and obscure excitement.

It is hard to disentangle the mature men and women, acquaintances of my adult life, from the delightful companions of those childhood years. The brilliant, suave Chaim Zhitlovsky would be a welcome visitor even though he and my father differed heatedly on most issues. Sholem Asch, moody and self-centered, already with an air of grandeur though not yet internationally famous, would put in an occasional appearance. The Yiddish writer Liessin lived near us. I mention those that I happen to remember but there were many more. All the active intellectual and political currents in the Jewish life of the period touched our home at some point.

Outside diversions, too, had a heavy ideological cast. We went for boat trips up the Hudson organized by the Poale Zion. There would be "balls" bearing no resemblance to any type of function usually designated by the name except that speeches would be followed by dancing and refreshments of tea and sandwiches—an obvious hangover from the student "balls" of Russia and Switzerland, each of which was dedicated to a "cause." One might meet Alexander Berkman and Emma Goldman unaccountably turning up at a Social Democratic ball despite their anarchism. And there were endless public meetings lasting late into the night to which one had to go. Baby-sitters were an unheard of institution as far as I can judge; in any case, the cost would have been prohibitive. Besides, I believe my parents felt that a bright ten-year-old should be able to appreciate political discourse at any hour.

But the worm turned. I recall confiding to the guest of honor who asked how I had enjoyed his address on one such occasion that everyone in the audience had been wishing for him to conclude because he spoke much too long. I was not being smart or rude; the truth was sacred and that was the truth. When I met my parents' subsequent remonstrances with this argument I felt beyond reproach and they were both uneasy: could they risk infecting their child's probity by inoculation with some of the whiter lies? The problem was to recur.

Our family finances, despite my father's public acclaim, remained at a low ebb. Paying the rent was always postponed to the last possible day; the landlord turned out to be an admirer of my father's and was prepared to be as elastic as possible in his construction of what date constituted that last day. The grocery storekeeper was apparently a less zealous reader of the Yiddish press. These difficulties were new only in that I was developing a great awareness of them, though by no means a painful one. What changed the situation was my mother's decision to find work in a factory.

It sounds simple enough today. Why not? One must reconstruct the state of mind of these European intellectuals of middle-class origin to appreciate that for both my father and mother, despite their socialism and "proletarian" ideology, this represented social decline.

To be a hungry student or a chronically indigent intellectual was proper and vaguely praiseworthy, but for my mother to seek work in a factory was as great a loss of caste as if my father had become a petty shopkeeper. To have become a peasant or farmer might have been in the *narodnik* or Tolstoian tradition and tolerable as such. This was different. For the first time I was told to keep a secret. Our friends were not to know.

My mother's only training was that received in two years of medical school before her marriage, but she was a clever needle-woman, as her intrepid insistence on making black alpaca suits for my father in Paris attested. She applied for work in a millinery

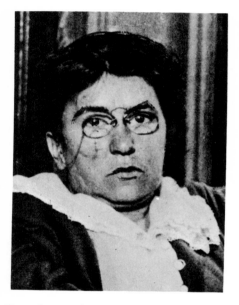

Famed anarchist and feminist Emma Goldman (1869–1940).

factory on the East Side—under an assumed name for fear that some erudite foreman would recognize Syrkin's wife and provide a bit of unwelcome publicity. After a few fumbling days she learned how to stitch the straw but though the few dollars she earned were badly needed my father was so depressed by our solvency that the experiment was abandoned after a few weeks.

It was to be resumed once more in my father's absence. The party may not have had money for its editor and foremost ideologist, but there was no question that once back in the socialist-Zionist fold he had to be sent to the Zionist congress held in Germany in 1909. I don't know what arrangements for his family's support had been made but they rapidly collapsed. Shortly after my father left, my mother pledged me once more to secrecy—I was to write none of this to papa. Being "experienced" she got another job at "hats." I was left with the apartment key and, when I returned from school, would wait till she came home. . . . My father left daily for the Astor Library, which served him as research center and office. Any crank or lunatic who wanted to find him—and the tribe was numerous—knew that he could discover Syrkin either at work in the Jewish Room or pacing meditatively up and down the corridor. To save the cost of lunch my mother would give him a sandwich cut into bite-size pieces which he would keep in his pocket and eat while reading.

I must be careful not to leave a false impression. As a child it would never have occurred to me to think of our family as "poor." My father's constant intellectual excitement, his marvelous exuberance, set the tone of the house.

Lektsies—lectures. Who can quite explain the passion of the immigrant Jews (and, sometimes, their children and grandchildren) for this form of education, entertainment, and boredom? Cut off from most educational institutions in America by lack of time and money, as well as by feelings of shyness and inadequacy, the intellectually aspiring immigrants found in the lecture their own improvised substitute. The lecture was held at union halls, after meetings of fraternal societies, in the headquarters of political groups, everywhere. The lecture could be a serious effort at communicating knowledge and ideas; it could be a counterfeit display, exploiting the innocence of listeners.

But good or bad, serious or farcical, profound or superficial, the lecture was the Jewish immigrant's own: in his language, at his place, by his intellectuals. And it's interesting to note that while some aspects of immigrant life have gradually withered away, the passion of the Jews for lectures still seems to survive. Hardly a community center or temple or synagogue doesn't have at least a few each year, again ranging wildly in quality, but still . . . people come, they sit; who knows, perhaps they listen.

David Shub, a veteran Forward writer, recalls in his Yiddish memoirs an especially spectacular group of lectures on the East Side.

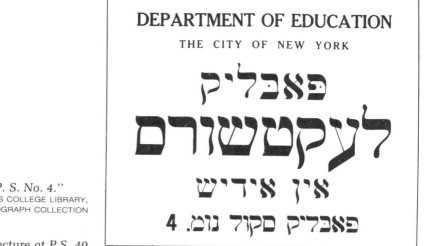

"Public Lectures in Yiddish, P. S. No. 4."
TEACHERS COLLEGE LIBRARY,
BOARD OF EDUCATION PHOTOGRAPH COLLECTION

*Self-improvement. A public lecture at P.S. 40
sponsored by the Board of Education.*
TEACHERS COLLEGE LIBRARY,
BOARD OF EDUCATION PHOTOGRAPH COLLECTION

RIGHT AFTER the 1904 presidential elections the Russian Socialist-Revolutionaries announced a series of ten lectures in Russian by Dr. Chaim Zhitlovsky on "Materialism and Synthetic Monism." That very few of the audience had any idea what that meant did not matter. The massive Clinton Hall was filled by the entire Russian-Jewish and Russian radical intelligentsia: name socialists, anarchists, Zionists, any literate Russian speaker. I attended all ten sessions.

Zhitlovsky, a handsome, middle-aged man with a very pleasant voice, spoke a lovely literary Russian and was a splendid lecturer— the best I'd heard. He was trying to prove that Marxism was not scientific, that Russian Social Democratic theory was false. I was not the only one there not to understand even half his talks.

The first half of each lecture attacked dialectical materialism with traditional and modern philosophy references hurled all over the place. Only in the latter half of the talks did the speaker get to actual Marxist thinkers like Plekhanov.

I had no idea if his critique made any sense or not but I did not like the tone of his polemics. He attacked from the left, attempting to prove that the opposition was not sufficiently radical. "In this respect we agree with the anarchists," was a typical comment, at which point the anarchists applauded vigorously.

Social Democrats and Bundists would rise to oppose Zhitlovsky but among the then New York branches of those bodies he had no equal. In philosophical debates Zhitlovsky always won, although some of us believed he was playing on our ignorance.

In one lecture he fell upon Plekhanov—the chief Russian Marxist theoretician—with quotes from Beltov, a "young Marxist philosopher." In 1895, Plekhanov, under the name Beltov, published legally in St. Petersburg a book called A *Monistic View of History*, an account of materialism and an anti-Russian populist argument. The book was very successful, until the government found out Beltov's identity and banned the work. Having read the book in Vilna in 1903 I knew who Beltov was. Zhitlovsky must have known, too, even years before that, but he assumed no one in New York would. Citing the work he tried to prove Plekhanov lacks philosophical judgment and misinterprets materialism.

Dr. S. Ingerman, head of New York's Social Democrat Russians, and longtime friend of Plekhanov's, came to the platform after the speaker and exposed him: "It's no secret to any intelligent Russian socialist that Beltov is Plekhanov, and you know it, too—for ten years at least. Nevertheless you dare attack Plekhanov with quotes from "the philosophically sophisticated Russian Marxist, Beltov. On what level is this polemic?"

Zhitlovsky reddened and answered that he's "not accustomed to tracking down pseudonyms of revolutionary literary figures."

Within a few weeks Zhitlovsky was back attacking Plekhanov's dialectics, with references to "refutations by the Italian Marxist,

Professor Antonio Labriola, and the young Russian Marxist Kamensky." Kamensky's article had appeared years earlier in an aboveground Petersburg Marxist journal, later banned. Zhitlovsky also knew that Kamensky was Plekhanov's most recent pen name. Zhitlovsky again gambled that the journal either did not reach New York or that the author's identity was not apparent.

Zhitlovsky tripped up again. I was not the only Russian socialist to have read the Kamensky articles in the Astor Library. Nor was I alone in my loss of faith in Zhitlovsky, which did not, however, diminish the colossal influence he retained over the radical Russo-Jewish intelligentsia wavering between anarchism and socialism. Followers were also won over from the older New York anarchist contingent.

The 1904–5 lecturers were delivered in Russian as was a subsequent six-lecture series. In rebuttal Abraham Cahan followed the second series with one of his own in Russian: "Is Marxism Scientific?" Zhitlovsky was present, in opposition.

Cahan tried to show that Zhitlovsky's philosophical edifice had nothing to do with Marxism because Marx had nothing to do with philosophy. Marx was an economist, argued Cahan. His doctrine is economic, Cahan added, and correct.

Zhitlovsky had no trouble demolishing Cahan. Cahan, he said, had simply had not understood the lecture he was trying to refute. Cahan's rejoinder was, "If Abraham Cahan doesn't understand Zhitlovsky's lectures, what good are they?" My sympathies were with Cahan but he did not convince me that Marxism is scientific. Cahan admitted defeat to me a few decades later.

Zhitlovsky, official United States representative of the Russian Socialist-Revolutionaries, who delivered his 1904–5 addresses in Russian, later became a Yiddishist, who steered radical assimilationists to Jewish nationalism.

NOTICE
Tonight, November 19, 1897
LECTURE about ASTRONOMY in the *William Morris Forward Club*
Admission free

November 20, 1897
LECTURE in *William Morris Club*
about ANARCHISM and SOCIALISM.

NOTICE
The Arbeiter Bildung Shule announces that Dr. Ingerman will start a series of lectures about the "HISTORY OF ANCIENT GREECE." All students who have missed a couple of lectures can come again, and also new students.

The proliferation of lectures, like everything else in the immigrant Jewish world, did not escape the caustic eye of the Forward. *And while many of these lecturers were political allies of the* Forward, *it wrote in 1904 a sharply critical analysis of the flaws—the superficialities, the self-indulgences, the frequent ignorance—of the lecture system.*

FORWARD, 10/25/'04

EVERY YEAR, when the women return from the Catskills, and the cantors begin to tie rags around their throats, the progressive portion of the Jewish quarter gets busy with lectures. Committee members scurry over the streets in pairs looking for forgotten intellectuals; people wear out the doorknobs of the *Forward* office asking for addresses of the lecturers. There is fierce competition among the societies to get good lecturers.

Friday, Saturday, and Sunday there are lectures. Hundreds of listeners—brides and grooms, boarders and *boarderkehs*, fill the halls. The lecturers talk about living things and dead things. What do these lectures accomplish?

Our people are getting a chaotic education; they are not getting what they need, but whatever is available. Our lecturers are seizing on topics that do not require exact knowledge or explanation. In addition, the listeners do not understand what is being said; the lectures do not enlighten or inspire them; instead of a ray of light, they are like clouds of dampness. After the lecture when the chairman asks for questions or debate, nobody responds. If someone does, the question has nothing to do with the lecture. It reminds one of the third act of *Enemy of the People*, in which only the drunkard speaks the truth. Sometimes the questioner is a fanatic, and the lecturer who had talked about the difference between a novel and a drama has to convince the audience that he had no intention of insulting the Socialist Labor party.

Always and everywhere the same audience. During the winter there are several hundred lectures. Big societies have series of lectures; the tiny ones have single, irregular ones. Some big clubs attract several hundred people. Statistics would show that there are thousands and thousands of Jews coming to be educated, which means that the most illiterate masses are being reached. . . . The observant lecturer or listener sees the same faces at every lecture. There are numerous young men and girls whom you can see at every talk, unless there are several in one evening. They come to hear about socialism on East Broadway and about literature on Forsythe Street; about a play in Harlem, and even a lecture in Russian on Grand Street. Although they hardly know the language, it doesn't matter—they sit and sweat and listen.

"And she talks . . ." *A satirical attack on the* Forward. *Drawing by William Gropper.*

Second only to the network of lectures, and in part an extension of it, was the network of cafés at which the more intellectual and bohemian segments of the immigrant world spent its evenings in talk and tea. The café had a long and honorable history in Europe which it has never been able to match in America. But there was another reason for congregating at Goodman and Levine's or Sholem's, or later at the most famous of all, the Café Royale. Apartments were so crowded, there was often no room for guests; sometimes so threadbare, one was ashamed to invite people. At the café you could get away from the burdens of family, children, bills; you could forget yourself in the pleasures of literary conversation, roaming over the cultures of Europe and America, or you could criticize expertly the latest performances of Jacob Adler or David Kessler. In the cafés, for a minimal expenditure for a glass of tea and a piece of cake, you could live out in the evenings a fantasy of freedom and largesse.

HERMAN YABLOKOFF

PEOPLE SIT IN THE Royale all day and night. The aristocrats of the theater family sit on the right; the lesser actors, writers, and general public on the left. It is an unwritten law. When an actor gets a good review in Friday's paper, he automatically goes to the right. The waiters know all the customers by heart. The *trombeniks* who can't afford a meal are not driven out. They have enough sense to vacate the tables at dinnertime for those who can afford a good Hungarian meal. Minor actors grab a bite in Ratner's or Rappaport's dairy restaurants, the Fourteenth Street Automat or a Jewish deli, then rush back to the Royale.

Kibbitzing in a literary café: Abraham Reisen, seated third from left; Sholom Asch, standing fourth from left; Joseph Opatoshu, seated fifth from left; B. Rifkin, standing third from right.
YIVO INSTITUTE
FOR JEWISH RESEARCH

Many actors call themselves to the telephone, so that Herman, the busboy, should call out their names and the managers will remember them. As soon as they see Guskin or a theater director enter the Royale, they rush out to a candy store and call themselves on the phone. Herman shouts: "Just left," or "Not in." When the actor returns Herman tells him: "You just had a call; a Broadway theater manager," he jokes. He understands the "plot" and for that alone he is worth a nickel. If he doesn't get it, he'll refuse to call the actors' names.

COMMERCIAL ADVERTISER, 4/22/'99

THE OTHER DAY a Hebrew scholar, a Yiddish actor, a Hebrew poet, and the editor of an East Side Yiddish paper were talking together in the lobby of the Windsor Theater. The scholar was explaining how it is that the Hebrew language is greater than any other. "It is the only language," he said, "which means more than it says. When you say 'a chair' in English or in Russian or in Yiddish, you mean simply a chair, but when you say 'a chair' in Hebrew you mean almost everything, for the word is connected with an infinite number of things."

The four men proceeded to a café where a discussion of the Hebrew language ensued. The poet began to discuss with the Yiddish editor an intricate point in Hebrew. Soon the actor, the poet, the scholar, and the editor were industriously scribbling and arguing about various points of the dead language. The discussion lasted about half an hour, with the participants using several languages—Russian, German, Yiddish, and English, as well as Hebrew—to convey the delicacy of their meanings.

And they talked of things too which were not so minute. They talked of realistic art, of the degradation of the theater; they gossiped intelligently about their friends, about literature. The actor spoke of having seen Sonnenthal, the great German actor, the night before in *Nathan der Weise*. The scholar deplored the rarity of excellence and the prevalence of frivolity in art and literature. It was a serious and elevated conversation and had an added interest in view of the fact that there are several hundred men in the East Side who form a community where general ideas are nightly discussed in the various little cafés of the neighborhood. These men meet late at night, and instead of getting drunk discuss high thoughts with cheerful indifference to the squalor and dirt of their environment.

BERNARD RICHARDS

"YES," SAID KEIDANSKY, "I fully believe in the Americanization of the Russian Jews, but in order to bring this about in the best manner American Jews should first become somewhat Russianized. . . .

"There is something earnest, something serious, something solid, about the Russian that seems to him deplorably lacking in the average Americanized Jew. The Americanized Jew seems to become so superficial, so frivolous, so light-minded and narrow that he does not appeal to the studious European Jew, who looks always for thought and for depth of character. . . ."

Keidansky took a sip of his tea, a puff at his cigarette, greeted a fellow scribe, who had just entered the café and continued:

". . . Here is a bargain. Please publish it for me. If the American Jews will help to put Ibsen and Hauptmann and Gorky on the American stage, I promise to shave twice a week (to begin with), cut my hair short and have my nails—what do you call it?—yes, manicured. So long as these plays are given only in German and Yiddish I refuse to enter America beyond Fourteenth Street. I agree even to learn table manners on condition that the American Jews furnish good after-dinner conversation. Otherwise I will continue to eat with my knife.

"I like America immensely, but I like it served in Russian style."

In 1922 Oswald Garrison Villard, a once-famous liberal writer who for many years edited The Nation, *turned his eyes southward in Manhattan and took a close look at the* Jewish Daily Forward. *His report was accurate and sympathetic.*

OSWALD GARRISON VILLARD

WHICH IS THE MOST VITAL, the most interesting, the most democratic of New York's daily journals? In my judgment it is the *Forward*, or the *Vorwärts*, to use its Yiddish name. I doubt if the publishers of other American journals know much about it. They must have heard vaguely of the superb office building which it has erected on the East Side in the midst of its constituency and they must, most of them, gasp with envy when they hear that its circulation is now 200,000—far beyond that of the *Tribune* or *Globe* or *Herald* or *Sun!* But what must startle them most is the fact that a large part of the net profits of this newspaper go not to the owners or the editors but are under the bylaws of the Forward Association distributed among the exponents of the causes to which the *Forward* is devoted. During the last ten years the *Forward* has earned one and a half million dollars, of which it has, after providing for its splendid up-to-date plant, donated $350,000 to union labor and to other causes for which it battles. Often in enterprises like this the profit is distributed in large salaries and expenses; yet the editor-in-chief of this amazing publication recently strenuously resisted his colleagues' efforts to advance his salary to a figure which would be scorned by a city editor of any of our English-language morning dailies. But its lower-placed workers are well remunerated. Even when one has to find fault with a given policy—the dollar motive is not attributed to its conductors. When there was an investigation during the war of our foreign press, an

The Forward building on East Broadway. JEWISH DAILY FORWARD

investigator testified that the *Forward* was the only foreign language daily in America which could not be bought. . . .

The *Forward* progressed slowly enough until the idea of a purely socialist propaganda organ was abandoned, and Mr. Cahan came to the front, making the *Forward* a newspaper first, and only secondarily a political instrument. Fortunately for him and his daily, his accession to the editorship was followed in 1903 by a vast increase in the Russian immigrants to the United States, in consequence of the Kishinev pogroms, by which immigration the *Forward* greatly profited.

Mr. Cahan has been governed by a double standard in dealing with his public. He struck first for popularity; hence he decided to make the writing in his journal so simple that the least intelligent on the East Side could understand it. He not only adopted the colloquialisms of the Yiddish of New York, showing no hostility whatever to the introduction of English words, but employed editors to susbstitute in the news manuscripts the shortest words possible for more learned ones. In his editorials he deals with topics of the widest appeal, like the famous editorial of his urging every mother who read the *Forward* to see that her child took a clean hand-kerchief to school with him. Over this editorial there raged a storm. East Side intellectuals denounced it as insulting. But Mr. Cahan felt that the learning of the learned Orthodox Jews was narrow and unsuited to the everyday needs of the hundreds and thousands of *Forward* readers. Mr. Cahan knows how to render his daily of personal service to his readers. There is no more striking feature than its letters from readers regarding their personal problems. Again there have appeared from time to time extraordinary symposia bearing upon some of the vital problems of the East Side, such as the tragedy of the growing apart of immigrant parents and their rapidly Americanized children. When there is suffering on the East Side, it is the *Forward* to which multitudes look for guidance and leadership as well as for financial aid.

What pabulum does this unusual newspaper supply to its followers? Its eight pages of eight columns each (28 or 32 pages on Sunday) offers a variegated bill of fare. Pictures, of course; occasional cartoons; little of crime (about two columns a day); often sensational matter; extraordinarily valuable correspondence from abroad, together with a great deal of Jewish and labor news, all with Hearst-like headlines. While the *Forward* writes down to its readers, it is printing today by far the best fiction and *belles lettres* of any newspaper in America. This is Mr. Cahan's second striking conception for his journal. He has employed an amazing array of remarkable writers whose names are almost unknown to the English-reading public but who are printing real literature in this East Side newspaper. Best of all, the whole spirit of the newspaper is really actuated by the old American ideals of liberty and justice. Hence it was hounded by the government during the war.

Abraham Cahan (1860–1951), editor of the Jewish Daily Forward.
JEWISH DAILY FORWARD

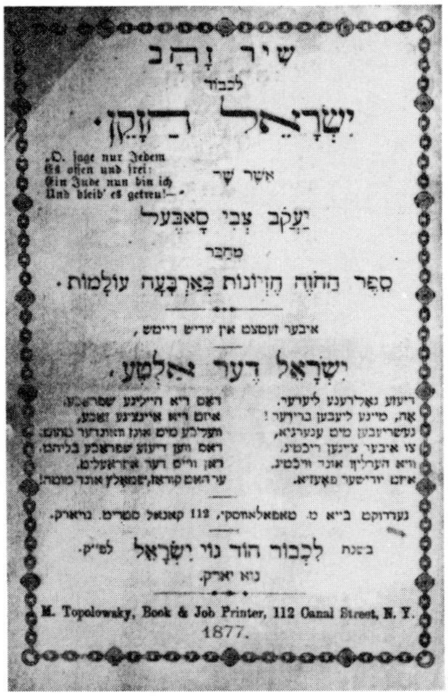

שִׁיר זָהָב
לכבוד
יִשְׂרָאֵל הַזָּקֵן

אשר ש

יַעֲקֹב צְבִי סאָבעל
מחבר
סֵפֶר הַחֹזֶה הַחִזְיוֹנוֹת בְּאַרְבָּעָה עוֹלָמוֹת

איבער זעצט אין יודיש דייטש

יִשְׂרָאֵל דער אַלטער

בשנת לכבוד הוד גוי יִשְׂרָאֵל לפ"ק
ניו יארק

M. Topolowsky, Book & Job Printer, 112 Canal Street, N. Y.
1877.

The first Yiddish book published in America, a volume of inspirational poems translated by Jacob Sobel from "The sacred tongue" into "Judeo-German."

Yiddish Voices

Of the rich harvest of Yiddish literature, its poetry and its prose, we can offer here only a few small samples, in the hope they will stimulate the reader to go to the work of the writers themselves. Let it be said, however, that in the decades between, say, 1890 and 1970 there was an outpouring of Yiddish creative work in America. Something of the situation and problems of that work is suggested in a poem by one of the Yiddish writers, Meyer Stiker.

MEYER STIKER

YIDDISH POETS IN NEW YORK

They came from small and from large towns,
In coats bulky, coarse, and shoes with patches,
Their eyes wide open and their lips in prayer
That their separated fathers might recognize them.

In rooms like hovels on Reed and on Pitt streets,
In meager parks with hardly any grass or trees,
They moved at first with halting, bashful steps,
Clinging to the seam of their dreams, dreams that

Had followed them from home, dazzling them
Like snow or rustling branches in bloom.
Now in dark alleys of granite and of brick
They have sown the kernels of a poem
Thereby to cover up old patches—and again
Their fathers do not recognize them.

Translated by Arthur Gregor

The first significant group of Yiddish poets to appear in the immigrant world was called the sweatshop, or labor, poets. They were men who were themselves workers, experiencing in the shops the same need and exhaustion, the same bleak humiliation as the mass of immigrants. Their poetry was sincere, if not sophisticated; it spoke directly out of the feelings of the masses, and sometimes spoke to them in accents of radical exhortation. Perhaps the most gifted of these poets was Morris Rosenfeld, a man of flaring personality and pathos.

HUTCHINS HAPGOOD

... MORRIS ROSENFELD WAS BORN in a small village in the province of Subalk, in Russian Poland, at the end of the last Polish revolution. The very night he was born the world began to oppress him, for insurgents threw rocks through the window. His grandfather was rich, but his father lost the money in business, and Morris received very little education—only the Talmud and a little German, which he got at a school in Warsaw. He married when he was sixteen, "because my father told me to," as the poet expressed it. He ran away from Poland to avoid being pressed into the army. "I would like to serve my country," he said, "if there had been any freedom for the Jew." Then he went to Holland and learned the trade of diamond cutting; then to London, where he took up tailoring.

Hearing that the tailors had won a strike in America, he came to New York, thinking he would need to work here only ten hours a day. "But what I heard," he said, "was a lie. I found the sweatshops in New York just as bad as they were in London."

In those places he worked for many years, worked away his health and strength, but at the same time composed many a sweetly sad song. "I worked in the sweatshop in the daytime," he said to me, "and at night I worked at my poems. I could not help writing them. My heart was full of bitterness. If my poems are sad and plaintive, it is because I expressed my own feelings, and because my surroundings were sad."

MORRIS ROSENFELD

THE SWEATSHOP

Corner of Pain and Anguish, there's a worn old house:
tavern on the street floor, Bible room upstairs.
Scoundrels sit below, and all day long they souse.
On the floor above them, Jews sob out their prayers.

Higher, on the third floor, there's another room:
not a single window welcomes in the sun.
Seldom does it know the blessing of a broom.
Rottenness and filth are blended into one.

Toiling without letup in that sunless den:
nimble-fingered and (or so it seems) content,
sit some thirty blighted women, blighted men,
with their spirits broken, and their bodies spent.

Scurf-head struts among them: always with a frown,
acting like His Royal Highness in a play;
for the shop is his, and here he wears the crown,
and they must obey him, silently obey.

The poet Morris Rosenfeld (1862–1923)
shortly after his arrival in New York in
1886.   YIVO INSTITUTE FOR JEWISH RESEARCH

MY LITTLE SON

I have a son, a little son,
a youngster very fine!
and when I look at him I feel
that all the world is mine.

But seldom do I see him when
he's wide awake and bright.
I always find him sound asleep;
I see him late at night.

The time clock drags me off at dawn;
at night it lets me go,
I hardly know my flesh and blood;
his eyes I hardly know. . . .

I climb the staircase wearily;
a figure wrapped in shade.
Each night my haggard wife describes
how well the youngster played;

how sweetly he's begun to talk;
how cleverly he said,
"When will my daddy come and leave
a penny near my bed?"

I listen, and I rush inside—
it must—yes, it must be!
My father-love begins to burn:
my child must look at me! . . .

I stand beside the little bed
and watch my sleeping son,
when hush! a dream bestirs his mouth:
"Where has my daddy gone?"

I touch his eyelids with my lips.
The blue eyes open then:
they look at me! they look at me!
and quickly shut again.

"Your daddy's right beside you, dear.
Here, here's a penny, son!"
A dream bestirs his little mouth:
"Where has my daddy gone?"

I watch him, wounded and depressed
by thoughts I cannot bear:
"One morning, when you wake—my child—
you'll find that I'm not here."

Translated by Aaron Kramer

An illustration from Tsukunft, a distinguished Yiddish literary magazine published for many years by the Forward Association.

די צוקונפט

No. 8 (20)   AUGUST, 1903   Volume 2

The greatest of all Yiddish writers, Sholom Aleichem, spent the last year and a half of his life in New York, living in the Bronx together with other immigrants and earning his living by writing sketches for the Yiddish papers. Here is an amusing memoir of Sholom Aleichem in New York by a Yiddish journalist.

N.B. LINDER

ONE SUNDAY MORNING on one of those warm, late-autumn New York days, I accompanied Sholom Aleichem on a short walk along Westchester Avenue in the Bronx.

Sholom Aleichem was asking me about the *Saturday Evening Post*. Someone had suggested he translate some of his stories for publication in that magazine. So he wanted to know: what sort of readers did it have, how large was its circulation, what kind of stories did it print, were there very well-known Jewish writers among its contributors?

Speaking about these things, we went on to a discussion of American literature in general. Sholom Aleichem mentioned Edgar Allan Poe, Mark Twain and a few other famous American authors whom he had read in Russian translation. Hardly any of the modern American authors were familiar to him, he said.

As we were walking along, a young man whom Sholom Aleichem had met previously broke into our conversation and asked whether he couldn't walk along with us. He was a "partly-Americanized" Russian intellectual who had been here about ten years. As we continued our conversation, he told Sholom Aleichem something about the new works that were appearing in American literature and mentioned a number of writers, speaking with particular respect about the influence of H.L. Mencken on the younger literary figures in America.

Sholom Aleichem wanted to know: Who is Mencken and what does he represent? The young man then told him everything he knew about Mencken and in passing said that Mencken was known as a fanatical woman-hater. This interested Sholom Aleichem greatly and the following dialogue ensued.

Sholom Aleichem: "Probably had a shrew of a wife who made his life miserable?"

The Young Man: "No. He never married."

S.A.: "Is that so? A bachelor then. Was he ever betrothed? Did he ever have a sweetheart?"

T. Y. M.: "This I cannot tell you for certain."

S.A.: "Did he have sisters? Sisters-in-law?"

T.Y.M.: "I don't know. I know nothing about his family. But if you're really interested, I can find out and let you know."

S. A.: "Yes. Find out, for God's sake! And while you're about it, try to find out too whether he at least had a mother!"

Sholom Aleichem with his wife in America.

IT WAS A COLD, wet day. Sholom Aleichem had not been feeling well and, to make matters worse, was extremely tired. He had been standing all morning, as was his custom, writing at a high table in his workroom. He had an appointment to meet someone on Forty-second Street that afternoon and I was to go with him. His family was reluctant to let him go outdoors in such weather but, since the arrangements had been made some time ago, there was nothing for it but to "go into the city," as Sholom Aleichem used to say.

He felt so little like talking that when we sat down in the subway train he allowed me to read a newspaper—something he never permitted me to do when I accompanied him on his trips. He closed his eyes and occupied himself with his own thoughts. But it was not one of Sholom Aleichem's lucky days. We had just sat down when a man moved over to us and said that he had recognized Sholom

Aleichem and wanted his opinion on certain political matters. He began to fire questions at Sholom Aleichem: What did he think about the war? How did he like Hindenburg's dealings with the Russians? etc. etc.

Sholom Aleichem listened and answered with a short "yes" or "no" or "who knows" and kept looking at me beseechingly to rescue him from this ambush. I tried to draw the man's attention away from Sholom Aleichem but he had attached himself like a leech and refused to be brushed off.

Suddenly he noticed that Sholom Aleichem was wearing a pair of foreign galoshes made of red leather. "Funny-looking galoshes," he observed. "First time I ever saw such galoshes! How come galoshes red?"

This time Sholom Aleichem opened his eyes and inspected his besieger. "The cook in our house accidentally spilled a plate of Passover borscht on them; that's why the're red. . . ."

The man smiled—he understood, that is, that Sholom Aleichem was joking. But he had another question, just as difficult: He had noticed that the lenses in Sholom Aleichem's glasses were unusual. (Sholom Aleichem was farsighted and needed glasses only for reading; he wore especially-made half-lenses.) "How come you wear half-glasses—not whole ones like everybody else?"

I was afraid that Sholom Aleichem would lose his patience, but he replied quietly and easily: "I have a cat at home who loves to eat. She'll eat anything and, as you see, she ate up half my glasses. . . ."

The man enjoyed this joke very much. He burst out laughing, and in order to show that he too knew something about humor, he assumed a naïve expression and said: "A likely story! A cat? I never saw a cat who would eat glass!"

"And a man who chews cotton—did you ever see that?" asked Sholom Aleichem.

"What does that mean—'chew cotton'? I don't understand."

"To chew cotton," explained Sholom Aleichem very patiently, "is to attach yourself to another human being, uninvited, and bend his ear with foolish talk which he doesn't care a fig about. Now do you understand?"

Our uninvited guest asked no further questions. He didn't even stay on the same train!

The masthead of The Big Stick, *an East Side journal of "humor, wit and satire."*

Poets, painters, thinkers: Rear (left to right) Peretz Hirsch-bein (?), S. Drimmer, unidentified, Moses Soyer, Reuben Iceland, Jennings Tofel, Sasha Ostrofsky, David Ignatov. Front (left to right) Chaim Gross, three unidentified women, Mani Leib, two unidentified women, Shaye Boudin, Julia Levien.

A period of Yiddish creativity starts in about 1907 with the group of poets called Di Yunge *("the Young Ones")—Mani Leib, Zisha Landau, Moishe Leib Halpern, H. Leivick, and others. They soon would go their different ways, but for a time what linked them was their desire to create a poetry that would not just be propagandistic, either for Jewish socialism or Jewish nationalism. They wanted a poetry that would be free, autonomous, dealing with personal experience. The majority of them were still shop workers, but they hoped, in Landau's witticism, to create a poetry that would no longer be "the rhyme department of the Jewish labor movement." They purified the Jewish language of* Deutschmarish, *the heavy Germanisms beloved by earlier writers; they wrote as individuals, though individuals still living in the immigrant streets.*

MANI LEIB

I AM

I am Mani Leib, whose name is sung—
In Brownsville, Yehupetz and farther, they know it:
Among cobblers, a splendid cobbler; among
Poetical circles, a splendid poet.

A boy straining over the cobbler's last
On moonlit nights . . . like a command,
Some hymn struck at my heart, and fast
The awl fell from my trembling hand.

Gracious, the first Muse came to meet
The cobbler with a kiss, and, young,
I tasted the Word that comes in a sweet
Shuddering fist to the speechless tongue.

And my tongue flowed like a limpid stream,
My song rose as from some other place;
My world's doors opened onto dream;
My labor, my bread, were sweet with grace.

And all of the others, the shoemaker boys
Thought that my singing was simply grand:
For their bitter hearts, my poems were joys.
Their source? They could never understand.

For despair in their working day's vacuity
They mocked me, spat at me a good deal,
And gave me the title, in perpetuity,
Of Purple Patchmaker, Poet and Heel.

Farewell then, brothers, I must depart:
Your cobbler's bench is not for me.
With songs in my breast, the Muse in my heart,
I went among poets, a poet to be.

When I came, then, among their company,
Newly fledged from out my shell,
They lauded and they laureled me,
Making me one of their number as well.

O Poets, inspired and pale, and free
As all the winged singers of the air,
We sang of beauties wild to see
Like happy beggars at a fair.

We sang, and the echoing world resounded.
From pole to pole chained hearts were hurled,
While we gagged on hunger, our sick chests pounded:
More than one of us left this world.

And God, who feedeth even the worm—
Was not quite lavish with his grace,
So I crept back, threadbare and infirm,
To sweat for bread at my working place.

But blessed be, Muse, for your bounties still,
Though your granaries will yield no bread—
At my bench, with a pure and lasting will,
I'll serve you solely until I am dead.

In Brownsville, Yehupetz, beyond them, even,
My name shall ever be known, O Muse.
And I'm not a cobbler who writes, thank Heaven,
But a poet, who makes shoes.

Translated by John Hollander

*Yiddish poets Mani Leib and
Rochelle Weprinsky.*
> *Let us meet again:
> two gravestones
> standing
> with wind
> between.*
> ROCHELLE WEPRINSKY

MANI LEIB

EAST BROADWAY

Of all rich streets, most dear to me
Is my shabby Jewish East Broadway.
Graying houses—two uneven rows:
Frail, restless and exhausted bodies:
The worry tinged with God's old fire—
It barely glows, yet it does not die.
And on the corners, seers and rebels
Who shout a nation's woe unto the sky.
And the poets. O rhapsodic brothers!

On the grime of each stone, you transmute
A nation's heart—finely—
Into the strains of a new hymnal.
Long after you, each stone will join
Your people in the prayer of your song.

Translated by Nathan Halper

MOISHE LEIB HALPERN

THE BIRD

So this bird comes, and under his wing is a crutch,
And he asks why I keep my door on the latch;
So I tell him that right outside the gate
Many robbers watch and wait
To get at the hidden bit of cheese,
Under my ass, behind my knees.

Then through the keyhole and the crack in the jamb
The bird bawls out he's my brother Sam,
And tells me I'll never begin to believe
How sorely he was made to grieve
On shipboard, where he had to ride
Out on deck, he says, from the other side.

So I get a whiff of what's in the air,
And leave the bird just standing there.
Meanwhile—because one never knows,
I mean—I'm keeping on my toes,
Further pushing my bit of cheese
Under my ass and toward my knees.

The bird bends his wing to shade his eyes
—Just like my brother Sam—and cries,
Through the keyhole, that *his* luck should shine
Maybe so blindingly as mine,
Because, he says, he's seen my bit
Of cheese, and he'll crack my skull for it.

It's not so nice here any more.
So I wiggle slowly toward the door,
Holding my chair and that bit of cheese
Under my ass, behind my knees,
Quietly. But then, as if I care,
I ask him whether it's cold out there.

They are frozen totally,
Both his poor ears, he answers me,

Declaring with a frightful moan
That, while he lay asleep alone
He ate up his leg—the one he's lost.
If I let him in, I can hear the rest.

When I hear the words "ate up," you can bet
That I'm terrified; I almost forget
To guard my bit of hidden cheese
Under my ass there, behind my knees.
But I reach below and, yes, it's still here,
So I haven't the slightest thing to fear.

Then I move that we should try a bout
Of waiting, to see which first gives out,
His patience, there, behind the door,
Or mine, in my own house. And more
And more I feel it's funny, what
A lot of patience I have got.

And that's the way it's stayed, although
That was some seven years ago.
I still call out "Hi, there!" through the door.
He screams back "'Lo, there" as before.
"Let me out" I plead, "don't be a louse"
And he answers, "Let me in the house."

But I know what he wants. So I bide
My time and let him wait outside.
He inquires about the bit of cheese
Under my ass, behind my knees;
Scared, I reach down, but, yes, it's still here.
I haven't the slightest thing to fear.

Translated by John Hollander

MAN, THAT APE
Man, that ape, the first time in his life
He sees an elephant at night,
In all that darkness, the elephant's
Wearing, it seems, a pair of pants.
He broods about this for a while,
Then from some fig leaves, constructs a pair
of pants, a pull-over, and underwear,

A shirt and shoes and then a hat,
And a skullcap for wearing under that.
Man, that ape.

That's nothing—the first time in his life
He sees the risen moon on high,
He locks his wife in an embrace
To singe the hair from off her face;
And after that, to make her gleam,
First he smears on a chalky cream,
Then sticks on all the gold he's got.
She doesn't emanate one beam.
He howls and bays and starts to scream.
Man, that ape.

That's nothing—the first time in his life
He sees the sun ascending where
The mountaintop and heaven meet,
He raises his right fist to swear
That he will follow it up there;
Since when, too short of time, he's run
From east to west, just like the sun.
The sun comes up, the sun descends:
He climbs, and falls—it never ends.
Man, that ape.

Translated by John Hollander

LONG FOR HOME
Long for home and hate your homeland.
What can you be
But a tiny twig
Snapped from a withered tree?
An ashen speck
In a burning tower?
Little soul, raging on your day of woe,
When a man here goes astray
What can he aspire to
But insanity,
To rend himself and be alone?
Weep, then, for your passing years.
Like rain upon the ocean
Fall your tears.

Translated by Meyer Schapiro

KADIA MOLODOWSKY

WHITE NIGHT

White night, my painful joy,
your light is brighter than the dawn.
A white ship is sailing from East Broadway
where I see no sail by day.

A quiet star hands me a ticket
open for all the seas.
I put on my time-worn jacket
and entrust myself to the night.

Where are you taking me, ship?
Who charted us on this course?
The hieroglyphs of the map escape me,
and the arrows of your compass.

I am the one who sees and does not see.
I go along on your deck of secrets,
squeeze shut my baggage on the wreath of sorrows
from all my plucked-out homes.

Four Yiddish poets in America—
Malka Lee, Bertha Kling, Ida Glazer,
Shifra Weiss.
YIVO INSTITUTE FOR JEWISH RESEARCH

—Pack in all my blackened pots,
their split lids, the chipped crockeries,
pack in my chaos with its gold-encrusted buttons
since chaos will always be in fashion.

—Pack the letters stamped *Unknown at This Address*—
vanished addresses that sear my eyes,
postmarked with more than years and days;
sucked into my bones and marrow.

—Pack up my shadow that weighs more than my body,
that comes along with its endless exhortations.
Weekdays or holidays, time of flowers or withering,
my shadow is with me, muttering its troubles.

Find me a place of honey cakes and sweetness
where angels and children picnic together
(this is the dream I love best of all),
where the sacred wine fizzes in bottles.

Let me have one sip, here on East Broadway,
for the sake of those old Jews crying in the dark.
I cry my heretic's tears with them,
their sobbing is my sobbing.

I'm a difficult passenger, my ship
is packed with the heavy horns, the *shofars* of grief.
Tighten the sails of night as far as you can,
for the daylight cannot carry me.

Take me somewhere to a place of rest,
of goats in belled hats playing on trombones—
to the Almighty's fresh white sheets
where the hunter's shadow cannot fall.

Take me . . . Yes, take me . . . But you know best
where the sea calmly opens its blue road.
I'm wearier than your oldest tower;
somewhere I've left my heart aside.

Translated by Adrienne Rich

ANNA MARGOLIN

GIRLS IN CROTONA PARK
As in a faded picture,
Girls have woven themselves
Into the autumn evening,
Their eyes cool, their smiles wild and thin,
Their clothes lavender, old-rose, and apple-green.
Dew flows through their veins,
Their words are bright and clear.
Botticelli once loved them in a dream.

As Yiddish fiction and poetry developed in the United States, there began also to appear a serious and sophisticated literary criticism in Yiddish. In its earlier phases, this criticism necessarily focused on two central questions: What is the distinctive character, or "mission," of Yiddish literature that distinguishes it from all others? How have the all-but-unique conditions of modern Jewish experience—religious tradition, geographical dispersion, persecution, cultural renaissance—affected the outbreak of secular imaginative writing in Yiddish? One of the most ingenious of Yiddish critics, B. Rivkin, developed a theory that Yiddish literature served as a substitute for the Jewish nation not-yet-formed, providing the substance of cultural identity. The most influential Yiddish critic, S. Niger, wrote learnedly about the depth of the Yiddish cultural experience itself, showing the seldom-noticed ties between modern Yiddish writing and the scattered homiletic and popular writings in Yiddish over the centuries.

All of this tended to take Yiddish literature in bulk, but the best literary criticism is usually written about individual figures. So too in Yiddish. Niger, for example, wrote a first-rate historical and literary study of I.L. Peretz, the major Yiddish fiction writer who borrowed heavily from folk and Hasidic sources. Gradually, literary criticism in Yiddish turned away from "national tasks" and "cultural obligations," and began to listen to individual voices, the tenderness, for example, of Abraham Reisen, a poet and storyteller who became a legendary figure among the Jewish immigrants, or Moishe Leib Halpern, a tormented, rebellious, sardonic poet who lived most of his life in New York. Among these more literary of literary critics, two of the notable were A. Tabachnik, who devoted himself mainly to writing about Di Yunge, the lyrical poets who flourished in New York shortly before the First World War; and Jacob Glatstein, himself a major Yiddish poet, whose caustic style and capacity for making comparisons between Yiddish and American writers made him a notable critic as well.

A. TABACHNIK

WE HAVE TO REMEMBER that, historically, *Di Yunge* were matching themselves against poets whose work was then regarded as the loftiest and last word in the art of poetry. It hardly seemed possible to imagine that anything better, or more beautiful, could follow the lyrics of Rosenfeld and Yehoash. Hence the *Yunge* had to struggle and put up with the greatest mockery and persecution. They were thought of not merely as "decadents," but as plain barbarians and defilers of the Yiddish word. Still, in the long run the *Yunge* were triumphant, and their successes were of an epoch-making nature: they altered forever the character of the Yiddish poem. After them it was impossible to write the way one had written before. . . .

The revolt of the *Yunge*, though it set forth artistically pure goals and zealously marked itself off from social questions, was nevertheless essentially an expression of deep social changes in Jewish life. Before the revolt of the *Yunge* could occur, Jewish life had to gather up new strengths and open up new sources of spirit while revivifying ancient ones; there had to be deep changes in the relationship between the individual and the community, and the ripening of a new sensibility; new cultural needs had to come about, and a fresh look at the meaning and purpose of life. Still, an artistic revolution is not the same as a social revolution. Often the more radical artistic revolutions are nothing short of reactionary in their social import, while by contrast the reversion to ancient traditions may turn out in fact to be progessive and democratic, indeed folkish in character.

The history of our literature declares something else: that as Yiddish poetry became more modern, as it increasingly adopted such subtle and sophisticated movements as symbolism, impressionism, neo-Romanticism, as its very texture became more refined and sophisticated, it also began paradoxically to draw nearer to those crevices in the Jewish soul that harbor the "Hidden Light," the undisclosed, or—as David Ignatov, one of the chief leaders of the *Yunge*, called one of his pieces—the "Buried Light." And on the other hand, wherever our poetry remained didactic, old-fashioned, conventional, unsophisticated, that was exactly where it turned out to be less Jewish in its artistic particulars (rhythm, symbol, imagery), and where it failed to give rise to any expression of our Sabbath-life or even our weekday life—that ordinary dailiness which later poets like Y. Y. Segal elevated to a poetic Sabbath-sanctity: to the beauty and holiness, in fact, of a sacred legend.

As Yiddish poetry grew more modern, even modernistic, as it grew freer in rhythm, subtler in tonality, more artful and sophisticated in imagery, it also grew more Jewish—I was almost going to say more Hasidic, in the Reb Nachman Bratzlaver sense of the word. The very first revolt in Yiddish poetry, that of the *Yunge*, was expressed in a turning back to origins—origins which Peretz calls "barely experienced"—to the religious vision of the Jewish people, its sorrow and rapture, its Messianic longing-and-redemption mythos.

You can see this not only in Leivick, but also in Moishe Leib Halpern, that mutineer and blasphemer. It is apparent in his images, the free skip of his apocalyptic fancies, his grotesquerie which contains so much of Yiddish *Purim*-theatricality, his bright rhythms redolent of traditional *Gemara*-tunes. And not only in Leivick and Moishe Leib—there is the same spirit in Mani Leib, that master of Yiddish idiom whom some like to consider not, God forbid, a Jew, but rather a sort of Russian in disguise. Certainly no one can deny or minimize the influence of Russian poetry on Mani Leib. Nevertheless no one else has set forth a poetry of Jewish faith in Mani Leib's particular manner and with his beauty and artistry. If we count Leivick (in verse only, of course) in the tradition of those cabalists who were not satisfied to await the Messiah but wanted to wrest him forth by force, then Mani Leib must be the poet of quiet folk-piety, the poet of belief who finds his expression in the common people's faith that God will not abandon them, that the miracle is not far off and can occur at the last second.

In Mani Leib, Elijah appears exactly as the common people conceived him—not the Elijah who flies up to heaven in a fiery chariot, but the one who secretly wanders over the earth, often disguised as a peasant. And who takes on still another incarnation in Mani Leib. "Only another whistler," Mani Leib calls himself—but who and what is he if not comfort-bringer, consoler, singer of lullabies? He is almost an Elijah himself. Look how the two resemble each other:

Love and sorrow fill his eyes,
Love smiles on his lips.
Among the poor, in peasant's guise,
From house to house Elijah slips.

And the poet goes among the same houses and "whistles like a wondrous flute the ballads of the poor," and as he whistles "[Jews] stand and hear, and in the stillness swallow tears, and their hearts rejoice that they are poor." Rosenfeld had sung "On a mute word hangs my people's dream." Modern Yiddish poets have lifted the dream out of muteness and given it tongue.

S. Niger (1883–1955), Yiddish literary critic.   YIVO INSTITUTE FOR JEWISH RESEARCH

S. NIGER

THERE IS NO DOUBT that a poem should exist for its own sake, not as a means to express ideas. Certainly it is good that poetry has declared its liberation. But . . . what does it mean for poetry to be free and not serve anyone or anything? What is the meaning of "poetry has its own place and unique functions"? Does it mean that all other "places" and all other "functions" in our life have no relation to it? That the creation and enjoyment of poetry is isolated from all other spheres of life? That creation and enjoyment of it exist in a vacuum? I am convinced that this is not what the *Yunge* meant when they talked about the freedom and specific functions of poetry. . . .

In the days of Edelstadt and Bovshover most of Yiddish poetry was subjugated to ideas and movements. . . . The verses and rhymes that were merely a means to an end.

At a time when art was crushed in the name of ideology, it was natural that poets who wanted to be poets should cry out: "We are not agitators, we are poets! We are the first to introduce the 'poetry of pure artistry.'"

The theory which proclaims that art has its own life and functions played a positive role in the development of Yiddish literature and world literature. I have no intention of minimizing its historical and psychological impact. But we must understand what it means for poetry and for all the arts to have "independent existence and functions." Does it mean that "the rest of life" no longer exists for the poet? That there is a barrier between ideas and poetry? Of course not!

The *Yunge* said that "poetic themes" should be discarded and everyday, drab life should be a source of poetry. True, but the "personal, everyday life," just like the "poetic" motiv, is insufficient by itself. It must be charged with deep response by the poet, and these responses must be revealed by means of words, sounds, and rhythms.

What does "pure" art and "free" poetry really mean? Of what must poetry be cleansed and from what must it liberate itself? From "political agitation and banal nationalist and social ideas," they tell us. In the days of our pioneer poetry this made sense. It was a "reaction to the banalities that were strangling it," proclaimed the *Yunge*, and therefore they "avoided nationalist motives," etc.

Isn't this a one-sided reaction? Is it really necessary to "cleanse poetry of social themes in order not to become bombastic"? By the same token, one would have to avoid "intimate-lyrical" emotions, because there are plenty of rhymesters whose hollow verses destroy and desecrate such feelings.

But intimate experiences are acceptable to the *Yunge*. Why then should not social or national responses be acceptable, if they are profound and meaningful? There are always hacks for every theme, while a living pen brings it to life.

The whole separation of themes into "individual" on the one hand and "social" on the other is senseless. Social and nationalist stimuli, when profoundly felt by the poet, can be the stuff of poetry. They must, in other words, become "I" experiences, and then there is no difference between individual and universal. Deeper analysis of poems with a social or national theme will reveal traces of the poet's most intimate subjective experiences, just as the anatomy of personal lyricism leads us, through subterranean darkness, to social and nationalist influences.

JOSEPH OPATOSHU

WITH THE NEW IMMIGRANTS came the new writers. They went into the factories and on the farms and at first did not even dream of making the written word their life's pursuit. Having burned their bridges behind them, these young writers never considered returning to the land of their birth. They immediately sought to strike new roots and unwittingly created a new Yiddish literature. This orientation was an inner process, an organic union of Yiddish literature with its new environment. Because this new literature developed very rapidly, it quickly overtook and outgrew the average reader. Indeed, for a reader who smacked his lips over a trashy novel by Zelikovitch, what enjoyment could he get out of a quality novel like Raboy's *Her Goldenbarg?*

Outwardly the writings of *Di Yunge* were a protest both against Odessa, Kiev, and Warsaw and, even more, against the haphazard state of Yiddish; against the American Yiddish press, whose leaders looked upon Yiddish as a means soon to be discarded; against the process which eliminated the savory kernels of Yiddish speech and left only the empty chaff. Besides, the sentimentality had to be smoked out. Among our Yiddish writers, the trees swayed too often in afternoon prayer, the sky was too often enveloped in a prayer shawl. And, to go from the sublime to the profane, the yellow press had one stock female: "She was like a 'baby doll,' but strong as an animal. When she lifted a leg, all the men drooled."

Protests of this kind united the young writers. Their trees ceased to sway in prayer, their skies ceased to be pure-blue prayer shawls. That was the only way to emancipate Yiddish literature from traditional sentimentalism. And once emancipated, the authentic Jewish strengths which had been tightly pent up in every genuine writer began to surge anew.

JACOB GLATSTEIN

THE CAREER OF A YIDDISH WRITER in America grows out of his abnormal situation. He hunts for readers. He comes to his readers because he believes he must speak to them personally. He always has something to say to them and something to scold them for. The several hours an author spends at his desk are nothing compared with his other literary activities. Lectures; dosing

Poet Jacob Glatstein (1896–1971).
YIVO INSTITUTE FOR JEWISH RESEARCH

his readers with tablespoonfuls of culture, critique, and heartache; literary relationships; stepping on colleagues' toes; the narrow corridor of general uselessness; and the constant attention to one's own immortality.

A Literary Community: The literary life of the Yiddish poets and novelists was peculiarly intense during the first several decades of the century. There were abundant talents; there was a strong, active readership; politics abrasively cut across literature; and temperament, sometimes in a vividly "Russian" style, flared up repeatedly. Here the novelist Isaac Raboy recalls a quarrel within the group of writers calling themselves Di Yunge, *not very different, when you come to think of it, from endless other quarrels among writers everywhere.*

ISAAC RABOY

DAVID IGNATOV CAME TO VISIT US and told me that "Opatoshu's going to break from us."

"Why?"

"Why, I don't know," Ignatov answered in pain. "I hear he's going to publish his own collection. This'll shatter our strength and we won't be able to produce anything. We'll never get the money."

"Someone has to speak to Opatoshu."

"You're a naïve young man," Ignatov interrupted. "Talking won't help. Let him go his way and we'll go ours."

The following Sunday Mani Leib visited; we were very happy to see him.

As we sat together for lunch Mani Leib told how Opatoshu was taking with him the writers Haimovich, Schwartz, and Rolnik and that that evening the entire group was meeting in Schwartz's house. "Maybe something can be saved by talking things through," Mani Leib suggested. "Two collections dare not appear; with so few readers, even one is too much."

That evening I went to the home of I. J. Schwartz, the Yiddish poet, together with Mani Leib [the leader of *Di Yunge*]. The whole group was gathered there. They chose me to act as chairman—my first time. I said that dissension would lead to nothing more than the ruin of so important a literary institution as *Shriftn*. I didn't speak as clearly then as I write now. I stammered, searched for language, grew confused. Then I gave each side the floor. Mani Leib spoke first and really let loose. Schwartz's wife ran in to denounce all of us as irresponsible and destructive—she would not allow such things to go on in her house!

We broke off the meeting, and Ignatov's side left. We had not made peace. Those who remained with *Shriftn* were Ignatov, Mani Leib, Halpern, Landau, Iceland, and I, all of us people who might have been expected to conduct ourselves a little more sensibly.

We left the house like a gang of boys, talking and shouting at the top of our voices, swearing to have nothing to do with the others the rest of our lives.

"They have no talent among them."

"They have poets?"

"Nobody with whom to put out a collection."

"Good for them."

"We'll finish them off."

Such were the sounds spilling into the empty Bronx streets.

Personally, I felt I'd wasted a day, and, bidding good night to my friends, went home.

Arriving there I found my wife waiting for me. She could tell something was wrong.

"So, you patched things up?"

"No we fought even worse."

"What are you fighting about?"

"I don't know myself. I don't think they know either."

"How can you fight over nothing?"

"Children," I threw off with a wave of the hand.

Like most European writers, though not many American ones, the Yiddish writers of the East Side spent an important part of their lives in cafés. Here there developed a camaraderie away from home and work, wives and children, burdens and bills. Here they could talk the evenings away, or scribble early drafts of poems. Here there were admiring spectators who sometimes stopped by for a word. The Yiddish poet and critic Reuben Iceland warmly summons memories of Goodman and Levine's, one of the cafés where the Yiddish writers used to hang out.

REUBEN ICELAND

ONLY FOUR OR FIVE of the tables in this cellar were "reserved" for writers. These stood in a corner to the left of the entrance, between kitchen and buffet.

No good came to us from either direction. From the buffet, we would be stabbed by the large, hostile eyes of one of the partners, especially if the restaurant was full and it didn't occur to these beggars that it might be the decent thing to leave the tables to more respectable customers. And out of the kitchen we would always get fumes, a bad smell of frying, a clang of tableware and the clatter of dishes getting washed. Our eyes would frequently smart because of the smoke that, beating through the kitchen door, would gather under the low ceiling: to which there would be added the reek of numberless cigarettes. Summer was frightfully hot. In the winter, one's feet would often freeze from the cold which blew along the floor or came in from the street when the door was opened. The food—as in most East Side eating places of the time—was barely endurable. The coffee simply horrible. The comments that you heard about yourself as writer were frequently enough to curdle your mother's milk—yet the cellar drew us. It drew us like a magnet.

I have already mentioned that in those days the majority of the young writers were shop workers. To miss a day's pay often meant not to have money to buy a pair of shoes for your child or be short three dollars toward the rent. Nonetheless, whenever you came into the cellar, you would find a crowd of people who, as you knew, were supposed to be in the shop. Several of *Di Yunge* were paperhangers and painters, and it wasn't unusual for them to get off the ladders in the middle of a job and come into the café in spattered work clothes which had once been white and with streaks of color on their face and hands. For a long time I used to have my lunch in the shop, fearful that if I went down to a restaurant I would not have the strength of will to complete the day's work.

Once on a Saturday in summer, when I worked only half a day, I came home and, after having my lunch, went to a barber to be shaved. In the evening, I was going to take my wife and six-month-old daughter to see one of our relations. I lived on Fourth Street, close to Avenue B; the barbershop was somewhere on Houston. In the chair, however, I suddenly felt the call of the café and was hardly able to wait for the barber to finish my shave.

It did enter my mind that it might be sensible to go home first and say where I was going. But my feet already were turning toward East Broadway. The day being hot, I expected to find only a couple of my colleagues in the café. For this reason, if no other, I would probably stay only an hour or two. It turned out, however, that the cellar was full. Out of a sea of faces and the clouds of smoke, there began to emerge the image of Mani Leib—a finger rocking in front of his nose like a pointer—his green, visionary eyes squinting at the homely, freckled, yet vital and insolent face of Moishe Leib Halpern.

I no longer remember what subject they were so passionate about at the time I came in. All I know is that in a moment I was in the midst of it myself. And it continued to boil—an hour, two, three. From one topic we would leap into a second, from a second to a third. Soon we were back at the first, each trying to prove a point with a quotation from an essay or a poem. In the same fashion, others tried to prove the opposite and for this purpose were also able to find crushing statements from a different authority.

Some left, others came. More of the writers left—and others took their place. We kept moistening our throats with coffee or with tea, at the same time nibbling on pancakes, on *blini*, cookies, rolls— especially on cigarettes. Hours flew. Night fell: no one noticed. Half the crowd had vanished; yet we, the other half, continued to sit there. The sweat kept pouring; yet we sat—talking. Goodman, at the buffet, sent sharp and contemptuous glances. Not seeing him or his eyes, we continued the discussion. Finally, Goodman exclaimed, "Even in hell there is a time when they rest. Go in good health!" But it sounded like—Go to the devil!

It was already two in the morning. Those of us who were left set out through Seward Park to Delancey Street . . . to the river, where one of us knew a wonderful place near a lumberyard.

After a while, the group started to get smaller, till only two of us were left, Mani Leib and I. It wasn't far from my house but he lived in Brooklyn and began to feel gloomy about having to go back, so he asked me to walk him as far as Delancey Street, where he would take the trolley that would bring him home. On Delancey, he decided to walk me back to my house. Then, in the middle of this, we turned again on Delancey.

Our literary conversation had run down. It was just before sunrise, yet we now had reached the haunting wistfulness of sunset. We began to speak about the workday week, about the hardship of that life, about the fretting and yearning that fills the nights at home, and how all this, these long and boring talks, are at bottom no more than an escape, an attempt to hush the yearnings in oneself. He told me that when he comes home late at night he gets into his apartment not by way of the door, but climbs up to the roof and from there moves down the fire escape to a window in his flat, and that he creeps into his house like a thief—so his wife shouldn't hear him; and that, once, he happened to get lost and opened the window of a neighbor, an Italian, and how the other, thinking he was a thief, attacked him with a knife.

When Mani Leib finally got on the streetcar, the sun had already risen on the Brooklyn side of the East River. Only now did I realize that I'd stayed away the whole night, that I had not told my wife I might be delayed, and that we were supposed to visit a relation. It was with a troubled heart that I began approaching Fourth Street. When I came to the building in which I lived, the grocery downstairs was already open and the grocer, standing by the door, looked at me severely and said, "Young man, wasn't it your wife who ran to the police to look for you?"

A Yiddish folkshule *play.*
YIVO INSTITUTE
FOR JEWISH RESEARCH

11

BEYOND NEW YORK

Chicago ghetto, circa 1900.   CHICAGO HISTORICAL SOCIETY

*Life was different for those immigrant Jews who settled beyond
New York. But to what extent and in which ways? Very different?
Not so different? Just a little different? It all depends, since the
answer will be shaped by whether you are thinking about large
cities or small towns, the East Coast or the Midwest.*

*As a rule of thumb, we'd say that the larger the city in which
Jews settled, the more likely it was that their community would
resemble that of the Jews in New York. The largest immigrant
communities were established, in the decades before the First
World War, in cities like Chicago, Philadelphia, Boston. Here, if
you walked through certain neighborhoods (say, the West Side of
Chicago), you could easily suppose yourself back in the Lower East
Side of New York. The same kosher restaurants, the same noise on
the streets, the same kids playing potsy and stickball, the same
candy stores selling the same Yiddish papers (though there might
be fewer five-story tenements than in New York). Look a little
deeper and you'd still think these neighborhoods were very much
like the Lower East Side, since here, too, a great many immigrants
worked in the garment trades or ran little grocery and butcher
shops. The surface of street life and the occupational structure—
not so different. But once you really looked deeper, then you'd
begin to see important differences.*

*In New York the immigrant Jews formed so large and thick a
community it provided them with a sort of social padding, the
protection of massed numbers. The Lower East Side could almost
be regarded as a separate city. But this was decidedly less true in
the other cities, where the Jews, though packed tightly enough, did
not form such a great mass as in New York.*

*The immigrant Jewish community in New York, perhaps
because of its sheer size, established its own, largely self-sufficient,
cultural life. It had its own institutions, theater, cafés, social
clubhouses, party headquarters, union buildings. There could
hardly be any question: New York was the center of immigrant
Jewish culture and every other place was a part of the provinces.
The major Yiddish theatrical companies did most of their work in
New York; the major Yiddish papers had their offices in New York.*

*In the early years of the century, Jewish immigrant communities
in the larger cities—Chicago, Boston, Philadelphia—also had their
own theaters, their own Yiddish papers and schools, their own
branches of the Jewish political groups. The Forward, during its
flush years, printed special editions for Philadelphia and Chicago.
Yiddish theatrical groups made regular appearances in all of these
cities.*

*Still, the difference seems notable. It was in New York that most
of the cultural energy had gathered, in New York that the main
ideas were advanced and the best creative work was being done.*

*Go to the smaller cities and the small towns, and the life of the
Jews, even those who were recent immigrants and continued to
speak Yiddish, took on a character distinctively its own. A Jewish
community of a few thousand souls in, say, Louisville, Kentucky,
would try to maintain itself, but it could hardly afford the luxury of
those numerous and stimulating differences of opinion and
organization that prevailed in New York and Chicago. It also had*

to adapt itself somewhat more cautiously and self-consciously to the dominant Gentile setting than did the Jews of the large cities. As for those who lived in more or less isolated small towns, or areas of the country with small Jewish populations (the South, the Northwest), their experiences were very different and cannot really be touched upon in these pages.

We've tried here, in any case, to present a modest sampling of portraits and incidents concerning the life of those immigrant Jews—venturesome souls—who went beyond New York.

Country Life

We start with an account of an effort in 1881 to set up a Jewish agricultural community in Louisiana, which, like most such efforts, collapsed in tragedy and disaster. Then comes a piquant item, the diary of a Jewish settler, Charles K. Davis, who led some sixty immigrant Jews to settle on a piece of land near Cimarron, a town in southwest Kansas not far from Dodge City.

JEWISH TRIBUNE, 9/27/'29

LATE IN 1881 A GROUP of immigrants left for New Orleans under the leadership of Herman Rosenthal, a wealthy merchant from Kiev, a man of erudition and culture, a writer and poet. The group comprised twenty families and some single men, in all about 125 students, teachers, artists, merchants, craftsmen and peddlers—educated and illiterate. None had ever farmed and few were accustomed to manual work.

. . . After correspondence between a "geographical committee" of the prospective colonists and leading Jews in various parts of the country, a tract of land located on Sicily Island in Catahoula County on the Ouachita River, a tributary of the Mississippi, was bought. The Alliance Israelite Universelle, through a New York committee, granted a loan of $8,800 to help the undertaking. . . .

The colonists found much of the land in splendid timber. The clatter of the axes soon mingled with the rhythm of Russian folk songs as big trees yielded to the blows of amateur woodsmen. Cotton and corn were to be the main products and a small amount of gardening was to be done for home use. A German farmer was employed as agricultural adviser, but he came only once or twice a week and his instruction was of little value.

There were three big houses on the plantation and a few old shacks where Negro slaves had been quartered. Rosenthal occupied a room in one of the big houses. Another room was used as an office. The rest were herded ten and more to a room. New Orleans Jews planned to help build forty small houses, each of which was to serve for a family or for four single men. Ten or twelve houses were actually put up. . . .

The colony's life was short. Surrounded by deserted plantations, cut off from the world, with Negroes of the most ignorant type as their neighbors, with rattlesnakes infesting the country, and mosquitoes "eating them alive," with malaria taking its toll among the children. . . . And as if the cup of misery were not full enough, the Mississippi overflowed in the spring of 1882, washing away houses, cattle, implements, and the small crops.

The New Orleans committee was willing to continue its aid, but most of the colonists were utterly discouraged. Rosenthal went to New York to raise funds to enable the rest to leave. Some, impatient at the delay, simply walked away. Yet the back-to-the-land persisted so strongly in others that they joined colonies launched shortly thereafter in Arkansas, Dakota, Kansas, and elsewhere. There the tragedy of Louisiana was reenacted.

CHARLES K. DAVIS

JULY 26, 1882
TODAY LEO WISE AND I left Cincinnati in charge of the Beer Sheeba Colony consisting of about sixty souls. We arrived in Indianapolis at midnight where the engine jumped the track before reaching the depot.

JULY 28
THIS MORNING I awoke feeling very blue. Mr. Sadler drove me out to the stockyards where a number of cowboys expressed very unfavorable opinions about the land we had selected.

JULY 29
THE UNION PACIFIC land agent told us that the impression has gained ground that these Russian refugees are a lot of beggars and paupers whom the relief committee of Cincinnati are trying to get rid of.

JULY 30
THIS AFTERNOON I went to Wyandotte, Kansas, where the local committee have placed four Russian families on a farm of sixty acres. The land is very poor and sandy but they are raising a fair crop of corn.

JULY 31
CHALE GEDANSKI'S wife complained of her breasts aching. I sent Liebersohn's wife to attend her and she reported it was nothing serious. They come to me, each one, with his or her troubles, and at such times I feel the responsibility is too great for a young man.

AUGUST 3
OUR EXPENSE at Kansas City was enormous. Every hotel

keeper overcharged us and we had no alternative but to pay. At about six I checked all our baggage at the depot for Cimarron. I then ordered all our people to the waiting room and gave them money to buy provisions for the journey. While we were waiting, the Sante Fe railroad agent announced he had received orders from headquarters to send us on an immigrant train. This in spite of the fact that our tickets entitled us to travel on an express train.

AUGUST 4

AT LARNED I was glad to see Leo, who explained to me why immigration to Cimarron is discouraged. In the first place, as long as a country is unsettled the railroad pays no taxes on its lands. It is therefore to their interest to keep the immigration east. Secondly, it is to protect the interests of stock men whose cattle are run up in droves through here from Texas. The owners are responsible for all damages they may do any farmer, and as people don't have fences out here, it is no easy job to keep the cattle from destroying crops. Also, all Texas cattle have what they term Texas fever, and whenever they go near domestic cattle, these become infected with the disease and die. For this the owners of the herds are responsible. Consequently, they have to ship their cattle through a point farther west which causes a greater expense.

AUGUST 5

THIS MORNING I took the ten men to the U.S. Land Office and had their entries made for government lands. When it came to signing their names they refused because it was the Sabbath. Finally, all signed or made their marks but Edelherts who refused flatly, saying he would rather not have the land than compromise his conscience. Then came the trying business of buying supplies, implements, stock, etc. We were green, the merchants knew it, and we were at their mercy. . . . Our expenses have been enormous, and now we have almost expended our money and not bought near what we actually need—sheep, milk cows, and other cattle, besides lumber and a thousand and one other things that at present we have no time to think of.

AUGUST 6

AT 9:30 WE ARRIVED at Cimarron. There are only 150 inhabitants in the entire county of which about a hundred live here. All the farmers received me kindly and offered me their teams for our freight free of charge. The farmers told me that they would lend us all the aid in their power so as to keep the stock men with their herds from eating off the grass that retains the moisture in the soil. . . . Almost every man in this section carries his *shot iron*, as they call it.

AUGUST 7

IN ORDER TO BE IN STYLE here, I put on my old

blue suit, a blue flannel shirt and a broad-brimmed straw hat. Together with the fact that I have not been shaved since last Wednesday, I think I compare favorably with the natives, excepting I can't get used to carrying my pistol around all the time. It's too heavy, and beside it's only a .38 caliber while a .44 is regulation out here.

AUGUST 11

STARTED FOR OUR SETTLEMENT on the Pawnee before daylight this morning. Before leaving us, our agent held forth the inducement of dinner and some water when we got there, but upon arriving we found the house unoccupied and the well in ruins. Imagine our feelings—tired and hungry and thirsty and eight miles across the prairies with the thermometer at 110. While we were studying the situation a cowboy rode up and told us that we could get some *shuck*, as he called it, at his camp two miles away. We finally got there after tramping in the hot sun. The camp consisted of a tent adjoining a corral into which the stock was driven at night. The man in charge got us up a dinner of antelope steak, onions, bread, and coffee. Although the grass was flying all over, I never enjoyed a meal so much in my life.

Farmers don't figure prominently in the mythology of the immigrant Jews, yet there were some—not many, but some. Mostly, they were dairy and poultry farmers selling milk and eggs to surrounding communities. There were Jewish farming settlements in New Jersey, New York, and Connecticut, and some have survived to the present time.

NEW YORK POST, 9/5/'94

IN THE SPRING OF 1890 an intelligent Russian named Kazan arrived in New York with $2,000. He had been employed upon a large farm in southern Russia, and after a few days in New York decided anything was better than our tenements. Upon consultation with a jeweler named Louis Hahn, Kazan learned that he could buy abandoned farms cheap in Connecticut. After looking over the field, Mr. Kazan bought a farm at Chesterfield, on the post road from Norwich to New London. With the money that remained to him, he bought six cows and restocked his farm with tools.

As soon as Kazan had settled in, he sent word to others among his acquaintances in New York and Russia. Before the first year was over there were twenty-eight Russian families here. Kazan's twenty-eight associates brought with them some money with which they paid down one-third or one-half the purchase money. The banks of New London were willing to advance some money on mortgage, and I am told that the Russians have proven worthy of trust. Whatever money is to be made must be obtained from the sale of

Jewish farmer Morris Cohen in his extensive vegetable garden in Arpin, Wisconsin. September 1, 1905.

milk, butter, and cheese. The soil is not rich enough to make garden crops profitable.

The first year at Chesterfield proved so encouraging that Mr. Kazan expected to have by this time at least a hundred families in the colony. Events have shown him to be rather too sanguine. Some of the colonists got tired of farming; others failed to make it pay. Of the twenty-eight original families, fifteen remain and are doing well. Eighteen other families have joined since and remained, making the present colony consist of nearly two hundred souls.

Some of the men knew absolutely nothing of farming or livestock. I heard of one man who fed his horse every second day, and wondered at his poor condition. Another man's method of feeding his cow was to turn her into a barn full of hay, thinking that she would eat what was good for her and then stop. Still another Russian farmer was discovered trying to cut a field of wheat with a reaping machine without knives. Making allowances for a certain amount of failures, the results so far are encouraging. The milk is sold either at a creamery built with the help of the Baron de Hirsch fund, or is made into butter and sent to New London. That and the manufacture of hats, pocketbooks, and clothing in winter gives enough money for such supplies as they cannot raise.

I asked Kazan how it was that he and his friends could make a living where the Yankee farmer was driven to the wall.

"The trouble," he answered, "from what I see of the American farmers about me, was that they were not willing to do the actual hard work themselves. Every Yankee I know around here wants a man or two to do the rough work. He will 'boss' the job and work hard himself, but he thinks it essential to have a hired man. These farms will not pay enough at present to warrant the hiring of help. The American women and girls are also above the 'hard labor' which we expect our wives to do. The American farmer's wife wants a piano and a buggy. She will not get up at four o'clock in the morning to milk the cows and make butter, as our wives and daughters expect to do."

In addition to the creamery, a pretty synagogue has been built. When this synagogue was opened, invitations were sent to the neighboring clergy, and to the gratification of Mr. Kazan, who is the head of the congregation, several clergymen came and made addresses of welcome to the Russians. The Presbyterian and Baptist clergymen from New London and the mayor of that city all spoke in the kindest way to the newcomers. This modern spirit is seen everywhere. It was a strange sight for me to see a group of typical little Russian Jews gathered in the schoolhouse listening open-eyed to lessons from a Yankee schoolteacher from the next village. In six months after coming from Russia, they talk English as well as if they had been born here. On the way back to New London I saw the local baseball club, composed of Russian lads, at work with all the enthusiasm of our native born experts.

ARTHUR GOLDHAFT

A DELEGATION FROM the Hebrew Emigrant Aid Society went down to New Jersey in 1881 to look over the area. They saw two advantages. The place was on a railway line so produce could be sent to the big markets in Philadelphia and New York, and it was far enough away so that the settlers couldn't simply pack up and go back to town. At least, the delegates thought they couldn't. And so they bought a tract of land near a railroad siding, named the place Alliance, and hired some local carpenters. First, they put up a large, barnlike house called a *gebeida*, which simply means building. It was hardly more than four walls and a roof, another *kesselgodden* where the immigrants could camp until their individual homes were built. Sometimes, as you look at the present-day farmhouses, if with your mind's eye you take away a side wing, a front porch and a couple of other additions, you can see a frame dwelling about twenty feet wide by twelve feet deep, one room downstairs and one room upstairs. This was to be the beginning for

Catskills synagogue.

each family. They were to draw lots for ten-acre farms, all laid out next to each other, and each group of forty or fifty families was going to have a synagogue and a *Talmud Torah*.

My parents arrived here in 1881. From the tales of mama and some of her cronies, I can still imagine how it was. Those first nights, I recall mama telling me, they all slept in a great circle on the floor of the *gebeida*, with their clothes on. I don't know what the cooking facilities were in that house, but I remember tales about a huge iron pot in the yard. In those first years, in Alliance, my mother lost three babies. . . .

The good Jews of Philadelphia did their best to help make a success of the farm experiment. Members of some of the finest families kept contact with the Alliance Israelite Universelle and the Hebrew Emigrant Aid and Shelter Society. There was the Fels family, of Fels Naphtha soap fame. A bachelor son devoted a good deal of time and money to the immigrants. He would come out and listen to their personal troubles, and he would assemble them for lectures on agriculture. In time, he even started a model farm, to employ some of the men under skilled leadership. . . .

In later years, Alliance was no longer an isolated and lonely little settlement. Several other colonies had been started. A few miles up the road was Mizpah, and in the opposite direction was Rosenhayn. The original Alliance colony was large enough so that a group had split off calling itself "The Seventeen," to take up a piece of land a few miles away.

But the liveliest addition was an entirely new group, in Carmel; these were the real intellectuals. While there had been philosophers and members of the intelligentsia in my parents' group, it had nevertheless been a haphazard mixture of refugees. The new group was strictly composed of intellectuals, even atheists, anarchists, and the like. It was actually whispered that certain couples among them were unmarried, and were practicing free love.

One of the settlers was the father of Gilbert Seldes, the well-known critic, and the sons of others became writers, scholars. The Roxy Theater, no less, was built by one of their descendants. Later, the settlers of Carmel used to have the leading radical personalities of the time as lecturers—Eugene Debs, Emma Goldman, and people like that.

The "Jew peddler" became a fixture of the American scene, trudging through distant parts of the country, penetrating small towns where he was regarded as an exotic, making friends with Baptists who enjoyed his biblical knowledge, bringing words of respect to black families. Some of these peddlers settled in one or another town, becoming the nucleus for a small Jewish community; others remained wanderers, on foot or with horse and wagon—pioneers, too, in bringing to isolated, native Americans some sense of cultural difference.

MORRIS H. WITCOWSKY

FOR THE FIRST FOUR YEARS I peddled with a pack on my back. This pack when full of merchandise weighed about a hundred and twenty pounds, eighty pounds strapped to the back and a forty-pound "balancer" in front. It is not as serious as it sounds. You get used to it. Anyway it gives you tremendous shoulders and arm and leg muscles. Leather suspenders and a wide leather girdle helped a peddler support the pack. It relieved the peddler of all the pressure in one area. You learned early how to remove the pack, lay it neatly on the ground, open it, and choose exactly the merchandise ordered or what you wanted to show. I sold mostly soft goods and notions: ribbons, thread, needles, piece goods, garters, men's socks, and women's stockings. I also carried buttons, both bone and pewter, and combs.

There were quite a few people who would have nothing to do with us. Perhaps they were prejudiced against the first peddler they saw and they just never bothered to test others. At any rate, you learned who these people were and avoided them, and you made certain that you were not stranded before nightfall near a home where you were not welcome. These homes, however, were few and far between. Even those customers who shook their heads and said, "Nothing today," were nice to us. You would be surprised how often they refused to take anything for a night's lodging. But, when this happened, you immediately opened your packs and put some little things on the table for each of the children and the presents were always accepted with thanks.

On the road I ate eggs, vegetables, and fruits. Later on, when I had a horse and wagon, I even carried my own dishes. My route took me through Reidsville, North Carolina, up into Danville, Virginia, and through the towns of South Boston, Alta Vista, Buena

Vista, and Appomattox. I made friends on all these routes. I remember a family in Rustburg, Virginia, who always insisted that I stay overnight and discuss the Bible with them. Jewish peddlers who couldn't even speak the language well had a special status with the Protestant Christians in the South. I was reminded of this feeling for the Hebrew religion wherever I went. I read such names as Pisgah, Cedars of Lebanon, Mount Olive, Mount Gilead, Mount Hebron, Nebo, Ararat. This familiarity with the *Torah* was good for both the Jewish peddlers and the people to whom we sold, particularly the Negro people.

Selling on credit to the Negro was called "having a book on the *shvartzers*." Do not misunderstand me. *Shvartzers* was not a sign of disrespect. As a matter of fact, I look back on it and realize that we performed a great service for the Negroes of the South between the years 1900 and 1920. We were probably the first white people in the South who paid the Negro people any respect at all. Once I learned their names, I did not say "Uncle" or "Auntie" but "Mr." or "Mrs." whatever their name was.

Collections were good. The Negro women always had the money for me, and even when they moved away, they caught up with me somewhere and paid me. I sold gold wedding bands to many Negro women. These cost ten dollars, paid at the rate of twenty-five cents a week. Clocks were popular. They bought one of two models, the "half-hour strike" or the "banjo type." The price was eight dollars and the installments were also twenty-five cents a week. The Negro women bought mostly ready-to-wear things—aprons for forty cents and housedresses at eighty cents.

. . . I knew maybe twenty peddlers in my territory, and none of us ever became rich. We all knew the dollar was hard to come by and we all learned to respect it. When you peddle for an entire week with a pack on your back and have $8.40 for your share at the end of the week, it is a lesson for work and its rewards, no matter how small . . . I think I was in a valuable profession. I do not know how many others, in different trades and professions, can say, "With each customer I left not only the joy of a new possession but perhaps a bit of information, some news maybe or even an interpretation of a biblical text."

Moving beyond New York, we first reach those once-distant areas of the city that we now assume to be part of it. But when Morris Raphael Cohen and his family moved to Brownsville (a section of Brooklyn) in the early 1890s, it really was not part of the city. Legally, Brooklyn was a separate city. Culturally, it was also very different. Consider only the fact that young Morris was the only Jewish boy at the Brownsville public school during the first half-year he went there. What a difference from the East Side!

MORRIS RAPHAEL COHEN

BROWNSVILLE WAS AT THAT TIME a Jewish boom town whose bloom had been nipped in the bud. It had a number of newly built houses, as well as a scattering of houses belonging to old settlers. Everywhere there were vacant fields and in the direction of Canarsie, meadows, woods, brooks, and marshes. Almost all of the natives, old and young, played baseball and so did the Jewish boys of my age. . . .

In the heart of Brownsville.
BROOKLYN PUBLIC LIBRARY,
BROOKLYN COLLECTION

When I applied for admission to the Brownsville Public School I was asked in what grade I had been in New York, and when I told them the truth, they told me that the Brooklyn schools were more advanced and that I would have to enter the last primary grade. . . . For the first half-year I was the only Jew in the school; however I got along fairly well with my classmates. But on the way to school I had difficulties. Beyond Dean Street I passed a number of houses inhabited by Germans who delighted to set their young children after me.

As there was no public library in Brownsville, my intellectual food was restricted to *Die Arbeiter Zeitung* and the few paper books in my brother Sam's collection. But the lack of reading matter was fully balanced by the opportunity to play with the Jewish boys of the neighborhood, far more than I had done in New York or even in Minsk. It was in Brownsville that I was introduced to the various forms of boy's baseball. I played for a considerable time in the fall of 1893, and I began again early in the spring of 1894—the first year of my life in which I had anything like a proper share of exercise and outdoor existence.

Flatbush Boys Club.
BROOKLYN   PUBLIC   LIBRARY,
BROOKLYN COLLECTION

In 1912 the famous English novelist Arnold Bennett made a trip to the Bronx. This, too, was then hardly a part of New York—more like an outlying suburb. Bennett had a good pair of eyes and a reasonably warm heart: He noted the amenities of the place, as well as its harshness, and he was keen in observing that it showed no trace of that artistic civilization "whose charm seems subtly to pervade the internationalism of the East Side."

ARNOLD BENNETT

. . . I   W A S   U R G E N T L Y   I N V I T E D   to go and see how the folk lived in the Bronx; and, feeling convinced that a place with a name so remarkable must itself be remarkable, I went. The center of the Bronx is a racket of Elevated, bordered by banks, theaters, and other places of amusement. As a spectacle it is decent, inspiring confidence but not awe, and being rather repellent to the sense of beauty. Nobody could call it impressive. Yet I departed from the Bronx very considerably impressed. It is the interiors of the Bronx homes that are impressive. I was led to a part of the Bronx where five years previously there had been six families, and where there are now over two thousand families. This was newest New York.

No obstacle impeded my invasion of the domestic privacies of the Bronx. The mistresses of flats showed me round everything with politeness and with obvious satisfaction. A stout lady, whose husband was either an artisan or a clerk, I forget which, inducted me into a flat of four rooms, of which the rent was twenty-six dollars a month. She enjoyed the advantages of central heating, gas, and electricity; and among the landlord's fixtures were a refrigerator, a kitchen range, a bookcase, and a sideboard. Such amenities for the people—for the *petits gens*—simply do not exist in Europe; they do not even exist for the wealthy in Europe. But there was also the telephone, the house exchange being in charge of the janitor's daughter—a pleasing occupant of the entrance hall. I was told that the telephone, with a "nickel" call, increased the occupancy of the Bronx flats by ten per cent.

Thence I visited the flat of a doctor—a practitioner who would be the equivalent of a "shilling" doctor in a similar quarter of London. Here were seven rooms, at a rent of forty-five dollars a month, and no end of conveniences—certainly many more than in any flat that I had ever occupied myself! I visited another house and saw similar interiors. And now I began to be struck by the splendor and the cleanliness of the halls, landings, and staircases: marble halls, tessellated landings, and stairs out of Holland; the whole producing a gorgeous effect—to match the glory of the embroidered pillowcases in the bedrooms. On the roofs were drying grounds, upon which each tenant had her rightful "day," so that altercations might not arise. I saw an empty flat. The professional vermin exterminator had just gone—for the landlord-company took no chances in this detail of management. . . .

The fittings and decorations of all these flats were artistically vulgar, just as they are in flats costing a thousand dollars a month, but they were well executed, and resulted in a general harmonious effect of innocent prosperity. The people whom I met showed no trace of the influence of those older artistic civilizations whose charm seems subtly to pervade the internationalism of the East Side. In certain strata and streaks of society on the East Side things artistic and intellectual are comprehended with an intensity of emotion and understanding impossible to Anglo-Saxons. This I know.

The Bronx is different. The Bronx is beginning again, at a stage earlier than art, and beginning better. It is a place for those who have learnt that physical righteousness has got to be the basis of all future progress. It is a place to which the fit will be attracted, and where the fit will survive. It has rather a harsh quality. It reminded me of a phrase used by an American at the head of an enormous business. He had been explaining to me how he tried a man in one department, and, if he did not shine in that, then in another, and in another, and so on. "And if you find in the end that he's honest but not efficient?" I asked. "Then," was the answer, "we think he's entitled to die, and we fire him."

The Bronx presented itself to me as a place where the right of the inefficient to expire would be cheerfully recognized.

Winter 1915 by
Abraham Walkowitz.
COLLECTION OF THE WHITNEY MUSEUM
OF AMERICAN ART, NEW YORK

Going beyond New York in the early days could almost be like going to a foreign country, still another foreign country. The Industrial Removal Office of New York, started by philanthropic German Jews, tried conscientiously to place immigrants in outlying cities, but sometimes things didn't work out so well. So they wrote back from Columbus, Pensacola, Chicago.

APPEALS TO THE REMOVAL OFFICE

Columbus, Ga.
May 7, 1910

David M. Bressler
New York, N.Y.

Dear Sir & Friend:

Abe Feinberg of this city has just appealed to me to aid him in securing the release of his mother from Ellis Island where she has been held for the past several days because she is a mute. Knowing Feinberg as I do, I have no hesitancy in assuring you that he is a man worthy of every aid that you may be able to set forth in the matter of securing the release of his mother and her admission to this country. Kindly take hold of this case, as I am sanguine that your help will mean much to this unfortunate woman who is held up without just cause, as well as to her son, who can care for his mother in an excellent manner.

I am sincerely yours,
F. L. Rosenthal
Rabbi
Congregation B'Nai Israel

Pensacola, Florida
September 28, 1909

Mr. D. Bressler
Manager of the Removal Office
New York

Dear Sir,

I Max Fruchtman who excepted a position as a taylor by Mr. A. Friedman, Pensacola, Fla., presently have in my way a few difficulties for which my wife, two little children and I are compelled to appeal to you for help!! When last November I learned that Mr. Friedman is looking for a ladies taylor for $20 per week, I excepted the offer and was sent through the removal office to Mr. Friedman. Landing in this location, I learned that Mr. Friedman wanted to employ me as a scab. Fortunately, Mr. Rosenberg my countryman gave me permission to work there.

Consequently, I learned that Mr. Friedman is not a gentleman to his words. During the season I worked much more harder than in New York at the shops, from 8 A.M. till 10 P.M. and Saturday till 11 P.M., having only one hour for dinner. I never kicked, always fulfilled his desires and was as a slave. My only consolation was that I am getting $20 a week all year round. But one day Mr. Friedman announced that he only can pay me $15 a week from June the first until August the first. Yet I am working till October the first and he still did not increase my pay. My dear sir! If you could know the condition in which I am. For four months my family has not had a piece of meat in the house. Our diet consists of bread, potatoes, and cheap sardines. I have to pay $4 a week rent, and $4 a week for furniture. If not, they will take it away from us. This is my fever which I am asking you, not to send any body to Mr. A. Friedman, because this man has already ruined three families. My dear sir, I am going to ask you a second fever, which consists only of giving me an advice where to go from Pensacola. If you know that anybody in this vicinity wants a taylor, then let me know as soon as you can.

Trusting that you will pay attention to my fever

I remain very truly yours
Max Fruchtman
117 W. Lovement St.

Chicago
June 25, 1907

Mr. President
Industrial Removal Office
New York

Dear Sir!

My parents Edel and Sofia Kanner and sisters and brother Fanny, Dora and Jacob, are at present in New York at 196 Eldridge Street, and are for over four weeks without work or any means of support; which I am sure, if they were in Chicago, I could help them get work and provide for them, but as I am only a workingman, it is impossible for me to bring them over here as I lack the necessary funds for the means of transportation. Therefore I wish to entreat you to do us a favor and have them sent to Chicago thru your office for which kindness, I assure you our everlasting gratitude.

Your very respectfully

Joe D. Kanner
180 Barber Street

Chicago,
Feb. 12, 1906

Dear Sirs;

I and my brother Abraham Hecht and my cousin Israel whom you sent to Chicago to Mr. Moshe Siegel got work, and we thank you very much.

Now I wish to ask you to send my brother Chaim Jacob and his wife and a sister-in-law Hinde Abramowitz. We will secure work for them.

With many thanks & regards,

i am yours

H. Hecht
414 14th Place
in the rear

Chicago
9/18 1906

Mr. David M. Bressler

Dear Sir

Please be so kind and take pity on my 2 orphans. the big girl was sick just came from the hospital I am not able to give them anything she is my sisters child they are my neices. all I want you to send them to me if its possible as she is not able to work the big girl and the little are those two I would like to have you send them to me. I would like, to send them money but I am not able too all I can do is to keep them I have no children myself. so I am willing to have them as I am their Aunt. so please be so kind and do it for me. they are by Mr. Fleisher. their address is Violet Lupescu Amelia
      113 E. 8th Str.
      New York
I also wish you a happy New Years

Resp.

Mrs. Jennie Schwartz
72 Washburn Avenue

What was immigrant Jewish Chicago like compared with immigrant Jewish New York? Bernard Horwich, one of the first east European Jews to find out, offers a few insights.

BERNARD HORWICH

I WAS TOLD I would find conditions much more to my liking in the "second America," so after three days on a very hot and dusty train I arrived one morning about ten o'clock at the Polk Street Station in Chicago. I can still remember the wooden sidewalks between Canal and Halsted streets, with steps on each side leading to the houses. My first job was with Wartz & Nathan, dealers in scrap iron. My coworkers, big husky Irishmen and Poles, pushed me around and on one occasion deliberately dropped a heavy piece of rail right beside me. The men burst into laughter; I was amazed at their grim sense of humor. Much as I disliked the idea, I next tried peddling. There I was, out on the street with a pack on my back and a basket in front, going wherever chance might take me. For three hours I went from house to house, but no one would see me. At last I came to the home of a Swedish woman who purchased two dollars' worth of goods. This was the first success I experienced since giving up the handkerchief business in New York. The work was not terribly hard, but I suffered a lot. Boys on the street saw only the incongruous appearance I made, and I was good prey for them. To add to my difficulties, streetcar conductors often refused me passage. One afternoon about five o'clock I jumped on a streetcar with my packs of merchandise. The conductor was in the front so I got on in the rear. Soon enough, the conductor noticed me. "You had better take your bundles and go back to Jerusalem," he remarked. Most of the people in the car looked at me and laughed. One day, after I had been peddling several months, fate took me to the house of a friendly Irishwoman who told me about the Milwaukee Avenue district. There were a good many well-to-do families of various nationalities in that locality. Furthermore, the boys were less menacing. Within a year I no longer carried a big pack around all the time. Instead, I would see my customers on certain days of the week. Then I would go to Marshall Field & Company's wholesale house on the corner of Market and Randolph streets, purchase the necessary goods, and deliver them.

NEW YORK POST, 8/29/'03

NEW YORK AND CHICAGO, to begin with, have been laid out and developed very differently. New York, wedged in as it is by two rivers, has no chance to expand except upward. A vacant lot is an unknown quantity, and the swarms of East Side children are left with no natural playground but the street. Chicago, unlike New York, has few walled streets with towering tenements on each side.

A straggling country road as in London was the original form of some of the tenement streets, and a generosity of breadth is still left as a sign of former comfort. Rickety hovels and houses, one story, two stories, rarely more than three stories high, are the characteristic note of a tenement street. Tumble down, grimy with soot, these living places under a gray sky are inexpressibly dreary. An independent investigation after an epidemic of typhoid fever not long ago showed that the sanitary conditions of these regions were deplorably bad, a verdict which ruffled greatly the feelings of a rather complacent board of health. As to interiors, Chicago has, alas, as bad ones as New York. Yet the air blows in through open windows, and sunshine floods the little rooms. The need for playgrounds is real but not so urgent as in New York. Yet Chicago has not been so successful as New York in laying siege to the city's pocketbook. It has no gardens in its playgrounds and no evening centers in the schools in the winter which keep thousands of little Gothamites out of the streets every week night. Indeed, New York's thorough use of its school property makes it an example to most of the other cities in the United States.

MEYER LESER

AT FIRST the market was Jefferson Street—even before that it was Canal. But Jefferson began to overflow. There weren't enough stores or space for stands. In about 1912 people began renting space on Maxwell Street. And soon you couldn't walk down the street because you were pulled in. On Sunday for blocks and blocks it was thick with people shoulder to shoulder. The more people came streaming from Europe, the bigger the neighborhood got.

Bernard Richards was one of the veterans of American Jewish journalism; he lived for a while in Boston, and apparently felt it was, for a lively Jewish intellectual, something of a backwater.

BERNARD RICHARDS

"I AM GOING TO BUY a book on Salem Street," said my friend when we suddenly met on Tremont Row. "Do you wish to come along?"

I was bent on any adventure, and so we started for the quarter, down through Hanover Street. . . . It was but a short distance, and before we knew it . . . we were near Bersowsky's Bookstore. [From the other side of the street] we could see the books and periodicals, phylacteries and newspapers, holy fringe-garments and sheets of Jewish music in the windows . . . and as we came nearer we could see [a] very aged woman, bewigged and kerchiefed, wan, wrinkled and wry . . . sitting on her high stool, drinking a glass of tea and selling newspapers. There were several simple prints and chromos

A mikvah on Barton
Street in Boston, 1910.
BOSTON PUBLIC LIBRARY, PRINT
DEPARTMENT

in the window, reproductions from pictures of Jewish life, parents
blessing their children, the Day of Atonement, the Feast of
Passover, high priests lighting the candles in the temple—these were
their subjects. . . .

"This," Keidansky explained, "is the leading Jewish bookstore in
Boston, and it is in a sense also the spiritual center of the
ghetto. . . . All the symbolism of our old faith is here incarnated.
And yet side by side with these are the things which tend toward the
transformation or dissolution of the ancient religion—the publica-
tions of the radicals, the destroying utterances of the revolutionists.
Here come [together] the Orthodox prayer books and the antireligious . . . pamphlets. And this old lady, who stands for all that is
pious and ancient, hands out the anarchist *Freie Arbeiter Stimme*
and the socialist *Vorwärts*. . . . Is it not strange how soon we come
up-to-date and ahead of our date?

I wanted to break away for a while from the sameness and
solemnness, the routine and respectability of this town, from my
weary idleness, empty labors, and uniformity of our ideas here, so
when the opportunity was available I took a little journey to the big
metropolis. One becomes rusty and falls into a rut in this suburb. I
was becoming so sedate, stale, and quiet that I was beginning to be
afraid of myself. . . . Anti-imperialism, Christian Science, and the
New Thought are amusing, but there is not enough excitement

here. Boston is not progressive; there are not enough foreigners in this city. People from many lands with all sorts of ideas and the friction that arises between them—that causes progress. New York is the place. . . . The refuse of all radicals, revolutionaries and good people whom the wicked old world has cast out . . . New York with its Germans and Russians and Jews is a characteristic American city. Boston and other places are too much like Europe—cold, narrow, and provincial.

THE IMMIGRANT JEW
IN THE UNITED STATES

WHAT OPPORTUNITIES FOR AMUSEMENT does Philadelphia offer? A few cheap theaters, many cheaper dance halls, and occasional rooms given over to higher social purposes. The Standard, centrally located at Twelfth and South streets in the heart of the ghetto, presents a weekly bill with afternoon and evening performances. Old popular plays of five acts, supplemented by vaudeville turns, often extend the matinee from two until six o'clock. The majority of the audience are first-generation Jews who jump to their feet when real flames envelop the heroine. If the hero demands the whereabouts of the concealed heroine, someone in the audience tells him. The National provides scenery and property richer than at the Standard. *The Great Train Robbery* enjoyed a long run there this season.

Next to Hall Weddings the Pleasure Social is the most popular form of social intercourse. Window placards advertising dances read like this:

ROUDIOS SOCIAL

December 2nd

KILGALLON, America's White Champion CAKE WALKER

Last Chance to See Him Prior to Him Going

to NEW YORK

PRIZE WALTZ **for Up-towners and Down-towners**

GREAT SPORT

Ad. 15 cents   Pennsylvania Hall

The 2 Harts comes to Philadelphia.
MUSEUM OF THE CITY OF NEW YORK, THEATER COLLECTION

That splendid chronicler of immigrant Jewish life, Samuel Chotzinoff, found himself as a boy living for a little while in Waterbury, Connecticut. Here he suffered one of those painful encounters with native prejudice, the inherited mythology of the Christian world, which almost every Jewish child sooner or later had to confront. Acute as always, Chotzinoff noted the ways in which being a Jew in this small town differed radically from being one back on East Broadway.

SAMUEL CHOTZINOFF

. . . I C O U L D N O T M I N D being called a *sheeny* in Cherry Street, because Cherry Street represented a small, self-contained, violently antisocial perimeter that threatened me only when I invaded it. But to be called a *sheeny* in Burton Street obliged me to reexamine the image of America I had pieced together from the security of the New York ghetto and from the absence of any racial discrimination in the books of Horatio Alger. I had seen two boys attempt to stone an old man, seemingly because he had a beard. But I had met Christian men with beards who walked the streets of Waterbury unmolested. It was not, then, the beard of the rabbi that had offended his assailants, but the Jew behind it. It was clear that in Burton Street Jews were not considered Americans.

. . . Who could tell what Christians really thought of me, of all Jews? I looked back with longing to my former unclouded life on East Broadway and in Rutgers Place. There Jews with beards walked not only with impunity, but with pride in their ancestry and beliefs. Rabbis were respected, even by the children of anarchists and atheists. Yet I could not conceal from myself that but for the difference in status of Jews Waterbury was a more desirable place to live than the ghetto, especially in summer. There had been nothing in the ghetto so pleasant as the windowboxes and little flower gardens on Burton Street, and the great horse-chestnut tree in our front yard. . . . Instead of fetid tenements, there were individual houses set at a polite distance one from another. Windows were curtained, and at night front parlors were lit softly and deeply by gas lamps with shades of subdued colors over them.

S. N. Behrman, the playwright known for his clever comedies, grew up in another small town, Worcester, Massachusetts. Somewhat irreverently, he recalls a Yom Kippur there and at the end of the passage comes to the shock of recognizing, as a boy, that only for Jews does this day have significance. For others it is "quite commonplace." It was a discovery much more likely in Worcester, Massachusetts, than in the Lower East Side.

S. N. BEHRMAN

B E F O R E I E V E N E N T E R E D the synagogue, I began to visualize what was going on Above on the Day of Atonement: the

All-Seeing, like a celestial Actuary, a kind of immense Mosaic statistician, graving prophetic casualties onto some vast double-entry ledger of stone, with a quill that was a gleaming and pointed pillar of quartz. The short walk across the street to the synagogue . . . was like a stroll across the Bridge of Sighs. Descending doom was already upon us; we did not know precisely what it was we had done or how we had sinned, but we knew that we had to pay for it. It was the vagueness of the mass guilt that gave it its special, terrorizing quality. . . .

Once we were outdoors, our sense of release was almost unbearable, and to work off some of our energy we always hurried off "down the line," as we called it, down the main street of town, in a parade of liberty. Down Providence Street hill we ran, past the Providence Street School, past the humble little Balbirishocker Schul. We heard its cantor singing from inside. His petition sounded ineffectual to us; we felt he could not possibly receive for his congregation the same favorable attention from the Celestial Scribe that ours did. We went on through Grafton to Front Street. In the winy October forenoon, with the air fermenting and mellowing in the warm sun, the vigilance of the Actuary seemed somehow relaxed, and the world was more intensely ours because we had lately been so confined. *Yom Kippur* did not decimate the pedestrian population of Worcester's streets, as it was said to do in New York. There were the usual people about, but they had the anemic, unzestful look of the unliberated. They walked Providence and Front streets as if it were quite commonplace to be doing so. We were always mystified by their casualness.

The New York Store in Phoenix, Arizona, 1896.
COURTESY OF ED KORRICK

Finally, after the Second World War, when the American Jews experienced a dramatic improvement in their economic conditions and social standing, there began the move to the suburbs. It is a process not yet completed, nor completely reckoned, but here, from World of Our Fathers, *are a few comments that try to pin down meanings and possibilities.*

IRVING HOWE

MOVING INTO THE SUBURBS required that people decide whether or not they wanted to declare themselves as Jews. At first everyone seemed amiable and anonymous, young and shiny, not stamped with an encrusted ethnicity. But that was just the trouble, since merely to surrender to the ways of suburbia was in effect a declaration about what one wanted to be.

The inner tone and structure of Jewish life underwent major changes during this shift from city to suburb. Whatever spoke too emphatically of traditional ways in religious practice, or too stridently of traditional ideologies in Yiddish secular life, was left behind. A few Yiddish groups, like the Workmen's Circle, did try to adapt themselves to the new setting, and in some of the plainer suburbs, like certain towns on Long Island, succeeded in establishing a foothold. But most immigrant institutions held little appeal for the new suburbanites—they were at once too keen in memory and too inharmonious with present desires. Only after life in the suburbs had settled into a measure of stability could they speak openly of their Yiddish origins and memories, giving vent to those feelings of affection they had found it prudent to suppress.

Among Jewish intellectuals and semi-intellectuals, as well as the more sophisticated children of the suburbs, it became a commonplace to disparage the suburban Jews as philistine and vulgar—in books, lectures, and articles there were frequent sneers at "bagel and lox" Jewishness. Of philistinism there was of course plenty in the Jewish suburban communities, though one would be hard put to show there was any more of it than in Yiddish-speaking immigrant neighborhoods or, for that matter, in American society as a whole. Those who loftily dismissed "bagel and lox" Jewishness failed or preferred not to grasp that certain pinched qualities of suburban Jewish life—residual attachments to foods, a few customs, and a garbled Yiddish phrase—might signify not merely self-serving nostalgia but also blocked yearnings for elements of the past that seemed spiritually vital. The suburban Jews had come upon the scene at a moment when Jewish culture in America no longer possessed its earlier assurance and vigor; they lived with whatever remnants of their youthful experience they could salvage; and "bagels and lox" (not to be sneered at in their own right!) were part of what they still had left, tokens of the past to which they clung partly because it reminded them of all that was gone.

Adaptations had to be made to a new order of life: learning how to take care of a lawn and cope with a "garden shop," fixing correctly the tonalities of suburban social life, discovering those softenings of opinion and voice that might be needed at a local school meeting, and finding the kinds of people with whom more could be shared than the accident of proximity. There were pleasures, too, mild but genuine. It was good to bask in a luxury of space, as if all the elements in one's field of vision had been expanded. It was pleasant "to walk on your own earth and feel your own green grass, and plan your own mysteries of birth and bloom and death. Only in our wildest dreams, the ones we didn't tell each other, did we include the ownership of broad acres, half acres, quarter acres."

Glossary

alef   the first letter of the Hebrew alphabet

alrightnik   nouveau riche

arba kosos   the four cups of wine drunk at the Passover *seder*

baal-agola   wagon driver

baiz   second letter of the Hebrew alphabet

balbatim   substantial members of a Jewish community

Bar Mitzva   a confirmation ceremony for a thirteen-year-old boy

Bintel Brief   a letter and answer column in *The Jewish Daily Forward*

boarderkeh   a female boarder

boolkes   rolls

bris   ritual circumcision

challa   a braided loaf of white bread, glazed with egg white

Chanukah   festival commemorating the rededication of Jerusalem's Holy Temple

chassen   bridegroom

chazzen   cantor

cheder   an elementary Hebrew school, usually occupying a single room

Chumash   the five books of the Torah

chupah   wedding canopy

daven   to pray

di alte heym   the old country

di goldeneh medina   the golden land

dos klayne menshele   the little man; the ordinary Jew

dybbuk   a condemned spirit who enters and possesses the body of a living person

echt   correct, proper

eili, eili   "My God, My God," a popular song

emes   truth

erev Pesach   Passover eve

farbrente   a passionate female advocate

fleyshiks   of meat, incompatible with *milkhiks* under Jewish dietary law

gazlen   thief

gemara   expository portion of the Talmud

gemilath chassodim   a free loan association

get (pl. gittin)   rabbinical bill of divorcement

gevalt!   a cry of pain, outrage or need

golem   human creature without a soul; a dummy; an automaton created by magical means

goy   a Gentile

Hasid   a member of an orthodox religious sect

Haskala   movement for Jewish westernization which arose in

Germany and eastern Europe in the eighteenth and nineteenth centuries

ivre   literally, Hebrew; proper recitation of liturgical Hebrew

Kaddish   a prayer glorifying God's name; also a mourner's prayer

kalleh   bride

kapote   caftan, gabardine

kashrut   Jewish dietary code

khometz   ritually unfit for Passover consumption

Kiddush   blessing said over a cup of wine to celebrate the Sabbath or a holiday

Kiddush Hashem   a glorification of the Jewish religion achieved by following God's commandments

kinder   children

kittel   a white gown worn by males on the High Holidays, on Passover and after death

koch alayn   a room or bungalow in a summer resort with shared cooking facilities

kohen (pl. kohanim)   descendants of Aaron, priests

kosher   ritually fit

kugel   pudding

landsman (pl. landsleit)   one who comes from the same town in the old country

landsmanshaft   society of immigrants from the same town or region in the old country

l'chayim   a toast to a long life and good health

luftmenshn   literally, people of the air; those who live without visible means of support

machetunim   in-laws

maggid   a teacher-preacher, usually itinerant

makhzor   holiday prayer book

maskil   learned man

matzo   unleavened bread, eaten at Passover

mazel tov   congratulations, good luck

med   a drink made with honey

melamed   teacher in a Hebrew school

mensh   man; used as a term of approbation for someone possessing qualities of humaneness and responsibility

midrash   a body of homilies

milkhiks   of milk; incompatible with *fleyshiks* under Jewish dietary law

mincha   afternoon prayers

minyan   the quorum of ten Jewish males required for religious services

mitzva   good deed

mohel   ritual circumciser

molodyetz   a lover of life loved all the more for violating social conventions

Moyshe   one of the masses, often used in a derogatory way

neshoma yeseroh   the expansiveness of one's soul on the Sabbath

nudnik   a nuisance

oren kodish   Torah scroll ark

Pentateuch   the five books of the Torah

Pesach   Passover, a holiday commemorating Jewish liberation from Egyptian bondage

pflommen   prunes

Purim   a holiday commemorating the defeat of Haman as recorded in The Book of Esther

rebbe   teacher, rabbi, learned man

Rosh Hashanah   Jewish New Year beginning ten days of penitence

Sanhedrin   the highest court and council of the ancient Jewish nation

schav   a soup made of sorrel

seder   Passover evening meal at which the Jewish liberation from Egyptian bondage is celebrated

sefer   a holy book

shabbes   the Sabbath

sheytl   a wig worn by a Jewish wife

shlemiel   an innocent bumbler

shlimazl   a hapless creature

shmendrik   an apprentice shlemiel; the opposite of a mensh

shnaps   whiskey

shochet   ritual slaughterer

shofar   a ram's horn blown in the synagogue during the High Holidays

sholom aleichem   a traditional greeting or salutation

shtetl   a small town or village in eastern Europe inhabited principally by Jews

shul   synagogue

shund   literary trash

Siddur   prayer book

Simchas Torah   a joyous holiday immediately following the last day of *Succoth* on which the reading of the Torah is both completed and begun anew

skebikhes   strikebreakers

sliches   penitential prayers

Succoth   a holiday in which wooden huts with thatched roofs covered with green twigs are built to commemorate the Jewish wanderings in the desert after emancipation from Egyptian bondage

tallis   prayer shawl

Talmud   a massive compendium of commentaries and debates on the Torah

Talmud Torah   traditional Hebrew school

Tashlikh   the ceremony of throwing one's sins into a river or stream on *Rosh Hashanah*

Torah   a parchment scroll containing the first five books of the Old Testament

trayf   ritually unfit, unclean, defiled

trombenik   a braggart

tsedaka   charity

tsimmes   dessert or stew; also used colloquially to suggest making a fuss

tsitsilisten socialists

vaiz variant of *baiz*

vaytik room literally, room of pain; refers ironically to a doctor's waiting room

yarmulkah skullcap

yeshiva school for Talmud study

Yiddishlach true to the spirit of Jewishness

yold a jerk

Yom Kippur The Day of Atonement, the last of the ten days of penitence beginning with *Rosh Hashanah*

yom tov ritual holiday

zaftig pleasingly plump

Sources: Books, Magazines and Unpublished Manuscripts

(Newspaper sources may be found in the text.)

I ORIGINS

THE OLD WAYS

Mendele Mokher Sforim, *Shlomo Reb Chaim's*; Marcus Ravage, *An American in the Making*, 1917; Morris Raphael Cohen, *A Dreamer's Journey*, 1949; Bernard Horwich, *My First Eighty Years*, 1939; Abraham Cahan, *The Education of . . .* 1969; Maurice Samuel, *The World of Sholom Aleichem*, 1943; David Blaustein, *Memoirs*, 1913; Sholom Aleichem, *Alleverk fun . . .* 1937; Isaac Babel, "The Story of My Dovecot," in *Lyubka the Cossack and Other Stories*, 1963.

ENLIGHTENMENT

Morris Raphael Cohen, *A Dreamer's Journey*; Abraham Cahan, *The Education of . . .* ; I. L. Peretz, *Zikhroynes*, 1920; Abraham Cahan, *The Education of . . .* ; Simon Dubnow, "Jewish Rights Between Red and Black," in *The Golden Treasury*, edited by Lucy Dawidowicz, 1967.

OFF TO AMERICA

Abraham Cahan, *The Rise of David Levinsky*, 1917; Marcus Ravage, *An American in the Making*; Anzia Yezierska, *Hungry Hearts*, 1920; Chone Gottesfeld, *Tales From the Old World and the New*, 1964; Sholom Aleichem, *Off for America*, in the *New York World*, January–May, 1916.

II THE SCENE

THE SHOCK OF AMERICA

Marcus Ravage, *An American in the Making*; Isaac Raboy, *Ikh dertsayl*, 1920; Bernard Weinstein, *Fertsik yor in der yidisher arbeter-bavegung*, 1924; Leon Kobrin, *Mayne fuftsik yor in amerika*, 1955; Isaac Raboy, *Ikh dertsaye*; A. M. Sharansky in Israel Davidson, *Parody in Jewish Literature*, 1907; A. J. Rongy, in *Medical Leaves*, 1937; Moshe Nadir, *Teg fun mayne teg*, 1935; Z. Libin, in *Geklibene skizzen*, 1902;

William Dean Howells, *Impressions and Experiences*, 1896.

IN THE HOME

Zalmen Yoffeh, "The Passing of the East Side," in *Menorah Journal*, December 1929; Sammy Aaronson, *High As My Heart*, 1957; Marcus Ravage, *An American in the Making*; Hutchins Hapgood, *The Spirit of the Ghetto*, 1902; Henry Roth, *Call It Sleep*, 1934; Irving Howe with Kenneth Libo, *World of Our Fathers*, 1976.

GROWING UP IN THE GHETTO

Samuel Chotzinoff, *A Lost Paradise*, 1955; Jacob Epstein *Autobiography*, 1955; Sophie Ruskay, *Horsecars and Cobblestones*, 1948; Sam Franko, *Chords and Discords*, 1938; Maurice Hindus, *Green Worlds*, 1938; Samuel Goldberg, Interview, January 20, 1967; Herbert Asbury, *The Gangs of New York*, 1928.

WORKING THEIR WAY UP

Hutchins Hapgood, "The Earnestness That Wins Wealth," in *The World's Work*, May 1903; Stanley Bero, "Gemilath Chassodim," in *The New Era*, December 1904; Samuel H. Cohen, *Transplanted*, 1937; I. Benequit, *Durchgelebt un durkhgetrakht*, 1934; Isaac Raboy, *Iz gekumen a yid kayn amerika*, 1944; Barney Ross, *No Man Stands Alone*, 1957; Charles Bernheimer, in *The Russian Jew in the United States*, 1905.

A SENSE OF COMMUNITY

S. P. Schoenfeld, *Zikhroynes fun a shriftzetser*, 1946; Lillian Wald, *The House on Henry Street*, 1915; Samuel Chotzinoff, *A Lost Paradise*; Michael Gold, "East Side Memories," in *American Mercury*, September 1929.

IV RELIGION

DISRUPTION

Abraham Cahan, *The Rise of David Levinsky*; Hirsh Maslianski, *Zikhroynes: fertsik yor lebn un kemfn*, 1924; E. Lisitsky, *In the Grip of Cross Currents*, 1959; S. Gurwitz, *Zikhroynes fun tsvey doyres*, 1935; Aaron Rothkoff, "The American Sojourn of Ridbaz," in *The American Jewish Historical Quarterly*, June 1968; S. P. Schoenfeld, *Zikhroynes fun a shriftzetser*; Zalmen Yoffeh, in *Menorah Journal*, September 1929; Hutchins Hapgood, *The Spirit of the Ghetto*; Ray Stannard Baker, *The Spiritual Unrest*, 1910.

RABBIS AND CANTORS

Abraham Cahan, *The Commercial Advertiser*, July 14,

1900; S. Gurwitz, *Zikhroynes*; S. Kwartin, *Mein lebn*, 1952; Samuel Rosenblatt, *Yossele Rosenblatt, The Story of His Life as Told by His Son*, 1954.

SHUL, CHEDER, YESHIVA

David Blaustein, in *University Settlement Report*, July 1905; Abraham Cahan, *The Commercial Advertiser*; Alexander Dushkin, *Jewish Education in New York*, 1918; Henry Roth, *Call It Sleep*; E. Lisitsky, *In the Grip of Cross Currents*, 1959; Hirsh Maslianski, *Zikhroynes* . . .

ORTHODOX AND SECULAR

Leon Kobrin, *Meine fuftzig yor in amerika*; Chiam Zhitlovsky, "The Jewish Factor in My Socialism," in *Voices from the Yiddish*, edited by Irving Howe and Eliezer Greenberg, 1972; Bernard Richards, "The Russianization of American Jews," in *The New Era*, January 1905.

HOLIDAYS

Charles Angoff, "Memoirs of Boston," in *Menorah Journal*, Autumn–Winter, 1962.

V WOMEN

MOTHERS AND DAUGHTERS

Rose Pastor Stokes, *Unpublished Memoir*; Rose Cohen, *Out of the Shadow*, 1918; Elizabeth Stern, *My Mother and I*, 1917.

DAUGHTERS AND FATHERS

Marie Syrkin, *Nachman Syrkin*, 1960; Golda Meir, *A Land of Our Own*, 1973; Rose Cohen, *Out of the Shadow*; Anzia Yezierska, *Red Ribbon on a White Horse*, 1950.

THOUGHTS AND FEELINGS

Rose Schneiderman, *All for One*, 1967.

WOMEN AT WORK

Rose Cohen, *Out of the Shadow*; Marie Ganz, *Rebels*, 1919; Anonymous, Unpublished Memoir, 1917; S. P. Schoenfeld, *Zikhroynes* . . .

GETTING ORGANIZED

Rose Schneiderman, *All for One*; Louis Levine, *The Women's Garment Workers*, 1924.

MODERN PROBLEMS

Hutchins Hapgood, *The Spirit of the Ghetto*; Marie Ganz, *Rebels*; Anzia Yezierska, *Breadgivers*, 1925.

VI LABOR AND SOCIALISM

SWEATSHOP

Ray Stannard Baker, "The Rise of the Tailors," in *McClure's Magazine*, December 1904; Jacob Riis, *How the Other Half Lives*, 1890; Sam Liptzin, *Tales of a Tailor*, 1965; Isaac Raboy, *Iz gekumen a yid* . . . ; I. Benequit, *Durkhgelebt un durkhgetrakht*, 1934.

EARLY UNIONS, EARLY REBELLION

Marcus Ravage, *An American in the Making*; Morris Hillquit, *Loose Leaves From a Busy Life*, 1934; I. Benequit, *Durkhgelebt* . . . ; Leon Kobrin, *Mayne fuftzig yor* . . . ; Rose Pastor Stokes, *Unpublished Memoir*; Bernard Weinstein, *Fertsik yor* . . . ; Sam Schaeffer in "The Rise of the Tailors," by Roy Stannard Baker, in *McClures*, December 1904.

STRUGGLES AND VICTORIES

World of Our Fathers; Jacob Panken, *Unpublished Memoir*, Tamiment Institute, NYU; Abraham Rosenberg, in *Out of the Sweatshop*, edited by Leon Stein, 1977; Rose Schneiderman, *Milwaukee Journal*, March 27, 1911; Morris Hillquit, *Loose Leaves* . . .

VII EDUCATION

EDUCATING THE IMMIGRANTS

Gregory Weinstein, *The Ardent Eighties and After*, 1947; Abraham Cahan, *The Rise of David Levinsky* and *The Education of* . . .

EDUCATING THE CHILDREN

Samuel Chotzinoff, *A Lost Paradise*; Samuel Tenenbaum, "Brownsville's Age of Learning," in *Commentary*, August 1949; Marcus Ravage, *An American in the Making*; Morris Raphael Cohen, *A Dreamer's Journey*; Steven Duggan, *A Professor at Large*, 1943; David Steinman, in *City College Alumnus*, Fall 1950; Meyer Liben, "CCNY—a Memoir," in *Commentary*, September 1965.

VIII POLITICS

TAMMANY AND THE JEWS

Abraham Cahan, *The Education of* . . . ; S. L. Blumenson, "The Politicians," in *Commentary*, March 1956; Bernard Weinstein, *Fertsik yor* . . .

REFORM AND THE JEWS

Lawrence Veiller, *Oral Memoir*, Columbia University; Morris Hillquit, *Loose Leaves* . . . ; Eddie Cantor, *My Life Is in Your Hands*, 1928; Jonah Goldstein, *Oral Memoir*, Columbia University; Henry Moskowitz, in *The Outlook*, February 27, 1918; Jacob Panken, *Unpublished Manuscript*, Tamiment Institute, NYU; Richard O. Boyer, "Boy Orator Grows Older," in *The New Yorker*, November 5, 1938.

IX THEATER
EARLY YEARS, EARLY PLAYS
David Kessler, *Unpublished Memoir*; Jacob Mestel, *Unzer teyater*, 1943; Leon Kobrin, *Mayne fuftzig yor* . . . ; Samuel Chotzinoff, *A Lost Paradise*.

THE ADLER PERIOD
Hutchins Hapgood, *Commercial Advertiser*, March 3, 1899; Jacob Adler, in *Theatre Magazine*, January 14, 1901; Harold Clurman, in *Midstream*, January 1968; Melech Epstein, *Profiles of Eleven*, 1965; Ronald Sanders, *The Downtown Jews*, 1969; Hutchins Hapgood, *The Morning Telegraph*, c. 1905; A. Mukdoyni, *Teyater*, 1927; Celia Adler, *Celia Adler dertsaylt*, 1959; David Kessler, *Commercial Advertiser*, December 4, 1898.

IN THE MODERN STYLE
Ludwig Lewisohn, in *The Nation*, December 13, 1919; Samuel Grossman, "Five Years of the Yiddish Art Theatre," in *Menorah Journal*, August 1923; Stark Young, *Immortal Shadows*, 1948; Stark Young, *Flower in Drama*, 1923; James Agate, *Red Letter Nights*, 1944; Ludwig Satz, *New York Times*, September, 26, 1926.

X CULTURE
A PLEBEIAN YEARNING
Marcus Ravage, *An American in the Making*; Gregory Weinstein, *The Ardent Eighties* . . . ; Marie Syrkin, *Nachman Syrkin*; David Shub, *Fun di amolike yorn*, 1970; Herman Yablokoff, *Arum der velt mitn yidishn teyater*, 1968; Bernard Richards, in *The New Era*, January 1905; Oswald Garrison Villard, in *The Nation*, September 27, 1922.

YIDDISH VOICES
Meyer Stiker, in *A Treasury of Yiddish Poetry*, edited by Irving Howe and Eliezer Greenberg, 1969; Hutchins Hapgood, *The Spirit of the Ghetto*; Morris Rosenfeld, in *A Treasury of Yiddish Poetry*; N. B. Lindner, "Sholom Aleichem in New York," in *Jewish Currents*, November 1958; Mani Leib, Moishe Leib Halpern, Kadia Molodowsky, in *A Treasury of Yiddish Poetry*; A Tabachnik in *Voices from the Yiddish*; S. Niger, *Dertsayler un romanistn*, 1949; Joseph Opatoshu, in *Voices From the Yiddish*; Jacob Glatstein, in *Voices From the Yiddish*; Isaac Raboy, *Ikh dertsayl*; Reuben Iceland, in *Voices From the Yiddish*.

XI BEYOND NEW YORK
COUNTRY LIFE
Charles K. Davis, in *American Jewish Archives*,

Volume XVII (1965); Arthur Goldhaft, *The Golden Egg*, 1957; Morris H. Witcowsky, in *Forgotten Pioneer*, edited by Harry Golden, 1963.

CITY LIFE

Morris Raphael Cohen, A *Dreamer's Journey*; Arnold Bennett, *Your United States*, 1912; Industrial Removal Office Letters, Archives of the American Jewish Historical Society, Waltham, Mass.; Bernard Horwich, *My First Eighty Years*; Meyer Leser, in Ira Berkow, *Maxwell Street*, 1977; Bernard Richards, *Discourses of Keidansky*, 1903; *The Immigrant Jew in the United States*, edited by Charles Bernheimer; Samuel Chotzinoff, A *Lost Paradise*; S. N. Behrman, *The Worcester Account*, 1954; *World of Our Fathers*.

Text Permissions

The editors wish to thank the following for permission to quote from the sources listed:

Martin Abramson for *No Man Stands Alone* by Barney Ross and Martin Abramson.

The American Jewish Archives for the diary of Charles K. Davis.

Charles Angoff, author of a series of novels about Jewish-American life, known collectively as *The Potansky Saga*; and for "Memories of Boston."

A.S. Barnes & Company, Inc., for *Tales From the Old World and the New* by Chone Gottesfeld.

Brandt & Brandt for *Awake and Sing* by Clifford Odets, copyright 1933, 1935 by Clifford Odets, copyright renewed 1961, 1963 by Clifford Odets; and for *The Worcester Account* by S. N. Behrman.

Harold Clurman for "Ida Kaminska and the Yiddish Theater."

Commentary for "Brownsville Age of Learning" by Samuel Tenenbaum, copyright © 1949 by the American Jewish Committee; for "The Politicians" by S. L. Blumenson, copyright © 1956 by the American Jewish Committee; *Commentary* and Diana Liben for "CCNY—A Memoir" by Meyer Liben, copyright © 1965 by the American Jewish Committee.

Coward, McCann & Geoghegan, Inc., for *As High As My Heart* by Sammy Aaronson and Albert S. Hirshberg, copyright © 1957 by Al Hirshberg.

Dodd, Mead & Company for *Rebels* by Marie Ganz.

Doubleday & Company, Inc., for *Maxwell Street: Survival in a Bazaar* by Ida Berkow, copyright © 1977 by Ira Berkow; for *Out of the Shadow* by Rose Cohen, copyright 1918 by Rose Cohen; and for *The Breadgivers* by Anzia Yezierska, copyright 1925 by Doubleday & Company, Inc, and for *Your United States* by Arnold Bennett.

Paul S. Eriksson for *All for One* by Rose Schneiderman.

Farrar, Straus & Giroux, Inc., for *Yossele Rosenblatt* by Samuel Rosenblatt, copyright 1954 by Samuel Rosenblatt.

Harcourt Brace Jovanovich, Inc., for *A Walker in the City* by Alfred Kazin, copyright 1951 by Alfred Kazin.

Harper & Row, Publishers, Inc., for *The Rise of David Levinsky* by Abraham Cahan, copyright 1917 by Harper & Row Publishers, Inc., renewed 1945 by Abraham Cahan; for *An American in the Making* by M. E. Ravage, copyright 1917 by Harper & Row, Publishers, Inc., renewed 1945 by Mark Eli Ravage; for *The Downtown Jews* by Ronald Sanders, copyright © 1969 by Ronald Sanders; for *Forgotten Pioneer* by Harry Golden.

The Hebrew Publishing Company for *Days of Our Lives* by Israel Kasovich.

Holt, Rinehart & Winston, Inc., for *A Treasury of Yiddish Poetry*, edited by Irving Howe and Eliezer Greenberg, copyright © 1969 by Irving Howe and Eliezer Greenberg; for *The House on*

Louis Levine, copyright 1924 by the International Ladies' Garment Workers Union; and for *Chords and Discords* by Sam Franko, copyright 1938 by Sam Franko.

Yale University Library for the Rose Pastor Stokes papers.

The estates of Stark Young and William McKnight Bowman for "After the Play" by Stark Young from the 1/4/22 issue of *The New Republic*.

The family of Sholom Aleichem.

Picture Permissions

Well over half of the two hundred and more illustrations in this book come from five principal sources: the YIVO Institute for Jewish Research; the Museum of the City of New York; the Library of Congress; the *Jewish Daily Forward*; and the New York Public Library. To a number of individuals at these institutions we owe a debt of gratitude: to YIVO's photo archivist Marek Web and his associate Fruma Mohrer for showing us a unique collection of photos of immigrant personalities and activities; to senior curator A.K. Baragwanath and his associates Steve Miller and Esther Brumberg of the Museum of the City of New York for assisting us in looking through their incredibly rich Riis, Byron and Yiddish Theater collections; to Jerry Kearns and his associate Leroy Bellamy of Prints and Photographs for their help in locating glass slides from the Library of Congress's priceless Bain Collection; to Simon Weber and Meyer Stiker, editor-in-chief and city editor of the *Jewish Daily Forward*, for permitting us to inspect the photo morgue of that venerable newspaper; and to the New York Public Library's Edwin S. Holmgren, director of Branch Libraries, and his associate Don Allyn, for assisting us in every way possible.

For their courtesies and kindnesses we would also like to thank the following curators, archivists, librarians, and directors: Mercy P. Kellogg, New York Public Library, Seward Park Branch; Gunther E. Pohl and Timothy Field, New York Public Library, Local History and Genealogy Section; Richard M. Buck and Paul Myers, New York Public Library, Lincoln Center Branch; Carol Corey and Mary Corless, Museum of Modern Art/Film Stills Archive; Arlene Schneider, New York Board of Education Archives, Special Collections, Teachers College Library, Columbia University; Andrzej Rottermund, Warsaw National Museum; Margaret E. Knowles, Community Service Society of New York; Anita Duquette, Whitney Museum of American Art; Ethel Lobman and Jeffrey Eichler, Tamiment Collection, New York University; Sinclair Hitchings and R. Eugene Zepp, the Print Department, Boston Public Library; Marie Cimino Spina, History Division, Brooklyn Collection, Brooklyn Public Library; Rita Arsht Bunin, the Children's Aid Society of New York; Mitchell Grubler, Staten Island Historical Society; Wendy Shadwell and Mary Black, The New York Historical Society; Ernest Greizman, University Settlement; Nathan M. Kaganoff and Martha Katz-Hyman, American Jewish Historical Society, Waltham, Massachusetts; Leon Stein, JUSTICE/ILGWU, New York City; Mary Lean, The Bostonian Society, Boston, Massachusetts; Judith Endelman, the Jewish Theological Seminary of America, New York City; Abraham J. Peck, American Jewish Archives, Cincinnati, Ohio; Burton Beck and Henrietta Dabney, the Amalgamated Clothing Workers Union,

New York City; Nat Andriani, UPI; Jane Stevens, Chicago Historical Society; Rudolf Ellenbogen, Rare Books and Manuscript Library, Columbia University; Barbara Dunlap, Archives and Special Collections, the City College Library; Ben-Zion and Ronald Norman Clarke.